Literacies Across Educational Contexts

Mediating Learning
and Teaching

Literacies Across Educational Contexts

Mediating Learning and Teaching

Edited by

Brian V. Street

Foreword by

Katherine Schultz

with 26 Contributors

Caslon Publishing
Philadelphia

Caslon, Inc.
P.O. Box 3248
Philadelphia, Pennsylvania 19130

www.caslonpublishing.com

Library of Congress Cataloging-in-Publication Data
Literacies across educational contexts : mediating learning and teaching /
edited by Brian V. Street ; with a foreword by Katherine Schultz ; with 26
contributors.
    p.   cm.
    Summary: "International scholars and practitioners apply the principles
of the New Literacy Studies, which views literacy as a social practice, to
diverse educational contexts. Sixteen case studies explore what it means for
students of all ages to learn and teachers to teach across diverse contexts"—
Provided by the publisher.
    Includes bibliographical references and index.
    ISBN 0-9727507-2-X (paper cover : alk. paper) — ISBN 0-9727507-3-8
(case cover : alk. paper)
    1. Literacy. 2. Literacy—Case studies. 3. Literacy—Cross-cultural
studies. I. Street, Brian V. II. Title.

    LC149.L47 2005
    302.2′244—dc22

                                                    2004027452

Printed and bound in Canada

Contributors

Patricia Ames, PhD
Researcher and Lecturer
Faculty of Education
Univesidad Peruana Cayetano Heredia
Instituto de Estudios Peruanos
Lima

Glen Barnard, MSW
Research Associate
Institute for International Research on
    Youth at Risk
National Development and Research
    Institutes, Inc.
New York City

Sarah Kathleen Bazzi, MA
Honolulu

Penny Jane Burke, PhD
Lecturer
Educational Foundations and Policy
    Studies
Institute of Education
University of London
London

Hye-sun Cho, MA
Doctoral Candidate
Second Language Studies
University of Hawai`i at Manoa
Honolulu

Michael Clatts, PhD
Director
Institute for International Research on
    Youth at Risk
National Development and Research
    Institutes, Inc.
New York City

Peter M. Cowan, PhD
Assistant Professor
Language Education
School of Education
Indiana University
Bloomington

Sue Cox, MA
Lecturer
School of Education and Lifelong Learning
University of East Anglia
Norwich

Maryann Cucchiara, MA
Senior Associate
National Center on Education and the
    Economy
New York City

Kathryn A. Davis, PhD
Associate Professor
Second Language Studies
University of Hawai`i at Manoa
Honolulu

Monika Hermerschmidt, MA
Lecturer in Education
School of Culture, Language and
    Communication
Institute of Education
University of London
London

Julie Eastlack Hopson, PhD
Instructor
Department of English
Madison Area Technical College
Madison

Joanne Larson, PhD
Associate Professor and Chair
Teaching and Curriculum
University of Rochester
Warner Graduate School of Education
    and Human Development
Rochester

Constant Leung, PhD
Senior Lecturer
Education and Professional Studies
King's College London
London

Bronwen E. Low, PhD
Assistant Professor
Integrated Studies in Education
Faculty of Education
McGill University
Montreal

Tshidi Mamabolo, PGCE
Head, Foundation Phase
Olifantsvlei Primary School
Johannesburg

Joanna Oldham, PGCE
Department of Education
Liverpool Hope University
Liverpool

Dorothy Rajaratnam, B Ed
ESL and Primary Teacher
Toronto District School Board
Toronto

Anna Robinson-Pant, PhD
Senior Lecturer
Centre for Applied Research in Education
School of Education and Professional
    Development
University of East Anglia
Norwich

Alan Rogers, PhD
Visiting Professor
School of Education
University of Nottingham
Nottingham
School of Education
University of East Anglia
Norwich

Jennifer Rowsell, PhD
Curriculum, Teaching, and Learning
Ontario Institute for the Study of
    Education
University of Toronto
Toronto

Kimberly Safford, MA
Research Officer
Center for Literacy in Primary Education
London

Katherine Schultz, PhD
Associate Professor and Chair
Educational Leadership Division
The Graduate School of Education
University of Pennsylvania
Philadelphia

Rob Simon, MTS
Doctoral Candidate
Reading, Writing and Literacy
Graduate School of Education
University of Pennsylvania
Philadelphia

Pippa Stein, PhD
Associate Professor
Applied English Language Studies
University of Witwatersrand
Johannesburg

Brian V. Street, PhD
Professor of Language in Education
Department of Education and
　Professional Studies
King's College London
London

Md. Aftab Uddin, MA
Research Scholar
School of Education
University of Nottingham
Nottingham

Dorinda Welle, PhD
Director
Youth and Community Development
　Research
Institute for International Research on
　Youth at Risk
National Development and Research
　Institutes, Inc.
New York

Foreword

Katherine Schultz

During the final week of August 2004, U.S. Department of Education Secretary Rod Paige spoke at the Republican Convention in support of President George W. Bush. The central theme of his speech can be summed up in a single sentence from the middle of his speech: "Ladies and gentlemen, No Child Left Behind is working." As he spoke about this controversial piece of legislation in the United States, one of the television cameras found a young boy in the audience. While Paige described the higher standards in schools and the increased levels of achievement in math and science, the boy concentrated on his handheld Game Boy, ignoring the speech about his schooling. Later that evening and in the following days, Jon Stewart's T.V. comedy, The Daily Show, replayed this on a split screen to suggest the humor in official talk about success in schools juxtaposed with a bored youth playing electronic games.

However, as this timely volume illustrates, there are and should be many possible connections between this boy's explorations with electronic games outside of school and the work that occurs during the school day. In other words, *if* schools were set up to reflect the understandings of education explored in this volume, then the image of a boy concentrating on his Game Boy could be understood not as an illustration of boredom during a politician's speech but rather of successful education practice and progress. Rather than ironic, it would be viewed as apt.

We live in a time of emerging digital technologies in which our lives are increasingly mediated by visual popular culture (e.g., Hull 2003; Kress 2003; Luke 2003; Schultz, in press). At the same time that youth are exploring and learning from new technologies in their lives outside of schools, national legislation has been passed to regulate teaching in the United States, Great Britain, and elsewhere. As a result, while possibilities for learning are rapidly expanding outside of school, mandated curricula inside of classrooms are becoming increasingly restrictive. Legislation, like the No Child Left Behind Act in the United States, has directed teachers and curricula toward a narrow range of assessment measures and prescriptive teaching that ignores the knowledge and interests of youth. Schools do not value the knowledge students derive from experimentation with Game Boys and other venues of learning that fall outside of their purview and do not teach them the information they need to score well on tests. Most standardized curriculum guides overlook the connection between the young boy's deep engagement in learning and playing on his Game Boy and the possibilities for teaching him in the classroom.

This volume presents a radically different picture of education—one that is more in tune with the times and that takes advantages of the educational opportunities available in the new literacies and technologies found in many communities around the world. What this book does so well—by presenting a panoply of images of learning across multiple contexts—is to argue for broader and more generative definitions and understandings of literacy, learning, schooling, and education. These understandings are embedded in descriptions of a multigrade school in the Peruvian Amazon, a linguistically diverse Hawai`i high school, and a teacher preparation program in Canada, among other richly described contexts.

Over the years practitioners in and out of schools have demanded that researchers illustrate large theoretical claims with concrete examples in practice. Several recent edited volumes have collected ethnographic studies that use the theoretical perspectives of New Literacy Studies and that are situated in a wide range of contexts, including taxis in South Africa (Breier, Taetsane, and Sait 1996), cattle auctions in Wales (Jones 2000), a high-tech workplace in the Silicon Valley of California (Hull and Schultz 2002), and households in Lancaster, England (Barton and Hamilton 1998). Such descriptive studies give us rich portraits of the literacy practices of people from around the world, strengthening the theoretical claims of literacy scholars. This volume adds to this body of work by braiding together theory and practice. Each author has consciously made a critical link between theory and educational practice. Several of the authors are or have been classroom teachers or practitioners in after-school or out-of-school programs. As a result the volume is both theoretically strong and filled with implications for teaching and learning in and out of school.

The need for such a volume raises the critical question of why—when researchers have so painstakingly documented the rich literacy practices that youth and adults engage in outside of formal school settings—so many schools, and an increasing number of out-of-school programs, are moving toward standardized curricula that ignore this knowledge. If researchers have argued for years that pedagogy should be based on careful attention to students' interests, knowledge, and experience, then why are school curricula built instead on the ideas of policy makers often located at a great distance from the school and students (Schultz and Fecho, in press)?

One frequent response to this question is that most research reports are written in language that is inaccessible to school leaders and policy makers. It is also argued that research grounded in single, localized examples are not compelling enough for broad policy decisions, or even practice decisions, a point that Simon (this volume) makes when he suggests the need to mediate local and global contexts. Through its grounded examples of how the theoretical perspectives of the New Literacy Studies can be applied and used as a frame for understanding classroom practice, this volume provides a resounding response to that concern.

A further possibility is that scholars have not yet made a compelling enough case for valuing out-of-school learning in the assessment of students inside of school and during the school day (Schultz 2003). This suggests that we need to describe in better detail the permeability of the boundaries between school and out-of-school learning (Hull and Schultz 2002) and offer a more expansive notion of learning in classrooms that includes all the knowledge students acquire across various contexts. A recurring theme in this volume is the need to erase artificial boundaries, including lines that divide learning that occurs during the school day and learning outside of school. Stated affirmatively, this volume argues for the recognition of literacy practices that bridge a wide range of domains in education. These include field trips, service learning projects, participation in school councils, and the like.

In our edited volume, *School's Out* (2002), Glynda Hull and I argue against the tendency to reify the divide between schools and out-of-school contexts. In its descriptions of literacy and learning in a wide range of out-of-school settings and in the responses from school-based practitioners, our book suggests that researchers and educators look for ways that each site can inform the other, breaking down the false and useless borders that are too often constructed between them. For instance, we ask, how can research on literacy and out-of-school learning help us think again and anew about literacy teaching and learning across a range of contexts, including school? At the same time, we wonder how might out-of-school identities, social practices, and literacies be leveraged in the classroom (Hull and Schultz 2002, pp. 2–3)?

In *Literacies Across Educational Contexts: Mediating Learning and Teaching* each contributor adds to the dialogue addressing these issues in a range of settings. The book is structured to make critical linkages across several domains, including learning that occurs in and out of school; formal and informal learning; and learning in primary, higher education, and adult education settings. There are examples of programs, such as the Project Freire program in New York City, an early childhood classroom in South Africa, and adult literacy classes in Bangladesh, that challenge commonly held assumptions about boundaries between in- and out-of-school learning.

Finally, policy makers and school leaders may not count out-of-school learning in their assessment of students and construction of curricula because they do not yet realize the full impact of new technologies on the ways literacy and learning have been reconceptualized. Standardized curricula often reflect only text-based understandings of reading and writing. New practices and technologies, such as the visual texts and improvisational performances produced by students in the Hispanic Academic Program in California, draw on students' cultural knowledge and resources. Such examples contribute to new understandings of multimedia and the various modalities available to youth and adults for composing. These emerging practices raise questions such as those posed by Allan Luke (2003, p. 133) and referenced throughout this book:

> How will literacy practices be redefined in relation not only to the emergence of digital technologies but also to the emergent, blended forms of social identity, work, civic and institutional life, and the redistributions of wealth and power that accompany economic and cultural globalization?

To this question we can add, how will these new literacies and technologies reshape our understanding of curricula and educational practice in and out of school? This collection of fine pieces begins to respond to this critical question by bringing together rich descriptions of diverse educational contexts from around the globe to illustrate the enormous possibilities of bridging the life worlds and school worlds of youth and adults.

We stand at a crossroads. Researchers and practitioners can continue to go down separate paths to the detriment of each group, or we can begin to bring these perspectives together to re-imagine educational practice, research, and theory. This volume takes an important step in that critical direction. It is a direction that embraces the richness of youth and adults' lives and allows us to understand the tremendous resources that every learner brings to the classroom and educational programs outside of school.

References

Barton, D., and Hamilton, M. 1998. *Local literacies: Reading and writing in one community.* London: Routledge.

Breier, M., Taetsane, M., and Sait, L. 1996. Taking literacy for a ride—reading and writing in the taxi industry. In: M. Prinsloo and M. Breier (eds.), *The social uses of literacy: Theory and practice in contemporary South Africa.* Cape Town: Sached Books, pp. 213–233.

Hull, G. 2003. Youth culture and digital media: New literacies for new times, *Research in the Teaching of English 38*(2): 229–233.

Hull, G., and Schultz, K. (eds.) 2002. *School's out!: Bridging out-of-school literacy with classroom practices.* New York: Teachers College Press.

Jones, K. 2000. Becoming just another alphanumeric code: Farmers' encounters with the literacy and discourse practices of agricultural bureaucracy at the livestock auction. In: D. Barton, M. Hamilton, and R. Ivanic (eds.), *Situated literacies: Reading and writing in context.* London: Routledge, pp. 70–90.

Kress, G. 2003. *Literacy in the new media age.* London: Routledge.

Luke, A. 2003. Literacy and the other: A sociological approach to literacy research and policy in multilingual societies. *Reading Research Quarterly 38* (1): 132–141.

Schultz, K. 2003. *Listening: A framework for teaching across differences.* New York: Teachers College Press.

Schultz, K. (in press). Qualitative research on writing. To appear in *Handbook of writing research.* New York: Guilford Publications.

Schultz, K. and Fecho, B. (in press). Literacies in adolescence: An analysis of policies from the United States and Queensland, Australia. To appear in *International handbook of educational policy.* The Netherlands: Kluwer Academic Publishers.

Contents

Section II Literacies in the Adolescent Years

Section III Adult Literacies

1

Introduction
New Literacy Studies and Literacies across Educational Contexts

Brian V. Street

This volume aims to provide an 'application' of theory to practice, not in the static 'cookie cutter' sense, but as a dynamic dialogue between the two. The authors have taken on the challenge of applying to diverse educational contexts some of the principles entailed in viewing literacy as a social practice—and in particular the approaches labeled as New Literacy Studies (NLS) (Gee 1991; Street 1993). They do so not just by invoking the general principles of NLS but through offering practical critiques of its application that force us to refine the original concepts. Indeed, the authors were invited to contribute precisely because, while well versed in NLS approaches, they were also able to bring to bear a range of other theoretical and disciplinary perspectives and because they were all also involved in practical educational projects that seriously tested and challenged such approaches.

The educational contexts in which these approaches are followed through include both formal and informal learning in and out of school, in institutional and 'everyday' settings. While differentiated from the 'everyday' learning everyone engages in throughout the life span, such education has, as Rogers claims (this volume), much to learn from Lifelong Learning. The focus here is on the uses and meanings of literacy across such contexts. We see the differences cited here, between supported education and everyday learning and between literacy in education and literacy in use, as on a continuum rather than as binary oppositions. The authors are committed to avoiding the reification and essentializing that often goes with these categories and would reject the kind of value statements that privilege one above the other in general terms. In this endeavor, the authors draw upon Hull and Schultz in their ground-breaking *School's Out* (2002), and in the same spirit Kathy Schulz provides a Preface to the whole volume. Like them we do not want to appear simply as school bashers, privileging the 'home', while at the same time we do not want to passively accept the dominant discourse of current times that assumes schooled literacy is the standard against which all other literacies of the Lifeworld are assessed. Rather, a social practice approach to literacy in use pushes us towards recognizing the considerable overlap across these boundaries as people, texts, and practices track through different settings and scenes: Children move between home and school; teachers and facilitators bring 'sedimented' features of their background and 'habitus' to bear on their educational practice; schools and other formal institutions of education bring in moving-image media, performances, and cultural models from outside of the school walls; while projects involving literacy, rap music, and oral and visual performance may bring in features of schooled education.

So, we start with a different terminology than has tended to dominate the literacy field, especially as it is embedded in education, testing, and international comparison. The authors here variously refer to 'mediating', 'bridging', and 'crossing', referring not only to school/home relations as in Hull and Schultz's approach, but more broadly to communicative boundaries—spoken and written language, performance and other semiotic modes of communication, as in Low's 'blurring' the boundaries and Cowan's 'transculturation', and more broadly still to what Simon terms "the symbiotic interconnectivity between the 'local' and the 'trans-local'." In different ways, all of the authors could be seen to be, as Simon puts it, conceptualizing a dialectical and recursive relationship between "social events and social relations 'at distance' [and] local contextualities" (Giddens 1991, 21), between policy, theory, and practice.

Starting from the school and moving outwards in this dialectical way, Larson, for instance, describes school as "an everyday discursive practice in which language and literacy mediate learning across multiple contexts . . . and communicative boundaries." She links such mediation to broader changes in contemporary life, citing "the multiple literacies needed for participation in a global information economy." In this context, she and others quote Luke (2003) as calling for "an expanded understanding of what it means to learn across local and more global contexts as [people] move between cultures and communities." The issue of what it means to learn in these new contexts is, then, central to the papers here. As Hopson states: "I also adopted the NLS frame because it builds on the notion that inquiries into the nature of 'cultural models', such as learning theories (Gee 1991) of different social groups, may help to explain what literacy learning means in different situations." Learning, from this perspective, is seen not so much as imbibing what experts provide or 'deliver', in the language of much current educational prescription, but as 'taking hold', as Kulick and Stroud (1993) famously put it in an earlier study of New Guinea villagers' response to missionary literacy. It is for these reasons that, in the title of this volume, we have inverted the usual collocation 'teaching and learning' to that of 'learning and teaching', in order to stress the primary focus on learning, at whatever age and stage of life and in whatever context. The two themes—of blurring boundaries and of learners 'taking hold'—are linked in the different settings described here. As Leander (2001) puts it, "the division between 'inside' and 'outside' is blurred as learning occurs across time and space."

The volume, then, attempts to follow through some of the consequences of applying these ideas to diverse educational contexts. The studies reported here show a range of things going on, in and out of formal institutions, that affect both learning and teaching and that are not always highlighted by traditional approaches to either pedagogy or research. The accounts describe processes of learning in school and out of school, through field trips, school councils, service learning, Widening Participation; among LGBTQ (lesbian, gay, bisexual, transgender, and questioning) youth and in the Project Freire Saturday Literacy Academies in New York City and a Hispanic Academic Program in Northern California; via multigrade schooling, linking literacy learning in home, community, and school in the Peruvian Amazon; in a San Francisco experimental charter high school Life Learning Academy (LLA or Life Learning), where school is, for some participants at least, 'like home'; and in an Hawai'i high school where teachers, students, parents, community members, and university researchers are "collectively working towards positively transforming educational practices and linguistic attitudes within a predominately Filipino, Samoan, and Hawaiian high school" context. That is, all cross the boundaries between traditional educational institutions and the everyday lives of learners. Likewise, those authors who describe literacy practices within traditional institutions, such as primary schools, teacher training programs, secondary schools, and higher education, also take into account the practices and experiences that participants bring from outside and that also, therefore, mediate their learning.

The volume began with the circulation to authors of a provisional check list of the principles on which application of NLS to education could be based (Street 1997; 1999), and the authors have since both built on these and adapted them to their own settings and theoretical perspectives. The check list was originally presented in the UK journal *English in Education*, published by the National Association of Teachers in English.

a. Literacy is more complex than current curriculum and assessment allows.
b. Curriculum and assessment that reduce literacy to a few simple and mechanistic skills fail to do justice to the richness and complexity of actual literacy practices in people's lives.
c. If we want learners to develop and enhance the richness and complexity of literacy practices evident in society at large, then we need curriculum and assessment that are themselves rich and complex and based upon research into actual literacy practices.
d. In order to develop rich and complex curricula and assessment for literacy, we need models of literacy and of pedagogy that capture the richness and complexity of actual literacy practices.
e. In order to build upon the richness and complexity of learners' prior knowledge, we need to treat 'home background' not as a deficit but as affecting deep levels of identity and epistemology, and thereby the stance that learners take with respect to the 'new' literacy practices of the educational setting (Street 1997).

Since 1997, the publication of a great deal more literature on out-of-school literacies has enhanced this latter point (cf. Hull and Schultz 2002) while, as Rogers says, "learning programs which fail to take account of literacy practices and perceptions outside school are less effective" (personal communication; cf. Rogers 2003).

I suggested then that

The next stage of work in this area, then, is to move beyond simply theoretical critiques of the autonomous model [of literacy] and to develop positive proposals for interventions in curriculum, measurement criteria, and teacher education [based upon these principles]. It will be at this stage that the theoretical perspectives brought together in the 'New Literacy Studies' will face their sternest test: that of their practical applications to mainstream education (1997, 29).

It is that test which the present book addresses.

A particular lens offered by this approach, that emerged originally in the analysis of literacy in higher education (HE), is that of academic literacies (Lea and Street 1998; Jones et al. 2000; Lea and Stierer 2000; Street 1996). Many of the authors adopt and adapt this kind of analysis here. The academic literacies approach builds on NLS to direct educationalists' attention away from the narrow and formal features of literacy in education, such as, for example, initial acquisition and learning of the alphabet in primary school; mastery of English spelling and grammar for ESL learners in secondary schools; and development of study skills in HE. The academic literacies approach, rather, directs our attention to the broader and more socially based uses and meanings of literacy. In the educational context this means making explicit both the particular genres, styles, and discourses associated with the literacies required for educational purposes and the underlying institutional power relations in which such literacy practices are grounded.

The first theoretical principle embedded in this approach, then, is that just as NLS has established that everyday literacy practices vary across cultures and contexts, so the literacies associated with different educational domains and contexts are different from each other and from those of noneducational contexts in significant cultural and discursive ways. While education has a tendency to see its own practices as somehow universal, logical, neutral, transferable, objective even, an NLS approach in general and academic literacies in particular recognizes the extent to which such educational practices are socially constructed, vary across time and space, and have to be learned in specific ways (Hyland 1999), just as the other literacies that people encounter across a lifetime.

The 'academic literacies' approach, seen as a development beyond the study skills and academic socialization approaches to student learning (Lea and Street 1998), shifted attention from surface features of 'literacy' to deeper features of epistemology and of power, taking account of the institutional context and of ideological and discursive features of the writing required of students. Students approaching entry to university, for instance, have found that the literacy expectations of institutions of HE are very different from those of school, so that even the most successful pupils in formal examination terms may find themselves struggling to understand what is required at this level. While the emphasis in academic support for such students has tended to be on 'nontraditional' students in general and English language learners in particular, as though their language and cultural experience were the 'problem', the academic literacies approach suggests that all students experience such disjunctions as they encounter new sets of literacy practices. The approach, then, targets the institutions themselves and the professional development of tutors as well as the students' 'needs' for academic support and it stresses the need for unpacking and making explicit what is taken for granted in terms of literacy requirements.

In the present volume a number of authors adapt the academic literacies approach as a lens through which to view the literacy requirements of educational institutions at a number of levels (cf. Hermerschmidt and Burke for HE in the United Kingdom), extending the original focus on HE to such other domains as primary schooling (Stein and Mamabolo; Cox and Robinson-Pant); secondary schooling (Oldham); Widening Participation Programmes (Leung and Safford); service learning (Hopson); adult learning (Rogers); and teacher training (Rowsell and Rajaratnam). What if we were to treat all of these contexts as equally subject to the interpretation offered by the NLS lens in general and academic literacies in particular—that is, viewing their writing practices as culturally constructed, located in power structures, and varying in genre, discourse and textual characteristics? Such an approach would enable us to follow through the principles enunciated in NLS work in out-of-school contexts and to test their value in these more formal contexts (cf. Hull and Schultz 2002).

A major focus of the NLS approach is the relationship between literacy and language. The volume, then, addresses both educators who work with English Language Learners (ELL) and English as an Additional Language (EAL) learners as well as those working with native English speakers, and one finding of the research has been that the differences are not so great—or certainly not so stereotypical—as had previously been assumed. I suggested in an earlier paper, for instance, that

> an emphasis on EAL without this wider contextualization might over problematize the additional language dimension of many learners' language and writing: some of the problems associated with such language and writing may

be more general and shared across varieties of students, whether EAL, EFL, or L1, having to do with genre, discourse, and/or code switching of the kind all pupils moving into new educational contexts encounter (Street 1997, 1).

I argued therefore that "it is dangerous to generalize too quickly about the category EAL as an undifferentiated whole (cf. Gregory 1996). Many children from such backgrounds may experience less of a 'gap' between home or community and school learning practices than those from L1 English homes . . ." (Street 1997, 3).

Many of the authors in the present volume address these issues (Stein and Mamabolo; Davis et al.; Low; Cowan; Cucchaira). They note, for instance, that, while many educators believe that all EAL/ELL learners face the same challenges as they work to develop academic literacies (e.g., the problem is 'English'), this view does not sufficiently take into account how students' particular language and education backgrounds differently prepare them for the academic literacy demands of school (Leung and Tosi 1999). Furthermore, there may be similarities between academic literacy development for EAL/ELL learners and for L1 English speakers, again depending on their background experiences, expertise, and ideologies. How these differences interact with the specific demands of educational contexts, especially around student literacy, will vary. Understanding the problems students face requires recognition of the dynamic interplay of these features rather than a monolithic assumption of one target to be reached and of EAL/ELL students all facing the same difficulties in reaching it. The papers illustrate how different educators work with students from different educational and language backgrounds to enable those students to develop the range of academic literacies that educational institutions demand, at the same time as they extend that range to take into account much of what such students already know in their everyday communicative practices and what they bring to the educational institution. As Davis and her colleagues (this volume) in the Studies of Heritage and Academic Languages and Literacies (SHALL) project in Hawai`i explain: "Through drawing on community language and culture capital, students began to value bilingualism as a resource rather than consider it a problem for them and their parents to overcome." In this and other cases, such students may have been led to believe that their native languages, including creoles and pidgins, are somehow inferior and inadequate to the task of learning. An extreme version of this was the inspiration for

Cucchiara's work in the Project Freire Saturday Literacy Academies in New York, when a Haitian student said of a book she showed him about his own culture: "Don't read this. We have no culture."

A focus on the literacy practices of participants in such situations can help us see and perhaps explain aspects of the situation that are not immediately apparent on the surface, and that might lead to external pressures to disregard local language and literacies in this way. As Larson comments, "If we only looked at such activities in terms of narrow curriculum-based packages that could be picked off the shelf, with their privileging of a few selected features of literacy, we wouldn't see what is going on in these activities and would miss the potential to present them to children in an open-ended way or to encourage children to transform and develop them." Rowsell and Rajaratnam likewise encourage learners, in this case trainee teachers, to draw upon rather than disregard their own cultural heritage. They show how a trainee teacher from Sri Lanka brings to bear on her learning about pedagogy her own 'sedimented habitus', the track record and experience of growing up, learning, and teaching in Sri Lanka and then in Canada. She is then able to blend and combine the strengths (and evaluate the weaknesses) of these various traditions in her teaching practice in ways that are not captured by a focus solely on her and her pupils' accomplishment of the appropriate test scores. By looking at the social literacy dimension of school councils in the United Kingdom, Cox and Robinson-Pant likewise show how different literacy practices are deployed for different purposes, a theme also developed by Oldham, by Stein and Mamabolo and by Low. In this case, the reading of formal minutes and producing agendas are combined with visual communication and performance. These differences in communicative practices may have implications for how the school council idea works; for power relations; and for how children may be nurtured towards understanding 'democratic' procedures. Cox and Robinson-Pant combine these perspectives in observing that "promoting only the dominant literacy practices associated with meetings sometimes hindered genuine participation and decision making on the part of children themselves."

Hopson, similarly, shows how we can help explain the disparate views of participants about the success of a service-learning program for Appalachian children "by investigating literacy practices within the tutoring community itself." She looked at what the professors taught, what the college students did with their tutees, and what those tutees thought was going on, all of which are revealed in an ethnographic profile by the focus on literacy practices. And, moving beyond a narrow view of literacy, Stein and Mamabolo demonstrate the ways in which bringing in to a South African primary school performance traditions from the children's wider culture affects the perceptions of what is going on, and of academic success, by different participants. A key insight offered by the literacy practices focus, perhaps missed by an educational focus alone, is that this process is not just one way—'bringing in' outside cultures to the classroom, where they may be transformed and reduced to a narrow schooled agenda. Rather, as Mamabolo recognized in her village school, "pedagogy is not enough." She had to go out to the children's parents and home backgrounds. Likewise, Ames in trying to understand the role of multigrade schooling within the educational system in Peru, needed also to take account of "the literacy practices in different domains in the life of children such as home and community." Davis and her colleagues note how the multilingual situation in Hawai`i and in particular the central importance of 'Pidgin' and the evident inappropriateness of policies based on the U.S. No Child Left Behind Act of 2001 provide an ideal opportunity for developing a similarly imaginative and alternative approach, the SHALL curriculum: "These movements toward acknowledging diversity and seeking productive solutions to discriminatory federal policies have paved the way for increased appreciation for community languages, literacies, and cultures as resources in moving towards meeting the educational needs of immigrant and local populations."

Cowan, describing an Hispanic Academic Program (HAP) in California notes how one such 'productive solution' likewise built upon the premise that it is important to value students' own experience rather than treating it as deficit. In this case a similarly imaginative group of teachers encouraged bilingual students to write poems, in English or in Spanish, about their identity, narratives of their families' histories, stories of their journeys to the United States, or back to their families' places of origin. In this case, it turned out to be their artwork, including their engagement with what is called "lowrider art"[1]

[1] A lowrider is a genre of customized car associated with the Mexican-American community. Lowrider cars are lowered to the ground, ride on small custom wheels and skinny tires, and often feature elaborate paint schemes (frequently including icons found in the Mexican-American community). *Lowrider Arte* has been published since 1992 when the editors of *Lowrider* decided they were receiving enough art to publish a separate magazine devoted entirely to the genre of lowrider art" (Grady 2001, 175).

that particularly enabled such students to express their identities and experience, again making the point about local definitions of what counts and the importance of multimodal productions as cultural and educational mediators. And Simon, working with pupils traditionally defined as 'at risk' in the San Francisco experimental charter high school Life Learning Academy (LLA) shows how a program that similarly builds on what students actually bring can combine a flexible, self-questioning, and reflexive institutional model that is responsive to pupils' interests with a scheme that appeals to policy makers at federal, state, and local levels (cf. Heath and Mangiola 1991). In broader terms, Simon shows that the program is "at once local—growing from an attempt to meet the needs of its constituents, teachers and students, in a particular context—and trans-local—both in the sense that the school is linked to a broader educational system and goals and in that the school's questioning approach may speak to possibilities of meeting literacy needs of other students in other contexts."

Simon's attention to the goals of the education system in which the innovative projects described here are embedded suggests an important caveat entered by most of the authors in this volume: namely, that it is not enough to simply advocate 'local' languages and literacies without regard to the practical and power needs of students in these contexts. As Davis and her colleagues in Hawai'i argue: "Our conceptualization of a multilingual, multicultural, and hybrid approach to language instruction did not ignore the necessity of teaching the Discourse of power to students from non-mainstream language, dialect, and cultural backgrounds" (Delpit 1998). In bridging these Discourses, they, like Burke and Hermserschmidt and others in this volume, "had to ensure that classes were designed to expose students to academic discourses and apprentice them into an academic community of practice." In mainstream approaches, such an 'access' curriculum and pedagogy are often developed at the expense of students' home and community literacies. In romanticized approaches, home and community are emphasized at the expense of access, as Delpit's work strongly argues. The authors here attempt to bridge these extremes. While the focus on literacy as social practice has drawn all of these teachers/ researchers outward from the formal educational institution into settings where learning is going on in different ways, they have all remained firmly committed to providing students with access to the language of power. But the 'access' agenda in this context does not simply involve working within the standard norms of attainment and assessment (although many of the projects did report improved results in standard assessments, such as the SHALL project in Hawai'i, the Life Learning Academy in California, and the Project Freire Saturday Literacy Academies in New York, among others) but also entails a 'transformation' agenda. If we recognize the power and meaning of what students bring to the educational context, then that context too would have to change if 'access' is to be fully realized. As Rogers claims (this volume), in a definitive account of the relationship between the natural learning of literacy which many adults do and the formalized literacy learning programs for adults which are based on much children's schooling, "Adult learning is continuous and chaotic but it is also highly effective and it may be more appropriate for formal institutions to learn from this model than the direction to be always in favor of a 'single-injection' ideology of literacy learning."

These attempts to bridge and blur the traditional boundaries of language, literacy and learning, in and out of school, are not, then, simply accounts of variation but also, in all cases, accounts of power. If we recognize that literacy practices vary with context and that different practices may be appropriate for different kinds of activity, then we must also recognize that these differences are not simply neutral: The relation between communicative practices is also constitutive of power relations. In their account of school councils in the United Kingdom, for instance, Cox and Robinson-Pant argue that "the important factor influencing participation was not the kind of literacy practiced (e.g., dominant literacy as compared to 'local literacies') but the ways in which social practices shaped that literacy, e.g., the 'currently privileged' educational discourse." Their conclusion holds for most of the accounts provided here: "The wider ideological context and the institutional culture of the schools influenced how these [intervention] activities were shaped in practice." Intervention, then, is 'loaded' and researchers cannot simply 'apply' their theoretical perspective from outside as though it was just a matter of 'understanding': If the social practice approach to literacy assumes that literacy practices are always imbued with power relations, then interventions to challenge dominant literacies and to facilitate 'alternative' literacy practices should also be subject to the same analysis. The power dimension works within intervention practices themselves too. The authors, then, recognize the need to address the relationship of researcher/researched, to include the research process itself in their purview and to apply NLS and other principles reflexively to their own work. One of the ways in which this is attempted here is that many of the chapters embrace both researchers and teachers working together in various ways, e.g., Larson and Gatto; Stein and Mamabolo; Rowsell and Rajaratnam; Davis et al.; and Cox and Robinson-Pant.

A further theoretical claim, shared by many of the authors, is that we can no longer isolate the concept or the practice of literacy from other communicative practices. Literacy practices are integrally combined with visual communication and performance, a theme developed in particular by Oldham, by Stein and Mamabolo, by Conan, and by Low. Drawing upon such recent theorizing as that in the field of 'multiliteracies' (Cope and Kalantzis 2000) and of multimodality (Kress and van Leeuwen 1996), these authors attempt to move beyond a narrow schooled or linguistics-based notion of literacy and recognize the varied 'modes' of communication that surround all reading and writing and that are perhaps more evident in out-of-school contexts than in present-day curricula. Oldham, for instance, shows how some teachers in the United Kingdom are attempting to bring these understandings to bear in their classrooms. She describes how teachers in secondary schools not only recognize that their pupils are already fluent in moving image media, such as popular film, and that it can be used to 'motivate' them towards the canonical texts of school but, more profoundly, that the stance adopted towards such texts and the understanding of them is deeply rooted in the learner's awareness of different communicative practices. Drawing upon this metaknowledge may have more implications for such boundary crossing in school than simply 'motivating' pupils. For instance, pupils in this context are happy to engage in discussions of how film editors select scenes and characters from the original written texts for use in their new media text. Already accustomed to using communicative strategies that cross boundaries in their everyday lives, students in the school context are able to compare different versions of a canonical text in different media and thereby to attain insights and understandings not available when the focus is only on the single channel of traditional literacy. Stein and Mamabolo, describing a primary school in South Africa, similarly show how pupils cannot only draw upon out-of-school narrative and story-telling modes to enhance their own school communication and learning, but, again in a more novel way, are able to combine traditional and schooled modes in telling new stories from their own daily experience.

Cowan shows how a pupil at the Hispanic Academic Program, who later became an artist, deployed "a semiotic narrative that uses cultural icons to tell where he came from": Joaquin's teachers had to learn how to 'read' this production, since at first they saw it just as 'doodling'; only later did they recognize that "Joaquin and his peers were communicating messages about their cultural heritage through visual texts that they created and that we published." In providing an ethnographic account of such productions, Cowan is obliged to situate them historically and culturally: "In Latino visual discourse, drawings feature icons from Mexico, from indigenous Amerindian cultures, and from expressions of pachuco/a, cholo/a, and Chicano/a cultural identities that get invested with meanings that represent the experiences of Latino youth who create and circulate them." In this and the other cases cited here, the combination of mode awareness and learning is suggestive for future curricula and pedagogy. Low brings many of these themes together in relation to a theoretical frame derived from Cultural Studies. Here too, she describes classrooms where pupils' own performance, in rap and other musical styles, combining verbal play with musical improvization, provides "a resource of creative, provocative literate practices" for all children, both those already successful in schooled literacy and those whose out-of-school literacies have not been recognized.

The combination by Low of Cultural Studies approaches with those from NLS signals another key dimension of this volume, the crossing of disciplinary and field boundaries, content areas, and modalities. Cowan, for instance, "merged the New Literacy Studies" (NLS) focus on social practices with the New Visual Literacy's (NVL) conception of images as visual texts analyzable for cultural meanings (Kress and van Leeuwen 1996) situated in the social, historical, and cultural context of the intellectual colonization of Mesoameria." This combination of NLS and NVL traditions enables him to draw on the strengths of Kress and van Leeuwen's work, while at the same time criticizing them for "not contextualizing Western visual design in greater detail." His account, by "exploring and describing the social practices of Latino visual discourse and by invoking its social, historical and cultural context," in the tradition of NLS, "finds that social practices situated in a sociocultural context are integral parts of visual literacy and social semiotics." He further draws upon Latin American conceptions of 'transculturation'—the dynamic process by which new cultural forms are continuously being created and adapted across borders of race and class—to complement these traditions. Similarly, Stein and Mamabolo, as we have seen above, combine narrative traditions drawn from South Africa with those of multimodality and multiliteracies (Cope and Kalantzis 2000), while also bringing to bear a sociocultural approach to learning along with the contextualizing dynamic of NLS. They argue that we need such a combination of approaches to describe the complexities of their research and of projects that engaged children with "issues of culture and identity, across multiple semiotic modes of communication, in relation to their lifeworlds and language use outside of the classroom." Again, traditional literacy is not enough for such projects and traditional literacy theory is not enough for such research. As Cowan notes, "It isn't enough for Latino adolescents just to learn to copy icons, they want to know their cultural heritage and often learn it through the sponsorship of a more knowledgeable elder."

Cucchiara, in describing similar concerns for culture and identity in a youth project in New York, attempts to bring out "the theoretical underpinnings and intersections between Freirean principles and the New Literacy approach." Just as Welle and her colleagues, also working in New York, "use a 'bifocal lens' of literacy-and-sexuality practices," so Cucchiara says of her project, "Freire and the ideological model would be our lens as we worked." The application of the work of Paulo Freire, best known in projects in the South, to such educational activities in the North, complements Cox and Robinson-Pant's adaptation of Participatory Rural Appraisal (PRA), a methodology also used in many development projects in countries of the South to foster wider community involvement, to the work of school councils in the United Kingdom. Participatory Rural Appraisal incorporates specific visual approaches that the authors here link to the issues raised more broadly by multimodality. The intention of their project was for teachers and children to develop a range of communicative strategies appropriate to their particular context. They thus added PRA and multimodality to their NLS perspective, both for the project itself and also with respect to the analysis of it. Rowsell and Rajaratnam call upon another dimension of Gunther Kress's work, his argument in *Before Writing*, that "who we are and where we come from impinge on the way we learn and the way we *make* language" (Kress 1997, xvi). The concept of language-making draws attention to issues of identity, a key theme in their account, and here they draw upon anthropologist Dorothy Holland's notion of 'history in person' (Holland et al., 1998) to help them understand the 'dual identity' of the teacher trainee, Dorothy.

Hermerschmidt and Burke bring to bear both an NLS and its derivative academic literacies approach, but also extend them via what they term 'reflexive methodology', while Hopson adds to NLS, communities-of-practice learning theories (Lave 1996; Lave and Wenger 1991; Wenger 1998) linked to power (Foucault 1976) and identity, also calling upon recent work by Holland and Lave (2001). Similarly, Ames, writing about multigrade schooling in the Peruvian Amazon, invokes new pedagogical approaches and sociocultural constructivism, drawing upon theories of learning, such as those of Lave, Wertsch, and others, that run throughout this volume. As she argues, "This approach emphasizes that key aspects of mental functioning can be understood only by considering the social contexts in which they are embedded, since knowledge is achieved through participation in social practice." While Davis and her colleagues likewise call upon recent work that sees learning in the context of 'communities of practice', they also adopt a critical stance that warns of the dangers of reification in the approach to such 'communities'. Indeed, in the academic literacy courses they describe at an Hawai`i high school, teachers began discussion of language, literacy, and identity by asking students themselves to explore 'communities of practice' within their own neighborhoods. "Students found that they commonly navigate multiple and complex identities in the predominately Filipino and Samoan neighborhood where they live." This exposed "a rich tapestry of language and culture which students explore in view of their own emerging cultural identities." The participants and the authors are here drawing upon concepts of hybridity (cf. Willett and Solskein 1999; Egan-Roberston and Willett 1998) and Bhabha's (1994) third space (a concept also invoked by Rowsell and Rajaratnam) rather than simply reifying such language and culture or marginalizing it as in many mainstream programs. Welle and her colleagues, working with LGBTQ youth in New York City, demonstrate that such calling upon 'social context' in educational practices is not simply a matter of adding something from outside to an essentially static focus on schooling. Their account of sexuality provides a telling case of how such sources of meaning are deeply embedded in people's lives in ways that may force schooling to change and not just its clients. They note how recent understandings of sexuality, like those in literacy studies, reject the notion of an 'autonomous', reified category: "Not unlike autonomous definitions of literacy which privilege 'standard' practices such as reading and writing, what could be considered autonomous definitions of sexuality typically remain focused on a relatively limited set of 'standard' sexual practices anchored within discrete 'sexual events'." In both cases we need more nuanced, dynamic, and ideological conceptual frameworks if we are to understand the complexities. Simon, struggling with the critiques of NLS by Brandt and Clinton (2002) and by Collins and Blot (2002) as overemphasizing such 'local' approaches, suggests that the task of mediating local and global, to which all of the authors here are variously committed, may be helped by the work of Giddens (1991). This sociologist's theories of late Modernity—notably the concepts of time/space 'distanciation', 'disembedding' mechanisms, and 'institutional reflexivity'—'present a useful theoretical bridge from the NLS social practice view of literacy to the globalizing demands of educational policymakers" (cf. also Street 2004).

The authors in this volume, then, believe that the combination of NLS perspectives with such new theoretical approaches offers significant advantages for both research and practice. We hope that this work will help educators (both administrators and teachers) to understand how to make sense of the complexity across these areas so they can make informed decisions about curriculum, instruction, and assessment. That is, the volume is addressed across the cusp of theory and practice. While building on and extending theoretical work in NLS and academic literacies, it is also committed to working through the implications of these approaches. We are concerned not with one-directional 'applications' but rather, in attempting to work through the implications of these approaches for different sectors of education. We expect to find limitations and problems in the approaches that will require us to go back to their underpinning conceptual apparatus and to either adapt or even reject those parts of it that are evidently inadequate at least for this task. Theory as well as practice is subject to the critical perspective being adopted here.

Collectively, then, the authors work across languages, across disciplines, across modes of communication, across the life span, and across domains of education to highlight the kinds of questions that educators need to ask about their learners, whether in school or community contexts, to help them make grounded pedagogical decisions. While the case studies in this book aim to be theoretically and methodologically rigorous, at the same time they aim to be accessible to practitioners who work with students in schools and other educational institutions every day. As the series editors write in their mission statement, that entails researchers taking educators seriously as fellow scholars and it requires the authors to operate in both domains at once—that of researchers and that of practitioners. Indeed, that is the working experience of most of the authors and provides the basis for their contributions to this volume.

Organization of the Book

Following this introductory section, which lays out the ideas with which the authors are engaging, the substantive part of the book is divided into three sections, organized on the principle of learners' ages. While not wishing to reinforce narrow conceptions of 'stages' of learning, since we argue that the primary factor in learning is social context—for instance, as Rogers shows (this volume) children often learn in ways previously attributed only to adults—we also recognize that for educators the organization of learning into rough age groupings is often the most salient and visible starting point. Having started from there, we can then bring to bear all of the complicating features outlined by the authors in this volume—the mediating, crossing, and bridging whereby learners bring to bear features of the cultural environment on their learning of multiple literacies in and out of formal institutions. All of the authors were asked to circulate their papers to each other and to take account of what fellow authors have said as it affects their own paper, and these cross references help to bridge the 'levels' and ages highlighted by the division into sections. They also, we hope, give the volume coherence and density and are in keeping with the spirit of reflexivity that is crucial to this kind of approach.

The three sections are labeled 'Early Literacy Learning'; 'Literacies in the Adolescent Years'; and 'Adult Literacies'. This organization enables us to juxtapose within each section papers from different countries and from different kinds of learning institutions and projects, involving different mixes of modality along with the novel combinations of theoretical perspective outlined above. Each section begins with a keynote paper that provides, through close ethnographic-style detail of a specific project, some of the key theoretical principles that will be developed in the other papers. The keynote for Section I, 'Early Literacy Learning', is provided by Pippa Stein and Tshidi Mamabolo's '"Pedagogy is Not Enough:" Early Literacy Practices in a South African School'. The title quote "Pedagogy is Not Enough" signals the theme that runs through other papers. As Mambolo discovered, in trying to bring in outside literacies to the classroom, it was also necessary for her as the teacher to go out to the families and communities of her pupils and to listen to their wider experiences within which literacy learning took its meaning. The papers in Section I include a project for encouraging children in a United Kingdom primary school to engage in 'citizenship' activities, involving the communicative skills required for meetings, and the literacy skills associated with such 'democratic' practices as minute taking, keeping records, etc.; multigrade schooling in the Peruvian Amazon, where again the researcher focused also upon the literacy practices in different domains in the life of children such as home and community; and an elementary school in the United States, where field trips served as part of the wider aim to assist students' participation in the culturally valued activities of their communities. While the papers all focus, then, on the ways in which 'early' literacies are mediated to learners in the learning institutions, they also all take into account the 'outside' dimensions of literacy learning. At the same time, they all recognize that it is not enough just to 'add on' outside literacies to schooled literacy, nor is it, as Larson puts it, "simply a matter of nonformal vs. formal learning, but it is a matter of how students learn both the literacy demands of education and schooling and of life outside of school to critically understand and transform the connections between the local context, including the classroom, and the global or community context."

Section II, 'Literacies in the Adolescent Years', begins with a paper by Low that signals the theme of popular youth culture which figures in accounts of adolescents' engagement with literacy and learning both in and out of school, across countries and projects. She uses a Cultural Studies framework as a lens for viewing the ways music, poetry, and drama can bridge these domains. These cultural practices are also central to the accounts provided by other authors in this section. Simon describes the Life Learning Academy (LLA), a San Francisco experimental charter high school, which used an "extended family" model as a way to bridge students' in- and out-of-school literacies. Cowan, describing an Hispanic Academic Program (HAP) in California, shows how students' engagement with what is called "lowrider art" enabled them to express their identities and experience. Oldham, like Low, recognizes the power of students' out-of-school cultural knowledge, in this case regarding moving-image media and describes what happens when teachers in a United Kingdom secondary school attempt to draw upon this experience in teaching canonical literary texts. This section also provides an opportunity for a different 'cut' across formal education by including papers specifically focused on EAL/ELL learning contexts, as in the LLA, the HAP, and the work on Heritage languages in Hawai`i, where students' use of poetry from their own languages offers a bridge to schooled genres and literacy, building on their linguistic and cultural capital. And finally, Cucchiara describes a project for urban youth in Brooklyn that both engages with the EAL/ELL and the popular culture dimensions variously addresses throughout this section.

Section III of the book is entitled 'Adult Literacies', although it overlaps in both content and theory with the other two sections. The framing point is laid out by Rogers' argument concerning the continuous nature of the learning process and the ways in which the learning and literacies of adults have much to teach younger learners. Hopson's account of a service-learning project in the United States, in which college students get credit by offering tutoring to 'at risk' pupils from local high schools, engages with learners at different levels of the education system; the disjunctions between the conceptions of literacy and learning of the different parties, including the undergraduates' professors, reinforce the theme of bridging and crossing that runs throughout the book. The interface between schooling and higher education is also addressed by Leung and Safford, who provide a case study of a Widening Participation programme in the United Kingdom that highlights the underlying issues of academic literacies in both sectors, again considering the experiences of students crossing thresholds as they move from school to university. Finally, in this section, Hermerschmidt and Burke describe their academic literacies work in a higher education institution in the United Kingdom, highlighting the difficulties students face as they enter the new cultural environment of the academy and bringing out the disjunctions at this level too that have been evident across all of the levels described in the different sections.

References

Bhabha, H., 1994. *The location of culture.* London: Routledge.

Brandt, D., and Clinton, K. 2002. Limits of the local: Expanding perspectives on literacy as a social practice. *Journal of Literacy Research* 34(3):337–356.

Collins, J., and Blot, R. 2002. *Literacy and literacies: Texts, power and identity.* New York: Cambridge University Press.

Cope, B., and Kalantzis, M. (eds.). 2000. *Multiliteracies: Literacy learning and the design of social futures.* London and New York: Routledge.

Delpit, L., 1998. *Other people's children: Cultural conflict in the classroom.* New York: The New Press.

Egan-Robertson, A., and Willett, J. 1998. Students as ethnographers; thinking and doing ethnography: A bibliographic essay. In A. Egan-Robertson and D. Bloome (eds.), Cresskill: Hampton Press Inc., pp. 1–32.

Foucault, M. 1976. Power as knowledge. In: C. Lemert (ed.), *Social theory: The multicultural and classic readings.* Boulder: Westview Press, pp. 518–524.

Gee, J.P. 1991. *Social linguistics and literacies: Ideology in discourses.* 2nd ed. London: Taylor & Francis.

Giddens, A. 1991. *Modernity and self-identity: Self and society in the late modern age.* Stanford: Stanford University Press.

Gregory, E. 1996. *Making Sense of a new world: Learning to read in a second language.* London: P.C.P.

Heath, S.B. and Mangiola, L. 1991. *Children of promise: literate activity in linguistically and culturally diverse classrooms.* NEA School Restructuring Series. Washington, D.C.: NEA/AERA.

Holland, D., Skinner, D., Lachicotte, W., and Cain, C. 1998. *Identity and agency in cultural worlds.* Cambridge: Harvard University Press.

Holland, D., and Lave, J. 2001. *History in person: Enduring struggles, contentious practice, intimate identities.* Santa Fe: School of American Research Press.

Hull, G., and Schultz, K. (eds.). 2002. *School's out: Bridging out-of-school literacies with classroom practice.* New York: Teachers College Press, pp. 11–31.

Hyland, K. 1999. Academic attribution: Citation and the construction of disciplinary knowledge. *Applied Linguistics* 20(3): 341–367.

Jones, C., Turner, J., and Street, B. 2000. *Student writing in the university: Cultural and epistemological issues.* Amsterdam: John Benjamins.

Kress, G. 1997. *Before writing: Rethinking paths to literacy.* London: Routledge.

Kress, G., and van Leeuwen, T. 1996. *Reading images: The grammar of visual design.* London: Routledge.

Kulick, D., and Stroud, C. 1993. Conceptions and uses of literacy in a Papua New Guinean village. In: B. Street (ed.), *Cross-cultural approaches to literacy,* Cambridge: Cambridge University Press, pp. 30–61.

Lave, J. 1996. The practice of learning. In: S. Chaiklen and J. Lave (eds.), *Understanding practice: Perspectives on activity and context.* Cambridge: Cambridge University Press, pp. 1–31.

Lave, L., and Wenger, E. 1991. *Situated learning: Legitimate peripheral participation.* Cambridge: Cambridge University Press.

Lea, M., and Street, B. 1998. Student writing in higher education: An Academic Literacies Approach. *Studies in Higher Education* 23(2): 157–172. Reprinted in M. Lea and B. Stierer (eds.), *Student Writing in Higher Education: New contexts.* Buckingham/Society for Research into Higher Education: Open University Press, 2000, pp. 32–46.

Leander, K. 2001. "This is our freedom bus going home right now": Producing and hybridizing space-time contexts in pedagogical discourse. *Journal of Literacy Research* 33(4): 637–679.

Leung, C., and Tosi, A. 1999. *Rethinking language education.* London: CILT.

Luke, A. 2003. Literacy education for a new ethics of global community. *Language Arts* 81(2):20–22.

Luke, A., and Carrington, V. 2002. Globalisation, literacy, curriculum practice. In: R. Fisher, G. Brooks, and M. Lewis (eds.), *Raising Standards in Literacy.* London: Routledge/Falmer, pp. 231–250.

Rogers, A. 2003. *What is the Difference? A new critique of adult learning and teaching.* Leicester: NIACE.

Street, B. 1996. Academic literacies. In: D. Baker, J. Clay, and C. Fox (eds.), *Alternative ways of knowing: Literacies, numeracies, sciences.* London: Falmer Press, pp. 101–134.

Street, B. 1997. The implications of the New Literacy Studies for literacy education. *English in Education* (3): 26–39.

Street, B. 1999. New literacies in theory and practice: What are the implications for language in education? *Linguistics and Education* 10(1): 1–24.

Street, B. 2004. The limits of the local—'autonomous' or 'disembedding'? *International Journal of Learning*. In Press.

Wenger, E., 1998. *Communities of Practice-Learning meaning and identity.* CUP: Cambridge.

Willett, J., Solskein, J., and Wilson-Keenan, J., 1999. The (im)possibilities of constructing multicultural language practices in research and pedagogy. *Linguistics and Education* 10(2): 165–218.

Section I

Early Literacy Learning

2

"Pedagogy is Not Enough"

Early Literacy Practices in a South African School

Pippa Stein and Tshidi Mamabolo

Introduction

> In order to build upon the richness and complexity of learners' prior knowledge, we need to treat 'home background' not as a deficit but as affecting deep levels of identity and epistemology, and thereby the stance that learners take with respect to the 'new' literacy practices of the educational setting (Street 1997).

> What's the use of saying you are a teacher if you do not look into why your children are not performing well? At the end of the day, when you go home to your house, can you pat your shoulder and say, "I was a teacher today," if you know exactly what the causes of their problems are and yet you have done nothing to solve them? What kind of work is that? (Tshidi Mamabolo, interview, December 2003)

In this chapter we tell the story of how a Grade 1 teacher, Tshidi Mamabolo, in partnership with a teacher-educator, Pippa Stein, engaged with key issues around home-school relations in a semi-rural school serving children from 'shack' settlements on the edges of Johannesburg. Through this case study, which covers the period from 1999 up to the present, we provide a grounded account of where certain ideas from the New Literacy Studies (Street 1984; Barton 1994; Gee 1996; Prinsloo and Breier 1996) have taken us, and where we have taken them. We describe examples of early literacy pedagogy within a sociocultural framework, and show how ideas in related fields, including multiliteracies (Cope and Kalantzis 2000) and multimodality (Kress and Van Leeuwen 1996), have influenced our pedagogy. We explore how certain of these ideas have taken hold within a particular context, relationship, and historical moment, and how these ideas have evolved into forms of social action which have local cultural voice. Through our example of a dynamic dialogue between theories in the New Literacy Studies and their appropriation and translation in a real, complex site, we present challenges to the New Literacy Studies in relation to literacy pedagogy, poverty, and social justice.

Beginnings: Children's Early Literacy Learning Project

In 1999, we started working together on the Children's Early Literacy Learning (CELL) Project, an ethnographic-style research project investigating the key shaping influences which enable some children and not others to acquire literacy successfully in the early years.[1] The research focused on the uses of and meanings given to literacy and numeracy in home, local community, and school contexts, particularly among families and children who are poor and whose home language is not English. The relationship between literacy learning in schools and literacy practices in families included the exploration of how factors such as language and identity impact on early literacy learning within the context of a multilingual and multicultural South Africa.

The research started from the proposition that the contrast in the culture of literacy use across home and local community, on the one hand, and school sites, on the other, is a major reason for variable school achievement in South Africa. This is an important starting point in attempts to make schools more accessible to students from diverse cultural and language backgrounds. Drawing on the ethnographic research tradition established by a body of influential

[1]The CELL Project was led by Mastin Prinsloo (University of Cape Town), Carole Bloch (Project for Alternative Education in South Africa), and Pippa Stein (University of the Witwatersrand). It was funded with a Spencer Foundation grant. Assistant researcher Thandiwe Mkhabela worked on collecting data from Olifantsvlei Primary School.

literacy researchers in what has come to be known as the New Literacy Studies (Scribner and Cole 1981; Heath 1983; Street 1984; Barton 1994; Gee 1996; Prinsloo and Breier 1996), the key concept shaping the research direction is literacy as a social and cultural practice. A particular focus of this perspective is to see literacy as social action, and as distributed among coparticipants, rather than an autonomous, individualized skill. The CELL research methodology involved forms of participant observation, interviews, and the collection of artifacts and texts which formed part of activities around literacy in the focus on children's everyday lives.

A critical factor regarding literacy acquisition in South Africa is the state of early literacy pedagogy, which, broadly speaking, has worked within a tradition which emphasizes repetition, recitation, and decoding at the expense of meaning-making. Educators have only recently begun to note the differences between the long-standing international debate between phonic-centred and whole-language literacy pedagogies. A central aim of the research is to describe the range of literacy pedagogies which children are experiencing in local schools, and the extent to which these pedagogies are producing or hindering literacy acquisition. The issue of pedagogy needs to be seen in relation to the fact that the African National Congress government introduced a new outcomes-based national curriculum in 1997, which foregrounds learner-centred, participatory, interactive teaching. It also needs to be seen in relation to the turbulent history of language in education policy in South Africa. During the apartheid era, from 1948 until 1994, English and Afrikaans were the two official languages, and the nine other indigenous languages had no status. Children learned through the medium of their home languages until Grade 5, after which they switched to learning through the medium of English or Afrikaans. A progressive, inclusive, multilingual language policy based on eleven official languages was put in place through the new post-apartheid Constitution in 1996. Parents and communities are able to democratically decide on which languages their children should learn at school, both as medium and as subject. Because of the status of English as a global language, as well as its association in people's minds with 'democracy', parents and school communities have elected in the majority of schools to reject the idea of using indigenous languages as the medium of instruction and go 'straight for English' from Grade 1. This policy works effectively in schools which are well-resourced and where children who speak African languages at home have access to English-speaking environments. However, this is not the case in the majority of South African schools, where children live in rural, under-resourced areas and English is a foreign language.

Olifantsvlei Primary School, where Tshidi Mamabolo teaches, was chosen as a research site because of its access to large numbers of children (approximately 800) living in the surrounding informal settlements in conditions of childhood adversity and poverty. The school was built by the Johannesburg City Council in the early 1960s for children of the Council's black employees. It started functioning in a cowshed under the supervision of the farm manager and continued to do so until after the 1994 democratic elections, when the Moses Maren Mission leased the land from the City Council and raised funds to construct all the school buildings which exist today.

Children at Olifantsvlei are multilingual speakers of local and foreign African languages, and the school, in consultation with the parents, has chosen a 'straight for English' language policy in which English is the main language of teaching, learning, and literacy from Grade 1. The children attending this school live with parents, relatives, or caretakers who are variously employed, unemployed, or migrants from neighboring countries seeking work on the Witwatersrand. The majority of these children come from female, single-headed households and live in 'mkukus' or 'shacks' on small plots of land with no sanitation but, increasingly, with electricity. Some of the children do not live with adults, but with older brothers and sisters who care for them. With the HIV/AIDS pandemic, some children are living in child-headed households. The only form of social welfare for the poor is a child grant of R140.00 ($20) per month for a child who has a birth certificate.

In 1999, the Grade 1 and 2 teachers, Tshidi Mamabolo and Ntsoaki Senja, assisted Pippa Stein and Thandiwe Mkhabela, the CELL researchers, in selecting focus children from their classes who could be observed for eighteen months in their school and home contexts. They facilitated access to the parents and allowed the researchers to observe, tape record, and videotape their classes on a regular basis. Both teachers requested feedback on their literacy pedagogy during the fieldwork phase and asked for workshops to improve their teaching. As this kind of intervention might have affected the data collection process, Stein and Mkhabela agreed to work closely with all Grade 1 and 2 teachers in 2001 when the fieldwork was complete. During the fieldwork phase, however, the researchers were communicating with the teachers about the literacy practices they were observing in the classroom and in the focus children's homes.

Tshidi Mamabolo had joined the school as a new teacher in 1999. She had been teaching previously in a Soweto primary school. In reflecting on her shift from the Soweto school to Olifantsvlei, she says:

> As I went on with my duties at Olifantsvlei, I noticed that the children were behaving in ways that I was not used to, in the sense that they were not willing to participate in activities we did in class. They were reluctant, demotivated and also lacked interest and concentration. I reflected on this and decided that perhaps it was my fault and that I was using inappropriate teaching methods. Although I was using storytelling, question and answer and phonic drills, the children were still passive. My class was not learner-centred in the sense that I did not encourage children to express opinions, challenge each other and take initiative in class. (Interview, December 2003)

In our classroom observations of Tshidi Mamabolo's teaching at this time, it was evident that she was working carefully and systematically through a range of literacy activities which included phonic drills, story-reading, and handwriting practice. However, she provided few opportunities for children to engage in discussions, tell their own stories (it was always the teacher who told stories), and develop their creativity in different modes of communication. Although Mamabolo constantly switched between Zulu, Sotho, and English in her teaching, the target language of communication in speaking, reading, and writing was English. There is no doubt that one of the main reasons why the children were 'passive' was connected to their struggle with English. It may also have been related to hierarchical family practices in which children are not generally encouraged to engage in conversation with adults or challenge their elders.

The Fresh Stories Project

In 2001, Stein and Mkhabela worked with Mamabolo and Senja on a three-month story project in multimodal literacies in which children made images, performed, wrote about, and made three-dimensional objects which drew on the representational resources of their cultures, histories, and languages. Although the school's medium of instruction was English, Stein and Mkhabela insisted that the children could work through any languages they wished, including Zulu, Sotho, Tswana, and English. This was quite difficult for the teachers to accept in the light of their focus on English, but as the project was in the nature of an "innovation," they agreed to go along with a multilingual approach.

The teachers were accustomed to providing scaffolding and direction for all learning activities in this school. The intention in this project, however, was to create a more relaxed and playful environment for making, which would allow the children to respond to the creative tasks with little or no intervention from teachers. The purpose of this was to construct within the constraints of school 'an unpoliced zone' in order to investigate the choices the children would make in terms of the 'stuff' which was to hand—their resources for representation—and their interests within the specific social context of making (Kress 1997).

Drawing on ideas in New Literacy Studies on the relations between culture, identity, and learning (Gee 1996), this project engaged children with issues of culture and identity, across multiple semiotic modes of communication, in relation to their lifeworlds and language use outside of the classroom. Children were asked to produce 'fresh stories'—not stories which they had heard in oral storytelling traditions, or seen on television or radio. In order to provide a stimulus for inventing stories, the children were asked to think of someone in their homes, neighborhoods, or streets who interested them, and who could become a 'character' in a play, a visual text, and a written story. In one group, the children produced a collection of unusual hybridized traditional fertility doll figures which were made out of waste materials which they found in their environments (Stein 2003; Stein and Newfield 2004). Drawing on a range of oral, written, and visual resources, the children produced rich multimodal, multilingual texts which provided concrete evidence of their sophisticated understandings of their social conditions and their aspirations for the future.

Building on their teachers' interest in their out-of-school lives, children starting improvising plays which represented meaningful events and routines in their daily lives. Activities to do with literacy were a feature of almost every play. In one example, a group of children improvised a fifteen-minute play called "Home-School," a fascinatingly detailed performance of three children's daily traffic between home and school. The themes of this play return again and again to the connection between money, food, literacy, and school. The parents in this play are vulnerable: They do not know how to read and write. It is the children who are omnipotent, who have power through their literacy. In the extract which follows, we see the makers/performers of the play demonstrating an ironic and sophisticated understanding of the relationship between poverty and literacy. Child 2 argues that the single most important reason for knowing how to read is to be able "to count the money."

"Home-School" Play: Scene 3: AT HOME

Three children come home from school. They live in a small shack in an informal settlement. They knock on the door. Mother and Father are at home.

Mom: Dumelang bana.
[Hallo children.]

Children: Agee, mme.
[Hallo mom.]

Child 2: Agee, ntate.
[Hallo dad.]
The mother gives the children some books.

Mom: Mpheng dijo, ke lapile . . . ke lapile . . . Ke lapile ngwanaka.
[Give me some food, I am hungry . . . I am hungry . . . I am hungry, my child.]
She sits on a mat.

Child 2: Ntate, e re ke go balele.
[Daddy, let me read for you.]

Mom: To child 3.
A r'yo bala buka.
[Let's go and read the book.]
They go to join the father and child 2. Child 1 is washing the dishes.

Dad: To child 2.
Mpalele ngwanaka.
[Read for me, my child.]

Child 2: Child 2 picks up the book and 'reads' the following text, which she is making up as she goes along.
Ba re, "Motho ge a sa tsebe go bala a no bala boka." "Ha o sa tsebe ho bala fela, o nke pampiri o bale," ene ba ya ho jwetsa mo pampiring mona, hore

o bale pampiri enjani. Ene ha o sa bale, o dutse o shebile sona, jwale ho be
ho hlaha tshelete mona, a nkeke o tsebe ho bala niks. O tla bala jwang?
[They say, "If a person cannot read, he or she must just try to read a
book." They say, "If you only don't know how to read, you must just
take a paper and read," and you are told on the paper about the kind of
paper you must read. And if you don't read and you are only sitting
down and looking, and then you see some money, you won't know how
much it is. You won't know how much it is. How can you count it?]

Mom: *She has joined dad and children. To child 2.*
Tsamo nketsetsa tee.
[Go and make me tea.]

Child 1: Mme, ke sa hlatswa dijana.
[Mommy, I am still washing the dishes.]

Mom: O sa hlatswa dijana? Hei, 'nna a re mo hlatswise.
[You are still washing the dishes? Hei, we won't help you.]

The play demonstrates that children from an early age are active agents of literacy authority. Even at the age of 7 years, children are already active mediators
of literacy knowledge and authority within households where parents have limited access to literacy and literacy knowledge. What we witness in this representation of everyday life (whether real or imagined) is the impact of school
ways on the home (and not the other way around), the communal and interactive activity around text which echoes some of the New Literacy Studies
(Street and Street 1991), the important role of siblings in literacy acquisition
in households where parents are not print literate, the naturalization of literacy
activities in the flow of everyday life, and the ways in which children use their
literacy knowledge to have power and control over the parents: the rules and
codes around authority and knowledge relations in the household.[2]

The Manhattan Country School–Olifantsvlei Exchange

At the end of 2001, Mamabolo asked the principal if she could move with the
same class to the next grade. In 2002, she moved into Grade 2 with the same
children, whom she observed had undergone a metamorphosis:

[2]Lynne Slonimsky's insights into this play are incorporated into this analysis.

Children were starting to unfold and become creative. Their self-esteem was boosted. They were now able to reflect on themselves. They were enthusiastic and eager to learn. They would build their own words, write sentences, and help others in class who were experiencing problems. They were more interactive and their writing skills had improved tremendously. Children started to open up, ask more about their cultures, languages, religions; they were more interested in the people around them and children from other parts of the world. (Interview, December 2003).

That year Mamabolo met an art teacher, Janice Movson, from the Manhattan Country School in New York, and they set up a North-South exchange project between their two schools which aimed to build on the children's multiple literacies. The Grade 1 and 2 classes in both schools participated in the same task, which was to make a mural of their neighborhood to represent who they were and where they lived to the 'other'. Each group made a mural, took photographs of themselves, wrote letters about their aspirations, and painted self-portraits. These different forms of 'identity texts' were used by both teachers in forms of critical literacy, to introduce the children to notions of difference, to the gaps between the North and the South, the rich and the poor. In both schools, parents were invited to come into the school to see the mural which their children had made and, subsequently, to see the mural which had arrived from the other school. At Olifantsvlei, at least 15 parents [out of a class of 56 children] arrived for a very moving ceremony in which the mural from the Manhattan Country School was opened and displayed. In order to honor the children's efforts in front of their parents, Mamabolo organized this event in culturally familiar terms, as a kind of ritual ceremony in which the mural was seen as a 'gift' sent from the Manhattan children to the Olifantsvlei children and their parents. Parents, children, and teachers made speeches and sang praises. At the Manhattan Country School, the teacher, Janice Movson, informed her children that the mural from South Africa had arrived and was hanging in the art room. Children lined up and went to look at it before they met in a group to talk with animation and interest about the drawings, portraits, and letters. The teacher sent a note home to parents to inform them that the mural from Olifantsvlei had arrived and could be viewed in the art room. One parent came to see the mural and commented on how exciting the project was. Significantly, the technical person at the school who was filming the children's response to the mural was so inspired by the event that he informed the school director, who then invited Janice Movson to do a video presentation of the mural exchange project for all the staff. This proved to be a very fruitful and stimulating follow-up and reflection on the entire process.

Meanwhile, at Olifantsvlei, the ritual ceremony around the reception of the mural marked a turning point in terms of building home-school relationships. That year, parents came regularly to school meetings and took a more active interest in their children's learning. By the end of 2002, the children were assertive and responsive, eager to engage in new learning challenges. When the President of South Africa, Thabo Mbeki, invited all children to write to him telling what they thought of the 'new South Africa', the children in Mamabolo's class were the only group of children in the school who volunteered to write letters. Here is Tabia's letter:

> Dear Mr President, My name is Tabia. I am a girl. I want you to buy me a uniform. I want you to put electricity in Thembelihle squatter camp. I want you to put fence. My school need more classroom. Please come and make our school beautiful. This letter is from Tabia.

"Pedagogy is not enough"

In 2003, Tshidi Mamabolo started teaching a new intake of Grade 1 children. Within a few months, she became increasingly alarmed at the high levels of absenteeism and the numbers of children falling asleep early on in the school day. More children than ever were complaining of hunger. Very few parents from the new Grade 1 class attended school meetings or came to ask about their children's progress. One day, a desperately ill 7-year-old girl crawled into her classroom. Her mother was dead, her father was dead. She lay for days under a blanket, near to her teacher, dying of AIDS.

Mamabolo decided that some form of action had to be taken, but this time, she did not blame herself, or her pedagogy. She decided that the time had come to move out of her classroom and into the world, saying that "pedagogy was not enough." She felt she had to "look deeper into the social situations of the children, their home contexts and living conditions." Concentrating her energies on the children who seemed to be in difficulty—those who were regularly absent, sick, or sleepy in class—she talked to each child, asking them to explain to their parents/households that she would like to visit them in their homes to talk about their problems. She followed this up with personal letters to the parents asking them if she could visit them. Not one parent refused the invitation. On weekends and after school, she went from household to household, listening to parents telling their story about why their children were not at school. She received a very warm welcome. What she discovered shocked her. All that concerned these families was how to get food on the table. Some children were being fed by neighbors; others had been sent home to the farms in rural areas because there was no money to buy food to feed them. Some children were staying at home because there was no money for school fees, transport, or school uniforms. In her journal entry at the time, she wrote:

> In four households I visited, mothers are raising their children alone. They survive through their children's social grants, which they get if they can produce a birth certificate for the child. Sara Nthembu only gets R140.00 per month ($20) social grant. She has two children living with her, the other two are living in the Transkei with her sister. She says she couldn't come to school because she feels there is "nothing I can do for the school." Her child does not have stationery and other things needed at school. Her fear is that she will be told that she owes school fees. She is also afraid that her daughter will be expelled because she does not have a school uniform. The child is showing learning problems—she is not coping with her school work and she sleeps early on when she arrives at school. She also told me that the children don't eat breakfast because there is no food in the house. She is sometimes helped by neighbours who invite the children for supper. Her problems were causing her "not to face life but to withdraw." She says this makes her feel better. (Mamabolo, field notes, March 2003)

As a result of this visit to the family, Mamabolo organized food for Mrs. Nthembu's daughter when she was at school. She made arrangements for the payment of school fees. Mrs. Nthembu told her that she was relieved and promised to support her child and to attend meetings and class activities. After her visit, she came and asked if she could help her with other activities in the class. This led to other parents coming into her classroom to spend the morning sessions there, helping with the issuing of books and toilet routine. Mamabolo invited parents to come and tell stories in different languages, "but up until this point, no-one has come."

In another household, the children's mother could not read:

> Mrs. Zuma has three children. One of the children has epilepsy. She was sick when I visited them. Mrs. Zuma said she could not attend parents' meetings because she could not read the invitations from the school. Even if Sam brings home circulars, there is no one to read them and explain the contents. I arranged that I would send older children from the high school who live in the vicinity to read and explain the circular to her. She was pleased with the arrangement and I continue to visit her. (Mamabolo, field notes, March 2003)

Mamabolo made the decision that a sustained form of action which involved the parent community, the school, the teachers, and the children had to be found. She focused on the production of food, organizing a soup kitchen so that the children had one slice of bread each morning. She spoke to the principal, the school management team, and her colleague about using some land around the school for starting up a vegetable garden project for the parents and needy children. Significantly, she received much more support from her principal and colleagues for the garden project than she had ever got for her pedagogical innovations. She wrote a proposal to the school governing body, asking for support for the project, as it intended "to alleviate poverty, to create jobs by selling vegetables, develop skills, provide nutritious food and *bring parents closer to the school.*" The school body agreed to allocate land surrounding the school to vegetable gardens. Mamabolo and the school principal set up a series of meetings with the parents in order to form a community organization. This organization would make decisions about the allocation of the land, acquire equipment and seedlings, decide on the sharing of responsibilities, and establish time frames for the project. Parents and the school formed an organization called the Thembalihle Farming Project. Other teachers in the school offered to run cooking classes and needlework and computer courses for the parents. The Thembalihle Farming Project agreed to start Adult Basic Education and Training (ABET) classes to teach parents literacy. The Project organized fundraising activities to acquire equipment and seeds. Mamabolo and the principal approached the local government council and it contributed R5 000 to starting up the vegetable gardens as part of an HIV/AIDS outreach project supplying fresh food to HIV/AIDS sufferers. In December 2003, the first crop of vegetables was harvested and distributed to eighty hungry families. By June 2004 needy children were being fed by the school four times a week with a hot meal of vegetables and porridge.

Tshidi Mamabolo has become 'a literacy activist', in multiple senses of the word. Her attempts to change her literacy pedagogy have taken her on a journey she never imagined she would embark on. Through her own efforts and personal relationships, she has acquired new forms of literacy and new ways of 'reading the world'. In reflecting on what has happened at Olifantsvlei, she focuses on her need "to do something" in order to strengthen home-school relations:

> When teaching literacy, it is important to get everyone on board. I realised that to strengthen home-school relationships with learners and their households, I had *to do something* in order to achieve positive results, to bring parents closer to the school, to involve them in school activities which would in turn benefit their children, to show them that they are also role players in the education of their children. I realised how little I knew about the children's home backgrounds in my class—I know a few details like their date of birth, but who stays with the child, I sometimes don't even know. Sometimes you have children who stay with their sisters, sometimes children don't live with their parents, but with their grandparents, who cannot read or write, so you have to know that . . . Because I believe that if you have prior knowledge of the child, that opens up the world between yourself and the child so that you are able to continue and go forward. Hence I have to go out there and search for what children already know, and have, and their family backgrounds. With that in hand, I have really moved forward, it's like we have started together on one footing now, the children and myself. I now know where they come from, how to communicate with them. I know that every morning I have to say to Dumi, "Did you eat in the morning?" I have to ask Matsepo, "Was your sister home today?" because he lives with his older sister, who is in high school, and she often stays out at night. So I should think backgrounds of the children are definitely important. And it's what we have been leaving behind as teachers, we just want to teach the child as the child is in the classroom, but we don't want to go further, we think that is not our stuff, we are not connected to that, someone will do that for us, but since I have started visiting parents, the children are so free, they come to me and tell me things

about their lives. And it has helped me enormously in my teaching. It has changed my pedagogy. For those that I see have problems, and I know them, I don't say to them, go home and ask your parents to read to you because I know there is no-one who can do this. So what I do is ask an older child to be a guardian for this child, to help this child to read every day. We talk openly now, we work as a unit, there is a kind of freedom in my classroom which there wasn't before. We sort of decide as a group before doing things. When I used to teach them before, sometimes they were so passive, they couldn't say anything. Maybe they were frightened of me . . . it's like they were not free, it's like if you are in prison, you do not know what to do. In my head, I thought these children are so quiet, and even if I posed questions to them, there was no voluntary answering like I have now. Parents come to the meetings now, I have noticed they call me to communicate with me, they are now acknowledging and helping their children. (Interview, December, 2003)

Getting Everyone on Board

Kulick and Stroud (quoted in Street 2001) have argued that instead of talking about the impact of literacy, we should be asking the question, how do people *take hold of* literacy? Tshidi Mamabolo's story is a powerful example of how one teacher has taken hold of literacy *through reconfiguring the boundaries between home and school.* Her story begins within the four walls of her classroom, which in itself is a symbolic boundary between 'inside' and 'outside'. Through her involvement with literacy researchers and readings provided on the CELL Project, she became aware of alternative ways of thinking about and teaching literacy, in which literacy is seen as a multi-semiotic set of practices, such as plays, pictures etc., each connected to specific forms of language, activities, and identities. Influenced by these ideas, Mamabolo expanded her literacy pedagogy by blurring the boundaries between 'inside' and 'outside' through setting tasks which built on children's out-of-school literacies and knowledges, including their multilingualism and their cultural histories and identities. Children started bringing the outside world into the classroom world. Their motivation and interest in literacy learning increased substantially, as did their sense of agency and dignity in the world. Tshidi's own sense of empowerment as a literacy teacher increased. But in 2003, the outside world came crashing into her classroom in all its misery and messiness: children dying of AIDS, children starving, children constantly absent. She came to the conclusion that "pedagogy was not enough" and that crossing the boundary between home and school needed to happen in a new, different kind of way: that communities have to 'travel between', that there needs to be a constant traffic between homes and schools, a reciprocity from all sides. Going 'out' the classroom led to a series of events and actions which have opened up new spaces for home-school relations. Through this boundary breaking at multiple levels, Mamabolo has engaged in a form of disinvention of conventional schooling, a reconfiguring of structure and agency which has opened up new possibilities for action for all participants.

Mamabolo's concept of *literacy pedagogy* has moved from a focus on classroom-based instructional procedures to a more ecological model (cf. Barton 1994) in which teaching young children to read and write is linked into a much broader chain of sustainability, of taking hold of literacy. Those who care for the children need to be actively brought into this chain, a process Mamabolo calls "getting everyone on board," in the sense of building local support in order to sustain early literacy development. We would suggest that *"getting everyone on board" is the literacy pedagogy.* On the surface of things, one could well ask what the planting of vegetables has to do with taking hold of literacy. We would want to answer that through the planting of vegetables, different kinds of linkages have been made possible in relation to literacy development in this context. In a similar way to Larson's analysis of field trips (this volume) as more than extensions of classroom activities, as contexts in which students participate authentically in culturally valued everyday practices, taking hold of literacy for Mamabolo means working with local cultural practices and community needs as well as school models in a more local/central mix. Tshidi Mamabolo's initial decision to change her pedagogy by 'letting the world in' to her classroom brought the world in, in all its inchoate messiness. In letting the world in, she has not only extended the boundaries of what it means to teach literacy, but she has also extended her own sense of identity as a literacy teacher who through taking certain forms of action, has changed how others see her and how she sees herself. Mamabolo's capacity to improvise across the inside/outside divide, to move between the culture of the classroom and the home, can be likened to Dorothy Rajaratnam's experience (in Rowsell and Rajaratnam, this volume) who was able to work productively with the strengths, rather than the constraints, of her dual identity as an inhabitant of two cultural worlds. For Mamabolo, to be 'in the classroom' she understood that she had to 'be in the world' but being in the world in the context of social disintegration brought with it an unbounded set of moral and ethical dilemmas which she had to face. Through a reconceptualization of the whole literacy program within her specific context she has creatively engaged with these dilemmas, bringing new meanings to this situation which move beyond autonomous models to more inclusive ecology-based literacy pedagogies.

In presenting this case study, we show one example of where some ideas in the New Literacy Studies have taken us and where we have taken them. Through its focus on home-school literacies, the New Literacy Studies opens up the idea of 'inside' and 'outside'(Hull and Schultz 2002), of thinking about the resources that children bring to the school from their home environments and visa versa. What teachers see so often is the 'products', the effects of environments on children. What they often do not see are the processes and practices which produce these effects. But going on the journey, negotiating the 'traffic' between homes and schools, within the context of human distress and poverty, is fraught with ethical dilemmas. Mamabolo's journey led her into the heart of human misery. She felt she could not turn her back on it. If she did not take action, who else would? Many teachers will argue, understandably, that they are not social workers and their job is to teach effectively in the classroom. However, we think that the logics of the New Literacy Studies' position on home-school literacies lead teachers to confront *how to remake the conditions for reading*. But in contexts of poverty and social marginalization, where does 'remaking the conditions for reading' begin and end? And whose responsibility is it? As Dorinda Welle (personal communication) has noted, this case study demonstrates the centrality of the term 'home background' to new literacy approaches, and potentially to social work, or some synthesis of the two. In Mamabolo's journey, 'home background' was viewed by her initially as an important but 'backgrounded' factor in her struggle to teach her children literacy. From the moment she took the decision to step out of the classroom and into the worlds of 'home backgrounds', home background was transformed into a living, dynamic social context which demanded her attention. Her changed relation to 'home background' then became the material for her reconceptualization of literacy pedagogy. Welle has interpreted Mamabolo's transformation in the following way:

Home background is no longer static, a set of demographics, but is a context of social relations and social actors variously in crisis and variously resilient. In the passive view of home background, literacy must be seen as the 'source' of social action. Home background is passive, literacy is active. To me, you demonstrate that by the end of the chapter, we should call 'home background' something else, something that positively references a matrix of social relations, social conditions, and potentials for social action. (Dorinda Welle, personal communication, 2004)

Our story has shown how one teacher has tried to create a world in which literacy can occur through taking *forms of social action* because *pedagogy was not enough*. Literacy thrives on full stomachs. If running vegetable garden projects is a way of feeding children and, at the same time, bringing parents into the fold of the literacy on the school premises, perhaps the New Literacy Studies approach to literacy needs to encompass, in more explicit and substantive ways, *forms of social action* which address 'the literacy crisis'—not the fact that 'standards are falling', but the fact that not enough children are learning to read and write because there is no food on the table. It is time to solve the problem rather than explore or report on the problem. It seems to us that the New Literacy Studies' abiding interest in equity and social justice could be strengthened through a focused political program which incorporates new forms of activism, what one might call 'literacy activism', within the context of global politics, which will lead to remaking the conditions for reading for all our children.

Acknowledgements: We wish to thank the principal, teachers, children, and their parents from Olifantsvlei Primary School, Johannesburg, for participating in this research and Janice Movson, colleagues, and children from the Manhattan Country School, New York. Many thanks to the Wits Multiliteracies Project, and to Lynne Slonimsky and Dorinda Welle for their valuable insights into this work.

References

Barton, D. 1994. *Literacy: An introduction to the ecology of written language.* Oxford: Blackwell.
Barton, D., and Hamilton, M. 1998. *Local literacies.* London and New York: Routledge.

Gee, J.P. 1996. *Social linguistics and literacies: Ideology in discourses.* 2nd ed. London: Falmer Press.

Cope, B., and Kalantzis, M. (eds.). 2000. *Multiliteracies: Literacy learning and the design of social futures.* London and New York: Routledge.

Heath, S.B. 1983. *Ways with words: Language, life and work in communities and classrooms.* Cambridge: Cambridge University Press.

Hull, G., and Schultz, K. 2002. Locating literacy theory in out-of-school contexts. In: *School's out: Bridging out-of-school literacies with classroom practice.* New York: Teachers College Press, pp. 11–31.

Kress, G. 1997. *Before writing: Rethinking the paths to literacy.* London and New York: Routledge.

Kress, G., and Van Leeuwen, T. 1996. *Reading images: The grammar of visual design.* London: Routledge.

Prinsloo, M., and Breier, M. 1996. *The social uses of literacy: Theory and practice in contemporary South Africa.* Amsterdam and South Africa: John Benjamins and SACHED Books.

Scribner, S., and Cole, M. 1981. *The psychology of literacy.* Cambridge: Harvard University Press.

Stein, P. 2003. The Olifantsvlei 'Fresh Stories' Project: Multimodality, creativity and fixing in the semiotic chain. In: C. Jewitt and G. Kress (eds.), *Multimodal Literacy.* New York: Peter Lang.

Stein, P., and Newfield, D. 2004. Shifting the gaze in South African classrooms: New pedagogies, new publics, new democracies. *Thinking Classroom* 5(1): 28–36.

Street, B. 1984. *Literacy in theory and practice.* Cambridge: Cambridge University Press.

Street, B. 1997. The implications of the New Literacy Studies for literacy education. *English Education* 31(3): 26–39.

Street, B. (ed.). 2001. *Literacy and development: Ethnographic perspectives.* London and New York: Routledge.

Street, B., and Street, J. 1991. The Schooling of literacy. In: D. Barton and R. Ivanic (eds.), *Literacy in the Community.* Sage, pp. 143–166.

3

Communicative Practices and Participation in School Councils in Primary Schools in the United Kingdom

Sue Cox and Anna Robinson-Pant

Introduction

As part of the citizenship education initiatives in the United Kingdom, school councils have been increasingly promoted in primary schools: These provide an "opportunity for pupils to get more involved in the way a school is run" (Sutton 1999, 6). The training materials and packages available to teachers wanting to set up school councils generally place emphasis on conventional meeting structures and procedures, similar to those in adult contexts (see, for example, Clay 2000 and Sutton 1999). Inherent in these structures is a range of communicative practices, including specific literacy practices associated with running meetings, such as writing and circulating minutes. Setting up school councils in this way provides young citizens with a model of democratic processes, yet does not encourage teachers or students to look critically at the implicit communicative practices. By contrast, we view school councils from the perspective of the New Literacy Studies (NLS), challenging the notion of literacy as a set of neutral skills.

In this chapter, we explore what the school council means to both teachers and children and whether there could be more opportunity for children to 'take hold of' (Kulick and Stroud 1993) and shape the communicative practices in these settings. As Street states in a recent publication (2003, 1), this involves "focusing not so much on acquisition of skills, as in dominant approaches, but rather on what it means to think of literacy as a social practice." In our research, we understood the concept of 'communicative practices' to encompass the communication structures and procedures around school councils and the associated literacy, visual, and oral practices. In the following discussion, we use this as an entry point for analyzing the interaction and decision-making processes within and around school councils. The "recognition of multiple literacies, varying according to time and space but also contested in relations of power" (Street 2003) enabled us to look at the dominant 'literacy' of school councils. Drawing on the NLS framework, we analyze the wider implications of introducing children to what could be seen as a literacy of power. In particular, we explore the social practices associated with running democratic meetings on an adult model—and how this affected power relations between children and adults and within the school as a whole. Like Larson (this volume), we locate literacy in the broader social context rather than in the narrower educational one as an element of the school curriculum.

We draw here on our findings from an action-orientated research project[1] in which we collaborated with teachers from three primary schools in Norfolk who had set up school councils. The aim of the project was to look at how communication among children and between children and adults in the primary school could be enhanced through introducing visual approaches. We were keen to explore how visual ways of communicating could increase children's participation in decision-making and their control over their learning and learning environment. As a starting point, we used specific visual approaches derived from Participatory Rural Appraisal (PRA), a methodology used in development projects in countries of the South to foster wider community involvement (Chambers 1994). The intention was for teachers and children to develop a range of communicative strategies appropriate to their particular context. The first stage of our project entailed ethnographic observation of school council meetings and focus group discussions with children (both school council members and nonmembers). In this chapter, we investigate the data

[1]Empowering Children through Visual Communication, funded by CfBT from April 2002– October 2003: see Cox and Robinson-Pant, 2003, for full details of the project.

from this phase, as this focused on existing communicative practices within school councils and raised issues around the kind of literacy dominant in this setting.

The three schools involved in the project were different in a number of ways. Tuckswood Community First School (5–8 years age range) has the longest established school council. Hillside Avenue Primary School and Village Primary School[2] have larger school councils, reflecting the size of the schools and their wider age range (5–11 years). Village Primary School is located several miles outside Norwich, whereas the other two schools are in the city. Although there were differences in context and age range, the three schools had established similar structures and procedures, notably representatives elected within each class in the school who brought issues for discussion to the school council meetings. The school councils had an elected Chairperson and other officers, such as Secretary, Vice Chair and Treasurer. School councils met regularly, every week or fortnight, and some form of record was kept to report on related activities at a class level. In all cases, teachers were involved in the school council meetings. At Tuckswood Community First School, there are also a number of committees, such as the 'football committee' and the 'environment committee', which report to the school council with proposals and decisions from their weekly meetings.

Learning Through School Councils

Teachers in all three schools saw their school council as a way of teaching the children how to take part in democratic procedures, such as an election or meeting. While the teachers had a range of purposes—centrally "to get decisions; to get them talking"[3]—in the process children were actively involved in learning new oral and literacy practices associated with their roles within and beyond the school council meetings. While school council members were the only children who were learning *within* the school council meetings, other chil-

---

[2] We are using the pseudonym "Village Primary School," since this school prefers to remain anonymous.

[3] Teachers' and children's comments are quoted here from our field notes and transcriptions taken during project research activities (including workshops with teachers, school council meetings and focus group discussions).

dren were learning from their involvement in class council and from the effects of the school council within the school. Teaching approaches varied among the three schools, but teachers were always present in the meeting. In Tuckswood Community First School, the two teachers involved in the meeting had specific roles: one acted as a 'mentor' and the other as a staff representative at the school council. The mentor's role was to help the children understand how to run and participate in the meeting, while the staff representative was intended to be a member on an equal footing with the children. In the other two schools, teachers tended to switch between the two roles to varying degrees—discussing issues as a participant while also teaching children about democratic procedures. It can be seen from the following extract how a teacher at Hilllside Avenue Primary School contributes as a participant—"can I make a proposal?" At the same time, he reminds the school council of their wider role within the school and hands responsibility over to the children:

> *[Note: the 'envelope' was a way of gathering agenda items from classes in the school]*
>
> *Teacher:* But it's not just for people in here. Can I make a proposal? Unless things are on the agenda from the envelope, we shouldn't bring things up at the meeting. To try to force people to use the envelope. Someone else will need to propose it.
>
> *Child chairperson:* Who thinks it's a good idea that things can't be raised at the school council unless they're in the envelope for the agenda? [Hands up. He counts.] It's a majority.

Through school and class council meetings, children across the school were learning about democratic procedures and concepts in this way. In the context of their elected roles as class representatives and school council officers, school council members were learning how to chair a meeting and appropriate ways of participating in discussion and decision making. For example, the children became aware of the expectation that everyone should be included: Sometimes the chairperson asked children in turn; sometimes when they did not do this, there were objections from other children. The child chairs had learned that they could address the teacher as a member of the council, inviting them to speak when they had raised their hand.

At Tuckswood Community First School, the role of the teacher mentor in inducting children into appropriate procedures was evident throughout the meetings. The teacher guided the meeting through whispering and prompting, while encouraging the child chair to take the lead. There was a considerable emphasis, linked with their emphasis on teaching philosophy, on children presenting reasons to support their point of view, being encouraged to say: "I agree with so-and-so because . . ." or "I disagree because. . . ." At times there were more directive teaching interventions, for example, the teacher 'mentor' explained that it was inappropriate for the child chairperson to instruct a child to raise their hand when the children were having a vote. Similarly, the teacher talked to a child about not dominating the discussion:

> *Teacher:* Jake—you're absolutely brilliant—but don't go on and on—I don't want to stop you talking but . . .

He goes on to explain that Jake is a good thinker and talker but that he shouldn't take up all the time; that when he says things he should keep it short. They were also introduced to issues around confidentiality.

> *Teacher:* You mustn't mention people's names because they're not here to defend themselves. You can say the class name. It's all right [excusing child who had just done this] because we didn't tell you before.

The following extract from a meeting shows how teachers helped the children to use the minutes and how the children were learning to raise issues directly with adults.

> *Teacher (mentor):* (reading out) Remember Karl reported last week—there was a problem in assembly with talking and with teachers not being out in the playground before the children
> *Karl:* We talked to [headteacher] about it and talked to the teachers about the assembly rules. [Headteacher] said that the teachers should be going in with the children. Teachers need to be out before the children . . .

On one occasion the teacher explained to all the children that their role in school council meant that they must speak up and get involved and that it was unacceptable to be a member if they were not prepared to do this.

They were also introduced to new terminology and language. For example:

Karl (chairperson): Any apologies?

Teacher: Anyone away?

and

Teacher: We're making a list to talk about. It's called an agenda. We're not talking about them, just making a list, so we have:

Afghanistan Appeal . . . (reads out agenda)

An important part of learning to be a school council member revolved around the concept of representation. In one school, formal elections were conducted where candidates prepared and presented manifestos to the whole school and all children took part in a secret ballot. Their manifestos demonstrated the children's understanding of the kind of qualities that democratic representatives might have, such as: 'being sensible', 'being fair', 'helping other people', 'speaking up', 'not being shy', 'listening to people'. The school council meetings presented the opportunity for the children to acquire an understanding of the difference between putting forward their own view and that of others (their class):

Jayne: (reading from notes) Year 6 should play properly on the playground. We should get more sports equipment. Year 3 should play properly . . . They're sad they can't play with the basketballs. It's not me, it's they. They say they want to play with the basketballs.

Callum: They're not here so it doesn't matter (said humorously).

Chairperson (Year 6 boy): Shhh everyone, we've discussed this before and decided they can't play with the basketballs.

Jayne: It's not me, it's them.

Chairperson: Then just tell them.

An example of the children's understanding of the democratic purpose of the school council is provided by a child chair.

Child chairperson: [The school council is] to solve problems, take it to class, the reps talk about it and the class decides what to do.

The teachers placed a strong emphasis on learning the dominant literacy practices associated with the school council activities. For example, the manifestos presented by the candidates for election had to be written down and read out by each child. Every meeting used a written agenda and recorded the outcomes of the meeting as formal written minutes. Notes were referred to by school council members in feeding back information to their class. Children sometimes used the agenda as a reminder of what was discussed:

Rosie: Canteen [next item on agenda].

Sam: Noise in the canteen.

Teacher: What happened about the noise in the canteen?

Rosie: I can't remember.

Teacher: Can Sam remember? Did you make any notes? Does Sam want to carry on with the rest of the agenda while Rosie finds her notes.

Notes and minutes also served an important function in keeping other teachers informed of what had been discussed and decided at school council meetings. In both class and school council meetings, there was a strong message that literacy was essential to the process of decision-making. For example, when the school council were discussing ways of improving communication between school council and classes, it was interesting that writing was preferred by the teachers who promoted the idea of a notice board for reporting back to the rest of the school.

Reflecting on their school council meetings in our focus group discussions, the children also showed that they felt literacy to be central in the school council activities:

Louise: We've got class council and we write down things in a book and then you go down to the school council with our books and then we just talk about it to school council then it's OK.

Jaya: They write the stuff down on the paper and they bring it back and say what is good.

They therefore saw good literacy skills as necessary to participate fully as a school council representative:

Jack: That's one reason I'm not on it. I'm not a good reader.

and

> *Isobel:* Well you do have to write quite well, but you don't have to read well because you're talking all the time.

In discussion, children recognized that people who could not read and write could be on the school council, but nevertheless asserted that they would need help from those who could. They suggested that this might be why there were pairs of representatives from each class.

There were practical difficulties around maintaining clear communication in written form, such as younger children being unable to read or write fluently and it being very time-consuming to write. As a solution, teachers sometimes wrote up the minutes on the board for younger children to copy out, or took a leading role themselves in producing a written record:

> *Josh:* Every Friday we decide what problems there are to everyone. Miss C. writes them down and when the envelope comes, we put them in.

Our observations indicated that teachers were striving to achieve a variety of aims, some of which were in conflict. They saw the aims of the school council as being to 'give children greater voice' but from the way that meetings were set up, it seemed that there was potentially a tension between this intention and the educational agenda (of teaching about democratic procedures). The teachers' educational aims of teaching children about democratic procedures were sometimes incompatible with the aim of encouraging children's participation. In terms of literacy, in particular, the emphasis on promoting only the dominant literacy practices associated with meetings sometimes hindered genuine participation and decision-making on the part of children themselves. Given the recent focus on development of literacy skills within the United Kingdom curriculum, teachers were understandably keen to take the opportunity to use the 'real' context of the school council meeting to introduce children to different registers, text types, and genres.

As we will explore further in the next section, the fact that teachers were concerned to promote learning through explicit teaching, and that both children and teachers assumed that a certain kind of literacy should be integral to democratic procedures in meetings, meant that sometimes it was difficult for children to have ownership of the decision-making. Within the school council meetings we observed, we were keen to "problematise what counts as literacy at any time and place" and to ask "whose literacies are dominant and whose marginalized or resistant" (Street 2003, 1). As in Stein and Mamabolo's account from South Africa (this volume), we realized that within the primary school context, children's 'resistance' may be expressed only in their silence or their passivity. We were also aware that the emphasis on the formal 'schooled' literacy within meetings left little space for children to make meaning in their own ways through negotiation.

The School Council Discourse: Looking at Power and Participation

Viewing school council communicative practices as embedded in relationships of power, we were aware that the learning that occurred went beyond the apparently neutral development of skills and concepts associated with democracy and the 'school council' literacy. Children were to a certain extent empowered by learning explicitly about democratic procedures and associated new literacy practices. However, our observations of what actually happened during meetings and as a result of school council discussions, suggested that this was not the whole story. It became evident that both teachers and children were working within parameters about what was appropriate to bring up in school council. This was reflected in the limited range of agenda items, often focusing on fundraising, behavior issues in the school as a whole, and playground concerns—in other words, matters that were extraneous to the business of teaching and learning in the classroom. (This is also highlighted in previous research; see Wyse and Hawtin 2000 and Dobie 1998). These extracurricular issues were summed up by the teachers as 'toilets and playtime'. The culture of the school (where teachers had control over decisions around teaching and learning) seemed to be a restriction on the school council's sphere of influence, which the children implicitly accepted. Furthermore, children were learning that they had limited ownership over the process of decision-making and the decisions made as they became increasingly aware of the power of the key decision makers beyond the school council. At the same time, they were acquiring new identities within the context of the different structures and procedures that were being introduced. Looking from the perspective of the NLS, we were interested to explore how the communicative practices described earlier influenced existing hierarchical relationships between children and teachers.

Teacher-Child Interaction

The teachers' intention was to create a forum for participatory debate between students. Although this was sometimes achieved, there were other times when the perceived authority of the teacher to make decisions meant that discussion became a dialogue between teacher and child. From our observation and focus group discussions, we found that the children sometimes deferred to the teacher's opinion and that the council meeting was seen as a process of gaining permission from the teacher, rather than negotiating within the council as a whole.

> George (child chairperson): *First on the agenda today. The clock in the canteen. Who brought this up? Why? Presumably because you want a clock in the canteen.*
>
> Jack: Because if you want to go on the field when the bell goes, you need to know . . .
>
> Teacher: No problem.
>
> George: OK. So it's decided to put a clock in the canteen . . .

However the situation did enable teachers to learn more about children's perspectives, particularly outside the classroom. For example, in one of the schools, the teachers were surprised to hear about children's experiences with midday supervisors at lunchtime.

> Teacher 1: We talked about the times that are difficult, assembly and what was the other one?
>
> Sam: At dinner.
>
> Teacher 1: They have to wait for hours [to go to the toilet] so they are desperate.

Teacher 2: Why do you have to wait for a long time at dinner?

Jason: Because Miss is only usually making sure that the packed lunches and the school lunches are . . . she comes round to the hot dinners but by then you are probably gone because you really need it.

Teacher 2: So you are not allowed to go out of the dinner hall when you need to go to the toilet?

Sam: No, because when you want to, if you put your hand up the teacher tells you to put it down.

Teacher 2: I'm sorry, I didn't know . . . how do you, when you need to go to the toilet, what do you have to do?

Sam: You put your hand up.

Teacher 1: Just put your hand up and wait?

Teacher 2: So do they ignore you then? So what do you do?

Sam: We wait . . .

Teacher 2: So you can't leave the dinner hall until after you have finished your dinner even if you need to go to the toilet.

Teacher 2: But even then, they are saying they can't go, they are just ignored.

Teacher 1: Just ignored.

Children commented on the fact that teachers were more likely to listen to them through the forum of the school council than if they raised the same issues informally in the playground.

"If we said we wanted to run in the corridor, the teachers wouldn't listen. But we can say that in school council."

"You can't always tell the people on duty outside as the staff will say, why did you bring it to me? . . . It wouldn't be talked about in the staff room but it would in school council."

Children also felt that teachers gained more insight into their needs through the school council, even though they saw the teacher as the ultimate beneficiary.

"I think it makes a big difference to [headteacher]. Instead of thinking on his own what the children want, he can find out what they want."

It was also apparent that at times, the purpose of communication about what went on at school council was to keep teachers informed rather than children. The following extract is from a class council meeting:

> *Ross:* New coat pegs—because some of the coat pegs aren't big enough to put coats on and library books fall off.
>
> *Teacher 1:* What happened about that because we need those.
>
> *Rosie:* We are going to get new ones I think.
>
> *Teacher 2:* We're definitely going to get new ones.
>
> *Teacher 1:* So that was decided?

Teacher 2's comment suggests that the decision was made outside school council and that some teachers had already been informed.

The interaction between teachers and children in the school council meetings was constructed within the institutional discourse of the school. Although the children were able to raise different issues for discussion from those in the classroom, the power dynamics between teachers and children remained relatively unchallenged.

Decision-Making

It was clear from our discussions with children that they thought that the teachers had the ultimate say and were central figures in the school council. For example, in describing what happens at school council meetings, one child said, "Lots of people gather round [head teacher] and say what they want to sort out."

In our observation of meetings, we also noted occasions when the teacher over-ruled the children's ideas for discussion. In this extract, the teacher indicated a clear hierarchy of interested parties, and the governors' and parents' wishes counted above the children's:

> *Ruth (year 4):* Two people in our class don't want to wear uniform.
>
> *Teacher:* Who's that?
>
> *Ruth:* gives names).
>
> *Teacher:* The school uniform is set by governors and the majority of parents appreciate it. We're quite flexible and don't insist that you wear a par-

ticular type of shirt or whatever, just the right colour. They're not going to get that changed. It is set by the governors, listening to what parents think.

Often, when teachers had the final say, this could have been because children did not have sufficient understanding of the implications of their decisions (e.g., cost or safety). An alternative interpretation could be that there was a conflict of interests between teachers and children and children were implicitly learning that their own views could be over-ridden by the teachers'. This is exemplified in the following extracts:

[The children were discussing ideas for the playground at school council meeting]

Teacher: . . . we mentioned it in my class and [headteacher] mentioned it in assembly. No balls are to be brought into the playground. What other toys would be useful to bring?

Isobel: skipping ropes

Ross: hoops?

Teacher: If we say no to balls, any other toys could be misused too. We want to get some equipment . . .

Child: could bring marbles

Nina: tennis things

Teacher: that would be balls again . . .

[The children wanted a mirror in the boys' toilets.]

Teacher: I'll take up one thing—the mirror in the boys' toilets. We couldn't see the advantage . . . If we're trying to get children out of the toilets (further explaining about how this might encourage boys to congregate in the toilets at playtime).

Similarly in terms of the ways in which decisions made by children were followed through (or not), children were implicitly learning that their ideas might not always be taken seriously or acted upon by teachers. Sometimes this was due to practical constraints, such as time, but also could be an expression of differing priorities:

[Children are discussing in a school council meeting who should be invited to open their school fete: they had been hoping that Simon Thomas from Blue Peter would come.]

Kirsty: What about Simon Thomas?

Child Chairperson: Sorry, the Friends moved quickly and booked Lois Pearce to open the fete. We won't be able to get him now, only a month to go. She's on Anglia News and she is a district commissioner for the guides. She's very pleased to do it.

Annie: We liked Simon Thomas. We don't watch news.

Teacher: It's just time.

Chair: We can't say, go away, but we could say we've got someone more interesting than you!

In this case, the adults' decision generated a lot of discussion around the school. The children were concerned that their decision had not been implemented. The teachers saw the priority as to book someone who could definitely come and open the fete—and recognized that there was little chance of inviting the Blue Peter presenter in time. In other situations, children comment on the lack of feedback on their suggestions and the slow response:

Joe: I think they should make things quicker because I said about the shed a long time ago and I haven't heard anything.

This could be related to a general concern on the part of children that the school council could be seen as ineffective. Several children commented on the fact that the same agenda items came up again and again:

Candy: Normally the big things we don't decide. Like the school disco, we just kept talking about it and each week it was on the agenda and then we really never never . . .

George (chair): Discussed anything else . . . We did things. I think the things that we decide on are the little things that no one notices. And the things we like either forget or we decide we can't do them are the big things that people would quite like . . .

Candy: Cos the big things we always . . . we talk about it and then it just goes on the agenda again and again.

George: And then eventually they just get bored with it.

Although children expressed frustration at things not getting done, the context of making real decisions provided an opportunity to learn about the complexity of decision-making. Sometimes, this was a matter of understanding procedural difficulties—for example, the Tuckswood Community First School Charity Committee was responsible for collecting and organizing delivery of clothes to Afghanistan. The piles of clothes the children had collected, which were becoming 'smelly', were a reminder to the children that it was their responsibility to get things organized between the committee and the school council. In other cases, children gained an understanding that some problems could not be easily solved: for example, bullying in the school. They were able to see for themselves that their suggestion of naming bullies had undesirable consequences (such as people naming their 'enemies'). These examples show that while handing over responsibility to children is not straightforward, when this occurs in a real life context, it can provide positive educational opportunities.

Insofar as the school councils were about decision-making, it was evident that teachers were largely in control of the process. We noticed that the school councils provided a channel of communication between children and teachers, rather than necessarily handing over power to the children. Analysis of the literacy practices associated with the process illuminated the extent to which children were marginalized. For example, the teacher would sometimes write the minutes of the meeting for the children to copy into their books, which would then be read by their class teacher to the other children. This meant that children were not always communicating directly with their peers in their own way.

Interaction among Children

The transfer of responsibility from teachers to children was also problematic in that the school council practices intensified existing inequalities between children and their peers. Moreover, school council structures introduced new hierarchical power relations between children that to some extent mirrored those already established between teachers and students. In particular, age was an issue as the younger children were not only reluctant to talk in the formal context of the mixed-age meeting, but tended to be excluded from the literacy-based proceedings. The fact that older children took on the formal roles within the council, such as chairperson, meant that they had control over who participated in discussion. This did not go unnoticed by the younger children:

Amy: Our chairperson, he always chooses the years 5 and 6 so I'm not that happy.

In focus group discussions, younger children suggested a range of ways of gaining attention, such as banging a drum; they were aware that rules about turn-taking were not being followed. Longer meetings were too tiring for younger children, who fell asleep, found excuses such as going to the toilet for leaving the meeting, or were sent back to their classrooms by the teachers. This led to the perception by older children that the youngest children (particularly Reception class) should not be involved in the school council since "they wouldn't understand it, they [reception children] are too young. They'll probably start to do it next year" (KS1[4] School Council member). Even in the first school with a narrower age range, the year 3s assumed authority. The teacher did not see the younger children's relative lack of participation as problematic. Since the school council was seen to have an educational purpose, it was considered appropriate for the younger children to listen to and learn from the older children.

The new power relations set up by the school council were related to issues of identity as an 'insider' or 'outsider' and the fact that some noncouncil members sometimes had little knowledge of what was going on in meetings. For example, Rory, who was dyslexic, saw himself as unsuitable as a school council member but wanted to be involved. He had lots of ideas and felt frustrated that he did not have a voice on the council, complaining about its lack of effectiveness. As well as endorsing hierarchies associated with age, the school council thus created new divisions between children through assumed power and identities on the part of those who were members of the council. While privileging children who were school council members, the new structures and practices could implicitly disenfranchise other children in the school.

Alternative Strategies

Following the early stage of our project (described above), we worked in collaboration with the teachers to develop alternative strategies for facilitating school council meetings. The teachers' espoused aim in setting up school coun-

[4]KS1 refers to Key Stage 1 age group (5–7 years): Key Stage 2 covers 8–11 years. One of the primary schools involved (Hilllside Avenue) ran separate school councils for KS1 and KS2.

cils had been to give the children greater voice, though they were aware of the difficulties of doing this in practice. Through our workshops with the teachers, it became apparent that though the teachers wanted to encourage participation on a local level within their schools, they themselves were working in an institutional paradigm of accountability. Contextual influences, such as national programs for literacy teaching, the national curriculum, and regular inspections which require conformity to national 'standards', limited the extent to which the teachers felt able to challenge implicit hierarchies. The need to demonstrate that standards were being maintained in every area inevitably meant that teachers were cautious in handing over responsibility to children. Their frequent mention of time constraints illustrated how little flexibility they had to focus on school council activities.

Our intention in introducing visual strategies for communication was originally to enable younger children, and others who found that the dominant literacy practices limited their full participation in school council activities, to participate. We were keen to experiment with a range of multimodal communicative practices (see Kress 1997) which children would be able to shape in their own way. Starting from practical / visual approaches taken from PRA, teachers and children investigated the use of pictures and objects as an alternative form of representation to challenge the ways in which school councils had conventionally been run. Recognizing that the dominant literacy practices marginalized some children (in the ways discussed above), the teachers encouraged the children to construct the agenda using objects and pictures to represent the issues to be discussed, to make visual matrices and maps to explore and compare their ideas, to use counters to express individual preferences, and to record meeting outcomes through their own signs or drawings. Rather than assuming that meetings had to be recorded in written form, teachers and children also began to value alternatives: for example, counters representing children's preferences could be placed in boxes to become a permanent visual record in the classroom. In one school, children began to make their own drawings in place of written minutes, suggesting a shift towards forms of communication that better served their own purposes.

These strategies helped to address some of the power issues identified in the preceding section. Drawing, the construction of timelines and other representations of children's experience at school, and map-making contributed to extending the range of issues considered appropriate for discussion at school council. This helped to make visible the implicit parameters that had previously shaped the school council agenda. Other activities, such as using a matrix to structure discussion, enabled all children to contribute their view. The visual presence of the objects and counters provided a focus for decision-making which was accessible to all. Though the teachers acted as facilitators, their surprise at the outcome of the children's discussion showed that they had less influence over the decisions. For instance, when ranking and comparing options for improving their playground at Village Primary School, the children decided that they wanted a water feature, in preference to the other suggestions (anticipated by the teachers) such as playground equipment. When children used cards, drawings and artefacts to represent their ideas, those who normally found it difficult to speak in a group or who were ignored by other children, found that the picture or concrete object gave their views more weight. For example, in Hillside Avenue Primary School, mapping was used to discuss 'places that are important to us'. A child was adamant that his drawing of the classroom where he went for support for his special needs should be placed in the center of the diagram that the children were constructing. The others in the group disagreed but he was able to insist, by continually pushing his picture back into the center, saying, "but it's important to me." As he was not usually verbally assertive, using pieces of paper helped him to have his point heard. Likewise, the younger children were able to participate in the decision-making process on a more equal basis. They also found the practical activities enjoyable and more intrinsically motivating than listening in a meeting.

In the introduction to this book, Street quotes from his earlier article (1997, 29) on the need for educationalists to "move beyond simply theoretical critiques of the autonomous model of literacy and to develop positive proposals for interventions in curriculum . . . based upon these principles." Our alternative strategies were intended to offer a practical critique of the dominant literacy in school councils through extending the range of communicative practices. However this was not unproblematic. At the beginning of the project, our own assumption was that the visual approaches in themselves would revitalize the local literacies of children and school communities and encourage more participation. Our research revealed that the wider ideological context and the institutional culture of the schools influenced how these activities were shaped in practice. As Burke and Hermerschmidt (this volume) note with regard to research methodologies, "Methods are often understood as 'packages' that can be picked 'off the shelf'. The same goes with theoretical frameworks which are seen to be ready-made packages that can simply be selected and then applied to sets of data." Being already familiar with the context of current United Kingdom primary education practice—where curriculum innovations are often 'packaged' and promoted as 'activities', rather than as approaches to be critiqued and developed—we had anticipated that our visual approaches could be seen as yet another set of prescriptive activities. For this reason, as a group, we had developed a critical approach towards implementing these visual methods. As time went on, the ways in which the visual strategies were implemented and evolved enabled us all to become more aware of the theoretical frameworks which shaped our practice as teachers and researchers.

What are the Implications of This Study for the New Literacy Studies?

At the outset of this project, we used the NLS concept of multiliteracies to problematize the communicative practices being promoted in school council. The introduction of visual approaches was envisaged as a way of challenging the dominant literacy and the associated hierarchical relationships (between teachers and children, and between older/ younger children). As the project progressed, extending the range of literacies within school council activities helped to address some of the difficulties in communication and issues around unequal power relationships that we identified. However, we realized increasingly that this local initiative did not challenge the social practices of the school as an institution in the context of national educational priorities. The important factor influencing participation was not the kind of literacy practiced (e.g., dominant literacy as compared to 'local literacies') but the ways in which social practices shaped that literacy. Indeed, the introduction of PRA could be seen as another 'dominant' literacy (see Robinson-Pant 1996) imposed from outside the local context. Neither the context of the school council itself, with its potential for participation and child-owned decision-making, nor the PRA methods could challenge the dominant communicative practices of the school. These were shaped by the 'currently privileged'[5] educational discourse. As Street

[5] Burke and Hermerschmidt's chapter has made us more aware of the static concept of power associated with the word 'dominant'—their idea of more fluid relationships is particularly appropriate when analysing United Kingdom educational discourses.

(2003) comments, "there is more going on in a local literacy than just local practice."

While teachers were concerned to open up spaces for child participation and decision-making, the influence of the dominant institutional practices closed down many opportunities for the transfer of power to children in the ways discussed above. This was demonstrated, for instance, by the focus on specific literacy modes. It was interesting that children themselves would spontaneously conform to the dominant practices: For example, when using drawing to facilitate decision-making, they were distracted by the need to produce a 'nice' drawing, and they reverted to formal procedures (sitting round a table and choosing someone to be in charge) on an occasion when they were given a choice. This relates to Rogers' chapter in this book, where he notes that adult learners in countries of the South often opt for a model of education based on local formal primary school practice rather than informal adult education approaches.

The NLS approaches enabled us as researchers to analyze the power dimensions of the communicative practices within school council activities. However, we are aware that in using this framework implicitly rather than explicitly (see Burke and Hermerschmidt), we to some extent closed down the opportunities for the transfer of power to the teachers. Unlike action research approaches where the teachers themselves problematize their own practice, within NLS, there can be insufficient attention to the role of the researcher and how action is to be initiated. Once NLS researchers move into the area of 'positive interventions' (see Street's introduction), this contradiction can become more apparent: that the relationship between the researcher and the 'researched' is not always explicitly addressed.[6] In this case, we needed to look more closely at the relationship between 'insider' and 'outsider' researchers, and between researchers and children. While the goals for participation were shared between the teacher-researchers and ourselves, the teachers in the schools were to some extent constrained by institutional practices which worked against the project's aims. In adopting the standpoint of NLS, we analyzed the project in the wider ideological context, as well as local, power dimensions. However, we realized that the research process itself shaped the project, and vice versa, and should be similarly analyzed in the context of institutional relationships.

[6]This could be related to critiques of Freire's 'neutral facilitator' and relative lack of attention to 'praxis' as compared to 'conscientisation'; see, for example, Mayo 1995.

Acknowledgements: We would like to acknowledge the contributions made by Barbara Elliott, De Jarvis, Sue Lawes, Emily Millner, and Tim Taylor to the research project on which this chapter is based. Our thanks also go to their colleagues and the children in the schools involved.

References

Chambers, R. 1994. Participatory Rural Appraisal (PRA): Analysis of experience. *World Development* 22(9): 1253–68.

Clay, D., and Gold, J. 2000. *Primary School Councils Toolkit.* London: School Councils UK.

Cox, S., Robinson-Pant, A., Elliott, B., et al. 2003. *Empowering Children Through Visual Communication.* Norwich: University of East Anglia and CfBT.

Dobie, T. 1998. Pupil councils in Fife. In: D. Christie, H. Maitles, and J. Halliday, (eds.), *Values education for democracy and citizenship.* Strathclyde: University of Strathclyde.

Kress, G. 1997. *Before writing: Re-thinking the paths to literacy.* London: Routledge.

Kulick, D., and Stroud, C. 1993. Conceptions and uses of literacy in a Papua New Guinean village. In: B. Street (ed.), *Cross-cultural approaches to literacy.* Cambridge: Cambridge University Press.

Mayo, P. 1995. Critical literacy and emancipatory politics: The work of Paulo Freire. *International Journal of Educational Development.* 15(4): 363–379.

Robinson-Pant, A. 1996. PRA: A new literacy? *Journal of International Development* 8(4): 531–551.

Street, B.V. 1997. The implications of the New Literacy Studies for literacy education. *English in Education* 31(3): 101–134.

Street, B.V. 2003. What's new in NLS? Critical approaches to literacy in theory and practice. *Current Issues in Comparative Education,* Summer 2003. http//www.tc.columbia.edu/cice/articles/BS152.htm.

Sutton, F. 1999. *The school council: A children's guide.* London: Save the Children.

Wyse, D., and Hawtin, A. 2000. Children's rights. In: D. Wyse, and A. Hawtin (eds.), *Children: A multi-professional perspective.* London: Arnold.

4

Multigrade Schooling and Literacy

Linking Literacy Learning in Home, Community, and Primary School in the Peruvian Amazon

Patricia Ames

Introduction

This chapter deals with literacy learning in an educational context that, despite its widespread presence in the world, tends to remain invisible in educational research, administration, policy, and curriculum planning (Little 1995; 2001): the multigrade school. In the multigrade school one teacher teaches two or more grade groups in the same classroom at the same time. Although in some cases multigrade classrooms arise from pedagogical choice, in most cases they arise through necessity. In developing countries, multigrade schools are often necessary because of geographic, demographic, and material difficulties, and therefore these schools tend to be seen as inferior (Thomas and Shaw 1992).

However, research on multigrade schools in several countries suggests that there is little or no difference in students' achievement in multigrade and monograde classrooms (Veenman 1995; 1996; Miller 1991; 1991a; 1990; Psacharopoulos et al. 1992; McEwan 1998; Pratt 1986). Multigrade classrooms can be as effective as monograde classrooms, or even better in some aspects (i.e., students' affective development), *if* adequate training and resources are allocated. But because developing countries tend to retain single-grade pedagogical methods in multigrade situations, they fail to reap the potential benefits (Thomas and Shaw 1992).

Looking for an understanding and improvement of literacy learning in multigrade schools, I conducted an ethnographic study and later an action research project with teachers in a multigrade school in the Peruvian Amazon region. For this study, I drew on the New Literacy Studies approach (NLS), which challenges the conception of literacy as a technical skill that can be learned through a series of graded steps (the autonomous model). The technical aspect of literacy is seen as part of a broader conception that understands literacy as a social practice implicated in power relations and embedded in specific cultural meanings and practices (Street 1993; 1995; Barton 1994).

This perspective can also be related to new pedagogical approaches and sociocultural theories of learning that emphasize the importance of meaning and social context rather than only codification skills in literacy learning (Czerniewska 1996; Stromquist 1997; Crawford 1995; Fosnot 1996; Steffe and Gale 1995). As in other studies in this volume (see Larson; Roswell and Rajaratnam; Hopson) an educational perspective of this kind was a necessary complement in the conceptual framework of the study. However, in contrast with those studies, which used the communities-of-practice learning theories or cultural modeling approach to learning, I draw mainly on a sociocultural contructivism approach (Cobb 1996; Steffe and Gale 1995; Wertsch and Toma 1995; Konold 1995; Bauersfeld 1995), since constructivism played an important role in the current changes affecting the educational system I was studying in the Peruvian Amazon. Sociocultural constructivism emphasizes that key aspects of mental functioning can be understood only by considering the social contexts in which they are embedded, since knowledge is achieved through participation in social practice. Learning, like human action in general, is situated in cultural, historical, and institutional contexts. However, this approach has important points in common with the approaches mentioned above (i.e., communities-of-practice learning theories; cultural modeling) since all stress the socially and culturally situated nature of learning.

From both perspectives then, the NLS and the sociocultural constructivism, approach the traditional graded division inside schools (the monograde model as the predominant way of organising instruction), which has been seen as the ideal by most educational systems, could be rethought and compared with other learning experiences outside school. The research therefore focused not only on the multigrade school, but also on the literacy practices in different domains in the life of children such as home and community. It is argued here that a combined social and educational approach could pave the way for improved literacy learning in multigrade schools, by paying attention to literacy and learning practices inside and outside the school and questioning of the notion of literacy behind the model of single-grade literacy instruction.

This chapter focuses on three main topics of the broader study. First, it analyzes the multigrade-classroom teaching and learning strategies and teachers' ways of classroom management, uncovering the importance that particular notions of literacy, such as the autonomous model, have in shaping teachers' classroom practice. Second, an insight into literacy practices at community and home attempts to show the varied literacy experiences children can get from their social context, despite the widespread characterization of it as "deprived" of literacy. Finally, I highlight how central features of the ways of learning at home can be considered as useful resources for children to engage in literacy learning at multigrade classrooms.

The Context: A Multigrade School in the Peruvian Amazon

In many developing countries it is possible to find a great proportion of multigrade schools, that often serve rural, isolated, and low-population areas. Peru is not an exception. There are currently 23,419 multigrade schools in Peru. They represent 73 percent of public primary schools in the country, although in rural areas 90 percent of schools are multigrade (Montero et al. 2002). Given the importance of multigrade schools in the rural areas, the study focused on a rural village as a case study. The village, San Antonio, is located in the Ucayali region, where 85 percent of the schools are multigrade.

The fifty families who live in San Antonio are mainly dedicated to fishing and agriculture in the tropical rain forest. The inhabitants are *mestizos,* "mixed-race people," descendants of an indigenous population that has mixed with outsiders over the years. They speak Spanish, the majority language in Peru, although the village is also surrounded by Shipibo[1] villages. There is no electricity in San Antonio, no provision of water in the household (it is fetched from the river), nor sanitary services. Conditions of poverty characterize the village, as in other rural settlements in the country. However, in contrast with other small rural villages, San Antonio has a basic health center and preschool, primary, and secondary schools.

The village has a multigrade school with three teachers, providing all six years of primary education. Each teacher teaches two grades at the same time, but sometimes, when one of them is absent, another teacher might get three or four grades in his or her classroom.

Parents of San Antonio school children strongly support literacy acquisition for their children and believe it will offer them better opportunities in life. However, they perceive the school learning results as poor, but few can afford to send their children to an urban school. Looking through the lens of NLS studies it was possible to underscore many of the problems behind the school failure to enhance their children's literacy learning.

Literacy Learning in the Multigrade Classroom

Despite current efforts in the Peruvian educational system to introduce a New Pedagogical Model (NPM) encouraging an active pedagogy, a child-centered approach to learning and curricular diversification to acknowledge the cultural and social diversity of students, one finds the prevalence of traditional teaching and learning strategies, especially in rural schools.

The San Antonio multigrade school, for example, offers a narrow range of literacy events for their students to engage with, even though literacy learning is a major concern for teachers and they dedicate most of their lessons to it.[2] Teaching and learning strategies used by teachers are based mainly on copying,

---

[1] The Shipibo people is one of the largest native indigenous groups of the Peruvian Amazon. They speak Shipibo as their mother tongue and Spanish as second language. There are at least four shipibo villages close to San Antonio. A small number of students who attend the secondary school at San Antonio come from these villages.

[2] Fifty-five percent of all lessons observed and 57 percent of written-down lessons in a sample of children's notebooks in all grades.

dictation, reading aloud, and rote learning, although two teachers try to encourage more writing production and reading comprehension and are more keen to produce meaningful experiences.[3]

In addition, in examining the teaching and learning strategies in different subjects, it became evident that learning at school appears mediated by writing, which plays a central role in school activities. Children are expected to acquire school knowledge mainly through written means. Literacy practices, however, range from very mechanical to more creative ones. The latter are clearly related to innovations promoted by the NPM, while the former fall within a more "traditional" approach to teaching and learning. Nevertheless, school literacy in general remains largely decontextualized from the children's experiences and firmly attached to its internal uses in school. It is treated as an object to be known or a skill to be mastered. Its communicative and social nature rarely appears, despite the emphasis the NPM has tried to introduce.

This last point is of special importance in the context of the multigrade classroom, where instructional organization is strongly linked with teachers' notions of literacy learning. The five teachers[4] used three different strategies to manage the multigrade classroom. The first strategy treats each grade group as separate, thus delivering different activities for each one. The second one uses whole-class teaching, without differentiating grade groups and doing the same activities with the whole group. A third strategy combines whole-class teaching, but then the class is split into grade or mixed-grade groups for specific activities. The first and second strategies are the most common, while the third appears less frequently among two teachers.

These strategies also appear linked with students' grade and age. For example, the first strategy is used by Olga,[5] the 1st and 2nd grade teacher. For Olga, 1st graders must learn to write (and thus they get extensive copying of letters, syllables, and words), while 2nd graders already have some notions of this and can copy and write more. She, therefore, feels forced to choose this strategy because of the students' different literacy levels.

---

[3] Since the research spanned two consecutive school years, I observed three teachers during the first year and two new ones who came to replace previous ones, totaling five teachers. The school staff, however, was always composed of three teachers.

[4] See footnote 3.

[5] All personal names have been changed.

A particular conception about literacy underlies this apparently forced choice. As literacy is seen as a set of hierarchical and graded skills, teaching must take into account the level of development of coding and decoding skills. Children who are learning to write do this through copying bits of written signs before proceeding to more complex activities, such as reading and writing texts. Children who already have some coding/decoding skills can copy longer passages and lesson contents and begin to read.

If literacy were understood as a communicative and social practice, however, children with different levels of coding and decoding skills could engage in joint activities, such as shared reading, producing written texts with the help of older children, and managing the classroom library together.[6] What seems inevitable to this teacher is only so because of her approach to literacy.

The 3rd and 4th grade teacher, Mario, seemed to envisage this possibility when working with mixed-grade groups. He explained that, in this way, children with different skills and abilities can help each other when doing the same exercise and despite their grade. This teacher used the second strategy (whole-class teaching) more and sometimes introduced the third one (mixing whole-class teaching and separate activities). In addition, Mario used a greater variety of activities and resources than other teachers, such as maps, charts, books, workbooks, dialogue, writing exercises, calculation exercises with physical material, observation, drawing, reflection upon grammatical aspects of language, oral presentations, and copying. Most of the activities were conducted through group work. Literacy is an important component of these activities. Whether children are looking at the map, identifying the names of departments, listing them, looking for their own department, producing a chart or copying verbs, they are using and practicing their reading and writing skills. In these activities, one sees that literacy is used as a tool more than as an end in itself, corresponding to the teacher's interest in developing meaningful activities rather than mechanical exercises for practicing reading and writing.

For other teachers (Cesar, Penny, Maria) who use the whole-class teaching strategy, however, it is also linked to a notion of literacy as a set of graded skills. Thus, since they teach either 3rd and 4th grades or 5th and 6th grades, they explain the fact that the children "already know how to write," means they have

---

[6]These strategies were introduced later in the research as part of a collaborative action research project with teachers. See Ames, 2003.

the basic coding and decoding skills and therefore can engage in the same activity despite differences in grade. Nevertheless, they keep using copying, dictation, and drill as the main methods for children to learn. The only exception was Maria, also a 3rd and 4th grade teacher, who shares with Mario an interest in more active strategies and has a broad range of teaching strategies, using sometimes a mixed strategy of whole-class teaching and sometimes splitting into grade groups.

Without entering into a discussion of the advantages and disadvantages of each strategy to manage multigrade classrooms, I would like to emphasize how each one of them is tied in with particular conceptions about what is literacy, what literacy is for, and how children learn literacy (and knowledge in general). Thus, using a NLS approach it was possible to unpack the conceptions that sustain particular teaching and learning strategies and multigrade classroom management practices and thus initiate a process of reflection and change in classroom practices.

The NLS approach is useful not only in that one can analyze the impact of a particular view of literacy (i.e., autonomous) in the multigrade classroom, but also in how other literacy and learning practices might sustain children's learning at school. To do so, an exploration of home and community is necessary.

The "Illiterate" Rural Villages: Literacy in Daily Life

Although the Peruvian rural population had been historically excluded from schooling for most of the twentieth century, a significant change in the last few decades had led to the expansion of educational services throughout the country. The people of San Antonio have benefited from this, achieving more years of education than the national average for the rural population, although they still fall behind urban areas and most did not achieve secondary education (see Table 1).

This is worth noting, since a dominant discourse in Peru as in other developing countries had constructed the rural areas as "deprived" of literacy and rural people as mainly nonliterate (Godenzzi et al. 2000; Maddox 2001). This discourse had influenced teachers' preconceptions about rural villagers. Teachers tend to consider rural parents as little educated at best and ignorant at worst, and thus offering scarce support to children to learn literacy (cf. Chopra 2001 on the construction of the "illiterate village woman").

Table 1. Average Number of Years of Schooling for Population over Age 15

Population over age 15	San Antonio[7]	National Rural[8]	National Urban[9]
Men	7.4	5.1	9.2
Women	6.8	3.7	8.3

[7] Source: Population Census, San Antonio, November 2000.
[8] Source: INEI. *Encuesta Nacional de Hogares 1997* (cit. in Montero and Tovar 1999).
[9] Ibid.

However, research into community life and a sample of nine households showed a very different picture, as found by other authors in this book similarly using NLS approaches to investigate community life beyond the school (cf. Stein and Mamabolo; Davies et al.; Welle et al.). In Peru, as in these contexts, literacy is used in a variety of ways and is related to different purposes as part of daily activities in the community and the home.

In the San Antonio community, literacy plays a central role and is used intensively by local organizations, since they have to deal with different kinds of documents for different purposes related to the organization of community life. Literacy in this case allows people, on the one hand, to establish a relationship with the state and public institutions and to access goods and social services provided by them. On the other hand, literacy also plays a role in the internal organization of the community (e.g., organizing a local festivity, accounting for a community labor force). Besides these more collective uses of literacy, villagers also use literacy individually when approaching public institutions such as the school, the health center, and the Ministries of Fishery and Agriculture or when acquiring national identity papers. Thus, literacy appears as a central requirement of the state bureaucracy in both collective and individual dimensions. Literacy and numeracy are also used for commercial transactions in which villagers are usually involved. Finally, literacy constitutes a tool in the relationship with other social groups at the regional and national levels (to state one's position, to negotiate social identities). In this sense, literacy for San Antonio villagers conveys multiple meanings related to their identity, status, and citizenship not only in the local context but also in the context of a broader national society.

In the more intimate sphere of home, literacy also has several roles to play in daily life. It has a role in domestic organization, through the use of shopping lists for people traveling to the city. It also serves for communicating with relatives outside the village,[10] using either short messages or letters (and even a combination of telephone calls and letters). Literacy is also valued and used for getting information and entertainment through reading newspapers and books and moral advice through the reading of the Bible.

Literacy also plays a role in the expression of personal feelings such as affection and love. This is most evident in the use of love letters between teenagers and between adult lovers, but it also appeared in a teenager's personal journal and in short affective messages children wrote to the researcher. Love letters express, in a formal but explicit language, the feelings of writers and would allow an alternative way to do so when overt expressions of affection in speech appear to be less appropriate (Besnier 1993).[11]

Children do not appear directly involved in most of these literacy events. Nevertheless, from their indirect participation (observing, listening, carrying messages to and from the port) they seem to extract the many purposes and uses that the written word has in their homes. Besides, children do participate directly in an identifiable literacy event: doing homework.

Doing Homework: The School Way to Learn

In contrast with other literacy events that occur as part of family life, helping with homework appears to be more formal and structured and reveals a dynamic shaped by school procedures. Doing homework is an activity unto itself, in which an adult, usually the mother, and the child or children sit down together to review and do the day's homework. The mother reads the instructions and guides children in the task, usually providing answers or examples required for the exercise, following a pattern usually found at school: the mother determines the child's activity, provides directions, expects the child to practice reading and writing, identifies errors, corrects them, and provides answers to questions involved in the homework.

This interaction contrasts sharply with interaction between mothers and children in everyday activities, where the mother provides fewer explicit verbal

[10]Every family at the village has at least one relative living outside the village.

[11]Writing to express feelings and personal experiences is also reported in a study of another rural community in Peruvian highlands (De la Piedra 2003).

directions, involves the child through active participation and corrects mistakes without verbal sanction. In helping with homework, the interaction between mother and child appears to mirror the interaction between teachers and students at school. Mothers appear to apply their own experience as students, and they follow the teachers' advice about ways of supporting their children's schooling, applying what Street et al. (forthcoming) call 'school domain' practices in the 'home site'.

> Teacher Penny: (last year) there was a girl in third grade. I put her in the second grade group because she didn't know dictation. . . . I didn't let her pass, and her mother asked me why. . . . I had told her, you teach her dictation, you dictate words to her at home, you teach her the (multiplication) tables, at least teach her addition. I said to her, your girl only plays here all day, she has to practice. . . . She doesn't mind then. What can I do? I made her repeat the grade.

By mirroring school practices and learning routines, both teachers and parents privilege this way of learning. Other ways of learning (i.e., the spontaneous participation of children in home literacy events) are not considered to foster literacy learning. Indeed, the tendency to encourage parents to help with literacy learning at home through explicit instruction is common in many countries (Lareau 1989; Gregory and Williams 2000). Some studies, however, such as Taylor (1983), point out that there is little evidence to suggest that children who successfully learn to read and write are specially taught by their parents in this 'schooled' way. In the families participating in her study, literacy is deeply embedded in the social process of family life and is not some specific list of activities added to the family agenda to explicitly teach reading (Taylor 1983, 92–93). This is confirmed by current trends in literacy learning that emphasize how children build their understanding of the writing system based on the real uses it has in their immediate environment (Czerniewska 1996).

Nevertheless, spontaneous literacy events at home seem not to be considered either by teachers or parents as ways to foster literacy learning among children. Even less attention is paid to other language experiences of children at home (i.e., the rich oral tradition related to the natural, magical, and spiritual world) as part of their literacy learning process. Without denying the importance of mothers' support for children in their learning, one can question whether the school-type interaction for helping with homework (fostered by teachers) is the best approach. Instead, research leads us to suggest that more opportunities for children to engage in real literacy events at home and in the community (with purposes beyond the acquisition of literacy itself and for communicative purposes, real life situations, household organisation, etc.) would help children's literacy learning in general. Children's spontaneous attempts to make sense of the written word seem to confirm the value of such opportunities.

Children and Their Curiosity about the Written Word: Beyond Homework

San Antonio children are conscious that literacy plays and will play a role in their lives. They are told and taught by their parents about the importance of becoming literate. From the written landscape in the village (composed by shop signs, commercial advertising inside shops, public building signs, labels on food products and familiar objects, occasional posters for national elections, calendars, diplomas, and so on) it is evident that children find printing in their everyday life, both in home and in the community. Children react to this presence of literacy with a great deal of curiosity and undertake actions to determine how it works, developing their own interpretations and ways of gaining access to how literacy functions.[12]

An exercise I conducted with children from 3rd to 6th grades, in which they mapped out written signs along the main street and defined the purposes of such signs, showed that they came to an interpretation of the functions of written signs based on their knowledge of the commercial uses they saw daily in community life and during their visits to the city. They emphasized commercial uses of such signs because these are the uses they know best and experience most frequently.[13] This does not mean they cannot broaden their comprehension of the multiple uses of written signs, but it is interesting to note that they

[12]I observed closely fifteen children from 1st to 6th grade (nine boys, six girls) from the selected homes for in-depth observation. However, I use the plural *children* throughout the section since I could observe similar behavior in a larger group of children during informal interactions with them.

[13]Children are usually in charge of small shopping for their mothers in the village and accompany them when doing bigger shopping or selling of fish and agricultural products in the nearby city

use what they already know about social life to answer questions about the uses of written posters. This indicates that they understand some functions of print based on what they see and experience in the community and at home.

Another example of ways that children involve themselves with literacy was evident during their frequent visits to my home: The children, for instance, would read labels on food products, first trying to guess the name of the product through visual clues such as pictures. They sometimes recognized signs they had seen on television and related these to the product, identifying them though they could not read or had no direct knowledge of the product, as was the case with a pot of mayonnaise, a product none of the children had tried before, but which they had seen repeatedly advertised on TV. The same happened with the small logo on my hat, the face of Colonel Sanders, which the children quickly connected with a fried chicken store, although Kentucky Fried Chicken obviously does not exist in their town or in Pucallpa, the nearby city. Nevertheless, the children had seen TV advertisements and were able to relate a visual sign to its meaning based on the (limited?) knowledge they had. These examples show how children actively relate visual signs with meanings and information, a theme evident in a number of papers in this volume (e.g., Low; Stein). They also show how children use all kinds of knowledge that they already have to build a way to decipher written signs, beyond the technical skill of decoding. These brief examples demonstrate that children show an understanding of how written words represent meanings and convey a message, and that is the purpose of print.

At this point some readers might observe that these processes have been extensively observed in children in urban contexts. However, it is worth noting how they are also present in rural contexts, since it is not so frequently acknowledged by educators working in such environments, especially in developing countries.

I did not have the opportunity to see children's written production at home beyond school homework. In their constant visits to my home, however, school-age children engaged in several situations of spontaneous writing, drawing, and copying of pictures and texts from schoolbooks. They also wrote brief, affectionate messages to me about our friendship and their feelings, as reported above. On one occasion when a typewriter was stored in my house, children decided to explore it and produced texts, such as their names, affectionate messages, and songs they knew from school or TV.

Once I asked a group of children to write original stories on their own, an activity seldom practiced at school. After their initial confusion and attempts to copy stories from books (a more frequent activity at the school), a group of children produced twenty short stories. The stories were shared with other children and some of the authors kept writing more stories without being required. In producing stories, the children drew upon topics, characters, conventions, and words that were part of their immediate environment, daily life, and oral communication. Children therefore used their language experience, both written and oral, to produce stories. In this way, they showed that they could use more resources to develop their literacy skills than those usually required by school. They produced these stories at home but without adult assistance, showing a personal engagement with the task.

These three brief examples of engagement in out-of-school writing by children again show them enthusiastically involved with the development of their knowledge about the uses, purposes, and functions of literacy. They generated self-directed activities with the written word when they approached it outside an institutional context, drawing on their experiences at school and home. They also went further, however, as these activities (especially typewriting songs and producing written stories) were not common in any of these domains. Moreover, these examples show that children can engage in literacy activities as part of their play, although most of the time literacy is presented to them as work, both by home and school.

Fortunately, children have other learning experiences, of the kind we have seen, that allow them to make this shift and which contrast with the way literacy learning is conceptualized both in homes dominated by school domain conceptions of literacy and in the multigrade classroom itself. Such experiences offer further resources for children to cope with learning when they enter the educational setting, a theme stressed by Rogers (this volume) who alerts us that "learning programs which fail to take account of literacy practices and perceptions outside school are less effective."

Other Ways of Learning:
Multiage Groups as Part of Everyday Life

When looking at doing homework, it was evident how the school presents its instructional strategies as the legitimized way of learning, exercising a powerful influence over home. Despite this, when the home is examined, it is evident that children are also socialized in other ways of learning. A look into such ways of learning, in contrast with school strategies, allows a discussion of their potential for multigrade classrooms.

Children in San Antonio perform various tasks in the home and community to support domestic and productive work. Their work is not only an aid to family survival, but also a way of mastering domestic, agricultural, or fishing skills in preparation for becoming productive adults. In this sense, the life of San Antonio's children is similar to that of many other children in rural communities. Literature on children's socialization in the Andes for example (Anderson 1994; Ortiz y Yamamoto 1996) has shown that children are part of productive units (households) and are involved in productive and domestic activities from a very early age.

Thus, at home, children engage in a progressive process of learning skills related to productive and domestic activities. The main learning methods used involve direct participation of children in the activity, practice as a mean to developing skills, and observation, while fostering at the same time a sense of responsibility and autonomy when performing their tasks. Children have the support of adults and older children who carry out the activity with them. Through their active participation in the activity, children progressively develop the skills necessary to carry it out independently. Children get a feeling of achievement when doing these activities and show they are proud of the things they can do. Children also are aware of the purpose of these activities and how they contribute to their families' needs.

Thus, children learn in a context that provides a purposeful background for the activity and the necessary support to guide them until their learning is complete. More importantly, they learn in interaction with others in what I called mixed-age groups, composed some times by adults and children and some times by older and younger children.

Therefore, children go to school with a rich experience of learning from others and helping other children learn in the context of their daily life. Children spend a great deal of time in mixed-age groups, which are used to establish relationships with older and younger children. In doing this, they develop a strong sense of responsibility and care for each other, share their knowledge and activities, and learn from one another.

Children also use this experience spontaneously to cope with schoolwork requirements. In the classroom, children interact with each other, regardless of grades and ages, to receive support for school tasks. Some teachers encourage mutual support more than others. More importantly, some teachers have more flexibility in their classrooms, facilitating this interaction among children.

Nevertheless, the pedagogical uses of children's interaction in the classroom and their ways of learning outside school are still scarcely developed. In contrast with their learning experiences at home, most schoolwork fails to involve children actively and purposefully in learning activities. School strategies are still heavily linked with direct teaching and constant use of drill and repetition. Children are supposed to carry out the same activity at the same time and (ideally) at the same pace. Mistakes are sanctioned rather than corrected through guided practice.

Even though the school is multigrade, separation of grades is still considered a principle for instructional organization and linked with a view of literacy as a set of graded skills that have to be taught separately according to grade. Thus, teachers treat different groups either separately, giving them different activities, or as a single group, giving them the same activity. Both of these strategies operate under the model of a monograde classroom, with all children doing what corresponds to their grade. There is a lack of flexibility for mixing strategies and taking advantage of diversity in the classroom, although two teachers have taken some steps in this direction (using a third strategy).

It seems that multigrade schools could gain if more attention were paid to other ways of learning observed at home. In both home and school, learning is progressive. At home, however, there is no strict physical separation between age groups, as there is at school. On the contrary, the interaction among age groups (adults-children or older-younger children) is what makes learning possible.

The experience of multiage interaction that children bring to school is of special importance for multigrade classrooms. Teachers could use the children's experience in common activities in multiage groups. Different groups could engage in different activities without the teacher's direction, but with his or her close support at some point. Older children could help younger children in their learning, reinforcing their own learning in the process. Literature about multigrade teaching strategies has shown peer tutoring[14] to be a successful tool for multigrade classrooms (Collingwood 1991; Thomas and Shaw 1992). Even

[14]Although the concept of peer tutoring appears related to the collaborative work carried out by children of same age group, multigrade literature extends this concept to refer to activities carried out by children of different ages and grades.

in the context of monograde classrooms, different learning paradigms (i.e., social constructivism) have emphasized that learning is not an isolated activity, but a social process in which interaction with other children as well as with the teacher helps individual learning.

The exploration of the home context shows that some skills can be learned through a more interactive relationship among children. This could also be taken into account in school, especially if there is a multiage group in the same classroom. The school, however, seems to pay very little attention to ways of learning other than those institutionalized and legitimized by the school itself. Although this is characteristic of the school as institution, it is also reinforced by wider conceptions and views that teachers have about children's communities (the "deprivation" label) and strongly related to social hierarchies in the region and the wider society.

Conclusions

In using the NLS approach in combination with sociocultural approaches to learning, this chapter has tried to show how such a perspective can fruitfully illuminate not only the problems that an autonomous model of literacy has for multigrade classrooms, but also how a concept of literacy as a social practice can offer alternative strategies for work with multiage groups in the classroom. Moreover, I have tried to identify the resources children can draw from their home and community experiences to face literacy learning, in an attempt to overcome the tendency to label rural children as deprived of such experiences. I follow thus one of the central principles of NLS, as it is stated by Street in the introduction of this volume as well as in other chapters (see Davis, Cho, and Toohey; Stein and Mamabolo; Rowsell and Rajaratnam; Rogers): "To build upon the richness and complexity of learners' prior knowledge" we have to move from labeling home background as a deficit or as deprived learning context. This principle allows educators to not simply look for what children "lack" because of their belonging to non-mainstream social groups, but rather to look for how different social and cultural experiences can enrich their learning. Thus I arrive at a similar conclusion as other authors in this book (see Davies, Cho, and Toohey) and others (Gregory and Williams 2000; Moll et al. 1994; Moll 1992), namely, that diversity can be conceptualized not as a problem but as a resource upon which children can draw in the face of the demands of literacy learning at school.

In doing this, however, I have not overlooked the context of poverty, inequality, and social hierarchies that surround children's learning experiences. Although the available space here does not permit me to develop these issues, which are developed, strongly and dramatically, in some other chapters (Stein and Mamabolo; Cucchiara), I would like to add that multigrade schooling is also affected by structural inequalities and poverty. In Peru, as in many countries (see Little 1995; 2001), multigrade schools have fewer material resources, infrastructure, educational aids, and basic services, and their teachers have less training and less support from regional and central educational offices. Multigrade schools are often located in small, isolated villages with scarce facilities. Teachers, therefore, face additional problems. They have fewer resources and poorer living conditions than teachers in urban areas and often live in school accommodations separated from their families for long periods. Both factors produce dissatisfaction among teachers and affect their teaching in both material and attitudinal ways.

The study also show that literacy does not imply the end of poverty, as some optimistic literature seems to suggest (Anderson and Bowman 1966). Most people in San Antonio are literate, but they remain in poverty. The case of San Antonio underscores what has been signalled by other studies (Street 1995; Kalman 1998; Graff 1987), that illiteracy intersects with other social, political, and economic factors to reinforce poverty, but is not the only cause.

This study has shown the wealth of literacy experiences in the lives of rural children in San Antonio, despite the context of poverty and its material dimensions. The school system should not overlook these either. Educational policies oriented towards promoting equal access to education for all must both pay attention to the lack of material resources that rural families and multigrade schools face because of their poverty and recognize the rich cultural resources that such children nevertheless bring to their schooling.

Acknowledgements: The research on which this chapter is based was supported by the International Research Project "Multigrade Teaching in Peru, Sri Lanka and Vietnam," conducted by the Institute of Education, University of London, with the financial support of the Department for International Development, United Kingdom. I would like to also thank Brian Street, Francesca Uccelli, and Virginia Zavala for their helpful suggestions on this paper.

References

Ames, P. 2003. *Multigrade schools in context: Literacy in the community, the home and the school in the Peruvian Amazon*. PhD dissertation, University of London.

Anderson, J. 1994. *La socialización infantil en comunidades andinas y de migrantes urbanos en el Perú*. Documento de trabajo No. 1. Proyecto de innovaciones pedagógicas no formales. Lima: Fundación Bernar Van Leer–Ministerio de Educación.

Anderson, C. A., and Bowman, M. J. 1966. *Education and economic development*. London: Frank Cass.

Barton, D. 1994. *Literacy: An introduction to the ecology of written language*. Oxford: Blackwell.

Bauersfeld, H. 1995. The structuring of the structures: Development and function of mathematizing as a social practice. In: L. Steffe and J. Gale (eds.), *Constructivism in education*. Hillsdale: Lawrence Erlbaum, pp. 137–158.

Besnier, N. 1993. Literacy and feelings: The encoding of affect in Nukulaelae letters. In: B. Street (ed.), *Cross-cultural approaches to literacy*. Cambridge: Cambridge University Press, pp. 62–86.

Chopra, P. 2001. Betrayal and solidarity in ethnography on literacy: Revisiting research homework in a north Indian village. In: B. Street (ed.), *Literacy and development. Ethnographic perspectives*. London: Routledge, pp. 78–92.

Cobb, P. 1996. Where is the mind? A coordination of sociocultural and cognitive constructivist perspectives. In: C. T. Fosnot, (ed.), *Constructivism: Theory, Perspectives and Practice*. New York: Teachers College Press, Columbia University, pp. 34–52.

Collingwood, I. 1991. *Multiclass teaching in primary schools: A handbook for teachers in the Pacific*. Apia, Western Samoa: UNESCO Office for the Pacific States.

Crawford, P. 1995. Early literacy: Emerging perspectives. *Journal of Research in Childhood Education* 10(1): 71–86.

Czerniewska, P. 1996. Learning to read and write in English. In: N. Mercer and J. Swann (eds.), *Learning English: Development and diversity*. London: Routledge and Open University Press, pp. 76–106.

De la Piedra, M.T. 2003. *Literacy practices among Quechua-speakers: The case study of a rural community in the Peruvian Andes*. PhD dissertation, University of Texas at Austin.

Fosnot, C.T. 1996. Constructivism: A psychological theory of learning. In: C.T. Fosnot (ed.), *Constructivism: Theory, Perspectives and practice*. New York: Teachers College Press, Columbia University, pp. 8–33.

Godenzzi, J., Flores, E., and Ramierz, E. 2000. Quiero tomar la palabra: Comunicación e integración de las niñas en la escuela, la familia y en la comunidad. Paper presented to Il Conferencia Nacional de Educación de las niñas rurales, 28–29 de Setiembre, Lima.

Graff, H. 1987. *The labyrinths of literacy: Reflections on literacy past and present*. London: Falmer Press.

Gregory, E., and Williams, A. 2000. *City literacies: Learning to read across generations and cultures.* New York and London: Routledge.

Hargreaves, E., Montero, C., Chau, N., Sibli, M., and Thanh, T. 2001. Multigrade teaching in Peru. Sri Lanka and Vietnam: An overview. *International Journal of Educational Development* 21(6): 499–520.

Kalman, J. 1998. *Writing on the Plaza: Mediated literacy practice among scribes and clients in Mexico City.* Cresskill: Hampton Press.

Konold, C. 1995. Social and cultural dimensions of knowledge and classroom teaching. In: L. Steffe and J. Gale (eds.), *Constructivism in Education.* Hillsdale: Lawrence Erlbaum, pp. 175–183.

Lareau, A. 1989. *Home advantage: Social class and parental intervention in elementary education.* London: Falmer Press.

Little, A. 2001. Multigrade teaching: Towards an international research and policy agenda. *International Journal of Educational Development* 21(6): 481–497.

Little, A. 1995. *Multigrade teaching. A review of research and practice.* London: Overseas Development Administration, Serial No. 12.

Maddox, B. 2001. Literacy and the market: The economic uses of literacy among the peasantry in north-west Bangladesh. In: B. Street (ed.), *Literacy and development. Ethnographic perspectives.* London: Routledge, pp. 137–151.

McEwan, P. 1998. The effectiveness of multigrade schools in Colombia. *International Journal of Educational Development* 18(6): 435–452.

Miller, B. 1990. A review of the quantitative research on multigrade instruction. *Research in Rural Education* 7(1): 1–8.

Miller, B. 1991. Teaching and learning in multigrade classroom: Student performances and instructional routines. In: *ERIC Digest,* Region III Comprehensive Center, pp. 1–7.

Miller, B. 1991a. A review of the qualitative research on multigrade instruction. *Research in Rural Education* 7(2): 3–12.

Moll, L. 1994. Mediating knowledge between homes and classrooms. In: D. Keller-Cohen (ed.), *Literacy: Interdisciplinary conversations.* Creshill: Hampton Press, pp. 385–410.

Moll, L., Amanti, C., Neff, D., and Gonzales, N. 1992. Funds of knowledge for teaching: Using a qualitative approach to connect homes and classrooms. *Theory into Practice* 31(2): 132–141.

Montero, C., Ames, P., Cabrera, Z., León, E., Chirinos, A., and Fernández Dávila, M. 2002. *Propuesta metodológica para escuelas unidocentes y/o con aulas multigrado.* Documento de Trabajo No. 18. Lima: Ministerio de Educación.

Montero, C., and Tovar, T. 1999. *Agenda abierta para la educación de las niñas rurales.* Lima: CARE-Perú, IEP, Foro educativo.

Ortiz, A. And Yamamoto, J. 1996. *Un estudio sobre los grupos autónomos de niños a partir de un trabajo en Champacchocha, Andahuaylas.* Documento de trabajo No. 1, Proyecto de innovaciones pedagógicas no formales. Lima: Fundación Bernar Van Leer–Ministerio de Educación.

Pratt, D. 1986. On the merits of multiage classrooms. *Research in Rural education* 3(3): 111–115.

Psacharopoulos, G., Rojas C., and Velez, E. 1992. *Achievement evaluation of Colombia's Escuela Nueva. Is Multigrade the answer?* World Bank Working Paper 896. Washington D.C.: World Bank.

Schiefelbein, E. 1993. *En busca de la escuela del siglo XXI: ¿Puede darnos la pista la escuela Nueva de Colombia?* Santiago: UNESCO/UNICEF.

Street, B. 1993. *Cross-cultural approaches to literacy.* Cambridge: Cambridge University Press.

Street, B. 1995. *Social Literacies: Critical approaches to literacy in ethnography and development.* New York: Longman.

Street, B., Baker, D., and Tomlin, A. (Forthcoming). *Numeracy practices at home and at school.* Vol. 4, Leverhulme Numeracy Research Programme. Dordrecht: Kluwer.

Steffe, L., and Gale, J. (eds.). 1995. *Constructivism in education.* Hillsdale: Lawrence Erlbaum.

Stromquist, N. 1997. *Literacy for citizenship. Gender and grassroots in Brazil.* Albany: State University of New York Press.

Taylor, D. 1983. *Family Literacy: Young children learning to read and write.* Exeter: Heinemann.

Thomas, C., and Shaw, C. 1992. *Issues in the development of multigrade schools.* World Bank Technical Paper Number 172. Washington D.C.: World Bank.

Veenman, S. 1996. Effects of multigrade and multiage classes reconsidered. *Review of Educational Research* 66(3): 323–340.

Veenman, S. 1995. Cognitive and noncognitive effects of multigrade and multiage classes: A best-evidence synthesis. *Review of Educational Research* 65(4): 319–381.

Wertsch, J., and Toma, C. 1995. Discourse and learning in the classroom: A sociocultural approach. In: L. Steffe and J. Gale (eds.), *Constructivism in education.* Hillsdale: Lawrence Erlbaum, pp. 159–174.

5

Breaching the Classroom Walls

Literacy Learning across Time and Space in an Elementary School in the United States

Joanne Larson

> Perhaps we need a critical approach to literacy education that is about engaging with texts and discourses as a means of bridging space and time, critically understanding and altering the connections between the local and the global, moving between cultures and communities, and developing transnational understandings and collaborations (Luke 2003, 22).

Introduction

When considering literacy learning, educators typically look to schools and classrooms as primary sites of investigation. New Literacy Studies (NLS) has informed research on literacy learning by opening up our investigative lens to what happens beyond school boundaries through extensive ethnographies of everyday literacy practices. Recent critiques of NLS have challenged us to understand the relationship of literacies outside of school and school-based literacies in ways that can be applied to literacy learning in multiple contexts (Brandt and Clinton 2002; Collins and Blot 2002; Hull and Schultz 2002). This chapter looks at how one urban teacher uses field trips as part of a curriculum framework we have called inquiry as social practice (Larson and Gatto 2004) to breach the classroom walls. Drawing on a three-year ethnographic study in Lynn Gatto's[1] 2–4th grade looped[2] classroom, I argue that field trips are key mediating spaces for literacy learning that negotiate the tension between school and community discourses and mediate students' communicative competence across sociocultural contexts. I argue that NLS shows us that literacy learning is more than taking school literacy outside or bringing community literacies inside by allowing us to understand how to assist students' participation in the culturally valued activities of their communities. Finally, I argue that it is not simply a matter of nonformal vs. formal learning, but is a matter of how students learn both the literacy demands of education and schooling and of life outside of school to critically understand and transform the connections between the local context, including the classroom, and the global or community context (Luke 2003).

Understanding Field Trips: What Past Research Tells Us

Traditional research on field trips emphasizes educational effectiveness and cognitive consequences. Effectiveness studies tend to focus on pretrip preparation (Anderson and Lucas 1997; Cox-Peterson and Pfaffingler 1998) and linking field trip success to desired outcomes (Muse et al. 1982). For example, this work finds that advance preparation that reduces the novelty of the experience for students supports more learning—as measured on standardized tests—than for students that do not have preparation experiences (Anderson and Lucas 1997). Experimental designs dominate the research on cognitive effects with findings ranging from the role of real-world memory in the development of memory representations (Fivush et al. 1984) to the role of follow-up activities in supporting cognitive reinforcement of concepts (Farmer and Wott 1995). This research informs us about some basics of field trip planning. However, there is still much to learn about the meaning of field trips in the learning experiences of elementary-aged children. Recent research using interpretive research frameworks has deepened our understanding of how meaning is constructed through field trip experiences.

---

[1] This research represents a long-term collaboration between Lynn Gatto and myself. I use her real name here with her permission. I use pseudonyms for all students and for the school district.

[2] Looping is a term used to describe when a teacher works with the same group of students over the course of multiple academic years

From an interpretive stance, the meaning of field trips is a fluid interactional construction not determined by the setting but co-constructed in the social relations of the learning community (Leander 2001). Field trips are not simply in-school or out-of-school activities, but are interactional contexts for learning through which inside and outside are mutually constituted (e.g., school discourse is produced outside of school and out-of-school discourse is produced in school [Leander 2001]). The co-construction of inside and outside blurs the boundaries between school and community, between the local and the global, affording us a space to facilitate students' learning of literacy practices across contexts.

Nespor (2000) ethnographically examined the transformation of public spaces for children and the school's role in producing those spaces. The present research describes field trips as distillations of the relationships of schools to the worlds outside their walls, as Nespor puts it (39). The argument centers on the idea that public community spaces (e.g., museums, malls) are disintegrating and those that are available are particularly restrictive to children. Children are limited to public spaces that are constructed for them and that operate with the assumption that children must have something to do (e.g., children's museums or play spaces such as Chuck E Cheez). Restrictive public spaces have particular consequences for children in increasingly isolated urban contexts given a pervasive institutionalized racism that operates in developed countries such as the United States (Goldberg 1993; Ladson-Billings 1999). As Nespor (2000, 39) argues,

> It may be, as McLaughlin et al. (1004:107) suggest, that a 'critical opportunity inner-city youth want is the chance to break out of the boundaries imposed by their isolation, to imagine and experience new things previously unimagined or unimaginable.' But for field trips to serve these ends their destinations have to be something other than spaces, which memorialize a history from which kids are excluded, or define participation as the ability to purchase commodities and appreciate the aesthetic elements of a setting. Simply requiring teachers to align field trips more closely to school tasks (Confar, 1995; Griffin and Symington, 1997) does not help kids towards richer participatory roles in public space, and indeed could easily work against this end.

From this perspective, field trips are critical spaces for introducing inner-city children to social practices in public spaces that have been previously difficult for them to learn due to urban isolation and the increasing inaccessibility of public spaces in urban contexts (Davis 1990). Starting from this argument, I will ground this chapter in the theoretical work associated with NLS and sociocultural/sociohistorical learning theory described in the next section.

Theoretical Framing for New Understandings

Drawing on NLS, I define literacy as a critical social practice (Barton 1994; Cope and Kalantzis 2000; Lankshear and Knobel 2003; Luke 2003; 1994; Street 1995) constructed in everyday interactions, conversations, and narratives (Bloome et al. forthcoming; de Certeau 1984; Ochs and Capps 2001). For the children in the study reported here, school was an everyday discursive practice in which language and literacy mediated learning across multiple contexts. I will focus on how literacy learning was socially constructed in everyday interactions both in and out of school (across time and space), specifically in the context of field trips. I argue that the teacher used multimodal literacies in ways that provided students with "critical engagements with globalised flows of information, image, text and discourse" (Luke 2003, 20).

In addition to using the NLS as outlined by Street in the introduction to this book, I draw on sociocultural and sociohistorical learning theory to inform my understanding of the social processes of language and literacy learning in the context of field trips. In this framework children are active members of a constantly evolving community of learners in which literacy knowledge constructs and is constructed by larger cultural systems and learning is defined as the transformation of participation (Cole 1996; Duranti 1997; Dyson 1997; Gutierrez and Rogoff 2003; Lee 2001; Ochs 1992; Rogoff 1994, 2003; Vygotsky 1962; 1978; Wertsch 1991). To unpack children's understanding of both local and global literacy practices, we need to observe and document how language and literacy learning are co-constructed and used by both students and teachers in interaction in routine cultural practices such as the field trips I describe (Rogoff 1994; 2003). Using this framework, we can ask how and in what ways children's participation is situated in public spaces through field trips. As Nespor explains:

> If, as Rogoff (1994: 209) puts it, 'learning is a process of *transformation of participation* itself', if 'how people develop is a function of their transform-

ing roles and understanding in the activities in which they participate', the question to be asked of field trips and other school-based spatializing activities is how, and in what activity systems, they situate kids as participants (2000, 36).

If neighborhood public spaces are disappearing in general and in urban contexts in particular, as Nespor (2000) argues, then access to communal social practices may be limited, thus changing the lives of children in that they have fewer opportunities to participate in the everyday activities of, and across, communities. I suggest here that the way Gatto used field trips facilitated students' access to fuller participation in everyday community activities in ways that traditionally defined field trips do not.

Understanding Field Trips in Context

The urban district in which this study takes place, Northeast City School District (NCSD), is facing increasing and dramatic problems as it struggles under the pressure of standardization and accountability in the guise of the No Child Left Behind Act of 2001 (http://www.ed.gov/legislation/ESEA02/). As one of the "big five" urban districts in New York state, this district ranks second after New York City in poorest achieving schools and is under increasing surveillance by the state department of education and the general public. Recent data locate this district last in the state as measured by the 4th and 8th grade math tests. The district faces problems common in contemporary urban contexts: budgetary problems; reductions in both teaching and administration positions; imposition of reductionist curricula; high poverty; high mobility; low morale, and so on. Gatto has been teaching in this district for thirty years. She has received many prestigious awards that culminated in her being named the 2004 New York State Teacher of the Year. When she was teaching 4th grade three years ago, New York State's mandated standardized English Language Arts exam became a political tool to hold 4th grade teachers accountable for students' scores. Gatto successfully argued that to begin with a group of students in September and expect her to account for their performance on a February test was unacceptable and that she needed an extended time period with students in order to be meaningfully accountable. As a result, she was able to implement a looped classroom that spanned from 2nd to 4th grades. The data used in this chapter are drawn from an ethnographic study of the three years in which she looped with her students.

The Study

I will discuss the role of field trips in mediating literacy learning using data drawn from a three-year ethnographic study of Gatto's classroom. With the help of research assistant Gloria Jacobs, I interviewed both Gatto and her students over the course of the study, videotaped classroom interaction and took field notes at various times of the day, concentrating on literacy practices. Gatto implemented a science-based curriculum of her own design and integrated language arts across content areas throughout the day. Research questions for the larger study focused on understanding how the teacher constructed a meaningful context for literacy learning in an increasingly constraining context. For this chapter, I specifically focus on understanding students' perceptions of the role of field trips in learning the discourse and literacy practices of communities inside and outside of school.

The data corpus includes sixty-four hours of observation and coinciding field notes, forty-eight hours of videotape, four hours of formal teacher interviews (transcribed), two hours of formal student interviews and one hour of focus group interviews (transcribed), e-mails, and student and teacher writing. Over the course of three years, I had countless informal interviews with both Gatto and her students, which I recorded on video and in field notes. In addition, I had access to Gatto's classroom data which includes seventy-eight hours of video and thirty-eight hours of audiotape she has collected for her dissertation research. She has collected students' daily journals, informal and formal assessment data (including standardized test scores), and end-of-year feedback letters. I used position statements she wrote as part of the National Teacher of the Year award process as an additional data source. The excerpts I present here are representative of the larger data corpus.

For this chapter, I focused on children's interviews conducted in the second year of the study as a primary data source. The nineteen students in the class ranged in age from 8 years 9 months to 10 years 10 months old that year. The majority of the class was African-American (69 percent), with white (26 percent) students filling out the remaining balance. There was one Latino student who accounted for the last 5 percent. In the 2000–2001 academic year, 80 percent of the students qualified for free lunch (a statewide indicator of poverty). I interviewed the children individually, then clustered them into two focus groups: one group consisting of students who had been in the classroom for both years (old-timers) and one group who had been there for one year (newcomers).

Using Erickson's (1986) discussion of evidentiary warrants as a guide, I sought to ensure an adequacy of quantity and variety of evidence. Following each interview I analyzed the transcripts using the constant comparative method of coding (Bogdan and Biklen 1998; Strauss and Corbin 1990). I open-coded transcripts and then refined those codes into conceptual categories based on relationships between the codes. Consistent with the constant comparative method, I checked new coding against previously coded transcripts to further confirm and identify emerging patterns and relationships. Through this analytic process I found that the students perceive the teacher, the curriculum, and their learning as meaningful, relevant, and "fun" and that field trips were a key source of what they perceived as fun about their learning in this classroom.

How Do Students Understand Field Trips?

When we transcribed the first set of interviews, we found that a majority of the students (79 percent) described what they were doing as "fun." In the weekly response journals, 55 percent of students described various classroom activities as fun. All students mentioned field trips as activities they valued, several mentioning field trips as their favorite part of being in this classroom. As we began our second set of interviews and the focus interviews, the goal was to unpack the children's reference to "fun." We found that students defined fun as: the teacher being nice, going on field trips, being treated fairly, feeling valued, feeling listened to, and being able to talk freely about what they know (Larson and Gatto 2004). All the students connected field trips with what they considered to be fun about the classroom in general and what made Gatto a good teacher in particular.

Evidence of the importance of field trips appeared across the data corpus. Gatto discussed the role of field trips in her curriculum in an essay she wrote as part of her submission to the National Teacher of the Year award (a task all state teachers of the year need to do). She wrote, "My students understand that learning does not take place just in school; they leave my classroom with a passion for experiencing new places and meeting new people." In another one of the essays submitted for the National Teacher of the Year award, Gatto articulated her goal for field trips:

> I am determined to not only make learning come alive for my urban students, but to also provide the kinds of experiences that will give them equal access to the world.

Gatto's articulated goals align with points made earlier about shifting urban students experience from isolation to participation through meaningful field trips (Nespor 2000). Isolation is imposed by society through the institutionalized racism and poverty characterizing increasingly segregated urban contexts. Rather than accept this isolation as given, Gatto not only facilitated her students learning traditional school-based literacy in the course of preparing for and participating in field trips, but also facilitated their learning the cultural capital needed for full participation in diverse cultural practices. For example, students participated in travel practices that will give them cultural capital to which they may not otherwise have access (Nespor 2000).

Analyses revealed that the field trips taken over the course of three years fell into three categories: overnight trips, day trips, and "regular" trips typically taken in this district (see Table 1). I offer the idea of "cyber trip" as an additional category that falls into the overnight category because it is intimately related to the trip to Kentucky. Gatto used these videoconferences as key curriculum components representing academic literacies and to build social relationships across time and space that are picked up in physical space and real time when students go to Kentucky.

Gatto designs field trips along three principles: (1) trips are curriculum based; (2) trips provide authentic experiences beyond the students' everyday lives; and (3) trips are explicitly focused on community building. The science-based curriculum centers around in-depth theme study, and all field trips relate to or build on these themes. Her students learn the literacy practices of communities, both professional and everyday, through participation in unit studies and their related field trips. Only the nursing home trips are not based on one

Table 1. Categories of Field Trips Over Three Years

Overnight trips	*Day Trips*	*Typical District Trips*

• Camping (2 trips)
• Zoo
  –Animal hunt
  (planned)
  –Pillow fight
  (spontaneous)
  –Snake observation
  (spontaneous)
• Boston (ocean life)
  –Farmer's Museum
  –Children's Museum
  –Aquarium
  –Seafood restaurant
  –Beach study
• Kentucky
  –7 trips to local high school for video conferences (virtual field trips) with Kentucky classroom
  –Funeral home (is the original home in this rural town and is the history museum)
  –Partner classrooms
  –Family homes
  –Slumber party at school
  –Western Kentucky University (science labs, swimming, slept in dorms)
  –Nature Reserve sleepover
	• Nursing home (24 visits)
	• Local arts high school (2 trips to see plays)
	• Local college (1 trip to see play)
	• Niagara Falls
	  –Aquarium
	  –Vivarium
	  –The Falls
	• Ice skating
	• Local park for scientific exploration (12 trips for water quality study and botany study)
		• Art gallery
		• Children's Museum
		• Museum of Science (3 trips)
		• Local county museum
		• Neighborhood library
		• Neighborhood bank

of her thematic units. The goal for nursing home trips focuses on community membership in general and on helping students understand how they can serve the community through service to others in particular. These regular trips facilitated students' understanding of community at both the local (e.g., classroom) and global (e.g., community or societal) levels through experiencing the continuum of social relations across contexts. Students learn empathy for others even if the people they serve might have "nasty" or "scary" things about them. The residents of the nursing home are quite elderly and ill. Sometimes residents they have gotten to know die. Students see residents getting older and sicker as they return to the same floor each trip and over the three years they were together as a class. They always take a craft project and snack to eat with residents. Students have little experience with people this age. Typically their grandparents are quite a bit younger. Through sustained interaction with residents and staff, students gain experiential knowledge of the discourses of aging and community service to which they would not otherwise have access.

The second principle of providing experiences beyond students' everyday lives connects with what Nespor (2000) argues needs to be accounted for in field trip construction. He argues that field trip destinations for inner city youth must not just be restricted to child-oriented spaces that traditionally exclude urban children, such as commodified spaces (grocery stores, malls), and aesthetic spaces (museums), nor can they simply be designed to meet school-based learning goals. Field trips must move beyond "exposure" to genuine participation in experiences that give students access to literacy practices, cultural capital, and discourses of power that institutionalized racism commonly denies them. Gatto explicitly used field trips in her curriculum as one tool to accomplish these latter goals. For example, the cyber "scientific summits" afforded students an opportunity to participate in authentic scientific discourse using communicative practices common in academic and corporate contexts, giving students access to discourses of power that traditionally defined field trips or the textbook-based science curriculum do not.

Team building is an explicit goal of Gatto's overall curriculum and her field trips in particular. Overnight trips provide key opportunities for students to learn to care for one another. Gatto surprises them with midnight hikes on camping trips, for example, where only she has a flashlight. Students need to rely on each other in order to navigate the trails safely. She often veers off the established trails to further facilitate students 'reliance on one another to find their way. She stated that she finds interaction in the classroom to be much more relaxed and conversational after the first overnight each year. The students come together as a caring team as the year progresses and their learning deepens.

The trip to Kentucky provides a case example of the role of field trips in this classroom. As Table 1 indicates, this trip was a richly engaging long-distance event that took intensive coordination on the part of two teachers and their students over time and space. The "cybertrips" occurred in the months prior to Gatto's class leaving for Kentucky. Called scientific summits, these videoconferences were grounded in academic and scientific language and literacy practices. Students presented their research on curriculum-related topics to each other using the literacies, discourses, and practices of real scientists. She prepared them for air travel in the new high-security context in the United States by taking them to the airport to tour a plane and go through security, giving them access to the cultural capital associated with air travel (Nespor 2000). The day they left was an event that drew crowds of family, friends, well-wishers, and the local news media. Once in rural Kentucky, Gatto's students were paired with Kentucky students. They stayed at their homes and came to the joint events together on a chartered school bus. They had a slumber party at the local elementary school, toured the first home in the town (now a funeral home), and went to classrooms at Western Kentucky University for demonstrations in the science labs and to go swimming. They toured the local nature reserve and spent the night with their new friends.

This trip enacted the three principles Gatto uses to guide her fields trips in a unique and meaningful way. The trip brings together all the units the class studied throughout the year in the curriculum principle. The second principle of engaging in authentic sociocultural practices beyond the students' lives is accomplished in multiple ways. The relationships between the students and their new friends in Kentucky are real and sustained over time and across space. To develop these relationships, students participated in videoconferences, traveled by air to a southern rural community, and attended demonstrations in university classrooms. The curriculum principle connects to the authenticity principle in the scientific activities in which children engaged. The cyber "scientific summits" engaged students in authentic scientific discourse as they presented their research to each other and discussed findings and problems they encountered.

The community building principle was evident in the prolonged interaction between Gatto's students and the Kentucky students during the trip. The slumber party, university sleep over, and the night spent at local family homes all served to build a sense of a team on an adventure. Children grew closer as the week passed. Gatto's students shared a common meaningful experience they will remember a long time and developed friendships with new community members that were constructed over time and in both cyberspace and physical space.

Students connected field trips to Gatto as a person when they described her as fun and nice. Recent literature on culturally relevant teaching states that students were motivated to learn with teachers who made learning fun in a humorous and dramatic sense (Howard 2001; Parish and Parish 1989). Nieto (1999) found that students defined fun lessons as imaginative and exciting. Fun teachers were viewed as entertainers or performers. Gatto's students moved beyond seeing her as an entertainer by their understanding of her curriculum as experiential ("she lets us go on tons of field trips").

> *Larson:* What does it mean for to be nice for like what's nice about her.
>
> *Devon:* Like she take us on lots of field trips.
>
> *Larson:* You like the field trips. What's good, like what kind of field trips have you gone on.
>
> *Devon:* We goin to the nursin home to the nursin home to help to like make people make stuff for people there and we're going to Boston next year.

In the excerpt above, the student takes up Gatto's goal of community service through service to others when he states they go to the nursing home "to make stuff for people there." On the one hand he is talking about the craft projects they take each trip, but he is also talking about the raised wood planters the class constructed for residents. The planters were large wood boxes in which residents put planting soil for gardening. Students designed them so they were high enough above the ground for a person in a wheel chair to fit comfortably under while tending to plants. They spent a good deal of time building these planters in the classroom using multiple scientific and mathematical practices to accomplish the task.

Gatto uses a weekly dialogue journal as an additional space to interact with her students and build relationships. Our analysis of students' journal entries revealed references to their experiences of field trips: "The video conference was fun"; "I hope the zoo be cool tonight. It is going to be fun at the zoo." The two excerpts below illustrate how students relate field trips to content learning. One child predicts that the upcoming three-day field trip to the Boston seacoast as part of their ocean unit will be a fun learning experience. Another, a young girl, associated the upcoming museum visit to learning history.

> *Carl:* She teach like a fun projects and we're going to learn science by Boston we're gonna go to the aquarium and we're gonna have a little fun. Like we're gonna have a pool party and we're gonna go to McDonalds. But I think the best part is learning in the aquarium.
>
> *Jackie:* Everything that I saw at the Farmer's Museum was that you can learn history in a fun kind of way to look and to have fun with history cause it could be fun.

In both excerpts, the students link participation in the Boston trip to content learning, disrupting the binary opposition between in- and out-of-school learning. Jackie asserts a causal relationship between fun and learning history when she indexes learning history with the pronoun "it" toward the end of the utterance.

This alternation between school and nonschool spaces appears across the data. It may be evidence that students do not understand learning to be restricted to any one place or time, but rather acknowledge that it occurs in everyday activities in multiple contexts and at different times. In this way, they are developing an expanded understanding of what it means to learn across local and more global contexts as they move between cultures and communities (Luke 2003). The variation in learning spaces Gatto's students experienced provided rich opportunities for full participation in both everyday community activities and school-based learning events. As a result, the division between "inside" and "outside" is blurred as learning occurs across time and space (Leander 2000).

Gatto also constructs formal school activities in community spaces, as was done for the zoo overnight trip they went on in the context of an animal unit. In the excerpts below, students described their experiences as being on multiple levels, including play and both formal and spontaneous scientific exploration.

Larson: Did you go on that field trip to the zoo.

LaTiesha: Um hum.

Larson: Had you ever gone on a field trip where you slept over before?

LaTiesha: No.

Larson: What was that like?

LaTiesha: Fun.

Larson: Heh heh what did you do?

LaTiesha: We had a pillow fight an then we went then we went outside an looking for some animals that was still woke in the middle of the night. Or or we had just go inside the room where the two snakes sat and we'll just look at those cause we gotta snake our own inside our classroom cause it was one snake that look just like the snake that we have.

As the excerpt illustrates, students are learning meaningful scientific knowledge by participation in the observational practices of scientists. Gatto took them out in the middle of the night on a "midnight safari" to observe nocturnal animal behavior. We can see that children took up this observational practice spontaneously in LaTiesha's description of their comparative observation of snakes ("cause it was one snake that look just like the snake that we have"). In the next excerpt, Derrick even seems to have developed the passion of a dedicated scientist when he states in the last utterance "when you woke up you would feel the um fresh air of animal life."

Larson: Did you go on the zoo field trip?

Derrick: Yeah.

Larson: What was that like to sleep over?

Derrick: Um it was really cool because um when you woke up you would feel the um fresh air of animal life.

The trip to the zoo facilitated scientific content learning, such as understanding the interaction between plants and animals and the animal classification systems that they plotted in charts. As a result, students participated in authentic literacy practices common in the work of scientific observation and documentation and gained cultural capital in scientific discourse.

Using New Literacy Studies
to Understand the Role of Field Trips in Literacy Learning

The academic literacies approach in NLS suggests that all students experience disjunctions as they encounter new sets of literacy practices (Street, this volume). For Gatto's students, field trips afforded them the opportunity to experience diverse literacy practices in the contexts of their use that they may not have had access to in their everyday lives.

Field trips mediated students learning to cross communicative boundaries and the multiple literacies needed for participation in a global information economy. The Kentucky trip in particular facilitated students' access to literacies needed in today's global context. In this classroom, field trips are more that taking school outside. Instead, Gatto assists students' participation in culturally valued activities of their and others' communities and in the multimodal literacy practices of everyday life through her curriculum in general and authentic field trips in particular.

An NLS field trip practice is not just an issue of nonformal vs. formal learning, but is a practice in which the classroom walls are breached and students learn across contexts, time, and space. Students are learning the multimodal literacy practices of their and other's communities by participating in them with the guidance of their teacher, their parents, and community members. They learn the literacy demands not just of education and schooling but of life outside of school, literacies Luke (2003) argues are the kinds of literacies needed in a global information economy.

If, as sociocultural learning theory argues, learning is the transformation of participation in culturally valued activity (Rogoff 2003), then we need to ask in what ways did students' participation change in Gatto's classroom? Based on the discussion presented in this chapter, I argue that students moved beyond "exposure" to internalize authentic scientific discourses and practices; understood learning to be fun, engaging, and experiential in this classroom (as opposed to boring rote practices in previous classrooms); developed close relations in and out of the classroom over time and across space; and gained cultural capital and discourses of power they may not otherwise have acquired.

In sum, when the boundaries of the classroom are dissolved and the community becomes more than a place to visit but is a context students participate in as authentic members, friends, scientists, and helpers, students participation in culturally valued activities of everyday life is full and rich and their learning is deep (Stein and Mamabolo, this volume). Furthermore, as several authors in this book have also argued, grounding content learning in real life practices facilitates learning in ways that go beyond simply bringing in outside practices to an authentic reconceptualization of literacies in use (Welle, Low, Street, this volume). I have argued here that we need to understand field trips as more than extensions of classroom activities. Field trips can be opportunities for learning the literacy practices of everyday life in ways that are authentic to children and in ways that give them access to critical literacy practices with which to move between cultures and communities and transform their understandings of the local and global.

References

Anderson, D., and Lucas, K. 1997. The effectiveness of orienting students to the physical features of a science museum prior to visitation. *Research in science education* 27(4): 485–495.

Barton, D. 1994. *Literacy: An introduction to the ecology of written language,* Blackwell: Oxford.

Bogdan, R.C., and Biklen, S.K. 1998. *Qualitative research for education: An introduction to theory and methods.* Boston: Allyn and Bacon.

Bloome, D., Carter, S.P., Christian, B.M., Otto, S., and Shuart-Faris, N. Forthcoming. *Discourse analysis and the study of classroom language and literacy events: A microethnographic perspective.*

Brandt, D., and Clinton, K. 2002. Limits of the local: Explaining perspectives on literacy as a social practice. *Journal of Literacy Research* 34(3): 337–356.

Cole, M. 1996. *Cultural psychology: A once and future discipline.* Cambridge: Harvard University Press.

Confar, P. 1995. Field trips worth the effort: Open your students' eyes and show them the world firsthand. *Learning* 23(6): 34–36.

Cope, B., and Kalantzis, M. (eds.). 2000. *Multiliteracies: Literacy learning and the design of social futures.* London: Routledge.

Cox-Peterson, A., and Pfafflinger, J. 1998. Teacher preparation and teacher-student interaction at a Discovery Center of Natural History. *Journal of Elementary Science Education* 10(2): 20–35.

Davis, M. 1990. *City of quartz: Excavating the future in Los Angeles.* New York: Verso.

de Certeau, M. 1984. *The practice of everyday life.* Berkeley: University of California Press.

Duranti, A. 1997. *Linguistic anthropology.* Cambridge: Cambridge University Press.

Dyson, A. 1997. *Writing superheroes: Contemporary childhood, popular culture, and classroom literacy.* New York: Teachers College Press.

Erickson, F. 1986. Qualitative methods in research on teaching. In: C. Wittrock (ed.), *Handbook of research on teaching.* New York: Macmillan, pp. 119–161.

Farmer, A., and Wott, J. 1995. Field trips and follow up activities: Fourth graders in a public garden. *Journal of Environmental Education* 27(1): 33–35.

Fivush, R., et al. 1984. Children's long-term memory for a novel event: An exploratory study. *Merrill-Palmer Quarterly* 30(3): 303–316.

Goldberg, D. 1993. *Racist culture.* Oxford: Blackwell.

Griffin, J., and Symington, D. 1997. Moving from task-oriented to learning-oriented strategies on school excursions to museums. *Science Education* 81(6): 763–779.

Gutierrez, K., and Rogoff, B. 2003. Cultural ways of knowing: Individual traits or repertoires of practice. *Educational Researcher* 32(5): 19–25.

Howard, T. 2001. Telling their side of the story: African-American students' perceptions of culturally relevant teaching. *Urban Review* 33: 131–149.

Hull, G., and Schultz, K. 2002. *School's out! Bridging out-of-school literacies with classroom practice.* New York: Teachers College Press.

Ladson-Billings, G. 1999. Preparing teachers for diverse student populations: A critical race theory perspective. In: A. Iran-Najey and P.D. Pearson (eds.), *Review of Research in Education,* Volume 24. Washington, D.C.: American Educational Research Association.

Lankshear, C., and Knobel, M. 2003. *New literacies: Changing knowledge and classroom learning.* Buckingham: Open University Press.

Larson, J., and Gatto, L. 2004. Tactical underlife: Understanding students' perspectives. *Journal of Early Childhood Literacy* 4(1): 11–41.

Leander, K. 2001. "This is our freedom bus going home right now": Producing and hybridizing space-time contexts in pedagogical discourse. *Journal of Literacy Research* 33(4): 637–679.

Lee, C. 2001. Is October Brown Chinese? A cultural modeling activity system for underacheving students. *American Educational Research Journal* 38(1): 97–141.

Luke, A. 1994. *The social construction of literacy in the primary school.* Melbourne: Macmillan.

Luke, A. 2003. Literacy education for a new ethics of global community. *Language Arts.* 81(1): 20–22.

McLaughlin, M.W., Irby, M.A., and Langman, J. 1994. *Urban sanctuaries: Neighborhood organizations in the lives and futures of inner-city youth.* San Francisco: Jossey-Bass.

Muse, C., et al. 1982. Teachers' utilization of field trips: Prospects and problems. *Clearing House* 56(3): 22–26.

Nespor, J. 2000. School field trips and the curriculum of public spaces. *Journal of Curriculum Studies* 32(1): 25–43.

New London Group. 1996. A pedagogy of multiliteracies: Designing social futures. *Harvard Educational Review* 66(1): 60–92.

Nieto, S. 1999. *The light in their eyes: Creating multicultural learning communities.* New York: Teachers College Press.

Ochs, E. 1992. Indexing gender. In: A. Duranti and C. Goodwin (eds.), *Rethinking context: Language as an interactive phenomenon.* Cambridge: Cambridge University Press, pp. 335–358.

Ochs, E., and Capps, L. 2001. *Living narrative: Creating lives in everyday storytelling.* Cambridge: Harvard University Press.

Parish, J.G., and Parish, T.S. 1989. Helping under achievers succeed. *Reading Improvement* 26: 71–78.

Rogoff, B. 2003. *The cultural nature of human development.* Oxford: Oxford University Press.

Rogoff, B. 1994. Developing understanding of the idea of communities of learners. *Mind, Culture, and Activity* 1(4): 209–229.

Strauss, A., and Corbin, J. 1990. *Basics of qualitative research: Grounded theory procedures and techniques.* Newbury Park: Sage.

Street, B. 1995. *Social literacies: Critical approaches to literacy in development, ethnography, and education.* London: Longman.

United States Department of Education 2003. No Child Left Behind Act, 2001. (http://www.ed.gov/legislation/ESEA02/).

Vygotsky, L.S. 1962. *Thought and language.* Cambridge: The M.I.T. Press.

Vygotsky, L.S. 1978. *Mind in society: The development of higher psychological processes.* Cambridge: Harvard University Press.

Wertsch, J.V. 1991. *Voices of the mind: A sociocultural approach to mediated action.* Cambridge: Cambridge University Press.

Section II

Literacies
in the Adolescent Years

6

"Sayin' It in a Different Way"
Adolescent Literacies Through the Lens of Cultural Studies

Bronwen E. Low

In the opening of the movie *Dangerous Minds* (Simpson/Bruckheimer 1995) Louanne Johnson, played by Michelle Pfeiffer, peers into her new classroom: One group of African American students is "freestyle" rapping, improvising rhyming verse to a beat, while other youth listen and dance to rap music. "Noisy bunch, aren't they?" she comments nervously. After realizing that she's going to have to "rewrite" the curriculum in order to engage her class of disenfranchised Black and Hispanic adolescents, she appeals to a colleague for help finding a "gimmick" for teaching them poetry, to which he responds, "poetry— these kids?" The attention-grabber turns out to be the songs of Bob Dylan, and the poetry project a comparison of the work of this Dylan and Dylan Thomas. The students rise to the challenge of interpreting poetry, a plot point that insists they were without poetry to begin with, in contrast to the poetic force of the freestyle scene. Ms. Johnson and, by extension, Hollywood seem unable to imagine a student-centered literacy curriculum that draws on youths' lived experience and interests rather than those of the teachers, despite the trendy rap soundtrack signaling the generational specificity of popular culture. From the perspective of contemporary urban youth, Bob Dylan might be as foreign and dated a figure as Dylan Thomas. The urban students in *Dangerous Minds*—an instance of the white middle-class teacher rescue-fantasy genre—are imagined as culturally deficient, as without literacy or poetry, and thus their success with Ms. Johnson only points to their inherent failure. As these students are by definition alienated from schooling, any success is necessarily attributed to the school, while failure in school belongs solely to them.

Why should educators take youth popular culture seriously? In this paper, I argue for popular culture as an important site of knowledge about adolescent literacy practices, and for the value of cultural studies as a theoretical and methodological framework for such an inquiry. Cultural studies of popular culture offer insight into how contemporary youth communicate, express themselves, and make meaning, through practices constituting what might be thought of as a counterliteracy—outside of the formal practices of academic literacy, pedagogy, and curriculum, and evolving out of exclusion, necessity, and improvised pleasure. In order to better understand the "richness and complexity" of the contemporary literacy practices upon which curricula and assessment must be based (Street, Introduction), literacy educators need to take such oppositional literacies seriously. Which means moving beyond a pedagogical approach which casts popular culture as a bridge or "hook" to the real lessons of curriculum (Paul 2000) and which puts the popular (a mere gimmick) at the service of a static canon. Nor does a serious consideration mean "bringing popular culture into" the classroom. In the terms of sociocultural learning theory, culture does not just provide a context for individual learning (Rogoff 2003). Instead, the individual is embedded within culture, actively producing culture and being produced by it: Popular youth culture is always already present in classrooms. The challenge for literacy education is how to respond to this culture in meaningful ways.

New Literacy Studies (NLS) research on youth literacy practices in out-of-school contexts has convincingly demonstrated their complexity and the ideology-driven disconnect between these practices and schooled forms of literacy (Gee 1996; Street 1995) (e.g., see Welle, Barnard, and Clatts; Cucchiara; and Larson in this collection). Also made clear are ways the split between academic and home/community literacies furthers the social marginalization of racial, ethnic, and language minority youth (Street 1995; Luke and Freebody 1997). In response to such findings, Hull and Shultz (2001, 603) ask "How might out-of-school identities, social practices, and the literacies that they recruit be leveraged in the classroom?" and, "How might teachers incorporate students' out-of-school interests and predilections but also extend the range of the literacies with which they are conversant?" One significant barrier to the incorporation of nonacademic literacies into school is the deficit model that characterizes many teachers' attitudes towards such literacy practices, particularly those that stem from black popular culture—such as the freestyle rapping in Ms. Johnson's classroom. Not only is Bob Dylan from the 60s but he is also a white artist. Like NLS, cultural studies emphasizes that power shapes the separation of school and out-of-school literacy practices, as well as distinctions between high and low culture. It provides a lens for reading pop culture as central to student knowledge, skills, and interests—and to literate practices and identities in the rapidly evolving present, given that the popular both drives and reflects the evolution of culture more generally. In this chapter I model how cultural studies might help recruit the popular to the work of schooling, and help teachers better understand and so build upon youth interests and predilections, through a textual analysis of a rap song and a case study of a performance poetry curriculum unit in two senior English classrooms. Popular culture is transient, shifting, contradictory, and multifaceted, and academic frameworks will always be ten steps behind, struggling to keep up. Cultural studies embraces the chase, alert to the changing shapes and directions of the popular, and thus is a crucial framework for educators committed to understanding and engaging, rather than reifying, adolescents' out-of-school literacies.

The task of mapping out the field of cultural studies is a daunting one, given that one of its organizing questions is "what is cultural studies?" (cf. Storey 1996). Johnson (1996) describes cultural studies as a movement or network, and argues that it resists codification because of its

> openness and theoretical versatility, its reflexive even self-conscious mood, and especially the importance of critique . . . procedures by which other traditions are approached both for what they yield and for what they inhibit. Critique involves stealing away the more useful elements and rejecting the rest (75).

While there is some consensus about cultural studies' history, with trajectories beginning somewhere around the founding of the Birmingham Centre for Contemporary Cultural Studies (CCCS) in 1964 as an experiment in adult education, this network is now transnational. And as Johnson's theft metaphor makes clear, the work is explicitly interdisciplinary, and indeed might be "shaped by its rebellion against disciplinarity itself" (Frow and Morris 2000, 329). That said, there are some characteristic elements of cultural studies approaches to culture, and I concentrate here on those useful for the study of literacy as social practice.

Cultural studies shares with the NLS an anthropological definition of culture as a whole way of life, but defines this whole

> as the "whole process" by means of which meanings and definitions are socially constructed and historically transformed, with literature and art as only one, specially privileged, kind of social communication (Hall 1980/1992, 9).

Borrowing some of the methods of literary studies, linguistics, and semiotics, cultural studies' object is representation broadly defined, including the languages of the word, the image, and the body. Within the terms of Duranti's (1997) typology, cultural studies emphasizes "culture as communication," as meaning-making, over culture as "system of practices" and "system of participation." Raymond Williams (1985) notes that "culture" tends to designate "material" production within archeology and cultural anthropology and "symbolic" production in cultural studies and history, a distinction, Williams argues, that wrongly obscures "the central question of the relations between 'material' and 'symbolic' production" (91). The notion of literacy as social practice explicitly takes up the relation of the material to the symbolic: How is literacy used and how does it mean in specific contexts for specific purposes? However, the roots of NLS in anthropology and sociolinguistics have meant careful attention to what people *do* with language, oral and written, and less analysis of how people *are shaped* by forms of representation such as art, media, and literature. A cultural studies lens focuses on how identities and social relations are made within, through, and against available representations. And cultural studies pays particular attention to popular and media culture as central to contemporary social communication under the semiotic, political, social, and economic conditions of globalization. As a way into a more extensive discussion of what a cultural studies perspective might offer the study of adolescent literacies, I offer a cultural studies reading of one popular text, a rap song that illustrates some of the dynamics of contemporary youth identities and language use. This sample illustrates how one might enact some of the analytic principles of cultural studies.

"Bakardi Slang" and the Postmodern Language of Diaspora

Rap music is valuable for exploring culture under conditions of globalization as it is increasingly international. The term "rap music" generally refers to the combination of the deejay's rhythm tracks and the emcee's lyrics. "Hip hop," on the other hand, while often used as musical category which includes rap but also rap's hybrid forms, including crossovers with other genres, here designates rap's larger culture. Hip hop includes rap, but also the break dancing and graffiti art which preceded and accompanied the emergence of rap music, as well as a whole culture of style, including clothing, hair, accessories, an idiom of movement and gesture, and a rich and changing lexicon. The Canadian rap scene is relatively small, emergent—a group actively working to understand and define itself. A stock tale in Canadian rap music is the struggle to get produced and find an audience in the commercial and aesthetic shadow of the U.S. hip hop industry. In one song by Toronto (known as T-dot in the hip hop world) rapper Kardinal Offishall, the artist proudly announces his community's distinctness from the scene to the south. Not only is "Bakardi Slang" (2001) a rap "boast" that proclaims the supremacy of the rapper and his crew but it is also a celebration of T-dot's language practices. Unlike many rap albums, *Quest for Fire's* liner notes contain transcriptions of the lyrics to a number of the album's songs, including "Bakardi Slang." Here are several verses from this track:

> BAKARDI SLANG. We
> don't say, "You know what I'm
> saying," T dot say's "Ya dun
> know." We don't say, "hey that's
> the breaks," we say "Yo, a so it
> go." We don't say, "you get one
> chance," we say, "you better rip
> the show." Before bottles start
> flyin' and you runnin for the door.
> Y'll talkin' about "cuttin' and
> hittin' skins"; we talkin' 'bout
> "beat dat face." T dot niggaz[1]
> will eat your food before you cats
> say grace . . . .

[1] In the controversial manner of much rap music, Kardi here rekeyes the n-word from a racist pejorative into a term of affection and community. See Randall Kennedy (2002) for the history of this term.

Differently, still ya know
the circle gettin' ill ya know . . .

Chorus. (What the?. . ./ Chilllll.
My nigga's in the street
throwin' dot slang each and every
single time we meet. . . .
. . . . Kardinal rock
the party, T dot drinkin' Bakardi.
Kardi drinkin' Bakardi. T dot rockin'
the party. . . .

. . . . you think we
all Jamaican, when nuff man are
Trini's. Bajans, Grenadians, and
a hole heap of Haitians.
Guyanese and all of the West
Indies combined. To make the T
dot O dot, one of a kind.

"Bakardi Slang" performs and announces a complex theory of language. The speaker carves out a distinct linguistic space for the T-dot hip hop scene, with an idiom grounded in the creoles of Toronto's Caribbean populations. Kardi's Caribbean heritage plays an important part in his articulation of identity in this different, "chilll-ier" context, but does not confine him, for his new speech community is larger than any one island. This T-dot identity is shaped by the "dialectical" relationship between nation and diaspora (Walcott 1999), but is not limited by the bounds of either. Instead, it is its own hybrid West Indian/Canadian formation that speaks of these other places, and yet is also "one of a kind." Within what has been called the world's most multicultural city, shaped by waves of immigration from all parts of the globe, and in relation to hip hop culture that is both locally inflected and transnational, traditional identity categories are inadequate in making sense of the lived experiences of youth. (Rowsell and Rajaratnam, this volume, give a detailed account of hybrid forms of identity, shaped by immigration and cultural collisions, within a Toronto context. See also David, Cho, and Toohey, this volume, on hybrid adolescent identities in Hawaii, under conditions of globalization.)

Throughout "Bakardi Slang," language is used to define a "we" separate from "you." This "you" is never identified, but through its association with expressions such as "You know what I'm saying," designates the American hip hop community. Rather than bemoan or protest against the challenges faced by Canadian rappers, "Bakardi Slang" tabulates what makes T-dot culture different from the "you," in order to celebrate these differences as the grounds of T dot's uniqueness. For after all, in the midst of the confusion of tongues—"what the?"—the rapper advocates that people just "chilllll," for this language is the grounds and medium for "rockin' the party."

To add to the linguistic complexity of Kardi's creative world, "Bakardi Slang" is rapped both in the "slang" of its title and in a more standard English, from which the T-dot and American hip hop idioms are distinguished via the use of quotation marks. Other songs in the album are rapped entirely in a Caribbean creole. Also clear from the track is that while some of the idiom of American hip hop is rejected by the T-dot community, a number of its central expressions are still integrated into Kardi's language: Good things are "ill," lyrics get "thrown," and the community of Toronto rappers are referred to as "niggaz." Despite rap's rapid and growing internationalization, the U.S. hip hop scene still stands as the center against which others make a relation, even in opposition.

T-dot slang reinvents or reworks the languages available to Toronto rappers, including versions of Standard English, African American English, and hip hop English, into what Hall (1996a) calls a "meaning which fit their experiences" (143). This language relies on its active use by a community of speakers; it has a currency as a means of communication because it is "thrown" "each and every single time we meet." It includes playful word-smithing, as in the pun on "Bakardi" and in the rapper's name, a "creolized" version of two titles of importance. What might be most important about "Bakardi Slang" is not the language it chronicles but the stance towards language it embodies, an irreverent stance towards linguistic authority, hierarchies, and divisions that values creativity and pleasure over standards and correctness. This song and, I propose, rap more generally celebrate the power of what Toni Morrison (1995) calls "word-work" to forge new selves, worlds, and meanings. Three mass-market examples of this spirit of word-work and self-invention and expression in rap are Sean "Puffy" Combs' multiple reincarnations, first as Puff Daddy and now as P-Diddy; Shaun Carter/ Jay-Z/Jigga/and Jay- HOVA, the new God of rap; and, perhaps most infamously, the three personas of the character known alternately as Slim Shady, Marshall Mathers, and Eminem. Such an improvisational theory of language and identity is characteristic of hip hop's performative spirit, its perpetual reinvention of itself through what Walcott (1999) calls

> an engagement in continuous practices of parody, deferral, bricolage, pastiche, collage, indirection, reversal, and numerous other "postmodern" practices to articulate and invent representations that are excessive and push the limits of normativity (103).

Via practices such as sampling from musical history and electronically modifying such samples so that they are no longer recognizable, rap's performative acts celebrate and rework existing cultural traditions while resisting fixed notions of origin.

Lankshear and Knobel (2003) make the case that the performative actually characterizes knowledge production in the digital age, and describe this "performance epistemology" as an "epistemology of rule breaking and innovation: of knowing how to proceed in the absence of existing models and exemplars" (173). They emphasize the importance of seizing the spotlight in the "attention economy" through strategies that please, that appeal to the imagination. In light of Lankshear and Knobel's argument, rap's push against the limits of normativity should be normative. Hip hop deejays and producers might be thought of as prophets of such an epistemology; as Sobol (2002) notes, in the early 80s they were sampling beats and playing them back through a digital keyboard, before the World Wide Web and personal computers, in effect "unearthing the cut-and-paste ethos latent in digital culture—in ways that literate theorists could only hint at" (122) before the fluorescence of digital culture. Given that elements of popular culture can foreshadow more general cultural changes, adolescent out-of-school identities and literacy practices emerge as vital to a future-minded curriculum.

Within the circles of mainstream education, rap and larger hip hop culture have a bad reputation: the news media have "constructed rap, rappers, and rap fans as the deviant, lacking, undesirable, or evil other" (Koza 1999, 91), and thus for many educators, the epitome of "what they have dedicated their careers to opposing" (65). Cultural studies resists distinctions drawn between high and low culture and turns literary close-reading strategies, including attention to particular tropes, forms of narrative, and genre, and the tools of linguistic analysis to the task of closely reading the complexities of popular texts.

From the inception of cultural studies, popular culture has been understood as a central site for understanding everyday semiotic practices. This commitment to popular culture means grappling with rap music as what Rose (1994) calls "a tangle of some of the most complex social, cultural, and political issues in American society" (2). Its "contradictory articulations" are therefore "not signs of absent intellectual clarity: they are a common feature of community and popular cultural dialogues that always offer more than one cultural, social, or political viewpoint" (Rose 1994, 2). Rap music opens up a range of possible viewpoints and identity positions with which youth might identify, from representations of the "gangsta" and "pimp" rapper to the poet-activist actively engaged in sociopolitical commentary and critique. A cultural studies approach to rap enters the dialogue about such representations—what they suggest about the lives, needs, and fantasies of their authors and audiences, as well as the economic, social, political, geographic, and historical conditions that make them possible.

Street (1995), writing from the perspective of literacy studies, singled out the usefulness of cultural studies' text-analysis for understanding "'the cultural attitudes, sentiments, values, and traditions'" (CCCS publicity document, cited in Street 1995, 59) of a particular place and time, what Raymond Williams, from within cultural studies, has called its textures of feeling. Texts and textual production are analyzed in order to understand texts-in-use: the textual organization of "subjective or cultural forms" (Johnson 1996, 97), or how texts "are used to define social relations, values, particular notions of community, the future, and diverse definitions of the self" (Giroux 1994, 301). In turn, my reading of "Bakardi Slang" takes rap music seriously as a literate practice that embodies an improvisational theory of language as the raw material for the creative production of identities and communities. It examines what this rap song reveals about the ways contemporary youth are making meaning out of available representations such as discourses of nationalism, Creole languages, and American hip hop vernaculars. It is committed to better understanding the active production of culture: "what we *do* with the cultural commodities that we encounter and use in daily life ("practice") and thus what we *make* as culture" (Frow and Morris 2000, 331).

The making of culture is also the making of identity: The self within cultural studies emerges through processes of identification in relation to and against available narratives and representations. Yon (2000), drawing on Hall's description of the postmodern subject, explains that although this process of making identifications is "constructed and open-ended" (13), these representations serve to "anchor" the subject in the social world (14). Hall contrasts this postmodern theory of identity with the theory of the Enlightenment subject with its unfolding "autonomous inner core," and that of the sociological subject produced through symbolic interaction with the social world. Unlike the coherence and stability offered by the latter models, postmodern identities multiply, fragment, become contradictory, and remain unresolved (Yon 2000, 13) and "subjects are no longer perceived as fastened to cultures and external social structures" (14). "Bakardi Slang" exemplifies some of its characteristics: T-dot identities are fluid, performative, hybrid, and creative. Both new literacy studies and postmodern cultural studies reject the essentializing tendencies of an "autonomous" model, whether of literacy or identity.

The postmodern notion of multiple and fragmented subjectivities is not an abstract construct; instead, in the words of Luke and Luke (2001), it "appears to have strong experiential and phenomenological, empirical, and even experimental corroboration" (94). Adolescents participate in a culture whose "intellectual, laboring and signifying capacities . . . are in flux" (93) as a result of

> unprecedented and seemingly irresistible global and borderless flows of human laboring and thinking subjects, of capital both symbolic and material, and of information, discourse and texts having immediate and palpable impact on social formations, on cultural practices, and indeed, on human development (93).

The high-speed flows and transformations of culture within the information age and under conditions of globalization mean that "youth increasingly inhabit shifting cultural and social spheres marked by a plurality of languages and cultures" (Giroux 1994, 298)—and a crossing of boundaries. For Kardinall Offishall, this shifting, plural space is a source of creative self-expression.

Given this cultural flux, there continues to be a need for studies of literacy practices that are new, in both the chronological sense and new to schools (Lankshear and Knobel 2003), in conjunction with work on making meaningful relations between these practices and curriculum and pedagogy. As shown by research on the multimodal "multiliteracies" that are required and cultivated by new media and information technologies, the proliferation of communication channels, and the representational forms of a media-saturated culture (Lankshear and Knobel 2003; Cope and Kalantzis 2000), models of literacy are challenged to keep up with lived practices. It seems that models of language and literacy are only ever approximations, metaphors even, of the ways language is lived, and ongoing work is needed to question and refigure these models. Cultural studies is committed to evaluating the usefulness of existing theoretical frameworks for understanding new practices, and as such represents an

> ongoing attempt to measure old theories against the emergence of new historical articulations, new cultural events, changes in the tempo and texture of social life, new structures of social relationships and new subjectivities (Grossberg 1996, 180).

And cultural studies privileges and explores the central role played by the mass media "with its massive apparatuses of representation and its regulation of meaning" (Giroux 1994, 299) in the construction of these changing events, relationships, and identities.

Why should literacy educators and education be interested in better understanding changing youth identities? Because who one imagines oneself to be is vital to what and how one will learn. If literacy is a social practice, then it is necessarily tied to specific ways of being in the social, to particular identities. Street (Introduction) points out that "deep levels of identity and epistemology" affect "the stance that learners take with respect to the 'new' literacy practices of the educational setting." While Street's interest here lies in the ties between "home background" and these deep levels, a cultural studies lens widens the gaze to include the influence of mass media popular culture on the ontology of the literate subject, and what new modes of being and knowing suggest about new ways of reading and writing the world. Gee (2003) also makes a relation between identity and "deep" or " active, critical" learning, arguing that a commitment to the latter requires seeing oneself "in terms of a new identity . . . as the *kind of person* who can learn, use, and value the new semiotic domain" (59) that the learning engages. What kinds of people do adolescents imagine themselves to be? What kinds of people do they aspire to be? And what sorts of literacy practices are enabled, and restricted, by these imagined and model identities?

Cultural Studies in the Classroom

Cultural studies has made little impact on educational research (Giroux 1994) and arguably less on classroom practices. As Giroux also makes clear, cultural studies theorists have largely neglected pedagogy, this despite Raymond Williams' "desire to make learning part of the process of social change itself'" (cited in Giroux 1994, 283). The study I now describe is an example of what work in both cultural studies and NLS on adolescent out-of-school literacies has to offer education, and what education can offer them in return. In the spring of 2002, I began collaborating with a high-school English teacher at an urban arts school in a mid-sized, northeastern U.S. city, helping to develop and lead a performance poetry or "spoken word" unit in his two senior English classes. This curriculum development is informed by my cultural studies work on "spoken word" culture (Low 2001a; 2001b). Spoken word is an umbrella category designating performance in which an artist recites (rather than sings) poetry, sometimes to musical accompaniment that ranges from a bongo drum to a digitally sampled rhythm track (as in rap music). The teacher and I planned to draw and build upon student interests in rap music and freestyle oral poetry, and the class culminated in a competitive poetry "slam," a poetry mock-Olympics in which poets perform original work and are scored by a panel of judges on a scale of 1–10. (See Stein and Mamabolo, this volume, on the uses of performance in a South African classroom). The students (and research participants) were all 17 or 18 years of age. One class was an English IV class, designed as an alternative to the academic advanced placement class, and was composed only of male students who self-selected to be in a same-sex class. Their teacher called them "survivors"—students who have not traditionally done well in English, but have managed to persist into their senior year. Of the twenty-nine boys in the class, twenty-two are African-American, three are Hispanic, and four are European-American. The other class was an Advanced Poetry class, which attracted some of the top academic students in the grade and was coed, consisting of nine boys and ten girls. Fourteen students are European-American, two are African-American, two are Hispanic, and one is Palestinian-American. The teacher and university researchers are all European-American. My data from this project include audio- and video-recordings of full-class discussions and performances, students' in-class writing, and one-on-one interviews with the students and teacher. In the following discussion,

I draw on a class discussion about the slam held in each class at the end of the term.

Throughout the course students were immersed in spoken word forms through videos, CDs, visits by local poets, and a series of workshops in which students developed and rehearsed their own poems. We listened to rap and offered students a wider context for thinking about its experiments with word and sound, including sound poetry, modernist decompositions of language, jazz poetry, and blues poetry. In negotiating classroom guidelines for the poetry slam, we tackled some of rap's controversial language and representations head-on, which resulted in some thoughtful and heated discussions of the politics of language, audience, and interpretation. I played them "Bakardi Slang," and students in both classes discussed processes of language change; in the male class, students described the microlinguistic climate of their neighborhoods, in which they can identify the block someone lives on by their idiom. For this chapter, I want to concentrate on three themes that emerged out of this project: the expansion of the role and identity of poet; risky explorations of identity; and thoughtfulness.

One valuable aspect of rap music for literacy educators is its commitment to linguistic skill, with rappers proudly proclaiming themselves word warriors. The links between rap and the other spoken word forms we explored redefined what counts as poetry in school; in the words of one male from the boy's class, "I think people really like poetry they're just afraid to admit it." A number of students in this group wrote poetry for the first time or shared it, much to the surprise of some of their classmates. One student in the English IV group, Darren, read us a spontaneous poem he wrote in class, inspired by a visiting poet, which began "My notebook is my horse and saddle/With this/I ride/I ride into the creativity of my emotions and embrace them as one would their child." A classmate expressed shock that Darren and others wrote poetry, "because I didn't see that part of him and I was like oh—well they deserve my attention because this is something that I didn't know about." This sense of surprise emerged repeatedly in discussions about the slam with students in both classes. In the Advanced Poetry class, one male announced, "I've seen things come out of people that I didn't know they had in them, and like we've been together since the 9th grade." In this same class another student, commenting on his powerful invective that won the slam, said, "I didn't know I had that in me." Students who performed seemed to experiment with different identities, making themselves strange and new to their peers and themselves. In the spirit of hip hop performativity, these students tried on different personas for size in their poems.

Students in both classes took significant risks with their poems, contributing to the sense of surprise. One of the biggest surprises for many students, as well as for their teacher, was a poem entitled "Who can defeat me," that was delivered with force by Jamal, an African-American male from the Pacesetter class known for his soft-spoken, easygoing manner. I include it here as an example of students' self-exploration through the medium of performance poetry.

WHO CAN DEFEAT ME
Inside me
is an inner me
that inner me
wants to be free
but should I let it free
therefore releasing
my enemy
cause my inner me
is my enemy
So what would I be
if me and my enemy
join to be we
will that complete me
is it reality
to see
Rodney King join hands w/ his enemies
after his tragic police brutality
or to see Afghanistan Refugee
eat w/ the ones dat made them flee
they are people just like you + me
they just wanna be free
free from brutality, harsh analogies
incriminating formalities, and mental
government battery
we must join in unity
to strengthen our community

because the core is you and me
we pave the way for whats to be
back during slavery
our ancestors wanted to be free
their spirits live deep in me
telling me
"FREE ME" "free me"
my mind is the key to my individuality
telling me
no one can defeat me
but me.

The poem's ambiguity gets at some of the complexity of this "inner me," at once Jamal's "enemy," the voices of his slave ancestors whose spirits "live deep in me," and his "mind." I read this "inner me" as a personification of this student's anger at the injustices of the world, from the treatment of Rodney King to the bombing of Afghanistan. While he fears his anger, he also recognizes its source in historical and contemporary racial violence, and its potential for resistance, for working in particular towards the liberation of African-American people. He suggests that paths towards freedom lie both with the individual, particularly the individual mind, and the building of community. Craig delivered the poem with such vehemence and intensity that he was almost shouting, which suggested that this normally reserved student was using the poem as one vehicle for exploring different aspects of himself, part of the journey, perhaps, towards freedom.

Other students also experimented with different perspectives and ways of being. One student who identifies as "G," an acronym for both his name and "gangsta" rapper, and who performed a controversial rap celebrating gang violence at the school's talent show, shared a poem entitled "Cry" that critiqued gang violence, and implicitly, models of masculinity that suggest that men have no feelings. It begins: "Misunderstood is the definition of when a man cries" and ends with: "And you ask why? Why you think I'm crying you bastard?/ It's cause I'm at your funeral putting flowers on your casket." This poem draws on some common themes in rap music: poetry as pedagogy, as tool for healing, and as vehicle for street wisdom. While the Advanced Poetry students, many of whom were creative writing majors, were already comfortable writing and sharing poetry, they also made themselves vulnerable through honest explorations of identity. A white student named Kevin, the class clown, wrote a poem in which he began by joking about his weight: "a dose of truth/ no a large portion/ . . . ./ I can't fit in . . ./ to the damn pants/ I can't fit into the pants/ that I bought for fifty bucks/ cause I said to my mom/ they would fit/ shit." But then his tone turned, and he critiqued the girls who use him as a dating novelty item on their route to that "real guy." Three girls—one African-American, one European-American, and one who self-identified as mixed race—performed a group poem, "Me," in which they interrogated race and racial stereotyping, including being "Too Black," "Too White," and "two things combined, intertwined/ Through society's eyes blinded by color/ Do I have to be one or the other?"

In both classes we discussed possible reasons for the collective risk-taking in the poetry slam. Several students suggested that they were more willing to explore difficult subjects because performance allowed them greater control over the audience's interpretation of their message. A few students proposed that their risk-taking was in part due to the fact that they were graduating seniors, leaving this particular community behind in a few weeks. One student responded that "freedom" was at stake in their choice of topics, not "vulnerability," and that the slam presented the "perfect opportunity" if "you just want to express yourself." Rogoff (2003) explains how our thinking is shaped by the cultural tools we work with. Slam poetry—vernacular, urban, often politicized, playful, sexy—opens up certain possibilities for thinking, and for trying on new modes of expression and being (Low, forthcoming). Students described some reasons slam poetry seemed like the right vehicle for self-expression and exploration: for one student it is "written and read in the author's own voice" and for another it has "more emotions in it, more of the writer inside the piece."

The students grappled with important issues at the individual, local, and international level: Self-knowledge, stereotypes, romance, racism, gang violence, the city school budget crisis and proposals to cut arts funding, terrorism, and the war on Iraq. The spoken word poems we explored in class might have in part inspired and provoked students to be so thoughtful in their pieces. But it is also the case that the students were given a venue and permission to express themselves in their own language, to show their peers and teachers what they already think about. As Darren described his work: "My thoughts laid out on paper/for all to see/ . . ./that I myself/Am poetry." Or in the words of a male in the Advanced Poetry class, "I think everyone was saying things that needed to be said, but didn't know how to put them, but once everyone said them they were said so eloquently it was amazing." Another pointed out: "Racism, terrorism, image, society, love—you can tell exactly what runs through our minds every day." One Hispanic student in the Pacesetter class put out a call towards the beginning of the project for the group to be as thoughtful as possible:

> cause we think about a lot of things they don't know we think about, you know what I'm saying. We write a lot of things they don't know we write about. So we care about issues they don't know we care about. If we show them that we care about these issues and we learn about these things and we can do it in this creative way of language . . . with our poetry what I want us to do—me personally—is to have them leave the theatre thinking like damn those are some talented young men and women you know what I'm saying like damn—they got things to say—know something else . . . that's the future of all of us—we're the future and they got to know that . . . the things we have to say even though we might say it in a different way, that shit is important.

Carlo's appeal was heard; given the space to share what they think and write and care about, in their own creative language, the students treated their classmates and slam audience with their intelligence, wit, insight, honesty, and emotion.

A cultural studies approach to curriculum takes youth culture seriously as a resource of creative, provocative literate practices. Given that adolescents might be saying what they have to say in a "different way," the challenge for educators becomes learning how to listen differently. To return to Hull and Shultz's (2001) formulation, the language arts unit "leveraged" the youth out-of-school rap and freestyle literacies Ms. Johnson cast as noise. It also "extended" such literacies: The students who were accomplished rappers and freestylers experimented with performance poetry, written in advance and performed without musical accompaniment. Experienced creative writers placed greater emphasis on the performance of their works. Some familiar practices were made strange, worthy of analysis; others were situated within the historical and contemporary context of spoken word culture. And given the students' expressions of surprise, not only were the teachers and administrators shown that "we think about a lot of things they don't know we think about" but so were the "talented men and women" in question.

References

Cope, B., and Kalantzis, M. (eds.) 2000. *Multiliteracies: Literacy learning and the design of social futures.* London and New York: Routledge.

Duranti, A. 1997. *Linguistic anthropology.* Cambridge: Cambridge University Press.

Frow, J., and Morris, M. 2000. Cultural studies. In: N. Denzin and Y. Lincoln (eds.), *Handbook of qualitative research.* Thousand Oaks: Sage Publications, pp. 315–334.

Gee, J. 1996. Ideology and theory: The moral basis of discourse analysis. *Social linguistics and literacies.* 2nd ed. London: Taylor and Francis, pp. 1–21.

Giroux, H. 1994. Doing cultural studies: Youth and the challenge of pedagogy. *Harvard Educational Review* 64(3): 278–308.

Grossberg, L. 1996. The circulation of cultural studies. In: J. Storey (ed.), *What is cultural studies?* London: Arnold, pp. 178–186.

Hall, S. 1980/1992. Cultural studies and the center: Some problematics and problems. *Culture, media, language: Working papers in cultural studies, 1972–1979.* London: Routledge (in association with the Centre for Contemporary Cultural Studies, University of Birmingham), pp. 15–47.

Hall, S. 1996a. On post-modernism and articulation. Interview edited by Lawrence Grossberg. In: D. Morley and K.-H. Chen (eds.), *Stuart Hall: Critical dialogues in cultural studies.* London: Routledge, pp. 131–150.

Hall, S. 1996b. Cultural studies: Two paradigms. In: J. Storey (ed.), *What is cultural studies?* London: Arnold, pp. 31–48.

Hull, G., and Shultz, K. 2001. Literacy and learning out of school: A review of theory and research. *Review of Educational Research* 71(4): 575–611.

Johnson, R. 1996. What is cultural studies anyway? In: J. Storey (ed.), *What is cultural studies?* London: Arnold, pp. 75–114.

Kennedy, R. 2002. *Nigger: The strange career of a troublesome word.* New York: Pantheon Books.

Koza, J. 1999. Rap music: The cultural politics of official representation. In: C. McCarthy et al. (eds.), *Sound identities: Popular music and the cultural politics of education.* New York: Peter Lang, pp. 65–96.

Lankshear, C., and Knobel, M. 2003. *New literacies: Changing knowledge and classroom learning.* Buckingham: Open University Press.

Low, B. 2001a. "Bakardi Slang" and the language and poetics of T Dot hip hop. *Taboo* (Fall/Winter), 15–31.

Low, B. 2001b. *Spoken word: Exploring the language and poetics of the hip hop popular.* Unpublished dissertation, Toronto: York University.

Low, B. Forthcoming. Poetry on MTV?: Slam and the poetics of the popular. *Journal of Curriculum Theorizing.*

Luke, A., and Luke, C. 2001. Adolescence lost/childhood regained: On early intervention and the emergence of the techno-subject. *Journal of Early Childhood Literacy* 1(1): 94–111.

Luke, A., and Freebody, P. 1997. Critical literacy and the question of normativity: An introduction. In: S. Muspratt, A. Luke, and P. Freebody (eds.), *Constructing critical literacies: Teaching and learning textual practice.* New York: Teachers College Press.

Morrison, T. 1995. Nobel Lecture (7 December 1993). *The Georgia Review* 49(1): 318–323.

Offishall, Kardinal. 2001. *Quest for fire: Firestarter. Vol. 1* [CD]. MCA.

Paul, D.G. 2000. Rap and orality: Critical media literacy, pedagogy, and cultural synchronization. *Journal of Adolescent and Adult Literacy* 44(3): 246–251.

Rogoff, B. 2003. *The cultural nature of human development.* Oxford: Oxford University Press.

Rose, T. 1994. *Black noise: Rap music and black culture in contemporary America.* Hanover: University Press of New England.

Sobol, J. 2002. *Digitopia blues: Race, technology, and the American voice.* Banff: The Banff Center Press.

Street, B. 1995. *Social literacies: Critical approaches to literacy in development, ethnography, and education.* New York: Longman.

Walcott, R. 1999. Performing the (black) postmodern: Rap as incitement for cultural criticism. In: C. McCarthy et al. (eds.), *Sound identities: Popular music and the cultural politics of education.* New York: Peter Lang, pp. 97–118.

Williams, R. 1985. *Keywords: A vocabulary of culture and society.* New York: Oxford University Press.

Yon, D. 2000. *Elusive culture.* Albany: SUNY Press.

7

Bridging Life and Learning through Inquiry and Improvisation
Literacy Practices at a Model High School

Rob Simon

In this world, I feel like this school is my home. The reason I feel this way is because there are people there that I love, and at school you can get educated and respect. My school smells like food and looks beautiful.
—Life Learning Academy Student[1]

The afternoon vans left, and the real work started. From a group of students petitioning Principal Teri Lynch Delane to make the school "look more homey" came the Life Learning Academy school design class, taught by Teri herself; two months later, after meeting with volunteer interior designers and architects, sketching mock-ups, writing proposals and grants, they were ready to paint. Several Delancey Street mentors and Academy teachers helped, mostly with taping and laying tarps to protect the carpet, but the work was done by students, in paint smocks and blue jumpsuits, eager to test their color choices on real walls in the school's entryway: alternating green and yellow, the ubiquitous teal, and a stubborn orange that demanded four coats. A student, along with her photography teacher, took pictures. Near the front en-

---

[1] This and other quotes from Life Learning Academy students and teachers are taken from interviews conducted by LaFrance et al. (2001) as a part of their comprehensive program assessment of Life Learning Academy.

trance, past the receptionist's desk, two students painted bright yellow to frame the oversized-teal letters of the school motto: "The important thing is this: to be able, at any moment, to sacrifice what we are for what we could become."

Introduction

Anthropological studies emphasizing the deeply contextualized nature of literacy practices in local settings sparked a revolution in academic writing and research over the past twenty years (Heath 1983; Street 1984). This new focus on local "literacies" emphasized complex literacy practices of individuals and communities, intended, in part, to provide an alternative to institutionalized, narrow definitions of literacy, what Street (1984) has called "autonomous."

In academic research, the influence of a social practice view of literacy and the so-called New Literacy Studies (Gee 1996; Street 1984) has been significant. Yet in spite of this wide body of scholarship, public debate over the supposed "reading crisis" in America continues along a course distinct and distant from New Literacy Studies (NLS) and its constituents' claims. Rather than account for a social practice view in the creation of new school policy, which may necessitate reforming the ideological assumptions and institutions that underlie their approach (Gee 2001), policymakers tend toward cookie-cutter approaches to literacy education, such as the Reading First initiative, part of the No Child Left Behind Act of 2001 (NCLB), the latest salvo in the standards movement. If not bridged, the new "great divide" may well be one separating the efforts of proponents of a social practice paradigm of literacy from opportunities to shape policy and practice. As noted by Brian Street in his article "What's 'New' in New Literacy Studies" (2003) and reiterated in his introduction to this book, NLS is facing a need to construct a "more robust and less insular field of study," by adapting theory into "positive proposals for interventions in teaching, curriculum, [and] measurement criteria."

The reasons for the distance between policymakers and social-practice theorists may well be multiple. The increased emphasis on situating literacy in local contexts prevalent in NLS may have had the unintended effect of failing to address the larger enterprise of literacy education in a way that offers viable pedagogical alternatives to the "autonomous" model. Further, as Hull and Schultz (2003) note, NLS has focused predominantly on out-of-school literacy practices, less often looking at the production of local school literacies and pedagogical models. At best, social practice theories of multiple literacies are complicated and not easily translated into policy—certainly not into "quick fix" approaches currently in vogue (Larson 2002).

At worst, socially situated theories of literacy may have exaggerated the significance of local contexts (Brandt and Clinton 2002), creating a "universalist/particularist impasse" (Collins and Blot 2002)—a widening gap between deeply contextualized ethnographies of literacy and generalizable programmatic and practical concerns. It is possibly a conscious disaffection with universalizing definitions of literacy combined with distance between local contexts—what might be termed antitranscontextualization—which opens NLS claims to the criticism of being overly relativistic, resulting in an undesired defanging effect on what has become an increasingly national and transnational literacy stage hungry for theories that address general tendencies and include proposals for intervention.

In this chapter, I explore one possible way of bridging this apparent gap between theorizing of literacy in NLS and the ways literacy is currently addressed in schools in the United States. Beginning with an analysis of recent critiques of NLS by Brandt and Clinton (2002), Collins and Blot (2002), and Street (2003), I turn to the theories of sociologist Anthony Giddens (1991) to establish an understanding of literacy as both contextualized and transcontextual, creating the basis for, in the words of Deborah Brandt and Katie Clinton, "incorporating individual agents and their locales into the larger enterprises that play out away from the immediate scene" (2002). I emphasize the interconnections between localities not to develop a new "autonomy," but rather a way of conceiving the local that has implications for other localities, one which emphasizes the symbiotic interconnectivity between the "local" and the "translocal"—a theoretical step that may have important implications for future policy and pedagogy and developing proposals for reform that demonstrate sympathy with NLS.

In the latter section of this chapter, building from Giddens' notion of institutional reflexivity, I explore a school site that seems to resonate with some of the social practice tenets of NLS: Life Learning Academy (LLA or Life Learning), a San Francisco experimental charter high school. The Life Learning Academy example is not held up here as a virtuous paradigm, a model that can simply be put in place in all contexts in the same way, but rather as an approach to thinking of literacy and teaching in context that has the potential to influence the public literacy debate at the level of policy and may have implications for school reform, one which allows for creative tension and embraces a sustained commitment to inquiry and improvisation. As a founding teacher at Life Learning Academy, I have experienced firsthand the impact this school has on the lives and literacies of students who, like the Life Learning student whose words serve as an epigraph to this chapter, come to very much "feel like this school is [their] home." Life Learning Academy's "extended family" model is one example of a way to bridge students' in- and out-of-school literacies (Hull and Schultz 2003), consistent with NLS' sustained critique. Further, it is a "bottom-up" reform effort that speaks to some of the demands of "top-down actors" (Fuhrman 2003); successful in educating a particular group of students, the school has managed to catch the imagination of policymakers at federal, state, and local levels, who see Life Learning Academy as a program that works and has potential for future replication.

Life Learning provides an example of a flexible, self-questioning, and reflexive institutional model that is at once local—growing from an attempt to meet the needs of its constituents, teachers and students, in a particular context—and translocal—both in the sense that the school is linked to a broader educational system and goals and in that the school's questioning approach may speak to possibilities of meeting literacy needs of other students in other contexts. Unlike many schools, Life Learning Academy has questioned, challenged, and reshaped the fundamental "grammar" and the conventional wisdom about what constitutes a "real school."[2] Life Learning serves students who have fallen through the cracks—the sixty students there have been involved in, or are at risk of involvement in, the juvenile justice system—and their literacy needs according to standard assessment measures are profound; for example, in 2002, incoming students had an average GPA of .77 the semester prior to entering Life Learning Academy (LaFrance 2004). The Life Learning student body is made up predominantly of youth deemed "problem children" by the

[2]On the persistence of the "grammar of schooling," by which I mean the enduring form and function of schools, see David Tyack and Larry Cuban's *Tinkering Toward Utopia* (1995); as this concept underlies notions of what counts as a "real school," see "Real School: A Universal Drama amid Disparate Experience," by Mary Hayward Metz (1991).

educational mainstream. Rather than take a deficit approach, Life Learning Academy views its students not as zero-sum prisoners of past mistakes, but as young people with high potential confronting challenging obstacles. Fueling Life Learning's development of collaborative curriculum and pedagogy is an underlying "inquiry stance" (Cochran-Smith and Lytle 2001) toward students, teaching, learning and school structures—one that institutionalizes a questioning approach and builds substantive changes upon this inquiry. Thus the example of Life Learning Academy poses a challenge to policymakers and reformers: Does a school that asks real questions about the local needs of its students offer an approach with potential for replication and reform?

Recent Criticism of New Literacy Studies

Several recent articles critical of NLS approaches (Brandt and Clinton 2002; Collins and Blot 2002; Street 2004; 2003) emphasize the need to connect localized literacy practices, long the focus of social-practice ethnographies of literacy, to the broader terrain that has been co-opted by "autonomous" definitions of literacy. While NLS studies have revealed the complexity and meaning that local home and community literacy practices have in peoples' daily lives, there is now a growing contingency within NLS that sees limitations in further localized case studies. Further, if policymakers recognize such studies at all, they are deemed irrelevant to literacy as they have defined it—a universal set of linguistic markers, methods, and skills that can supposedly be imprinted on any population in any context with equal success (as in the direct instruction approach recommended by NCLB); worse still, they might well view local literacies as "failed attempts at the real thing" (Street 2002). Researchers in sympathy with NLS principles have begun to struggle with what Deborah Brandt and Katie Clinton (2002) call "the limits of the local."

While Brandt and Clinton claim that the social-practice paradigm has veered "too far in a reactive direction, exaggerating the power of local contexts to set or reveal the forms and meanings that literacy takes," James Collins and Richard Blot (2002) highlight the need to "explore why historical and ethnographic cases are necessary, but insufficient, for rethinking inherited viewpoints"; in other words, examining why a flawed "autonomous" conception of literacy has taken hold of public thinking and policy around literacy education—and why a complex understanding of multiple "literacies" has not—has become a vital undertaking. Thus, connecting local practices to general tendencies has become key, in the eyes of these researchers, to making NLS principles relevant to the mainstream.

To bridge the theoretical gap between the local and the general, Brandt and Clinton (2002) turn to the work of Bruno Latour, attempting to define literacy not as an "autonomous" skill set or a local manifestation, but instead as a participant in local literacy practices in the form of texts, technologies, and objects, an "'actant' in its own right." In Latour's view, objects act as stabilizing forces in human events, mediate human interactions, and build connections across time and space; thus literacy, as object, may be seen as connecting literacy events and practices temporally and geographically—in this light, "literacy" is not a result of these practices, but a participant in them.

Brandt and Clinton rightly establish the need for reframing the relationship between local and "general" literacies. In his own analysis of the "limits of the local," Street (2004) turns to the work of Anthony Giddens for a framework to characterize this relationship. Giddens' theories offer a conceptual tool that focuses more on the dialectical nature of local and global, allowing us to view literacy not as actor or outcome, but as a system of knowledge that functions as what Giddens (1991) terms a "disembedding mechanism." Street focuses his analysis primarily on disembedding mechanisms. A broader consideration of Gidden's three characteristics, or "conditions," of modernity, however, may provide a crucial link to programmatic levels, one that seems to have implications for considering practical program models like Life Learning Academy as a necessary step between theory and policy, providing a theoretical framework for conceptualizing a dialectical and recursive relationship between "social events and social relations 'at distance' [and] local contextualities" (Giddens 1991, 21), between policy, theory, and practice.

Literacy as 'Disembedding Mechanism'

Giddens' theories present a useful theoretical bridge from the NLS social practice view of literacy to the universalizing demands of educational policymakers. In *Modernity and Self-Identity* (1991), Giddens describes three characteristics of modernity. The last of these features, "institutional reflexivity," will be addressed later; the first two seem to be a fitting apparatus for locating a link between local literacy practices and "global" (Brandt and Clinton 2002) or "general" (Collins and Blot 2002) literacies without slipping into the trap of an "autonomous" conception.

The first of Giddens' characteristics of modernity, the "separation of time and space," describes the rootlessness or "runaway" quality of the modern world. Modern life is not "connected through the situatedness of place" (16); "when" and "where" are important aspects of social interaction, but geographic proximity is no longer the essential factor in human events. In other words, while coordination of time and location matters, our social options are less geographically bounded, allowing for, for example, distance learning, video conferencing, or Internet discussion groups, technologies at the heart of literacy work conducted by Internet-based teacher networks like the Bread Loaf School's BreadNet.[3]

This "emptying out" of time and space—or time/space distanciation—is an important basis of Gidden's second feature of modernity, "disembedding mechanisms," which involves "the 'lifting out' of social relations from local contexts and their rearticulation across indefinite tracts of time-space" (18). This disembedding happens through the use of "abstract systems," which take the form of "symbolic tokens," like money, or "expert systems"—specific technical knowledge fields that operate across time and space and are taken hold of locally. In Giddens' conception, expert systems inhabit all areas of modern life and exist in all professional fields, from medicine to education. These systems are not "autonomous," however, but interactive, reflexive, and dialectical, dependent upon local agents to take hold of them and integrate and alter them to suit their needs. Giddens specifically emphasizes the "global" dependence on the local, but the reverse may also be true; thus, the "disembedding mechanism" of literacy "dislodges" distant events and practices and situates them locally, or vice versa. Take media, for example, the content of which is taken hold of within local literacy practices and used for specific, locally situated ends: in this way the headline from today's *New York Times* may form the basis of a class debate in a social studies classroom in San Francisco. Further, Giddens' notes that this media does not form an "autonomous realm of hyperreality where the

---

[3] BreadNet uses technology to bridge distances between geographically remote groups of participating students and teachers. See www.middlebury.edu/blse/breadnet.

sign or image is everything" (27); in fact, we might assume that without local interests, such media remain empty of utility.

If Giddens' conceptions of distanciation and disembedding mechanisms are applied to literacy, it is possible to envision a literacy with "global" components that gain meaning only in highly contextualized local instantiations. We then arrive at an understanding of literacy not as an "autonomous" skill set with universal meaning in all contexts, rather, literacy may be seen as an expert system that is alternately embedded, "taken hold" of, as Street (2004) suggests, citing Kulick and Stroud (1993), or realized, in local practice and "disembedded," with implications for other localities. In this dialectical model, the "expert system," literacy in this case, does not remain unchanged by local practice, but is instead always altered by the interaction, a reflexive state that allows local practices to have translocal implications.

Institutional Reflexivity and Institutional Revisioning

The last of Giddens' characteristics of modernity is "institutional reflexivity." As conceived by Giddens, the modern world is increasingly multiple choice, a place where individuals and institutions are always reimagining and remolding themselves given new options and choices.[4] Reflexive revisioning is characteristic of mainstream modern life, for individuals, institutions, and "expert systems," among which there is continuous interaction. Witness, for example, the ever-advancing iteration that is a defining feature of technology within the so-called "new capitalism" (Gee 2000) or the frenetic, self-referent "cool hunting" and guerilla tactics of corporate marketing to teenagers (Vilbig 2002). Furthermore, as noted above, this reflexivity characterizes the relationship between the local and the "global" broadly cast: in other words, there is a constant "interplay between local involvements and globalizing tendencies" (Giddens 1991, 242).

Most importantly, Giddens' reflexivity is a force that "propels modern life from the hold of pre-established precepts or practices" (20). In practice, however, there is often tension between the impulse to revise and a desire to hold fast to tra-

---

[4]Importantly, this revision is delimited by "differential access to forms of self-actualization and empowerment" (Giddens 1991, 6). In other words, the "have-nots" have less access to new lifestyle choices, a significant factor in the case of public education.

dition—characterized by what Roberto Unger calls "institutional fetishization"[5] (1994, 7), or what Giddens refers to as "inertia of habit or the externalities of tradition" (1991, 150). Nowhere is this tension more apparent than in an educational context, where it is made manifest in the reality that we educate twenty-first century American schoolchildren in schools that have changed little in over fifty years, their structures and practices having proven historically to be profoundly resistant to significant change (Tyack and Cuban 1995). It presents a counterintuitive fact of life for students, one that begs the question: Can we imagine revised school structures, where, as Giddens puts it, "tradition can be 'reinvented' in settings that have become thoroughly posttraditional" (150)? Can schools reinvent themselves to better meet the needs of local communities of students?

Taking the institutional level of Giddens' theory into account, it may be the case that lodging a broader view of "literacies" in the recommendations of educational policymakers and the mandates of local school districts is impossible without a prior or simultaneous reinvention of accommodating educational methods, structures, and institutions. What might an alternative school model, one that tolerates successive questioning, improvisation, and tinkering look like? Tyack and Cuban (1995) note that departures from the "standard grammar of schooling" have most often taken hold "on the periphery of the system, in specialized niches," where serious examination and revision of unexamined institutional habits and "widespread cultural beliefs about what constitutes a 'real school'" may be encouraged (87–88). As seen in the Life Learning Academy example developed below, the small school and charter school movements may provide a much needed "niche" in which to develop institutional models that manifest this reflexive turn and may have some play in the mainstream, functioning as sites of socially situated inquiry with unique local characteristics and potentially broader implications.

Revising Educational Structures: Inquiry and Improvisation

> Modernity institutionalizes the principle of radical doubt and insists that all knowledge takes the form of hypotheses: claims which may very well be true,

[5]Regarding this point, see also Michelle Fine's *Framing Dropouts* (1991), particularly her discussion of the role of institutionalized "ideological fetishes" underlying the problem of high dropout rates (page 180 and following).

but which are in principle always open to revision and may have at some point to be abandoned. (Giddens 1991, 3)

The process of working here is reciprocal. We are challenged in several ways. But we are getting as much as we are giving. The dynamic is invigorating. (Life Learning Academy teacher)

Roberto Unger (1996) has criticized the American tendency to believe that "abstract institutional conceptions," like democracy, civil society, and free markets, "have a single natural and necessary institutional expression" (7). Similarly schools, the form and function of which have become almost universally taken for granted, are popularly viewed more as a primordial creation than a product of history (Tyack and Cuban 1995, 86). Through the lens of Roberto Unger's democratic experimentalism, such a limited and "fetishistic" view of school structures is a pervasive superstition that effectively cages innovation. While teachers and students contend firsthand with the ambiguity of teaching and learning (Lortie 1975), policymakers prefer the comfort of old certitudes. As a consequence, to use the language of one Life Learning Academy teacher, there has often been little "reciprocal" in the relationship between school structures and their constituent teachers and students.

Though schools have proven resistant to change, the impulse toward school reform is not new—schools have long carried what Heinz Elau (1972) termed the "utopian scent," an attraction to reformers who cast schools as a panacea for the crisis du jour. Numerous studies reaccount reform trends, noting the enduring patterns, the resilience and intransigence of fundamental features of schooling—grouping students by age (see Ames, this volume, on "multigrade" schools in Peru), subjects taught in isolation—and the cyclical nature of reform efforts (Angus and Mirel 1999; Tyack and Cuban 1995; Kirst and Meister 1985). Historians note that many onetime reforms—blackboards, the Carnegie unit—become absorbed into the grammar of the larger school narrative. Reform efforts that attempt to realign the fundamental architecture of structures and practices, that are top-heavy or overreaching, risk failure, as curriculum reformers of the 1950s and 1960s discovered, having underestimated "the extent to which local and family values excited deep feelings about what should be taught in schools" (Lazerson et al. 1985, 43). Noted above, the niches tend to accommodate significant change better than the system as a whole—thus new small schools may offer a unique opportunity for experimentation. As Nathan Glazer (2003) notes, "'whole school reform' might require the creation of new schools rather than the effort to reshape existing schools." Reform that percolates upward from a deep engagement with local imperatives, generated from local experiments that have inquiry at the center of their projects, and maintain a spirit of "adaptive tinkering" (Tyack and Cuban 1995, 136) may fare better than wholesale efforts.

Opportunities to design sufficiently rich curriculum and instruction to reflect New Literacy Studies' call to "capture the richness and complexity of actual literacy practices" (Street, Introduction) might be most possible in small schools that respect students' literacies, ask questions, and remain open to change. Such projects might reflect aspects of Street's "provisional checklist" of NLS principles articulated in the introduction to this volume. To be successful, these projects should attempt a sustained commitment to Giddensian reflexivity: Look upon past efforts and future possibilities through the lens of inquiry—become, as it were, institutional variations on Gerald Campano's (2003) vision of ideal teaching practice, what he terms "systematic improvisation." In this approach, schools would situate themselves within a recognition that generating healthy teaching environments is predicated on viewing students' unique backgrounds and experiences as relevant resources (not as deficits, per NLS's critique) and building from experience of what works while remaining open to revision, in a spirit of dialogue, constant questioning, testing of promising possibilities, and serial tinkering. Such a proposition has at its center the necessity of being highly contextualized, varied and progressive, remaining in flux, both reflexive and tentative, refusing reification. Small school experiments can be promising places for meeting these qualifications, if only for the fact that they often begin with the most essential sort of inquiry: asking how to best respond to the needs of a particular community of learners.

The Life Learning Academy Model

From the start, Life Learning Academy was formed out of an acknowledged need and inquiry. Recognizing that the city was failing to serve a growing population of perceived "problem children," the San Francisco Mayor's Office of Criminal Justice sought out help from Delancey Street Foundation and its president, Mimi Silbert, in the creation of an alternative charter school as a part of a citywide juvenile justice reform effort (Moore 1997).

Delancey Street offered an intriguing model for this project: a self-styled "community of last resort" for adult ex-addicts and ex-offenders, where people who have existed, often violently, in the margins learn values and literacies of "doing life" legitimately and successfully in the mainstream. The turn-of-the-century immigrant association of "crossing Delancey Street" with achieving success serves as a kind of guiding metaphor underlying their work there: The 450-plus residents in San Francisco (well over a thousand including four other Delancey facilities nationwide) are prior outcasts reframed as new immigrants working toward self- (and community-) betterment and success. Delancey takes no public money; it is entirely resident-run, sustained financially by sixteen on-the-job training schools, including a three-star restaurant. The facility itself, a neo-Mediterranean, triangle-shaped compound in the shadow of the Bay Bridge, was built by a group of Delancey residents with the consultation of professional contractors and architects. In 1997, inspired by this success and led by Silbert, a group of dedicated reformers asked itself the question: What might a Delancey Street for kids look like?

The answer has proven to be a work in constant and sustained progress. From its genesis, the school was predicated on a social constructivist model, though never explicitly named as such. In true Delancey fashion, the students, in collaboration with Delancey mentors, volunteer architects, and a small cadre of teachers, built the school literally (and figuratively) from the inside out; in a building on a reconstituted military base on Treasure Island, the initial cohort of 24 students built their own classrooms. Subsequent projects, such as the school design class described in the anecdote that opens this chapter, have maintained this neo-Deweyan synthesis of community construction and learning. Further, the school attempts a variation of what Cochran-Smith and Lytle (2001) call an "inquiry stance"—calling fundamental verities about schooling and "at-risk" children into question, generating new knowledge and further questions as a community in practice. The questioning and revising spirit of Life Learning Academy is visible in its willingness to literally and figuratively pursue the imperative of the school motto (now framed in yellow paint, although that too may change), to always be willing to sacrifice what it is for what it could become. This notion of change through sacrifice, of becoming or collectively building something new, is at the heart of the school's project.

One example is the Crossroads Café. Students and Delancey residents built a full-service café on Treasure Island in 2000, which was originally run as a kind of Life Learning Academy–Delancey Street collaborative project. In 2002, a group of Life Learning Academy teachers created a proposal for a "school within a school" for a cohort of older Life Learning students, based upon an expansive, interdisciplinary "café curriculum." The café now functions as a kind of extended learning site, team-taught by a group of four teachers and vocational instructors who integrate math, economics, art, and English lessons connected to the café, which is run by Life Learning students and teachers. Resulting lesson strands are multiple and project-based, braided into the operation and culture of the café, developed from student interests, tied to district standards and specific learning outcomes, and demonstrating a complex approach to literacy. For example, students created a photo essay of their café renovations and wrote extensively about their experiences there; they designed the café logo and all promotional materials, including program descriptions and brochures; they wrote and planned the menu and daily cooked the food sold there, self-publishing a book of recipes; they constructed spreadsheets to balance and track their café budget, used algebraic equations to measure and write-up their progress. Such café class projects are directly tied to needs and interests of the participating student group; thus many of the projects taught in this café cohort will not be repeated with the next.

This example does not fit an "egg crate" conception of schooling so common to the experience of most schoolchildren (Lortie 1975, 14), nor does it reflect a view of literacy as neutral, static, or "autonomous." Literacy practices at Life Learning Academy demonstrate affinity with both the revising impulse at the heart of Giddens and recent NLS calls for developing sufficiently rich curriculum to account for the complexity of literacy in context. Teaching previously disenfranchised students the literacies of "doing school" at Life Learning Academy is accomplished in part through the continued building and maintenance of one. In the process, these students gain a sense of agency, empowerment, and connection to school that they had not formerly known; they gain proficiency with school literacies while collectively reconceptualizing schooling itself, which is transformed into a place where "you can get educated and respect." Students and teachers at Life Learning Academy become accustomed to writing proposals for individual, group, and school-wide projects like the café and design classes; such curricular flexibility is inherent in the school design, which was created with a mandate for developing and continually revising innovative curriculum (Life Learning Academy 2000). The Life Learning example does not "[exaggerate] the power of local contexts to set or reveal the forms and meanings that literacy takes" (Brandt and Clinton 2002); rather, it presents an approach to teaching and learning that demonstrates a complex view of literacies.

Literacies of "doing school" are intimately related to literacies of "doing life" at Life Learning Academy. Students come to Life Learning with histories of significant and sustained school failure and dropout, and some have prior involvement with the juvenile justice system. Home and family life for many Life Learning students is unstable; many students have prior drug problems and gang involvements. Problems like these are not pathologized at Life Learning Academy, but they are confronted openly. A student- and teacher-run disciplinary council is responsible for handling infractions to school rules, and student council members co-facilitate weekly student and staff groups for airing issues and mediating student conflicts. Further, Life Learning students are very "known" by teachers and staff, who build strong relationships with them outside the classroom. Students have often experienced violence in their lives, but there has never been a fight there. This is likely due in significant part to student involvement in school leadership and the school's "surround services" model (Life Learning Academy 2000).

In the Life Learning Academy model, who students are as people is paramount; thus there is a heightened focus on how students "do life"—conduct themselves publicly, demonstrate respect for themselves and their environment, give back to the community, and find healthy alternatives for solving personal and social problems. Life Learning students participate in a variety of forums to talk through problems (see for comparison, the account of pupils' involvement in school councils in the United Kingdom by Cox and Robinson-Pant, this volume), including individual and group counseling sessions with Principal Delane, herself a Ph.D. in psychology and a Delancey graduate, as well as with outside counselors, Delancey residents who have survived lives on the streets and in the prison system, and Life Learning teachers and peers. Much learning at Life Learning Academy takes place in this alternate school space, an extension of what Campano (2003) terms the "second class," through talk in groups, in counseling sessions, on camping trips, or over lunch, served family style and cooked by students under the supervision of a professional chef (five-course Vietnamese meals are not uncommon).

Talk in an environment that is highly social is vital, made more so by the fact that Life Learning students often feel more comfortable expressing themselves verbally than in writing. Consequently, talk at Life Learning Academy is used to mediate oral and written literacies, as in the case of one student who learned to write essays by dictating her ideas to a teacher or student mentor; as noted above, room is made within the school day for students to learn to verbally address personal and social problems. In this way, talk at Life Learning Academy helps to bridge students' in-school and out-of-school "worlds" (Hull and Schultz 2002).

Oral literacies are also reflected in Life Learning Academy coursework, which often emphasizes discussion and performative elements, as well as multimodal literacies. Building on critical literacy work we were doing as a part of a senior English class I taught in the spring of 2002, a group of students interested in media representations of teenagers spent several weeks researching and analyzing the ways teenagers are portrayed in popular films, television, and print media (a project not unlike that described by Low, this volume). As a culminating project, they collectively wrote, filmed, and edited their own 25-minute docudrama about the school. Our class decided that the best way to tell a "real" story about the Life Learning Academy community was to interview a group of graduating seniors and follow them through their last weeks at school, showing representative snapshots of classwork and culture along the way. We contacted a documentary filmmaker to help us with storyboarding, logging tape, transcribing interview segments, and working out a final edit. Several students worked well into the summer following their own graduation to complete the film. This work has since had numerous public showings, including presentations at a 2004 California Charter School Association conference in Sacramento and a juvenile justice conference sponsored by the Judicial Council of California in San Diego in 2003.

Multimedia and technology-mediated projects emphasizing oral literacies like this one are quite common at Life Learning Academy, as in one culminating project in a world history class in which participating students recorded a CD of rap songs they had written about Mayan and Aztec history. Such projects are possible because of school structures and practices that stress inquiry and experimentation. Life Learning Academy assessment is equally inquiry-based: While students take state-mandated tests, coursework emphasizes varied assessment measures, including year-end "presentations of learning" (POLs).

Individual instruction is enhanced through heterogeneous age (14–18) and ability groupings and small class sizes (6–10 students). Further, scheduling is built around a flexible model that tolerates progressive tinkering and accommodations such as teaching teams and block scheduling, constructed around an extended school day (students stay until 5:00 or later most days). Most importantly, the school is willing (and able, due to its charter status and small size) to ask questions and make changes to benefit its students. Weekly staff meetings provide forums for asking questions, making recommendations for change, sharing feedback on class projects, and discussing particular students. Thus a rich program model is accompanied by a concomitantly rich view of teachers, who are highly professionalized, recast as authors of innovative curriculum, knowledgeable instructors, administrators, counselors, and mentors. Underlying this program design is a view of literacy that is explicitly social, oral and written, unapologetically constructivist, woven from perceived and changing assessment of communal and individual needs and talents, predicated on a spirit of hopeful, collective questioning, growth, and change.

Life Learning Academy Outcomes: Connections to New Literacies Studies Tenets and Implications for Reform

> We have developed a remarkable culture. At its best it feels like a good family. . . . (Life Learning Academy teacher)

> I am like a leaky boat and the people at the Academy help me stay afloat. (Life Learning Academy student)

It comes as little surprise that students and teachers at Life Learning Academy feel themselves to be part of an "extended family" (Life Learning Academy 2000), and see the school itself—which indeed "smells like food and looks beautiful"—as more of a home than an institution. In a recent comprehensive third-party evaluation of Life Learning Academy prepared for the San Francisco Mayor's Criminal Justice Council, 95 percent of students reported satisfaction with the school overall; 90 percent of students said they agreed with the statement "The Life Learning Academy is a warm and supportive community where I can learn and grow" (LaFrance 2001, ix–x). This is not a school in which students and teachers feel "held captive" (Lortie 1975 4). Further, the compulsory, custodial aspect of high school is ameliorated somewhat by the Life Learning Academy admissions policy; as outlined in the school charter, students choose to be there (Life Learning Academy 2000). The first question new students are asked in the intake interview conducted by Principal Delane is, why do you want to be here? It is a question that is modified, deepened, and challenged during students' time there. Those that are accepted respond to the question first by showing up: The average number of school days missed by Life Learning students their first semester is five, down from thirty-seven the semester prior to entry (LaFrance 2004).

The Life Learning Academy resonates with NLS principles in that the program is socially situated and strength-based; students are active agents in their education, in which they are viewed not as a rash of deficits, but as profound resources of knowledge, high potential, and opportunity. As a consequence, students feel very "known" and respected at school, and they are willing to change their lives to be there—in the 2002–2003 school year, only one Life Learning Academy student was arrested more than once, compared to twelve of twenty-five youth arrested more than once in the comparison group (LaFrance 2004). Schooling is reframed as a vehicle toward "sacrificing" self-destructive behavior for future opportunity:

> When I was younger, I wanted to sell drugs, but I was too young. Then, when I got older and saw the consequences and got arrested, I came to the Academy and I changed my life around. I have a lot of positive people around that care about me and want me to go in the right direction and I know they will help me get there.

Literacy at Life Learning Academy is not viewed as a floating, abstract skill set, but as a contextualized practice, both individual and social. Data reflecting formal assessment of individual Life Learning students supports the literacy and numeracy benefits of this approach, even by standard measures; one student gained three grade-levels in reading fluency, reading comprehension, and math after eight months there (LaFrance 2004). Literacies of "doing school" and "doing life" are interwoven at Life Learning Academy, which encourages students to take an activist and questioning stance toward past mistakes and potential futures. Among the 2002 graduating class who were the subject of our student film "Life Learning," fourteen of seventeen graduates went on to some form of "thirteenth grade," four-year colleges and universities, two-year associate programs, or vocational training. Significantly, numerous Life Learning graduates stay involved with the school, returning to work, visit, or participate in groups.

The Life Learning Academy model is highly flexible, meeting complex literacy needs with a sufficiently complex school design, allowing for—demanding—constant reflection and revision. Students and staff have significant input into the administration of the school, and therefore the structures are "reciprocal"—they accommodate the requirements of constituent members of the community, not the other way around, allowing faculty and students to feel like Life Learning Academy is "theirs."

Built into Life Learning Academy's flexible program model is ongoing accountability, connecting this local experiment to broader assessment and accountability measures—to the city school board, San Francisco Unified School District, state and federal standards—and also to private and public funding sources, including the California State Board of Corrections and federal Departments of Education and Juvenile Justice, which mandate third-party evaluation. This evaluation shows Life Learning Academy to be a "profoundly effective program" (LaFrance 2002) by a variety of measures, quantitative and qualitative. Evaluator Steven LaFrance's findings show that 10 percent of Life Learning students demonstrated attendance problems in the evaluation period (compared with 75 percent of a control group); 19 percent of juvenile justice–involved LLA students recidivated versus 51 percent of control group youth; Life Learning students demonstrated grade-point average improvement from a .77 average the semester prior to enrollment to a 2.49 average their first semester at Life Learning Academy (LaFrance 2004). While 53 percent of African-American students statewide passed the mandated California High School Exit Exam in 2003, 72.7 percent of African-American students at Life Learning Academy passed (LaFrance 2004).

Implications and Conclusion

That innovative practice influences policy is demonstrated by the fact that the federal Departments of Juvenile Justice and Education view the Life Learning Academy model as successful and replicable; they have required as part of their funding that Life Learning Academy publish its curriculum, a process built into teachers' job descriptions and the structure of the school (Life Learning Academy 2000). Last year, Life Learning Academy received a two-year grant from the California Department of Education for replication, used to disseminate information and training on the Life Learning model to California educators. In addition to formal presentations at conferences (as noted above), the school created the LLA Institute of Educational Renewal, which has already trained over 200 educators and youth advocates. A U.S. Senate Appropriations Committee bill from 2002 provides federal matching funds for states interested in creating new programs built on the model of Delancey Street Foundation, the adult rehabilitation program out of which Life Learning Academy was created. At this writing, Life Learning Academy is one of fifteen finalists chosen by the Harvard Kennedy School of Government's Ash Institute for Democratic Governance and Innovation for its Innovations in American Government Award—commonly referred to as the "Oscars of government awards"— presented annually to the nation's "most creative, forward thinking, results-driven government programs" (Ash Institute Website 2004). Thus this project functions itself as something of a means to "disembed" literacy theories developed in practice, connecting local involvements to general policy and reform dialogue.

Such recognition demonstrates the large potential impact of a small school. Reform-minded local programs like Life Learning Academy can capture the imagination of policymakers, potentially having broader implications for "the larger enterprises that play out away from the immediate scene" (Brandt and Clinton 2002). Schools that are founded on a spirit of inquiry and improvisation not only enter the twenty-first century as characterized by Giddens' "contours of high modernity"; most importantly, they attempt to meet the literacy needs of twenty-first century students. While the example of Life Learning Academy demonstrates an approach to address the lives and literacies of "disenfranchised" youth, schools predicated on building from individual student strengths may have quite promising implications for reaching more mainstream students as well, students like Katie, a "millennial kid" referred to in a study by Young, Dillon, and Moje (2002), who "instant messages" 90 different friends around the country, often engaging in three or four IM conversations simultaneously. In a comprehensive public high school, this would be viewed as a marginalized literacy practice at best; at a school like Life Learning Academy, Katie's skill and interest could provide the basis for a student-driven inquiry project that generates significant questions about language and literacy. The example of Life Learning Academy poses a challenge to educators and policymakers alike: What might schools built upon asking questions about students' lives and literacies look like in other contexts?

The Life Learning Academy example goes one necessary step further than Street's (2003) important call for "positive proposals" for intervention from NLS; at Life Learning Academy, they have manifested practice into theory, and vice-versa. Life Learning is true to its motto: This program is always willing to sacrifice what it is for what it could become. It may be the case, as Tyack and Cuban (1995) suggest, that the schooling mainstream is too resistant to change, that ambitious reform is the business of the more experimental niches on the periphery. All the better, if our energies are focused on the creation of small schools like Life Learning Academy, which generate local knowledge about "what works" in their communities with implications for the wider world in which literacy and learning are always realized.

References

Angus, D.L., and Mirel, J.E. 1999. *The failed promise of the American high school, 1890–1995.* New York: Teachers College Press.

Ash Institute Website. 2004. www.innovations.harvard.edu.

Brandt, D., and Clinton, K. 2002. Limits of the local: Expanding perspectives on literacy as a social practice. *Journal of Literacy Research* 34(3): 337–356.

Cochran-Smith, M., and Lytle, S. 2001. Beyond certainty: Taking an inquiry stance on practice. In: A. Lieberman and L. Miller (eds.), *Teachers caught in the action: Professional development that matters.* New York: Teachers College Press.

Collins, J., and Blot, R. 2002. *Literacy and literacies: Texts, power and identity.* New York: Cambridge University Press.

Campano, G. 2003. *From the heart to the world and back again: Co-constructing school literacy practices with children from immigrant, migrant, and refugee backgrounds.* Unpublished doctoral dissertation, University of Pennsylvania.

Eulau, H. 1972. Political science and education. In: M. Kirst (ed.), *State, school and politics.* Lexington: D.C. Heath and Company.

Fine, M. 1991. *Framing dropouts: Notes on the politics of an urban public high school.* Albany: State University of New York Press.

Fuhrman, S.H. 2003. Riding waves, trading horses: The twenty-year effort to reform education. In: D.T. Gordon (ed.), *A nation reformed? American education 20 years after A Nation at Risk.* Cambridge: Harvard Education Press, pp. 7–22.

Gatto, L.A. 2002. Success and guaranteed literacy programs: "I don't buy it!" In: J. Larson (ed.), *Literacy as snake oil.* Rochester: Peter Lang Publishing, pp. 71–88.

Gee, J.P. 2001. Reading, language abilities, and semiotic resources: Beyond limited perspectives on reading. In: J. Larson (ed.), *Literacy as snake oil.* Rochester: Peter Lang Publishing, pp. 7–26.

Gee, J.P. 2000. Teenagers in new times: A new literacy studies perspective. *Journal of Adolescent and Adult Literacy* 43(5): 412–420.

Gee, J.P. 1996. *Social linguistics and literacies: Ideology in discourses.* 2nd edition. New York: Routledge Falmer, Taylor & Francis, Inc.

Giddens, A. 1991. *Modernity and self-identity: Self and society in the late modern age.* Stanford: Stanford University Press.

Heath, S.B. 1983. *Ways with words: Language, life, and work in communities and classrooms.* New York: Cambridge University Press.

Hull, G., and Schultz, K. 2002. *School's out: Bridging out-of-school literacies with classroom practice.* New York: Teachers College Press.

Kirst, M.W., and Meister, G.R. 1985. Turbulence in American secondary schools: What reforms last? *Curriculum Inquiry* 15(2): 169–186.

Kulick, D., and Stroud, C. 1993. Conceptions and uses of literacy in a Papua New Guinean village. In: B. Street (ed.), *Cross-cultural approaches to literacy.* Cambridge: Cambridge University Press.

LaFrance, S., Twersky, F., Latham, N., Foley, E., Bott, C., and Lee, L. 2001. *Education leads to transformation: A comprehensive evaluation of the Life Learning Academy.* San Francisco: BTW Consultants, Inc.

LaFrance, S. 2004. Life Learning Academy student academic performance report, academic year: 2002–2003. San Francisco: LaFrance & Associates, LLC.

LaFrance, S. 2002. Summary of evaluation findings for Life Learning Academy. San Francisco: LaFrance & Associates, LLC.

Latour, B. 1993. *We have never been modern.* Cambridge: Harvard University Press.

Lazerson, M. et al. 1985. *An education of value: The purposes and practices of schools.* Cambridge: Cambridge University Press.

Life Learning Academy. 2000. School charter proposal. 2nd revised version.

Lortie, D.C. 1975. *Schoolteacher.* Chicago: University of Chicago Press.

Metz, M.H. 1991. Real school: A universal drama and disparate experience. In: D.E. Mitchell and M.E. Goetz (eds.), *Education Politics for the New Century.* New York: Falmer Press, pp. 75–91.

Moore, T. 1997. Juvenile reform plan wins state funding. *San Francisco Chronicle,* May 17.

Ostler, S. 2000. Second chance for young thugs. *San Francisco Chronicle,* April 3.

Ryan, M. 2000. This school teaches hope. *Parade Magazine,* October 8, p. 1.

Simon, R. 2003. *Teaching within a media milieu: Increasing student engagement through media literacy.* Unpublished master's thesis, San Francisco State University.

Street, B. 1984. *Literacy in theory and practice.* Cambridge: Cambridge University Press.

Street, B. 2003. What's new in new literacy studies? Critical approaches to literacy in theory and practice. *Current Issues in Comparative Education,* Summer 2003. Text available at http://www.tc.columbia.edu/cice/articles/BS152.htm.

Street, B. In press. *The limits of the local: "Autonomous" or "disembedding"?*

Tyack, D., and Cuban, M. 1995. *Tinkering toward utopia: A century of public school reform.* Cambridge: Harvard University Press.

Unger, R.M. 1996. *What should legal analysis become?* London: Verso Books.

Vilbig, P. 2002. Advertising's sneak attack. *The New York Times Upfront,* April 8.

Young, J., Dillon, D., and Moje, E. 2002. Shape-shifting portfolios: Millenial youth, literacies, and the game of life. In: D. Alvermann (ed.), *Adolescents and literacies in a digital world.* New York: Peter Lang.

8

Putting it Out There

Revealing Latino Visual Discourse
in the Hispanic Academic Summer Program
for Middle School Students

Peter M. Cowan

Introduction

In the late 1980s, I was hired right out of my teacher education program to
teach computers in the Hispanic Academic Summer Program, a program to encourage Latino[1] middle school students to aim for higher education. The Hispanic Academic Program met in donated classrooms at a Catholic high school
in the historically Latino, Oakdale neighborhood of Bayside,[2] a working-class
city in Northern California. Trained as a writing teacher, I saw the computers
as an opportunity to motivate Hispanic Academic Program (HAP) students to
write, revise, and publish an anthology of their writing. I wanted their pieces
of writing to be memorable and worth keeping, so I designed a literacy curriculum that explored their cultural heritage, and they wrote poems about their
identity, narratives of their families' histories, and stories of their journeys to

---

[1] I use *Latino* instead of *Hispanic* to distinguish a category of social and racial stratification
within the population of the United States. *Latino* identifies people who came to the United States
or who have ancestors who came from the territories in the Americas colonized by Latin Nations
(Oquendo 1998).

[2] I use pseudonyms to protect the confidentiality of the participants in this study.

the United States or back to their families' places of origin. Hispanic Academic Program students fell along a continuum of monolingual English speakers to monolingual Spanish speakers, but most were bilingual; they could choose to write in English or Spanish. Not sharing their ethnic and cultural background, I saw their writing as a way for me to learn about their lives and culture. We posted their pieces of writing on the walls. Some students gave us drawings and we posted those too. Toward the end of the program we asked students to submit writing and artwork for the anthology.

Almost a decade after teaching Joaquin in the final summer of the Hispanic Academic Program (1994), I had a chance to meet him again and to talk about the anthology. I was happy to learn that he had saved his anthology (although he was sorry that he couldn't find it after a recent move). Before we began talking, he spent several minutes going page-by-page through the copy I brought. Then he said, under his breath, "I wish I knew where it was." I asked, "Did you keep it for awhile?"

"Yeah. That's the thing, there's a lot of things I can't find that I actually took very good care of. . . . I know they're somewhere because I don't throw anything away. Especially things like this," he said. That he kept his anthology so long and regretted its disappearance satisfied the writing teacher in me. But the memorable text that Joaquin made for the anthology was different from the texts that I had imagined.

We had asked the HAP students to submit two or three pieces of writing and any artwork that they wanted. Joaquin submitted just one short piece of writing but two pieces of artwork, including a full-page drawing that used distinctive iconography (see Figure 1): an Aztec pyramid, an Aztec warrior, a mythological god in the figure of a feathered serpent, and a Mexican flag. This kind of artwork, most often created by Latino adolescents in the United States and identifiable by its use of distinctive iconography like Mesoamerican pyramids, figures from Aztec and Mayan mythology, lowrider[3] cars, *cholos*[4] and

---

[3] A lowrider is a genre of customized car associated with the Mexican American community. Lowrider cars are lowered to the ground, ride on small, custom wheels and skinny tires, and often feature elaborate paint schemes (frequently including icons found in the Mexican American community).

[4] The term *cholo* generally refers to Mexican American working class youth who dress distinctively and who often organize themselves into clubs or barrio-centered gangs. The cholo dress style is frequently associated with lowriding (Stone 1990, 120). The close associations of lowriders,

Figure 1. Joaquin's drawing published in the 1994 Hispanic Academic Summer Program Anthology, with permission: The East Bay Consortium of Educational Institutions.

cholas, is commonly called 'lowrider art' because *Lowrider* magazine and *Lowrider Arte*[5] magazine publish drawings sent in by readers.

I asked Joaquin about how he chose what to submit.

> I really didn't know how to use certain words and use certain styles of writing to express everything. But I knew how to draw it and put it out there. . . . It's the same sort of thing, like when they found the first drawings in the caves. It was just the bison and people hunting, they didn't have written language but right there they were saying, we were hunters, we survive, we did it. So just by looking at that you read off of it.

When he was twelve, Joaquin felt better able to express his meanings visually than through his writing. He sees drawing as an ancient, efficient means of

cholos, and gangs means that the terms *lowriders* and *cholos* (denoting males) and *cholas* (denoting females) are considered derogatory by many people.

[5] *Lowrider Arte* has been published since 1992, when editors of *Lowrider* "decided they were receiving enough art to publish a separate magazine devoted entirely to the genre of lowrider art" (Grady 2001, 175).

making meaning, that a viewer has only to see an image and "read off of it" to apprehend its meaning. I asked Joaquin what he would have said about this drawing in 1994.

> Back then, I just would have been like, oh I like Aztecs so I put these here. And I like pyramids, they're here. . . . I would have said these were things that make up me. . . . I could have probably said something like that's actually me [Aztec warrior], that's actually my house [pyramid] and that's what I believe [feathered serpent] and that's where I come from [flag of Mexico]. It was that simple.

I asked Joaquin what he remembered about making this drawing.

> I had an idea of what I wanted to do. . . . I was like, man I should draw an Aztec pyramid because that's what I like, Aztecs, you know, people, structures, something to do with not really religion but faith and stuff like that. . . . This is a very early example of it, but nowadays I can pretty much tell a story in one picture.

Joaquin is now a skilled artist striving to become a film-maker, confident of his visual abilities and developing his writing abilities to translate his visions for films into screenplays.

In the summer of 1994, Joaquin created a memorable text, a drawing that "pretty much tell[s] a story in one picture," a semiotic narrative that uses cultural icons to tell where he came from, and that was worth keeping. He "put" his cultural heritage "out there" so that any reader of the anthology could "read off of it." But I couldn't read or comprehend it until years later, because I saw it as an elaborate doodle, not as a visual text communicating a particular meaning. Unbeknown to me when I was teaching HAP students, Joaquin and his peers were communicating messages about their cultural heritage through visual texts that they created and that we published.

This chapter reports the results of an ethnographic study of what I have come to call Latino visual discourse. I define Latino visual discourse as distinctive drawings featuring iconology commonly seen in U.S. Latino communities; the social practices of creating, displaying, and circulating these drawings that shape them into a visual code that is recognizable to and readable by someone who has been socialized into them; and how these drawings and social practices of their creation and display structure knowledge about and communicate perspectives on Latino cultural identities.

This study is particularly relevant to literacy researchers and teachers. It uses the New Literacy Studies' focus on social practices to describe how many Latino adolescents can and do act with their practices of visual literacy that are cultural resources they bring to their literacy educations. It is critical that literacy researchers and teachers pay careful attention to the resources, the social practices of cultural traditions of performance and visual representation that students bring with them to school (Stein & Mamabolo, this volume), even those aesthetic practices that might be disdained by educators as being 'low' art or popular youth culture (Low, this volume) or, worse, as evidence of prospective gang involvement (Cowan 1999; 2004). When as outsiders literacy researchers and teachers observe unfamiliar products of diverse practices of literacy, they risk (mis)judging them and missing the rich social practices of meaning-making that produce them and their affirming effects on children (Stein and Mamabolo; Low).

Conceptual Frame

A lens to apprehend Latino visual discourse needs to be constructed from diverse theoretical perspectives. This study merged the New Literacy Studies' (NLS) focus on social practices with the New Visual Literacy's conception of images as visual texts analyzable for cultural meanings (Kress and van Leeuwen 1996) situated in the social, historical, and cultural context of the intellectual colonization of Mesoameria.

New Literacy Studies

This study was originally undertaken along with a number of qualitative studies anchored in the perspectives of NLS (see Mahiri 2004, 1–17). Our purpose was "to research and identify the specific nature and functions of an array of literacy practices that young people appropriate for learning and expression" (1) with a particular focus on nonschool settings in urban scenes. We found diverse urban sites in which young people engaged with socially, culturally, historically, and politically situated practices. Engaging in these practices, they acquired and expressed certain values, beliefs, and identity associations that formed and transformed their identities. In our use of 'practices', we were drawing on Street's (1993, 12) conception of literacy practices that "incorporate not only literacy events, as empirical occasions to which literacy is integral, but also folk models of those events and the ideological preconceptions that underpin them." This ethnography attempts to describe practitioners' emic perspectives of Latino visual discourse, the "folk models" of visual literacy events and the "ideological preconceptions that underpin them" in a specific social, historical and cultural context.

New Visual Literacy

The challenge for this study was how to read drawings made by Latino adolescents like Joaquin and other HAP students. In their pursuit of understanding how images make meaning many theorists have concerned themselves with iconology, the layered meanings that accrue to icons as they are used in different contexts (Mitchell 1986). A new approach to visual literacy presents an alternative to iconology. It conceives of images as having visual grammar that encodes meaning. In *Reading Images: The Grammar of Visual Design* (1996), Gunther Kress and Theo van Leeuwen make a distinction between traditional visual semiotics with its focus on iconology and their focus on visual "grammar," on the way in which these depicted people, places, and things are combined into a meaningful whole.

Kress and van Leeuwen call their approach the New Visual Literacy and see their theory as social semiotics. Just as speakers and writers express social meanings, so do photographers and printmakers. Kress and van Leeuwen argue that visual images can be analyzed for cultural meanings by applying Halliday's definition of grammar, as a means of representing patterns of experience to build mental pictures of reality, to their description of patterns of visual composition in advertising, media, and book publishing. They show how Western visual design serves several communicational and representational requirements by adopting the three metafunctions from Halliday's theory of language. The ideational metafunction is how the semiotic system represents things in the world outside its system of signs. The interpersonal metafunction constitutes the interaction between the viewer and the image. The textual metafunction theorizes how a visual semiotic system forms texts.

Kress and van Leeuwen, however, leave out much of the social context of the New Visual Literacy by not considering the social uses of the images they analyze and by not contextualizing Western visual design in greater detail. By exploring and describing the social practices of Latino visual discourse and by invoking its social, historical, and cultural context, this study finds that social practices situated in a sociocultural context are integral parts of visual literacy and social semiotics.

Latin American Studies

Latino adolescents who participate in Latino visual discourse create and circulate distinctive drawings following conventions that are socially determined in a cultural context distinct from Western visual design. The social, historical, and cultural context of Latino visual discourse evolved out of the settling of the U.S. South and West and Mexico by Spanish-speaking, European and *mestizo*[6] migrants.

Early in the nineteenth century, the first nonindigenous resident and property owner in Bayside, a mestizo migrant from the U.S. Southwest, settled in Oakdale (Evanosky 1998, A-4). The peopling of California by the migration of Spanish-speaking and mestizo people from Spanish colonies in the U.S. South and West and Mexico, beginning in the late eighteenth century and continuing into the present with the ongoing migration of people from Mexico and other Latin American countries, created the conditions for transculturation.

"Transculturation," coined by the Cuban sociologist Fernando Ortiz (1940/1995), is set in counterpoint to assimilation, the dominant model of cultural integration. Assimilation conceives of cultural adaptation as a process of absorption into the dominant culture. A new immigrant has to shed ill-suited aspects of her old culture and adopt the new cultural practices of the dominant culture, to be absorbed into that culture. Assimilation implies that conforming to and being absorbed into the dominant culture is or should be the immigrant's end goal.

[6] *Mestizo* refers to the miscegenation of Europeans and Amerindians in the territories colonized by Spain beginning in the sixteenth century. It literally means: "People of mixed Indian and Spanish blood" (Anzaldúa 1987, 5).

In studying cultural integration in his native Cuba, Ortiz created a new paradigm. In transculturation, the dynamics of cultural change happen in three stages: deculturation, acculturation, and neoculturation. Deculturation describes the process by which voluntary and involuntary newcomers to Cuba were torn away from their old cultural roots. This is a violent process in which the conflicts created by competing cultures, and the violent imposition of one cultural system on another, lead to the destruction of old cultural forms. Acculturation is a process of adopting or adapting various cultural forms better suited to this different sociocultural context. Neoculturation is an on-going project, the syncretic creation of new cultural forms out of the contact and conflict among old forms; it is the transforming of culture into new forms to communicate new experiences and meanings. Finally, transculturation is the dynamic process by which new cultural forms are continuously being created and adapted across borders of race and class.

The Spanish colonization of Mesoamerica was intellectual as well as physical, social, and political. The Spanish brought and imposed Renaissance notions of reading, writing, historiography, and pictorial representation that were alien to the indigenous people (Gruzinski 1992; Mignolo 1995). The Mexica (Amerindians of Mexico), for example, practiced picto-ideographic writing. In the dynamic of deculturation, when confronted with Amerindian codices—the products of their picto-ideographic literacy practices and historiography—the Spanish judged them to be diabolical and destroyed them. In the dynamics of acculturation and neoculturation, Amerindians adopted and adapted Spanish literacy practices to their own uses, mixing them with their precolonial, indigenous practices (Lockhart 1992; Miller 1996; Pratt 1992).

> The colonization of indigenous literacy does not imply the devouring of those non-Western, pre-colonial conceptualizations but it banishes them from the view of those who belong to the dominant elite. This means that the dominant views of literacy become synonymous with the real by obstructing possible alternatives (Mignolo 1995, 5).

One can imagine that vestiges of Amerindian social practices of literacy, historiography, and visual representation could have survived, albeit hybridized through 500 years of transculturation, coexisting with and obscured by dominant practices of alphabetic literacy that are conceptualized as 'real' literacy.

The movement of people from south to north has meant, too, the migration of social practices and icons. In the United States, through transculturation, Latino youth have created new cultural identities. For example, *pachuco* is a name from the 1940s and 1950s adopted by Mexican American and Mexican immigrant youth who felt marginalized by both U.S. mainstream and Mexican societies. They developed a subculture that was distinct from and resistant to the dominant cultures of both societies. They were identified by their distinctive clothing, hairstyles, and language, mixing Spanish, English, and their own slang (Castro 2001, 177). Cholos and cholas are also distinguished by their clothing, hairstyles, language, and "[m]any believe the *cholo* subculture is directly descended from that of the *pachuco* of the 1940s" (Castro 2001, 54). Chicanos and Chicanas most generally are of Mexican descent born in the United States. Historically, and in some contexts in U.S. Latino communities still, 'Chicano' has pejorative connotations, but in the late 1960s it was adopted by Latino youth. In this more recent usage, it signals cultural pride in the Spanish language, in an indigenous heritage, and an understanding of racial oppression of and discrimination against Mexican-Americans (Castro 2001, 46). In Latino visual discourse, drawings feature icons from Mexico, from indigenous Amerindian cultures, and from expressions of pachuco/a, cholo/a, and Chicano/a cultural identities that are invested with meanings that represent the experiences of Latino youth who create and circulate them.

Methods

When I went back to the HAP anthologies to pursue my curiosity about connections between literacy and cultural identity, the drawings captivated me. I imagined that I could see intentionally constructed meanings and thought that if HAP drawings could be read for consistent meanings by people familiar with these kinds of drawings then they functioned as visual literacy. In an extended case study of Kress and van Leeuwen's (1996) theory of visual literacy, I wrote interview questions correspond to each of the three metafunctions. Using four drawings from HAP anthologies, I conducted semistructured interviews with seven, mostly young adults who grew up or lived in Oakdale and who were familiar with these kinds of drawings. I wanted to hear their retrospective accounts of when and where they saw these kinds of drawings, who drew them, what they meant, and how they interacted with them. Their answers to my questions about the drawings were consistent, which showed that they were being read for particular, analyzable meanings (Cowan 1999; 2004). In their interviews, the participants also described visual literacy events and the social interactions organized around the creation, display, and circulation of lowrider art.

Next, I became a participant observer in an after-school Lowrider Art class at the middle school in Oakdale that many of my HAP students had attended to observe and document the visual literacy events and social practices of Latino visual discourse as they had been described to me. One particular challenge was how to collect data about the out-of-school context of Latino visual discourse. Using money from a University of California Linguistic Minority Research Institute Dissertation Research Grant, I gave inexpensive 35mm cameras and provided film and developing to Lowrider Art students and encouraged them to photograph things they associated with lowrider art.

I analyzed the interview data according to categories I derived from Kress and van Leeuwen's three metafunctions (1996). But when I began analyzing field notes and photographs from Lowrider Art and integrating them with the interview data, I began to realize how limited Kress and van Leeuwen's metafunctions were a means of analyzing visual grammar in images to reveal potential meanings and possible interactions abstracted from social contexts. I redefined and reordered their three metafunctions into theoretical categories that would better describe the social dynamic of Latino visual discourse. Within this framework Latino visual discourse is made up of multiple visual literacy events that can be apprehended as belonging to three distinctive features of these social practices of taking meaning from one's surroundings and making meaning visually.

In my extension of Kress and van Leeuwen's theory, through the integration of a New Literacy Studies theoretical frame[7], the *contextual feature* of Latino visual discourse explores the context in and for which drawings are created. Given that literacies are situated in specific contexts, I explored the context of Latino visual discourse in two distinct ways: (a) the broader, sociohistorical context out of which the icons emerged and (b) the contemporary, sociocultural context and environmental context of Oakdale where Lowrider Art students saw, noted, and

[7]I borrowed two terms from Maybin (2000) after I realized that my data collection and analysis methods fit so well her description of New Literacy Studies' methods.

documented through their photographs the presence of icons in their familiar surroundings. In the *intertextual feature,* Latino adolescents draw on icons familiar to them to create new visual texts that encode particular meanings that can be read consistently by people who are familiar with them. The intertextual feature builds on Kress and van Leeuwen's ideational metafunction to reveal how Latino adolescents are initiated into the cultural knowledge embodied in the icons and how people draw on this iconological knowledge in their readings of the drawings. The *social feature* of Latino visual discourse describes visual literacy events with drawings at the center that engage Latino adolescents in social practices of visual literacy. These visual literacy events and social practices construct cultural meanings and knowledge that are particular to being a Latino youth within the wider social structures of U.S. racial and ethnic categories.

Study Site and Participants

Bayside is a heterogeneous, working-class city, and Oakdale is a poor, immigrant neighborhood. The Latino community in Bayside includes Americans of Mexican descent who have been residents for generations, as well as many recent immigrants predominantly from Mexico but also from Central America, South America, and the Caribbean. Hispanic Academic Program students and the participants in this study represented this range.

What follows is background information on the participants who are quoted. Marisa was a former student of mine. She is U.S. born of a Mexican-American father and a European-American mother who are both artists. When we spoke, she was in her early twenties, grew up in a mixed commercial and residential neighborhood on the edge of Oakdale, and was an undergraduate at a prestigious public university. Juana was a student at the community college where I was then teaching. She was born in the United States of Guatemalan parents, was in her mid-twenties, grew up in Bayside, and attended the Oakdale middle school that was the site of the Lowrider Art class I observed. Armando was a teaching colleague from another summer laboratory school. Armando was in his mid-thirties. He was born in Mexico, immigrated to the United States with his family when he was three, grew up in Oakdale, and taught at the same Oakdale middle school that he attended. Angel was a bilingual teacher at the same middle school, and created an after-school arts program that included the Lowrider Art class. He was in his late-twenties and is a

Figure 2. Karina's drawing published in the 1994 Hispanic Academic Summer Program Anthology, with permission: The East Bay Consortium of Educational Institutions.

native of Los Angeles: the son of a Mexican-descent mother whose family has lived in Southern California for five generations, and a Mexican immigrant father.

Over the course of a school year, fourteen 8th grade students (six young women and eight young men) cycled through the Lowrider Art class: eight left for a variety of reasons. Most had been in the United States from 3 to 5 years, although one young man had only been in the United States for several months. They came from a variety of family structures: Some lived with both parents, some with single parents, some with extended family. They all came from homes with financial means ranging from very modest to poverty level. In the section that follows, I explore one drawing created by Karina, (see Figure 2), a classmate of Joaquin's in the 1994 Hispanic Academic Summer Program.

Results

The Contextual Feature

I was curious about where Latino adolescents see and note the icons they feature in their drawings. The contextual feature documents the presence of icons in Oakdale that appear in Karina's drawing, and it describes visual literacy events with which participants become aware of these presences in familiar places.

Interview subjects described visual literacy events that corresponded to becoming aware of icons in one's environment and relating them to Latino visual discourse. Angel grew up in Los Angeles, but I can imagine his description of becoming aware of icons in his surroundings could be equally true for adolescents in Oakdale.

> It was in my mid-high school years when I first became aware of [lowrider art]. Then as time went by, I began to make connections with things I'd seen earlier but hadn't really associated with or had made a connection with. But I'd think back, oh yeah, I remember such and such, and maybe in middle school I had a binder that had things on it, or neighborhoods I might have been in where something was on the wall or even in stores.

Angel describes being an adolescent, becoming aware of previously unnoticed images and icons in his familiar surroundings, and making connections between these images and icons to images and icons in lowrider art.

When I asked Armando where one could see images and icons from the HAP drawings, he mentioned two murals in Oakdale, and "the ones that go to church see the Virgin everyday and some even wear medallions." For Latino adolescents, significant early visual literacy events have to do with noticing in a new way the presence of images and icons in murals on neighborhood walls, on binders, seeing the Virgin at mass, on medallions some wear, and even seeing images and icons for sale in stores.

Photographs taken by Lowrider Art students might be considered products of the visual literacy events that Angel and Armando described. Through their photographs, one can observe their awareness of these icons in spaces and places familiar to them, implying that, like Angel, they have made this connection between icons and lowrider art, and like Armando, they notice and mark these images in their surroundings.

The Virgin of Guadalupe is one of the most recognizable and potent icons circulating in Latino communities like Oakdale. Latino adolescents who attend mass at the landmark Catholic church in Oakdale see the Virgin because a version of her image hangs above the altar. A female Lowrider Art student showed me a photograph that she had taken of the interior of this church on what she said was "the Virgin's birthday," with the image of the Virgin barely visible. She was referring to December 12th, the date the appearance of the Virgin of Guadalupe is celebrated, an important celebration for Latino, particularly Mexican, Catholics (Garcia 1997, 1A).

The Virgin of Guadalupe is an icon of the transculturation of mestizo culture, and because Latino visual discourse comes out of a particular socio-cultural context, an iconological perspective on the Virgin is important to understand her ubiquity in communities like Oakdale. The original transculturation of the Christian Virgin Mary into the indigenous *La Virgen de Guadalupe* took place in 1531, a decade after the Conquest of Mexico. Juan Diego, a newly converted Indian, was walking on Tepeyac, a hill sacred to Tonantzin—the Aztec goddess of fertility. It was at dawn when a brown-skinned, Nahuatl-speaking apparition of the Virgin appeared to Diego against the rising sun. She commanded him to deliver a message to the Bishop to build a temple in her honor on Tepeyac. At first the Bishop did not believe Diego. The Virgin reappeared and filled Diego's poncho with roses. When he returned to the Bishop and spilled the roses, the image of *La Virgen* miraculously appeared on his poncho (see Figure 3 for a traditional image of the Virgin of Guadalupe). The ac-

201 REINA DE MEXICO Y EMPERATRIZ DE AMERICA

Figure 3. A print of the traditional depiction of the Virgin of Guadalupe (Cromos Y Novedades de Mexico, S.A. De C.V.)

Figure 4. The Virgin of Guadalupe at the center of an unfinished mural on the wall of a Mexican market in Oakdale.

ceptance of *La Virgen's* appearance to Juan Diego by the indigenous population of Mexico initiated Mexican Christianity and the widespread conversion of the Aztecs to Catholicism. The Virgin of Guadalupe "became the symbol of Indian Catholicism, different from European Catholicism of the Spaniards. As the Aztecs adapted the Catholic religion to their indigenous beliefs, they created a religion that met their own needs and own way of life" (Castro 2001, 239–240).

The icon of the Virgin of Guadalupe was frequently featured in photographs taken by Lowrider Art students, documenting both its ubiquity and their awareness of its presence in their familiar public surroundings. A male Lowrider Art student took the photograph in Figure 4. He passed this recently begun mural on the side of a Mexican market on his way to and from school: This Virgin's figure is complete, but her mantel of light, the angel beneath her crescent, and the frieze beneath both are only outlines. The Virgin of Guadalupe also appears in familiar private surroundings. When I visited Joaquin at his family's home in Oakdale, he let me photograph his mother's portrait of the Virgin hanging on the porch beside their front door (see Figure 5).

The contextual feature finds that Latino adolescents in Oakdale see and note the presence of cultural icons like the Virgin of Guadalupe in their neighborhood. The photographs confirm that there are particular places in Oakdale,

Figure 5. Joaquin's family's portrait of the Virgin of Guadalupe on their front porch beside their front door.

like church, homes, and murals, where kids see these icons, and they illustrate visual literacy events of becoming aware of icons that had always been around but that the Lowrider Art students may not have really noticed until they became aware of lowrider art.

The Intertextual Feature

In the intertextual feature, Latino adolescents draw on the semiotic resources in their environments to create new visual texts using icons like the Virgin of Guadalupe, but it is not enough just to draw these icons. The intertextual feature also describes visual literacy events that initiate Latino adolescents into the iconology and cultural stories of the images. The cultural knowledge embodied in the icons and their configurations in lowrider art construct particular meanings about Latino cultural identities that can be read consistently by people socialized into Latino visual discourse.

In Karina's drawing (Figure 2), against the background frame of the "Hispanic Academic Program" written in Old English calligraphy (a common feature of lowrider art), are a chola and cholo but drawn in the aspect of the traditional depiction of the Virgin of Guadalupe (Figure 4). In Karina's re-envisioning, a chola, identified by her hair and clothing styles, has replaced the

Virgin and beneath her, a cholo has replaced the angel, and between them a folded bandanna has replaced the crescent. Karina declined my request to interview her about her drawing, so I can only speculate what she might have had in mind. When one considers that the cholo style is held in low esteem by Mexican-descent high school students as well as by mainstream students and teachers (Matute-Bianchi 1991, 220); that 'cholo' is a pejorative term for low-caste Mexicans in Mexico (Acuna 1988, 111); that "*cholo,* [is] a word [that has been] used for centuries in Latin America to describe cultural or racial marginality (Vigil 1988; 1990)" (Vigil 2002); then Karina's drawing suggests a subversion of the pejorative assumption that cholas and cholos, with their links to indigenous cultures, are contemptible. Karina's drawing appears to challenge the negative associations of chola hair and clothing styles, the "outward physical features of the *chola* girl [that] appear to be heavily symbolic of a life that is neither Mexican nor American" (Castro 2001, 55). By drawing on the Virgin of Guadalupe, Karina's drawing references the original transculturation of the Virgin Mary and updates it. Instead of presenting the Virgin as a Nahuatl-speaking Mexica, she appears as a Mexican-descent mestiza, as a contemporary urban chola living in a barrio like Oakdale. The question is what meaning do members of this visual discourse community make of Karina's drawing?

The intertextual feature suggests that to comprehend this potential, ideological meaning from Karina's drawing, an individual needs background cultural knowledge. In her interview, Marisa described visual literacy events in which her aunt initiated her into this iconological and cultural knowledge. Juana, in her description of a similar visual literacy event, described how she became a mentor to her younger brother and her husband's cousins.

I ran into Marisa after she graduated, and remembering that she came from a family of artists I asked if she would look at some drawings and provide some information. Marisa drew lowrider art when she was in middle school, but she did not show her drawings to her parents. She showed them to her aunt, her father's sister, who is also an artist.

I wouldn't necessarily show my parents. . . . My mom, she's Caucasian and she's a very liberal woman. . . . but she saw these symbols and for her that means. . . . like gangs and like drugs and stuff. . . . She didn't want her daughter to be like that. . . . like a little chola. So I wouldn't show her these kinds of pictures, but I would show my *tia* [Spanish for "aunt"], and she would be like, oh that's great! My tia, she's like a Chicana, she collects Chicano posters. . . . She was the first person ever to teach me what it is to be Chicano, Chicana. . . . She started taking me to different people who would make these posters or to the Mission District, you know, the Mexican Museum. . . . The pictures that I see in here [the HAP anthologies] by the kids show like the traditional symbols of being Chicano or Latino in general. Even I can identify with these symbols even though I don't speak Spanish and even though maybe at times I wasn't really raised with a strong Mexican tradition. I can still identify with these symbols that unite all of us here who are Latino.

Marisa's comments highlight her mother's and aunt's differing perceptions of lowrider art. Her mother's perceptions are an outsider's (and reflect a parent's worries about her adolescent child). Her aunt's perceptions are an insider's allied with the insight that Marisa's interest in lowrider art was not about gangs and drugs but a signal that Marisa was interested in and ready to learn about the Mexican part of her heritage. Marisa turned to her aunt because she knew that learning to draw the "Mexican-type things" she saw around her was not enough. She wanted "to know about these things" and her aunt initiated her into this cultural knowledge, taught her "what it is to be Chicano, Chicana." Juana described a similar literacy event.

I have two folders of a lot of artwork. . . . As I got older a lot of my husband's cousins, they're just growing up, you know, they're eleven or twelve, thirteen, another is fourteen years old. . . . Even, I have a brother, he was like, oh you've got stuff, you should give some to me. . . . I said, here, I was like, oh here, take it. . . . You know, this is the young generation. . . . They would just take them and draw it and after a while I was, oh well then, draw me something. I want to see how your art is.

Juana assumes the role of mentor to her brother and her husband's cousins. She recognizes the significance of her relatives engaging with Latino visual discourse and becomes their mentor. This is part of the intertextual feature. It isn't enough for Latino adolescents just to learn to copy icons, they want to know their cultural heritage and often learn it through the sponsorship of a more knowledgeable elder. As they draw the icons that surround them, they also draw on their growing cultural knowledge to create new visual texts that make meaning of their Latino cultural identities and experiences.

Against the background of this iconological and cultural knowledge, I describe the meaning that participants, represented by Juana, consistently read in Karina's drawing. Even though Juana was born in the United States of Guatemalan parents, and Karina's drawing uses icons traditionally associated with the Mexican community, still Juana closely identified with Karina's drawing.

> I do remember seeing all this vivid stuff in junior high. . . . I have a whole bunch of different drawings that my friends drew for me, and I just kind of collect it all. I have it all in my room. Some are so old that they're falling apart. But it's just something that we identified ourselves with. I felt like I identified with, like this is us, looking at us the real way. . . . There were a lot of different images like the one, this one of the Virgin Mary. This one tripped me out though . . . because you always, we always identified the *Virgen de Guadalupe* as the leader of Mexico. I'm not Mexican, right, but it was a trip when I saw it for the first time. I was like, oh how cool! Because I mean it give us an image of a girl who we are, of the way we dress, you know, and the kind of lifestyle we live.

Even though Juana distinguishes herself as "not Mexican," she identifies closely with both the Virgin of Guadalupe and the chola, representing the kind of girls she and her friends were. The chola and the Virgin, in the context of Juana's adolescent social world in Oakdale, represent markers of membership in an Americanized Latina ethnic category.

Having lived this lifestyle, Juana also read the ideological challenge Karina's drawing represents to negative readings of the chola.

> When they put the rag here [pointing to the bandanna between the chola and cholo] it was identified more as a gang like situation, right. Not in a bad way 'cause there were girls that hung out with gang girls and stuff, but they weren't bad at all.

Juana knows that cholas are commonly associated with gangs, but in her experience one could be a chola or cholo and not be in a gang, not be "bad at all." To Juana, Karina's drawing reflects the way that she saw herself and her friends in middle school. It expresses their reality, that although they were cholas they were not necessarily in gangs and they were not bad, as they were often assumed to be.

Karina's drawing was read as an ideological representation of what it means to be a Latino adolescent—a member of a particular U.S. ethnic category. As such, it challenges the pejorative assumptions of people outside of the Latino visual discourse community who may lack this cultural knowledge and hold stereotypical assumptions about Latino youth. The intertextual feature reveals visual literacy events and social practices of initiating adolescents into culturally valued and contextualized knowledge that resonates with them, and that they use in their process of coming to identify with a larger, ethnic/cultural category within the stratification of the United States population.

The Social Feature

The social feature of Latino visual discourse identifies the visual literacy events in which drawings are created, displayed, and circulated. I describe the regular configurations of interactions centered on visual texts in the social feature. When I asked when and where people drew lowrider art, Marisa said

> People would just sit there and draw, like you'd be bored in class and you'd just sit there drawing stuff like this. You know, hey da da da da, look at this, oh that's cool.

Marisa's answer reveals that some students turn to drawing in response to the not uncommon experience of being bored in class, or out of a desire for attention from other students. Marisa's comments match a photograph taken by a Lowrider Art student (see Figure 6). She told me that this was a "loud" class and her friend always went to a back corner where she would not be noticed and drew. When I asked what people did with drawings when they were done, Marisa said

> You'd give them to somebody and they would put them in their binder. . . . they have a little clear pocket and you can stick them in there. Or put it in your locker, put it on the wall of your room. It shows again who you're affiliated with, who you are. I mean right there, blam, your locker, that's who you are

Figure 6. An Oakdale student drawing "lowrider" art in class.

right there. And to have [a drawing] in your binder you're always identified with that, you know, your *Raza*.[8] You go into class and you go sit with other Latino students, you go to lunch and you sit with them, and you all identify with these symbols, you know, of the cars and the Aztecs and stuff like that.

Marisa's description of keeping drawings in one's binder matches another photograph (see Figure 7). Here two Lowrider Art students are perusing the young man's drawings collected in clear plastic pockets in his binder. More significantly, Marisa's comments suggest that not only did the icons have the power to assert a Latino cultural identity, but having and displaying drawings in binders, in lockers, on walls in bedrooms, acted as assertions of Latino cultural identity.

These visual literacy events, the interactions centered on the creation, display, and circulation of lowrider art, suggest that it is not just the images and icons and drawings, but also the social practices, the participation in Latino visual literacy events, that construct cultural knowledge meaningful to some Latino youth.

[8] *Raza* is the collective name many U.S. Latinos use to refer to all Latinos collectively, regardless of nationality; it literally means "the race of people" (Polkinhorn, Velasco, and Lambert 1986, 54).

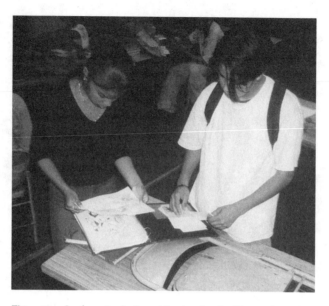

Figure 7. Students in the Lowrider Art class looking at drawings in a binder.

Conclusion

Exploring the contextual, intertextual, and social features of Latino visual discourse as it functions in Oakdale revealed that Latino visual discourse operates as a distinct form of visual literacy that many Latino adolescents engage in. It also reveals that participating in visual literacy events, being socialized into Latino visual discourse, and being initiated into the history of cultural icons was an important part of developing and asserting an affirming cultural identity for some Latino youth. Finally, this study shows that the ideological meaning constructed through icons in Karina's drawing challenged widely circulating stereotypes of Latino youth, asserting a Latino cultural identity that celebrates its indigenous heritage, and so resists the ideology of assimilation. Thus it appears that the drawings from the Hispanic Academic Program anthologies and the social practices described in the interviews operate as social practices of literacy communicating "shared cognitions represented in ideologies and social identities" (Barton and Hamilton 2000, 8).

My findings reveal that Latino visual discourse is a form of visual literacy and an epistemology that draws on Latin American/Amerindian ways of perceiving, thinking, and knowing that is subaltern (Mignolo 2000), because it exists outside of mainstream, Eurocentric cultural practices and institutions that conserve knowledge. The colonization of Mesoamerica resulted in the transculturation of practices of literacy (Gruzinski 1992; Mignolo 1995; Pratt 1992), and this process of cultural hybridization is at least as old as the Conquest. Transculturation and NLS theorize the journey of the social practices and icons of Latino visual discourse from south to north, and their neoculturation in Mexican-American/Latino communities in the United States where practitioners re-imagine, re-envision, and re-invest icons with meanings that Latino youth use to construct affirming cultural identities. Latino visual discourse is a culturally distinct form of visual literacy that some students bring to school, where it is overlooked, underestimated, and often denigrated by school officials who fail to see how these visual literacy practices are related to literacy (Cowan 1999; 2004).

The Hispanic Academic Program was a mediating institution operating between Bayside's large, urban public school district and its smaller Catholic school system to serve the needs of Latino middle school students who were, as neither high-achieving nor at-risk, benignly neglected and not being encouraged to pursue or prepare for higher education. As a literacy teacher, I was free to use the literacy practices that I was teaching to explore my students' cultural heritage. In the process, I became an unsuspecting observer of fascinating social practices of visual literacy. Now I have learned to recognize that HAP students like Joaquin and Karina brought their visual literacy practices across borders between community and school, and transculturated the HAP anthologies.

Joaquin, Karina, and other Latino adolescents took very seriously the opportunity to create memorable texts for the 1994 Hispanic Academic Program Anthology. While I was focused on creating an anthology of their school-based written texts, they were using their own, culturally situated, social practices of making meaning visually to create drawings that in the anthology blurred the boundaries between written and visual texts. These border crossers were drawing on their everyday social practices of Latino visual discourse to "put out there" images that afforded their HAP peers opportunities to take hold of the cultural knowledge encoded and communicated in their drawings. As Joaquin said, the written and visual texts in the anthology "go hand in hand"; they are meaningful, memorable statements of HAP students' cultural heritage. Joaquin and Karina put their cultural heritage out there for all readers to see and, for those who could, to "read off of it."

References

Acuna, R. 1988. *Occupied America: A history of Chicanos.* 3rd ed. New York: Harper Collins.

Anzaldua, G. 1987. *Borderlands/La frontera: The new mestiza.* San Francisco: Spinsters/Auntie Luke.

Barton, D., and Hamilton, M. 2000. Literacy practices. In: D. Barton, M. Hamilton, and R. Ivanic, (eds.), *Situated literacies: Reading and writing in context.* London and New York: Routledge, pp. 7–15.

Cowan, P. 1999. 'Drawn' into the community: Reconsidering the artwork of Latino adolescents. *Visual Sociology* 14: 91–107.

Cowan, P. 2004. Devils or angels: Literacy and discourse in lowrider culture. In: J. Mahiri (ed.), *What they don't learn in school: Literacy in the lives of urban youth.* New York: Peter Lang Publishing, pp. 47–75.

Elvanosky, D. 1998. Outlook: An enduring legacy in Peralta Park. *The Montclarian,* October 6, p. A-4.

Garcia, E. 1997. The 4am faithful: Mexican Americans crowd into churches for predawn celebration of the Virgin of Guadalupe, *San Jose Mercury News,* December 13, p. 1A.

Grady, K. 2001. Lowrider art and Latino students in the rural Midwest. In: S. Wortham, E.G. Murillo, and E.T. Hamann, (eds.), *Education in the new Latino Diaspora: Policy and the politics of identity.* Westport: Ablex Publishing, pp. 169–191.

Gruzinsky, S. 1992. *Painting the conquest: The Mexican Indians and the European Renaissance.* Translated by Deke Dusinberre. Paris: Flammarion.

Kress, G., and van Leeuwen, T. 1996. *Reading images: The grammar of visual design.* London and New York: Routledge.

Lockhart, J. 1992. *The Nahuas after the conquest.* Palo Alto: Stanford University Press.

Mahiri, J. 2004. *What they don't learn in school: Literacy in the lives of urban youth.* New York: Peter Lang Publishing.

Matutue-Bianchi, M.E. 1991. Situational ethnicity and patterns of school performance among immigrant and nonimmigrant Mexican-descent students. In: M.A. Gibson and J.U. Ogbu (eds.), *Minority status and schooling: A comparative study of immigrant and involuntary minorities.* New York: Garland Publishing, pp. 205–247.

Maybin, J. 2000. The new literacy studies: Context, intertextuality, and discourse. In: D. Barton, M. Hamilton, and R. Ivanic (eds.), *Situated literacies: Reading and writing in context.* London and New York: Routledge, pp. 197–207.

Mignolo, W.D. 1995. *The darker side of the Renaissance: Literacy, territoriality, and colonization.* Ann Arbor: University of Michigan Press.

Mignolo, W.D. 2000. *Local histories/global designs: Coloniality, subaltern knowledges, and border thinking.* Princeton: Princeton University Press.

Mitchell, W.J.T. 1986. *Iconology: Image, text, ideology.* Chicago and London: University of Chicago Press.

Oquendo, A.R. 1998. Re-imagining the Latino/a race. In: R. Delgado and J. Stephancic (eds.), *The Latino/a condition: A critical reader.* New York: New York University Press, pp. 60–71.

Ortiz, F. 1940/1995. *Cuban counterpoint: Tobacco and sugar.* Durham: Duke University Press.

Polkinhorn, H., Velasco, A., and Lambert, M. (1986). *El libro de calo: The dictionary of Chicano slang,* (revised edition). Mountain View: Floricanto Press.

Pratt, M.L. 1992. *Imperial eyes: Travel writing and transculturation.* London: Routledge.

Stone, M.C. 1990. Bajito y sauvecito [Low and slow]: Lowriding and the "class" of class. *Studies in Latin American popular culture* 9: 85–126.

Street, B.V. (ed.). 1993. *Cross-cultural approaches to literacy.* Cambridge: Cambridge University Press.

Vigil, J.D. 2002. Community dynamics and the rise of street gangs. In: M.M. Suarez-Orozco and M.M. Paez (eds.), *Latinos: Remaking America.* Berkeley: University of California Press, pp. 97–109.

9
Literacy and Media in Secondary Schools in the United Kingdom

Joanna Oldham

Introduction

In spite of a dearth of evidence, it has long been assumed that literacy and media are in opposition. In contrast, however, this chapter points to an interrelatedness between literacy and media within the context of secondary school English (the language arts domain of the curriculum within the United Kingdom). This interrelatedness can be seen in practices associated with teaching the development of reading and writing of print in this context.

A connection between literacy and media is perhaps not so surprising given that media has been defined as "a very general term . . . used to include a large range of aspects of twentieth century life (including) the worlds of advertising, fashion, 'pop' music, photography, film, newspapers, radio, television to be encompassed under that general heading as aspects of what we would term 'mass culture'," (Alvarardo and Barrett 1992, 20). In many of those examples, media can be seen to include print. In research I report here, however, I use 'media' to denote artefacts which use substantially, or in part, the principles of film and video narrative, including the technology for producing them (Bordwell and Thompson 1985). These artefacts (which I refer to as 'moving-image media' and abbreviate to MIM) generally exclude print. Nevertheless, research reported here suggests that MIM texts have the potential, in conjunction with specific practices described later on, to raise levels of literacy. This is in spite of the visuality of MIM texts, which might appear to be mutually exclusive from the verbality of printed ones.

The data on which this chapter relies come from a case study I conducted into the teaching of English by three teachers in state secondary schools across London. Each teacher had set out to teach English literature using MIM. In describing, problematizing and analyzing how literacy and media relate, I documented the texts and practices of each classroom. The texts included both print and MIM types (those received and those produced by students) and the practices included planning, teaching, learning, and assessment of and through the texts.

The updated account of literacy practices this chapter provides with respect to MIM is timely, since a vigorous debate I explore later, which has polarized literacy and media, has obscured understanding of what teachers do. The new evidence that this chapter reports as to what teachers are actually doing in English is significant because it suggests that teachers' practices equip students with an understanding of media and a facility with a range of multimodal texts. This has, I claim, implications for the debate about standards. Perhaps most significantly, however, this chapter is a refutation of notions of an essentialist relationship between literacy and media which have continued to dominate the design of the curriculum in the United Kingdom (e.g., by the National Literacy Strategy; Department of Education and Employment, 1997). Not only is facility with media not occurring at the expense of print as many had feared (Birkerts 1996); but also the ways in which performance is currently measured during assessment of English means that it fails to capture recent gains. This emphasizes a theme of this chapter and a contribution it makes to NLS research: The way we define literacy influences the measure of it and vice versa. The gains that currently remain unmeasured represent students' sophisticated multimodal knowledge, the result of teachers' multimodal practices.

There are three sections to this chapter. In the first, I establish a gap in the literature concerning schooled English. In the second, I present a case study concerning the teaching of English literature by three teachers. In the third, I discuss the findings of the analysis of the study. I conclude by suggesting that literacy in schooled English is more complex than current curricula and assessment suggest.

How Media Relate to Literacy in Schooled English

The case study of secondary school English in the United Kingdom that this chapter describes is to some extent a consideration of how taught English in schools is caught between two conflicting paradigms of literacy. Beyond schools, it has become increasingly difficult to discuss literacy in isolation from media in the sense of mass media, multimedia, and electronic hypermedia (Cope and Kalantzis 2000). All of these forms of media have juxtaposed written texts with other modes, including visuality, aurality, and spatiality (cf. Kress 2003). In doing so, they have arguably changed what it means to be literate. Within schooling, however, great store is set by a literacy concerned with the skills of reading and writing for the representation of language alone (Street and Street 1991; Street 1999). In each of these two paradigms, the relationship of MIM to literacy is different: In the former, media are an aspect of literacy; in the latter, media are irrelevant or possibly detrimental to literacy.

To establish how media actually relate to literacy in schooled English, it is necessary first to consider the sense in which any teaching of English includes literacy teaching. There are five possible perspectives on this. Firstly, there is the perspective that literacy, rather than being a 'sociocultural or educational goal', is instead "an outcome of the learning process" (Garton and Pratt 1989, 263). As such, schooled English presumably makes a contribution to literacy but is not solely responsible for making students literate. The significance of media within such a view is unclear.

The second perspective is that all teachers of English must be teaching literacy (reading and writing of print), since this is "what the outside world quite possibly considers the most important task of English teaching" (Davies 1996, 9). This is in spite of the fact that Davies' "cautious hypothesis" (when he was writing prior to the introduction of the National Literacy Strategy) was that "not a lot of direct teaching of literacy skills goes on in secondary English classrooms." From this perspective, media are mutually exclusive from literacy.

Thirdly, there is the significance of literature in being literate. Tracing historical definitions of 'literacy', MacCabe writes that "the word itself is a nineteenth-century coinage to describe the divorce of reading and writing from a full knowledge of literature. For Johnson and Milton it would have been impossible to separate the two" (MacCabe 1998, 32). Secondary school English, owing to the nature of its discipline, includes literacy in the sense that the study of literature is an aspect of the curriculum. Since literature is by definition a printed medium, MIM adaptations of literary printed texts are excluded from this definition of literacy (Eagleton 1997).

Fourthly, given the inclusion of media into secondary school English (Barratt 1998), there is perhaps another sense in which literacy is taught there. In its work aimed at reconceptualizing literacy, the New London Group (Cope and Kalantzis 2000) identifies that the term 'literacy' in general tends to signify the written and read representation of language only. Recognizing the communicative repertoire generated by radical societal and technological change, 'multiliteracy' has been proposed as a term which can capture facility with the multiplicity of communications channels and media and an increasing salience of cultural and linguistic diversity (Cope and Kalantzis 2000). In this sense, media are an aspect of literacy.

However, to a great extent, each of these four positions is an essentialist one. Each reifies literacy (and media), invoking autonomous models. Given the work of NLS, this is somewhat anachronistic. Fifthly, then, there is the view of NLS itself, which would argue that since reading and writing practices are embedded in schools in general and the study of English in particular, that consciously or otherwise, teachers and their practices transmit values related to ideologies of literacy to students. Moreover, this happens whether they consciously set out to teach literacy or not. The NLS perspective can therefore be invoked to argue, as this chapter does, that the relationship between literacy and media can only be understood through analysis of practice. For this reason, it is more accurate to discuss how literacy relates to *uses of* media rather than media per se.

What then is the relationship between literacy and uses of media in secondary school English? In spite of the dominance of print in school in general, such that "virtually all schooling after the first year or two assumes pupil literacy" (Hannon 2000, 8), English teachers routinely employ MIM (Barratt 1998). Whether such use of media is perceived to be the means or the ends of the study of English and whether or how it relates to literacy in this context has, however, hitherto been little understood.

Reference to media texts (including print and moving image) are included in the National Curriculum for English (Department for Education and Employment 2000); the statutory depiction of what teachers must teach and assess for students between the ages of 11 and 16 in the United Kingdom. However, this does not in itself tell us about the practice of English teaching. Moreover, there are suggestions that English teaching practices are neither monolithic nor uniform: by referring to "those teachers who assume that their task is to teach *through* Media Education" as "mistaken," Hart and Hicks (2002) suggest that some teachers are not aware of "the statutory requirements that English teachers are required to teach Media *in* English." While the interpretation of the statute's obligations on teachers may be correct, yet we do not have any systematic account of how teachers themselves conceptualize media in English and put this into practice.

Barratt's survey (1998) set out to audit uses of media and the extent of media education in English, and his data show that media have become part of the repertoire of English. His survey conceptualizes the majority of teaching of media within English as a discrete, polarized activity, however, which may, as data from the case studies of this chapter indicate, be a distortion of the true picture. Barratt's concern is the documentation of media in a bid to promote it, but we learn little about either how teachers themselves conceptualize use of media in their teaching of English or about how their conceptions influence their practices. This is a gap this chapter aims to fill.

Case Studies of the Teaching of English

In order to ascertain whether media represent an aspect of literacy, broadly conceived, in schooled English or whether they are used as a means to teaching a literacy which is concerned more narrowly with print, I researched the practices of three teachers. In addition to documenting literacy, NLS has offered a methodological frame for researching literacy. In writing not of 'literacy' but of 'literacies', NLS postulates no monolithic literacy; rather, there are patterns around uses of reading and writing within different communities. Using the word 'literacy' in conjunction with the word 'practices', as this chapter does, denotes the different sets of ways in which literacy is used by a community (secondary school English in this case). Drawn from Street in particular (cf. Street 1984), Baynham and Baker (2002) elucidate the concept of 'practices' as incorporating "the ideas, attitudes, ideologies and values that inform what people do" which links actions and actors closely via external and internalized worlds.

The practices approach has more recently been developed to incorporate 'figured worlds' (Bartlett and Holland 2002). These are defined as realms of interpretation which are "invoked, animated, contested and enacted through artefacts, activities, and identities in practice" (12). Both practices and figured worlds provide a conceptual framework for arguing, as this chapter does, that literacy and media's relationship in secondary school English is shaped by each individual teacher's conceptual frame as they mediate between curriculum and assessment, influencing whether and how literacy in schooled English relates to media. The differences between the practices of secondary school teachers Mr. Kite, Mr. Lightman, and Ms. Taylor pointed to different tacit conceptualizations of literacy which influenced how they used media.

In order to describe these conceptualizations, in each classroom, I documented the texts being used and produced (both print and media) and the elements of literacy (defined as reading and writing print) required of the students in each class. To understand media's relationship to reading and writing as construed by the figured world of each classroom, I needed to be able to distinguish between *what* (subject content) was being taught from *how* (methods) it was being taught. One indication of this was what was being assessed. The nature of the assessment task coupled with the teacher's discussion of students' assessment texts were used as indicators of the object of assessment. However, when I analyzed the relationship between what was taught and how on the one hand and what was assessed and how on the other, a rift between teaching and assessment was revealed. I will temporarily suspend discussion of this rift and continue by identifying the ways in which the case study teachers employed MIM. The teachers were unified by their claim to be using MIM in their teaching of literature to students between the ages of eleven and fourteen and while it is possible to debate whether the printed texts for study in each classroom were examples of Literature as each teacher claimed, this is less my concern than the relationship of reading and writing printed texts to the uses of media by the three teachers. Whereas Mr. Lightman teaches about media as texts in their own right, both Ms. Taylor and Mr. Kite harness media (differently) as tools in teaching and learning processes.

Mr. Kite had read Emily Bronte's *Wuthering Heights* with his 13- and 14-year-old students, who were then asked to independently select and read two other pre–twentieth century novels in order to write an essay which compared all three. Media in this sequence were represented, firstly, by excerpts from filmic adaptations of pre–twentieth century literary texts and, secondly, by television documentaries about the lives and times of selected authors of the nineteenth century. Mr. Kite chose to show the media texts at the point at which his students were being asked to select the two pre–twentieth century novels they had to read and compare with *Wuthering Heights* in their essay. In this way, media was used as an aid for students' selection of the literary print texts they had to read and write about and the essay comparing three literary texts was the means by which an assessment was made. In this assessment, the printed texts formed the object of study. For Mr. Kite's students, knowledge and understanding about media acquired during the teaching sequences was not a focus of the assessment task: Media in his sequence were teaching tools, not an object of study.

Mr. Kite explained the design of his teaching sequence in terms of the demands of statutory assessment, in particular, the specific criteria of the particular GCSE examination board syllabus his English department follows in teaching students between the ages of 14 and 16. "Firstly, pre–twentieth century literature fulfills the GCSE requirement of the comparative essay and pre–twentieth century literature; secondly, higher order reading skills." Going on to cite the relevance of examinations taken by eighteen-year-olds, Mr. Kite added, "and thirdly, critical literacy which will follow through to 'A' Level." In this, the influence of terminal assessment can be clearly observed. Had he not been so led by the demands of the terminal assessment, it is interesting to speculate about the kind of task Mr. Kite might have devised in which media and print knowledge were relevant. Previous research suggests that teachers' task setting is a mediating factor between literacy and media (Oldham 2003).

While Mr. Kite elected to use MIM as a teaching tool, he expressed some anxiety about its use in this context. Concerned that students might not read the printed versions , he said, "I hesitate about doing this in case the kids think 'oh can I just go and watch the video'." In spite of this somewhat ambiguous position about adaptations, Mr. Kite's teaching displays an equal interest in how texts of different types work.

> How does it set the scene. It uses a soundtrack. What's on the soundtrack? Yeh, you heard the sea. What can you see? It starts at the horizon and its panning round not the other way round. Which part of Britain? Note how quickly cinema can do this. Mood and place are set almost instantly. Writers take more words. Hardy, as I've said before, has a great sense of place. When you see the characters when you're watching a film, what do we need to know? We see them first. In some films you hear about them. How does this work in a novel? (Mr. Kite, English class)

In the preceding, Mr. Kite does not conform to the old medium-specific high / low culture divide in which printed texts are by definition better than media ones. Rather, in the assessment of literature, the filmic text is irrelevant and so he wishes to avoid the conflation of printed literary texts with filmic adaptations of them. He advocates wary navigation of filmic adaptations of literary printed works which are 'inferior versions' and those which are themselves 'works of art', as can be seen in his discussion of primary and secondary texts:

> Yesterday we looked at *Far From the Madding Crowd,* the screenplay of which was written by a man called Frederick Raphael and is a play in its own right. Is an adaptation a primary or a secondary source? If it's simply interpreting, it's secondary. If a film is a work of art, isn't there an argument for saying it's primary? What if Raphael is better than Hardy? (Mr. Kite, English class)

In this way, Mr. Kite's desire to make his students discriminating watchers of media is evident.

In the classroom of the second teacher, Mr. Lightman, two short stories connected by the theme of dystopian futures were read aloud by the teacher to his 12- and 13-year-old students: "Examination Day" by Henry Slesar and "The Pedestrian" by Ray Bradbury. In this class, MIM were represented by two complete film narratives: *Soylent Green* and *Blade Runner.* These texts were shown to the students in lessons producing an alternating pattern of print and media texts. The students were asked to construct a range of texts in response to these print and MIM texts. These included answers to tests of comprehension on both the print and media texts; newspaper articles; short stories; and pictorial representations of various aspects of life in the future. Assessments were made firstly of the tests of comprehension of both the printed texts and the moving image texts; secondly of the creative writing with dystopian visions of the future as a theme; and thirdly of the newspaper articles written about a dystopian futuristic news story. Media were crucial to some of these tasks in that students' were required to write responses to questions about the films they had seen. This made MIM texts in his sequence.

Mr. Lightman's talk showed a motivation for employing media different from Mr. Kite's. Although Mr. Lightman perceived that students respond to film more than printed media, he implied a discontinuity between what he teaches and what the curriculum requires:

> Ten years ago students were more malleable because you would design a curriculum based on what they do. They're not going to write letters about sailing holidays. (Mr. Lightman, interview)

In this, he regards the curriculum as too remote from students' experience, specifically where it relates to print. There is evidence that Mr. Lightman believes that media narratives are easier for students to understand: During didactic episodes in the classroom, he explains only the narrative of print texts not that of media texts. He connects his uses of MIM to the issue of ability and his claim that if the students' interest is engaged, that this spurs them on to read print texts:

> I use film for a lot for obvious reasons: to get them interested in anything in terms of issues, in terms of articulating what's happening. If I read them a story, they can't understand but if I show them a film then obviously, they get it then. They deal with the visual. (Mr. Lightman, interview)

In this way, Mr. Lightman regards MI texts as motivational. This can also be seen in his classroom interactions with students when they enter his class and ask, as they frequently do, if they will be watching a video in the lesson to which he responds, "No. Work." His reply, juxtaposing work on the one hand with watching films on the other, associates film with pleasure.

In Ms. Taylor's class, the 12-year-old students read aloud the script *Adam's Ark* by Harold Hodgson. Having written a synopsis of the play, they prepared work on how scripts were staged and performed. Ms. Taylor's use of MIM is, she explains, designed to develop students' reading and writing through study of drama and performance. Ms. Taylor told me that her objectives for this sequence were:

> To appreciate and understand the play from a written point of view. To learn how to write and how to accurately set out a play. To create a believable character through dialogue and action: writing and the physical. Setting out, speech and drama terminology, dialogue, scene, improvisation. (Ms. Taylor, interview)

Although she had originally planned to use film animation adaptations of Shakespeare's *A Midsummer Night's Dream* in her teaching sequence which concerned drama texts and scripts, Ms. Taylor later abandoned this in favor of using a video camera to record her students' performance of dramatic scenarios she had written. She videotaped these performances and then used the videotape as a vehicle for peer assessment. The criteria for this explicitly focused on modes other than reading and writing.

> We're going to examine ourselves and others to judge and observe things carefully in a theatrical as well as an English way. Watch and analyze. Think positively about the performance as though we were directors. Look at these auditions and choose the best and write about them. Think about imagination, movement, gesture, excitement. (Ms. Taylor; classroom observation)

Her learning outcomes were divided, she told me, between drama and English. She then added that "they're both the same to me." Ms. Taylor perceives a clear link between writing and drama and also reading and drama.

> We did a lot of talking about how character is a strong link between drama and English. The idea of being able to convey images in their head—one route in is how do you want your character to dress and also interpretation. (Ms. Taylor, interview)

Ms. Taylor's explanation about the link between performance and reading and writing conceptualizes her use of MIM as a learning tool, MIM being the means by which peer assessments were made.

One of her stated aims was to consider a play script as a performance rather than as a text. Although the students in her class were aged 12 and 13, Ms. Taylor told me that assessment criteria at GCSE (for assessing the work of 16-year-old students) influenced her teaching of younger students as well. "I'm applying GCSE techniques if you like but they're the same all the way through." Ms. Taylor's perception of terminal assessment thus influences the activities and tasks she sets. It is worth noting, however, how different the activities and tasks she sets are from those of Mr. Kite, who also cites the influence of (the same) terminal examination arrangements on his teaching sequence.

For Ms. Taylor, the design of the teaching sequence she taught was partly informed by the students' previous performance in an examination where "description was seriously lacking." Ms. Taylor explains that they lost marks in the examination because of a lack of use of similes and metaphors in their writing.

> I've got everything from a low 3 to a 6. I'm looking to increase their ability to write in complex sentences in different styles. Detail. How to write with in-

creasing accuracy. They would then need to focus on SPG [spelling, punctuation, and grammar], which has gone out of the window a little bit. (Ms. Taylor, interview)

While she herself is clear about the links between drama and English, I wonder how well the enactment of similes, for example, transfers to her students' writing.

Before I present additional data about assessment, I wish to summarize what can be drawn from the data so far. With regard to how they use MIM, teachers' practices appear to exist ahead of policy. I suggest that in addition to the read and written representation of language, additional modes, including drawing, sound, and performance, are valued in the figured worlds of English teaching. As such, the teaching of English is routinely multimodal. It also suggests that teachers mediate the use of media in the curriculum. Factors which affect the ways in which they do this include what is being taught (subject content) and how it is being taught (methods). In addition, however, the more significant mediating factor explaining how English is taught is which teacher is teaching. The case studies indicate how teachers' different uses of media are linked in complex ways to how they define literacy and how they interpret the requirements of curriculum and of assessment. As such, they have significant implications for our understanding of literacy in secondary school English.

It is not, however, the argument of this chapter that the case studies reveal yet more literacies such that we would need to invoke descriptions such as 'literacy in Ms. Jones' class' to acknowledge how they vary from teacher to teacher. Rather, what is at stake is how national assessment schemes and policy relate to such local practices. It is vital to remember that in order to be deemed accurate according to national 'standards', teachers' assessments of English have to be reliable (Wiliam 1998). The documented reliability of teacher assessment of English in the UK experience has been attributed to guild knowledge (Sadler 1987) which teachers use for the purposes of making assessments. Underrepresentation of media within such guild knowledge may explain why teachers teach MIM but exclude it from assessment.

Shortly I give an analysis of the same case study and teachers assessing the work of their own students and those of the other teachers. This reveals that, in spite of the multimodality with regard to their teaching practices, in assessment of English, the range of accepted communicative practices is more limited. A hierarchy of modes exists in curriculum and assessment with representation of language at the top. This limits teachers' ability to recognize and reward students' communicative repertoires in modes other than those concerned with the representation of language.

I continue with a depiction of this by showing the same three teachers assessing the work of one of Mr. Kite's students, Lorna. I use this to illustrate that within the assessment of language in its written form, analysis of the assessment aspect of the case studies revealed that English teachers rely on four referents: 'subject matter' denotes what the piece of writing is ostensibly about; 'technical features' denotes accuracy and surface correctness in, for example, spelling and punctuation and grammar; and the third code, 'style' denotes the students' facility with written language. The fourth code I label 'other referent' and it includes a miscellaneous set of aspects to which teachers additionally referred.

(Note that I have grouped the comments together, but each teacher was alone with me when the assessments were made.)

SUBJECT MATTER

> *Mr. Lightman:* Terrific on the ambiguities of emotions.

> *Ms. Taylor:* It doesn't actually say. The vocab. hints at more depth. She breaches up a whole load of ideas and follows one for a bit.

> *Mr. Kite:* This is very direct. (reads) "Of course there are many more contrasts, and small details that affect my emotions, but these are the things I feel have stirred the largest reactions in me, and have told the story so well for me, creating a large sense of atmosphere and involvement."

In terms of the teachers' evaluation of the subject matter of the piece of writing they are assessing, which is Lorna's personal response to chapters 1 to 12 of *Wuthering Heights,* there is apparent disagreement about which features of the subject matter are responsible for the judgement. Mr. Lightman cites Lorna's account of the emotions of the characters in the novel. Neither Ms. Taylor nor Mr. Kite comments on this directly. Ms. Taylor appears to be suggesting that Lorna has not discussed any of her personal responses fully enough, and Mr. Kite reads out an extract to demonstrate that the writing is very direct, which is apparently a good thing.

TECHNICAL FEATURES

> *Mr. Lightman:* I assume spelling errors are because of word processing.

> *Ms. Taylor:* (reads) "Thrushcross Grove"! Missed out a capital in the title and quotations need to be set out properly.

> *Mr. Kite:* Grammatically accurate.

Mr. Lightman's comment is very interesting. While he notes inaccuracies in spelling in Lorna's text, he rationalizes their existence, suggesting that Lorna is capable of better spelling; something he cannot know. He suggests that they are typographical errors. Ms. Taylor notes the incorrect naming of the house from the novel and refers to the omission of capital letters. Mr. Kite does not refer to the spelling at all, instead noting the accuracy in grammatical construction.

STYLE

> *Mr. Lightman:* Engaged, articulate. Fabulous vocabulary, sentence structure.

> *Ms. Taylor:* Lots of complicated vocab. which is nice. I like the use of vocab. It's very personable. I'd be very pleased with the phrasing. I'd like a bit more. She says things in a roundabout way. It wants more depth. Be nice to hone it down a bit.

> *Mr. Kite:* Very good mature writing style, good construction. The third thing is the referencing: I taught them to quote and to shadow the text. Appropriate use of opening and ending.

Mr. Lightman continues to praise Lorna's work. He and Ms. Taylor both make reference to the vocabulary. Mr. Kite unpacks his phrase about maturity in terms of construction rather than vocabulary.

OTHER REFERENT

> *Mr. Lightman:* 'Bloody hell! This is a mere 9th year is it? Good innit? It's terrific. (reads) "Of course, there are many more contrasts, and small details that affect my emotions, but these are the things I feel have stirred the largest reaction in me." Tremendous. From reading the book or seeing the film? Some 'A' Level students couldn't do this, could they? Rather interesting as well.

> *Ms. Taylor:* Very impressive for year 9. Obviously sensitive and positive reaction to texts, which is pleasing.

Mr. Kite: All the techniques of an adult, not seen in the less able. I encourage personal response: (reads) "One of the things I reacted to the most was the relationship between Catherine and Edgar Linton." A high level 6.

Mr. Lightman requests some clarification about the nature of the task: It is significant to Mr. Lightman whether the student was writing about the book or the film. In Mr. Lightman's case, the other referents he relies upon are norms. He expresses surprise that Lorna is in year 9, which suggests that her work is considerably better than he would expect for a student of this age. He also reads an extract from the text apparently to justify this comment. He again invokes a norm when he refers to a comparison between some 'A' level students and Lorna. Additionally, Mr. Lightman's use of 'other referent' also includes the extent to which he enjoyed reading the text. Ms. Taylor makes two uses of 'other referent': The first is a norm; the second is her judgement about the success of the teaching in terms of the apparent development of Lorna's sensibilities. Mr. Kite also uses a norm, comparing her level of maturity to that of an adult. He also comments on the extent to which the candidate has followed his teacherly instruction.

Discussion and Conclusion

What themes can be drawn from these case studies? Firstly, there is the relationship between teaching and assessment in English. While most of the work around teacher assessment of English has looked at the issue of reliability (Sadler 1987; Wiliam 1998), this chapter suggests that there may also be an issue for validity in teacher assessment: The case studies are an indication that taught literacy practices are more complex than the existing assessment arrangements allow. When teachers teach literature through media texts, as Mr. Kite does when he explains how films and novels construct setting differently, students' knowledge, skills, and understanding in this area are irrelevant to the assessment task and remain unassessed. When teachers teach about (rather than through) a media text, as Mr. Lightman does with *Blade Runner,* students' subsequent knowledge, skills, and understanding about some of the inherent modes of the media text (for example, the soundtrack, the editing) are beyond the remit of English and so remain unassessed. To remedy this rift, the academy would have to reconsider what it counts as knowledge in English.

Secondly, there are the values within assessment. In each of the three classes, students were asked to read printed texts (those framed as literary texts by the teachers) and to produce their own written texts (described above). In Mr. Lightman's and Ms. Taylor's class, however, the students were also asked to produce additional texts in modes other than print: Mr. Lightman asked students to design the bedroom of the teenager of the future; and Ms. Taylor asked students to design sets for plays and to perform the acting out of a script written by the teacher to video camera. These cannot be assessed under the present arrangements in English. Nor might we want them to be. However, it is perhaps less obvious but equally true that knowledge and understanding of MIM and other media cannot be assessed fully by an assessment frame which recognizes only speaking and listening and reading and writing as valid modes in English.

Thirdly, there is the extent to which schooled English, owing to the preceding, is an anachronism. Acknowledgement of the age of digitization has led Kress and Van Leeuwen (2001) to adopt a notion of multimodality to capture the choice-making required of contemporary communicators. Kress refers to this elsewhere as 'design' (Kress 2003), a word he uses to express the selection of modes of communication from a complex range of semiotic resources made available by technology. Kress and van Leeuwen consider that the range of alternatives means that "one multi skilled person can ask, at every point: 'Shall I express this with sound or music,' 'Shall I say this visually or verbally?,' and so on." (Kress and Van Leeuwen 2001, 2). This is not true of the assessment of secondary school English, however.

At the level of curriculum and assessment, it is significant that 'English' is divided not into categories such as language, literature, media, and drama, for example, but rather into the three domains of speaking and listening (which are counted as one), reading, and writing (Department for Education and Employment, 2000). The assessment domains of speaking and listening, reading, and writing do not take account, for instance, of Ms. Taylor's students' dramatic performances, which included movement and gestural modes; nor do they take account of the drawings of set designs. Assuming that 'reading' and 'writing' are literal categories which refer to print (and analysis of the curriculum suggests that this is what was intended by its authors), this means that only modes for the representation of language are signified as objects of teaching and assessment in English. Thus although practices associated with teaching and learning in English can be multimodal and/or multiliterate, as in the definitions above, assessment of English underrepresents media. This has two consequences: Firstly, for the validity of assessment of English, since the measure of performance in English may exclude aspects of what is taught and learned in English. Secondly, and perhaps more significantly for this chapter, it also means that students may actually be more (or differently) (multi)literate than assessment suggests.

The conclusion of the research this chapter reports suggests that ahead of policy, MIM is being used to scaffold learning in English in ways, predominantly undocumented, that differ from one teacher to another. The depictions of the uses of MIM in the case study are not exhaustive. Preliminary field work conducted prior to the case studies pointed to other tacit conceptualizations of media in the teaching of literature in the practices of other English teachers (Oldham, forthcoming). These included media as motivational tools (where adaptations of books students had studied were screened at the end of the teaching sequence) and media as student outcomes, where students' knowledge and understanding of poetry they had studied was assessed via audio-visual moving-image representations of poems made by the students. As such, I am confident that there are other conceptions of the media in existence, including ones which construe media as the learning objectives themselves.

The findings of the research are that there is a multimodality with regard to print and moving-image texts which exists in schools in spite of common sense notions about their mutual exclusivity and the prevailing trends of policy, a multimodaility which may have significant implications both for our understanding of students' and teachers' activities in secondary school English. This multimodality is not happening at the expense of print literacy, however. Far from resulting in the notorious falling standards, teachers' practices result in students developing a facility with media. This has led to recent gains in standards, but these are not apparent owing to the ways in which standards are currently indicated. It is, therefore, the contention of this chapter that literacy is constituted partly by the measure used as its index.

To finish, I invoke Street's terms (2000) 'events' and 'practices' to explain the relationship between literacy and media in schooled English. These terms distinguish, respectively, between "occasions when literacy is used" on the one hand and on the other attempts to "handle the events and the patterns of activity around literacy . . . to link them to something broader of a cultural and social kind." Although the teaching of English includes media, teaching English represents literacy events. What links these (diverse) events together is the practice of assessment; the ideology of which has been shown to exclude media. Eliminating the rift between teaching and assessment requires either the removal of media from taught English or the inclusion of the assessment of media within measures of performance of English. Each has significant implications for English in the future and the literacy that is learned there.

References

Alvarardo, M. 1992. M. Alvarardo and B. Barrett, (eds.), *Media Education: An introduction*. London: British Film Institute.

Barratt, A.J.B. 1998. *Audit of Media in English*. London: British Film Institute.

Bartlett, L., and Holland, D. 2002. Theorizing the space of literacy practices. *Ways of Knowing* 2(1): 10–22.

Barton, D. 1994. *Literacy: An introduction to the ecology of written language*. Oxford: Blackwell.

Baynham, V., and Baker, U. 2002. "Practice" in literacy and numeracy research: Multiple perspectives. *Ways of Knowing* 2(1): 1–9.

Birkerts, S. 1996. *The Gutenberg elegies*. London: Faber.

Bordwell, D., and Thompson, K. 1990. *Film art: An introduction*. New York: McGraw-Hill.

Cope, W., and Kalantzis, M. (ed.). 2000. *Multiliteracies: Literacy learning and the design of social futures*. London and New York: Routledge.

Davies, C. 1996. *What is English teaching?* Buckingham: Oxford University Press.

Department for Education and Employment. 2000. *The National Curriculum*. London: HMSO.

Department for Education and Employment. 1997. *The National Literacy Strategy*. London: HMSO.

Eagleton, T. 1997. *Literary theory*. Oxford: Blackwell.

Garton, A., and Pratt, C. 1989. *Learning to be literate*. Oxford: Blackwell.

Hannon, P. 2000. *Reflecting on literacy in education*. London: Routledge Falmer.

Hart, A., and Hicks, A. 2002. *Teaching media in the English curriculum*. London: Trentham Books Limited.

Kress, G. 2003. *Literacy in the new media age*. London: Routledge.

Kress, G., and Van Leeuwen, T. 2001. *Multimodal discourse*. London and New York: Arnold.

MacCabe, C. 1998. In: S. Cox (ed.), *Literacy is not enough*. Manchester and New York: Manchester University Press.

Oldham, J. 2003. Literacy and media in the teaching of English. *Nate News*, September 2003, Issue No. 24.

Oldham, J. (Forthcoming). The relationship between lieracy and media in secondary school English. PhD thesis, King's College, London.

Sadler, D.R. 1987. Specifying and promulgating achievement standards. *Oxford Review of Education* 13 (2): 191–209.

Street, B. 1984. *Literacy in theory and practice.* Cambridge: Cambridge University Press.

Street, B. 1996. *Social literacies.* London: Longman.

Street, B. 2000. Literacy events and literacy practices: Theory and practice in the New Literacy Studies. In: M. Martin-Jones and C. Jones (eds.), *Multilingual literacies: Reading and writing different worlds.* Amsterdam: John Benjamins.

Street, B., and Street, J. 1991. The schooling of literacy. In D. Barton and R. Ivanic (eds.), *Writing in the community.* London: Sage.

Street, B. 1999. New literacies in theory and practice: What are the implications for language in education? *Linguistics and Education* 10(1): 1–24.

William, D. 1998. The validity of teacher assessments. *Proceedings of the 22nd Annual Conference of the International Group for the Psychology of Mathematics Education,* Volume 2. South Africa: Stellenbosch.

10

"Where I'm from"
Transforming Education for Language Minorities in a Public High School in Hawai`i

*Kathryn A. Davis, Sarah Kathleen Bazzi,
and Hye-sun Cho*

> I am from the name Carlos,
> tall and chubby.
>
> I am from Pinakbet
> and Guinataan
> sweet and delicious.
>
> I am from Adidas shoes,
> sports clothes, and
> Jansport Bag.
>
> I am from TV, fan and
> stereo,
> From Bryan, Eric,
> and niece Precious.
>
> I am from masanting
> and maganaka,
> From the faces that we see,
>
> I am from the house
> by the papaya tree.

In the above poem, 15-year-old Carlos[1] shows multiple facets of his identity by creating a hybrid text which moves between English and his native Taga-

---

[1] All student names are changed to protect their privacy.

log language.[2] Carlos is at once an American teen wearing Adidas shoes and carrying a Jansport bag and a Filipino boy eating Pinakbet in Hawai`i by a mango tree. Carlos' rich and varied identity is not unique; rather, it represents the range of cultural and linguistic abilities of youth in public schools across Hawai`i. Yet despite the potential for building on the linguistic and cultural capital of students, the use of mainland and mainstream forms of schooling have resulted in students like Carlos failing to receive the academic preparation needed for educational and socioeconomic success.

Introduction

Recent legislation such as the federal No Child Left Behind (NCLB) Act has exacerbated already inadequate educational conditions for many minority students in Hawai`i and elsewhere in the United States (Crawford 2004). For example, the Reading First initiative, promoted by the Bush administration, advocates a return to an idealized direct instruction approach that ignores the contexts under which children develop literacy. Scholars and researchers (Friere 1970; Gee 1996; 2000a; 2000b; 2000c; Hopson, this volume; Maybin 2000; Richardson 1998; Stein and Mamabolo, this volume; and Street 1993; 1995; this volume) have challenged simplistic interpretations of literacy removed from social contexts. Richardson (1998) denounces the interpretation of reading and writing as "asocial individual cognitive skills dislodged from their socio-cultural moorings in human relationships and communities of practice" (116). Instead, the recent literature on promoting literacy development (e.g., Barton, Hamilton, and Ivanic 2000; Burke and Hermerschmidt, this volume; Cox and Robinson-Pant, this volume; Gee 1996; Low, this volume; Luke 1999; New London Group 1996; Street 1997; 1999; this volume) suggests the potential for building on language and cultural capital which extends beyond the notion of literacy as a set of static, decontextualized, and discrete skills to an understanding of literacy as dynamic, situated, and multifaceted. In other words, as suggested by Hull and Schultz (2002), since social and cultural practices are embedded in particular contexts, literacy is constantly being redefined

---

[2]The poem was the result of a classroom activity adapted from *Rethinking our schools: Teaching for equity and justice* (2001).

by individuals and social groups. Thus, allowing for a focus on the reader and writer's conceptions of their own literacy practices can bring individual students and their unique experiences and histories back into the educational equation (see Low, this volume). Willet, Solsken, and Wilson-Keenan (1999) point out that "effective literacy instruction [which] builds upon the cultural and linguistic backgrounds, ways of making meaning, and prior knowledge that all children bring to the classroom" (1) is especially important for non-mainstream children. Literacy practices most often taught in schools tend to represent the cultural and linguistic knowledge of students from dominant cultural and economic backgrounds. Those students whose backgrounds differ from dominant cultural values are likely to be at a significant sociocognitive disadvantage in mainstream schools (Heath 1983).

This chapter reports on a critical academic literacy project in which teachers, students, parents, community members, and university researchers attempt to alter currently unsatisfactory schooling conditions for linguistic minorities by collectively working towards positively transforming educational practices and linguistic attitudes within a predominately Filipino (Ilokano-speaking), Samoan, and Hawaiian high school. In many ways, Hawai`i is poised to accept alternative as opposed to mainstream forms of language and literacy development. Given that the majority population of Hawai`i is indigenous, immigrant, or from colonized situations (e.g., Micronesia), over the past thirty-five years residents have increasingly embraced the revitalization of Hawaiian and promotion of Hawai`i Creole English (HCE, or Pidgin, as is it known locally) for literary purposes. Thus, the transformation reported here not only promises to foster school success among linguistic minorities, but also has the potential for initiating state-wide change from the prevailing "language as problem" discourse to one of "language as resource." These efforts are congruent with the interventions in literacy curriculum evident throughout the accounts in this volume and closely parallel recent critical, participatory, and/or action research projects (cf. Pease-Alvarez and Schecter, in press). The following description of our critical academic literacy approach to literacy begins with a historical overview of past language repression in Hawai`i schools and recent movement towards greater acceptance of linguistic diversity. We also discuss how language use and attitudes in Hawai`i may reflect other U.S. and world-wide language minority circumstances. We then describe theories and activities utilized in the Hawai`i-based Studies of Heritage and Academic Languages and Literacies

(SHALL) community-school-university partnership program designed to pro-mote school success. We further link SHALL problems and potential to those of other programs described in this volume and propose implications for con-tinued literacy program development.

Language and Schooling in Hawai`i

Hawai`i represents the range of possible heritage language and cultural config-urations present in the United States and other multilingual societies and, as such, is a microcosm of educational conditions for linguistic minorities. First, the Hawaiian language suffered loss and near death through the decimation of the Hawaiian population and anti-Hawaiian/pro–Standard English school policies.[3] At the turn of the twentieth century, while the number of Hawaiians decreased, investment in sugarcane and pineapple production by the offspring of Caucasian missionaries resulted in an influx of immigrants from China, Por-tugal, Japan, the Philippines, Korea, and Puerto Rico to work on plantations. The language mix brought about by plantation conditions resulted in the cre-ation of a pidgin that eventually developed into a creole (Hawai`i Creole English or HCE) as children began to adopt pidgin as their first language (Sato 1991; Jenkins 2003).[4]

Today, 53 percent of the population is Asian, 33 percent is Caucasian, 10 percent is Hawaiian and other Pacific Islander, and 4 percent is from other ethnic backgrounds (2000 U.S. Census). Constant immigration to Hawai`i contributes to an ongoing diverse linguistic and cultural landscape. Ilokano, a Filipino language, and Samoan are among the leading languages spoken in the home. Other native languages of residents include Korean, Cantonese, Man-darin, Vietnamese, Tongan, Laotian, Spanish, and Thai. Recently, increasing im-migration from the Marshall Islands and Micronesia has resulted in immigrant native speakers of Marshallese, Yapese, Chuukese, Ponapean, and Kosraean.

---

[3]The indigenous population decreased drastically from 900,000 to 250,000 through the in-troduction of diseases carried by Caucasian sailors and missionaries in the late nineteenth century (Benham and Heck 1998).

[4]Pidgin is currently the native language of most Hawaii-born residents. Since residents use the term "Pidgin" for Hawaii Creole English (HCE), we will use Pidgin to mean HCE through-out this chapter. Cf. Jenkins (2003), especially comments on pidgins and creoles (6).

The 2000 U.S. Census reports that there are over 100 languages spoken in the home across a total Hawai'i population of less than 1.2 million. Thus, through a historical legacy of colonization and immigration, Hawai'i is now home to the indigenous Hawaiian language, the creole language HCE, known as Pidgin by the local population, and a vast range of immigrant languages.

Despite the linguistic and cultural diversity of the islands, U.S. mainstream norms have dominated language policies and schooling practices. Since the early 1900s, Americanization campaigns have resulted in the suppression of a multilingual press, the closure of heritage language schools, and ongoing attempts to eradicate HCE. English Standard Schools from the 1920s through the 1940s privileged speakers of mainstream U.S. English. This legacy of linguistic and economic privilege has continued in the form of private schools. Today, Hawai'i has the highest number of students (20 percent) who attend private school in the United States (Benham and Heck, 1998). In contrast, Hawai'i public schools have been charged in 1976, 1979, and 1999 for civil rights violations associated with neglecting the language and academic needs of immigrant students. These violations include the underidentification of language minorities, the lack of services for those who are identified, a disproportionate placement of language minorities in special education programs, inappropriate staffing of programs designed for language minority students, and improper mainstreaming procedures (Talmy 2002).

Department of Education (DOE) repression or neglect of multilingualism in Hawai'i has been exacerbated by increased use of standardized tests as a result of the No Child Left Behind (NCLB) legislation. These standardized tests fail to consider specific curricular needs in particular educational contexts serving diverse student populations (Cummins 1984; 1989; Neill and Medina 1989; Takala, Purves, and Buckmaster 1982; Valdes and Figueroa 1994).[5] In addition, NCLB supported programs such as the decontextualized Reading First literacy approach previously described have contributed to inadequate school progress for many minority youth (Coles 2003). At the local level,

[5]These programs have had devastating effects on schools in Hawaii. In the first statewide assessment of schools under the federal No Child Left Behind Act, 180 of 280 Hawaii public schools failed to meet academic standards for reading and math scores. At 46 schools, the state is considering federally recommended "major changes" that could include replacement of all or most of the staff, conversion to a charter school, and assigning school operations to a state or private organization (Hiller and Dayton 2003).

teachers and administrators often hold low expectations for academic achievement among economically disadvantaged students (Kadooka 2002). Reductive views of literacy and low expectations combine to produce an unfavorable environment for acquiring higher-level thinking skills, which, consequently, demotivates and isolates linguistic minorities while failing to adequately prepare them for higher education (Haycook 2001) . For example, Kadooka (2001), in her study of a Hawaiʻi public school program for low-income immigrants, found that these students spend much of their time doing busy work in the form of worksheets. Indeed, poor students are frequently academically underserved, often by limited educational practices with an emphasis on "low-level literacy and computational skills" which fail to adequately engage students intellectually (Moll 1994, 273).

The climate of high-stakes testing, decontextualized literacy instruction, and reduced academic expectations for many public school students in Hawaiʻi calls for alternative curricula geared to the unique and diverse needs of the multiethnic student population. In addition to a curricular approach which trusts students' academic capabilities, culturally appropriate literacy practices that reflect student diversity are clearly needed. As previously mentioned, in some respects, Hawaiʻi is poised to support alternative approaches to language and literacy development. Hawaiian language revitalization efforts since the mid-1970s have resulted in the establishment of K–12 immersion schools and university Hawaiian Language programs and Hawaiian Cultural Studies programs.[6] A strong literary movement in Pidgin (HCE) has transformed this language from one disdained to one with a place of acceptance within many classrooms and communities. The literary movement includes the production of the *Bamboo Ridge* journal devoted to Pidgin poetry and short stories; the production of plays in Pidgin that generally play to sell out audiences; and publication of books by local authors, some of whom (e.g., Lois-Ann Yamanaka) are experiencing national and international success. In addition, at least some educational administrators are aware of the special circumstances of educating immigrant and economically disadvantaged children. In response to low standardized test scores, the State Board of Education chairman cited an analysis of

[6]Over 2000 students in schools on all of the inhabited Hawaiian Islands are currently enrolled in the Kula Kaiapuni Immersion Schools. The Hawaiian Language program at the University of Hawaii serves primarily Hawaiian or part-Hawaiian students.

Hawai'i public school students that found 51 percent are "at risk" because they come from economically disadvantaged families, have limited English proficiency, or are special-education students (Hiller and Dayton 2003). The assistant superintendent for the Office of Curriculum, Instruction and Student Support indicated that the solution to low test scores was to "provide tremendous support for the schools rather than coming and hitting them over the head." These movements toward acknowledging diversity and seeking productive solutions to discriminatory federal policies have paved the way for increased appreciation for community languages, literacies, and cultures as resources in moving towards meeting the educational needs of immigrant and local populations. In the following section, we describe our efforts to participate in finding alternatives to restrictive legislation and educational practices.

A Critical Participatory Approach to Literacy Learning

The Studies of Heritage and Academic Languages and Literacies (SHALL) curriculum is being developed and implemented at the largest public high school in Hawai'i. In the school year 2000–2001, Filipinos and Samoans comprised 58.4 percent and 13.3 percent, respectively, of the high school student population (School Status and Improvement Report, Fall 2001). This school population represents the over-all predominance in the state of Ilokano-speaking Filipinos and an increasing Pacific Islander population and includes those who live in government-subsidized housing projects for the economically disadvantaged. Despite the school having a (most likely over-rated) reputation for violence and gangs (*Honolulu Advertiser*, Dec. 13, 2001), it enjoys an award-winning newspaper and more national award-wining artists than any other high school in Hawai'i.

The federally funded SHALL project[7] is directed by a University of Hawai'i faculty member in the Department of Second Language Studies who also directs the Center for Second Language Research (Kathryn A. Davis, co-author of this chapter) and employs a staff of experts in the areas of heritage language instruction (Julius Soria, Michelle Aquino, and Jacinta Galea'i), ESL/

---

[7]This project is supported by a Development and Implementation grant from the U.S. Department of Education, Office of English Language Acquisition.

academic English (Sarah Bazzi[8] and Gina Rupert), educational technology (Randy Gomabon), and assessment (Hye-sun Cho and Midori Ishida). The director worked with the principal, vice-principals, and key teachers at the school to incorporate SHALL courses into the pre-existing program.

From the beginning of the project in 2000 we were aware of what Cox and Robinson-Pant (this volume) describe as the ideological and institutional constraints which shape implementation of innovations. We felt that although a critical approach suggests involving in-service teachers from the start, previous research (e.g., Kadooka 2001; Talmy 2001) indicated that there could be struggles and tensions in the process of developing a project which challenged commonly accepted literacy curricula, time-honored pedagogical practices, and historically evolved attitudes towards language minority abilities and resources. Therefore, rather than engage in face-threatening encounters over conflicting ideologies, we chose a middle ground in which we develop and pilot courses; document the curriculum activities and outcomes through films, student products, and reports; and provide in-service courses which present the theories, practices, and products of the curriculum. As also indicated by many of the authors in this volume, we utilize this nonconfrontational approach in order to open dialogue with teachers and administrators and, thus, allow adaptation of modeled theories and practices rather than adoption of prescribed curriculum. Thus, it was arranged that SHALL instructors would develop and pilot curriculum which would then be shared with other high school teachers to use in ways that fit their particular needs and purposes.

Teachers in the SHALL program only teach one to two classes per semester to allow time for investigation of relevant literature; curriculum development based on cutting-edge theoretical perspectives; and ongoing program evaluation and curriculum revision. Block scheduling in which classes meet for ninety minutes per day five days per week allows time for creative project-oriented work. In addition, weekly meetings provide SHALL staff the opportunity for ongoing professional development, assessment, and alteration of curriculum and pedagogical practices to better meet student needs. We also engage in self-reflection and attempt to remediate ways in which we might "other" teachers, students, parents, and community members in the process of program implementation (Burke and Hermerschmidt, this volume; Fine et al. 2002).

[8]Sarah Bazzi, co-author of this chapter, has left the project to pursue a law degree.

The SHALL program is designed to meet the needs of Filipino and Samoan students by drawing on recent cross-disciplinary theoretical and ideological developments intended to redress inequitable schooling for linguistic minorities. First, we acknowledge heritage language and cultural resources through Ilokano for Filipinos and Samoan for Samoans language courses. These courses allow student exploration of multiple language and cultural identities while promoting linguistic proficiency. Second, we offer academic English courses to Filipino, Samoan, and Hawaiian students which are designed to help students develop an improved understanding of the social and educational expectations of teachers within classrooms and across disciplines. Third, in both the heritage and English language courses, students are provided with "third spaces" in which to negotiate or resist the hidden meanings of dominant discursive practices and knowledge frameworks. The importance of promoting critical literacy is also argued by Burke and Hermerschmidt (this volume), who suggest the need to move students from passive reading towards positioning themselves as readers, while Cox and Robinson-Pant (this volume) similarly suggest alternatives to school participation and literacy structures that marginalize some children. Hopson (this volume) additionally supports student self-determination of school literacy practices that have meaning for them inside and outside of classroom communities.

We see support for student-centered and critical heritage language/literacy and academic English literacy development as equally important in promoting positive self-esteem and achieving academic success. However, for the purposes of this chapter, we focus on academic English literacy courses that are designed to promote school achievement through community to school explorations of language and literacy discourses.

Community Language and Literacy Discourses

Recent literature on the identity of the learner (Canagarajah 1993; Norton 1997; Norton and Toohey 2000) views identities and contexts for learning as multiple and varied (Bourdieu 1991; Gee 1996; Wenger 1998). Such contexts extend beyond narrowly defined language and literacy skills to include the socially constructed values, understandings, and behaviors associated with language use. Wenger refers to these contexts as "communities of practice," which he defines as

A historical and social context that gives structure and meaning to what we do . . . it includes the language, tools, documents, images, symbols, well-defined roles, specified criteria, codified procedures . . . that various practices make explicit for a variety of purposes. But it also includes all the implicit relations, tacit conventions, subtle cues, untold rules of thumb, recognizable intuitions . . . and shared world views (1998, 47).

Communities of practice are similar to Gee's (1996) notion of Discourse, which he defines as "a sort of identity kit which comes complete with the appropriate costume and instructions on how to act, talk and often write, so as to take on a particular social role that others will recognize" (127). Gee further holds that individuals are socialized into a Primary Discourse while growing up within a particular linguistic and cultural community and then acquire Secondary Discourses outside the home and community such as schools and other institutions. Yet communities of practice theory (Wenger 1998) refutes the implication that Primary and Secondary Discourses are discrete, bounded, or static; rather, language, literacy, and cultural practices are dynamic, situated, and multifaceted (New London Group 1996; Street 1985; 1999; this volume).

In academic literacy courses at the high school, teachers began discussion of language, literacy, and identity by asking students to explore communities of practice within their own neighborhoods (also see Hopson, this volume). Students found that they commonly navigate multiple and complex identities in the predominately Filipino and Samoan neighborhood where they live. A constant influx of relatives from home countries provides a continuum of cross-generational linguistic abilities and cultural practices. Friendships and marriage across ethnic cultural communities; a unifying local language (Pidgin) and culture; (Local); and U.S. mainstream English and social influences insure a rich tapestry of language and culture which students explore in view of their own emerging cultural identities.

Students in the SHALL program commonly experience at least two Primary Discourses, one based on their heritage language and culture and the second involving the larger Hawai'i Creole English (Pidgin) local cultural community. However, in contrast to Gee's claims, multiple discourses are not always clearly demarcated. Students' spoken language often includes features of English, Pidgin, and one or more heritage languages, representing a mixture of discourses, or what is referred to as "hybridity" (Willett and Solskein 1999).

Egan-Roberston and Willett (1998) note that ". . . discourse shapes what we can think and say, and who we can be, as well as locates power in some places and instills control in others" (14). In classrooms, multiple discourses often intersect, yet the dominant discourse of the school tends to silence other practices. This silencing can create a language mismatch, which may exclude students weak in the dominant discourse or who feel participation in that discourse is threatening to their identity (Willet, Solsken, and Wilson-Keenan 1999; Burke and Hermerschmidt, this volume). To avoid the negative effects of silencing, academic English teachers worked towards creating a third space (Bhaba 1994), where students' primary and hybrid language practices were viewed as "an inherent feature of negotiation across differences," within the academic discourse of the classroom (see Low, this volume). This third space provided opportunities for "disrupting" the dominant classroom discourse and creating room for new and more inclusive discourses (Willet, Solsken, and Wilson-Keenan 1999, 168; Burke and Hermerschmidt, this volume).

Through third-space activities, students explored the features, perceptions, and roles of English, Hawai'i Creole English, Ilokano, Samoan, and other languages spoken in the community. While recognizing the need for developing academic literacy skills, teachers began exploration of multiple linguistic codes with students by providing pamphlets on the myths and realities of bilingualism written in Ilokano and Samoan (Hawai'i Council on Language Planning and Policy 1993; PREL 1995). Many students had never seen print media in their first language and were excited about reading bilingual materials and readily explored their own language use in written reflections. Students also read a local author's poem about her name and responded with a poem about the origins of their own names. One student wrote:

> Justin is my everyday name,
> Given to me by my mother,
> The best name in the world,
> It fits me.
>
> Taouli is my Samoan name,
> I got that name from my dad,
> All my pride is in that name,
> It is my Samoan heritage,
> It is my strength.

The author of the above poem, who has a Filipino surname and appearance, was able to reveal pride in the part of his identity not outwardly visible through claiming his Samoan name. Thus, affirming multiple identities allows students to claim selves that have been intentionally or unintentionally hidden.

Students often completed their multilingual assignments with the help of family members or friends. Through drawing on community language and culture capital, students began to value bilingualism as a resource rather than consider it a problem for them and their parents to overcome. Students were also encouraged to appreciate multilingualism through sharing texts that were important to them in languages other than HCE or their home language, such as the Philippines' Tagalog national anthem or a Hawaiian text advocating sovereignty. Students taking Japanese or Spanish classes enthusiastically included their developing language abilities into discussions and course assignments.[9]

Although students spoke a number of different heritage and foreign languages, Pidgin often served as a common language both in and outside the classroom. Teachers urged students to explore the historical roots of Pidgin by reading about and discussing the conditions that necessitated Pidgin and allowed it to develop into a fully formed language. They looked at Pidgin as a language in the linguistic sense, discussing syntax and lexicon, and conducted literature analyses as well that involved examining the social and political aspects of Pidgin literature such as audience (e.g., local, mainstream) and purpose (e.g., political statement, entertainment). For example, students critically analyzed literature about Hawai`i written by outsiders, such as *Hotel Honolulu* by Paul Theroux, in which Pidgin is compared to "birds squawking" (13). Reading and studying local literature had the additional effect of helping some students adopt a previously rejected identity of "reader." An academic English teacher described one such transformation as follows:

> Up until today I would have characterized Bruce as a reluctant reader. But now, Bruce thumbs through the Pidgin short story book *Da Word* by Lee

[9]One possible problem with student-produced heritage language work is that it may be difficult for teachers who do not speak the language to assess. However, students realized the importance of audience and translated their multilingual work for teachers. Additionally, teachers worked closely with the Ilokano and Samoan teachers, who not only helped with the linguistic aspects of the heritage languages but also provided assistance in interpreting cultural aspects of heritage discourses, such as the strategic use of silence in class to express anger.

Tonouchi, the proclaimed "Pidgin Guerilla." I am so pleased I try to ignore him sneakily reading it under the table after reading time. At the end of the class, eyes wide open, he proclaims, "Miss, I can read *this*. It's in *my* language!"

Given Fairclough's (1992) observation that schools operate under a hegemonic 'appropriacy' model that "uses the educational system to transmit shared language values (if not practices) based around the hegemony of a particular dialect" (43), teachers asked students to describe the observable and desirable usage of Pidgin in different contexts. Students discussed how, despite Pidgin's unifying effect within the local community, the use of the language in the classroom has often been forbidden and is still commonly frowned upon. In the process of examining anti-Pidgin school discourse, students read a poem called "If you talk Pidgin, you no can . . ." written by Lee Tonouchi[10] in collaboration with his students at Kapiloani Community College who compiled a list of all the things people had told them they could not do with Pidgin. Our high school students countered by writing poems entitled "If you talk Pidgin, you can . . ." One student wrote the following poem:

> Dey say if you talk pidgin you can . . .
> Communicate with other pidgin speakers
> Blend in with the locals
> Bad talk people that no understand pidgin
>
> Dey say if you talk pidgin you can . . .
> Go get kama'aina[11] rate
> Go swap meet and get discount
> Go Waikiki malls and fit in
> Go into Gucci and NOT be expected to buy anything!
>
> Dey say if you talk pidgin . . .
> YOU LOCAL!!!

Through drawing on the unifying influence of "being local" within the diverse Hawai`i society, this poem turns negative stereotypes of Pidgin speakers into

---

[10]Tonouchi is a local author who strives to alter the notion of language appropriateness by using Pidgin for most oral and literacy purposes, including a resume that gained him a job in higher education.

[11]A kama'aina (literally people of the land) rate refers to a discounted price that Hawaii residents receive on some products, services, and amenities.

positive features. Although the pervasive belief that Pidgin is unsuitable for most academic and institutional contexts means that it is seen as an obstacle to overcome, the writer reclaims power by suggesting using Pidgin to "bad talk" people who don't understand Pidgin, including outsiders who criticize it. Another stereotype about people who speak nonstandard English is that they are economically disadvantaged. However, the author uses this stereotype as an advantage; it allows her to go into Gucci without the expectation of buying anything and she can get a good deal at the already discounted swap meet, a biweekly market at the stadium that sells locally produced items such as clothing, snacks, and music. Thus, this poem exemplifies a sense of ownership and pride in a Pidgin identity as it critiques negative stereotypes about Pidgin speakers.

The exploration of community practices not only aids students in considering a possible hybrid cultural and language identity, but it can also contribute to parent and teacher valuing of students' ability to draw on a repertoire of cultural and linguistic knowledge for appropriate language use in particular interactional situations. Through community explorations, students begin to develop metalinguistic and metacognitive awareness of how language is structured and used, which they then can transfer to understanding school communities of practice.

Academic Language and Literacy Discourses

Our conceptualization of a multilingual, multicultural, and hybrid approach to language instruction did not ignore the necessity of teaching the Discourse of power to students from nonmainstream language, dialect, and cultural backgrounds (Delpit 1998). For this reason, as previously mentioned, the academic English classes were also designed to expose students to academic discourses and apprentice them into an academic community of practice. By academic discourses, we refer to the practices and skills necessary for students to succeed in mainstream U.S. academic contexts (see Burke and Hermerschmidt, this volume). Although instructors stressed the link between classroom assignments and the skills needed for college, they also encouraged students not currently interested in college to develop abilities that would give them the option of higher education, help them perform future job-related literacy tasks, and become critical and informed citizens.

Many of the students we work with have not been provided with an understanding of "how to do school" in the United States. Students utilize the metacognitive awareness developed through community explorations of language use to gain explicit knowledge of how school tasks are performed. To enhance academic metacognitive abilities, we draw from the work of Bourdieu (1991), Gee (1996), Wenger (1998), and Wertsch (1991) on a process approach to teaching and learning. Churchill (unpublished manuscript, 2003) describes a process approach as an apprenticeship. This apprenticeship involves acquiring strategies, learning processes, study skills, and other mechanisms that enhance learners' ability to teach themselves outside of the context of the classroom. Yet, rather than "passively awaiting the incorporation of the newcomer (apprentice), the community of practice strongly suggests trajectories of participation and exclusion" (Churchill, 13; Wenger 1998).

Our curricular purpose is to apprentice students to the discourses of schooling through providing opportunities for "trajectories of participation." While acknowledging students' rich repertoires of cultural and linguistic abilities, instructors provide the infrastructure for linguistic and ethnographic analyses of expectations for school practices. Students utilize student-as-ethnographer strategies of observing classroom interaction and collecting classroom documents to determine both oral and literacy expectations in school communities of practice. Through careful analyses of reading material and writing assignments, students begin to "notice," and thus have the capacity to reproduce, teacher expectations for classroom behavior and written work. Yet our curriculum rejects a purely "apprenticeship to" or "socialization into" the school community of practice. Rather, a central component of SHALL is critical analysis of texts and practices to provide students with a voice in their own schooling. These linguistic and critical analyses of text are based on McComiskey's (2000) position that successful language and literacy learning involves focusing on three interrelated levels of analysis: textual, rhetorical, and discursive. The following descriptions detail activities and outcomes of our student-as-researcher approach to developing academic English abilities at the textual, rhetorical, and discursive levels of analysis.

TEXTUAL ANALYSIS

The textual aspects of academic English were explored through a process approach to writing which allowed development of metaknowledge of the grammatical and stylistic features which would lead to cognitively complex writing.

As McComiskey (2000) notes, a process approach to writing is messy. Composition courses often view learning to write as a linear process, moving smoothly from prewriting to final draft. However, the reality is that revision is a continual, iterative, and interactive process. The teachers constantly engaged student-produced texts, challenging authors to elaborate ideas, commenting on interesting parts of their writing, and sharing their own writing anecdotes. Many students were not accustomed to this type of dialogue. At the beginning, a few students responded to marks on the paper as "corrections" and thought that they had done poorly. In most cases this was resolved by explanation and careful collaborative reading of comments. Other students said they enjoyed comments and felt like they were "having a conversation" with the teacher, remarking that they had never experienced so much feedback.[12] Through this interactive writing process approach, teachers found that students had a wide range of writing abilities, including those who had little experience with Standard American English; those who had a difficult time conceptualizing the nuances of formal versus informal language; and those who had highly developed Academic English skills and needed to refine them. One way instructors attended to the disparate levels of academic discourses in the class was by conducting miniconferences with individual students. Teachers also created grammar exercises as problem areas emerged in student writing and provided spontaneous grammar lessons during individual consultations as well.

Students also engaged in textual analysis through an oral history assignment in which they were asked to use their heritage language and/or Pidgin to interview a family or community member. Students were then asked to translate the interview into academic English and conduct analyses of the syntactic, phonological, and lexical similarities and differences between their heritage language and English. This and other comparison and contrast assignments helped students develop metalinguistic awareness as well as promoted new or enhanced multilingual literacy practices. For example, students utilized hybrid practices, such as code-switching, when producing different genres of writing. A student wrote the following note to a friend:[13]

[12]One of the benefits of coteaching and block scheduling was we had only 45 papers to comment on. It would be difficult for a teacher with 100 or more students to comment on papers at this level, as we had to work overtime to comment on half that. One solution could be giving extensive feedback on select assignments or rotating which class received this feedback.

[13]T = Tagalog, E = English.

(T) Kumusta ka na? Sana (E) ok (T) ka lang. . . . Wala akong magawa. . . .
Ginawa mo na ba yung (E) assignment (T) mo?

So, how are you? Hope you're doing fine. . . . I'm not doing anything. . . .
Did you do your homework?"

In discussing this note with academic English teachers, the student explored
the lexical features of the two languages as well as rhetorical features such as audience and purpose. She additionally noted the complexity of language evolution and use in remarking on the use of the loan word "assignment" which
translated into "homework" in English.

Through textual analyses, students developed metalinguistic awareness, or
the ability to see grammatical and stylistic features of written work, and then
use this awareness in creating increasingly complex school, home, community,
and personal texts.

RHETORICAL ANALYSIS

At the rhetorical level of analysis students focused on gaining an understanding of diverse literacy practices by beginning with those they encounter in their
everyday lives (see also Burke and Hermerschmidt, this volume; Hopson, this
volume). They brought in home and school writing samples which they then
analyzed in terms of the structure of texts, noticing the different organizational
patterns in various genres such as letters from the Philippines and science lab
reports. They also examined visual cues such as the use of art work in newspaper advertisements and paintings or photos in history books. Teachers differentiated between the intended audience and the actual audience and discussed
how differences could shape text and change interpretations. Part of the rhetorical analyses also involved a discursive critique of academic English use in terms
of how they might perceive it as a threat to their identities as well as an in-
comprehensible enterprise they had little or no access to. The instructors illustrated how students already had a mastery of several types of English genres by
using an adaptation of Peter Elbow's (1994) voices activity (see also Elbow
2000). The instructor dramatically performed three ways of describing the
same event: stream of consciousness writing, an e-mail message to a friend, and
an essay to a teacher. She then talked students through the differences in content, form, and audience before asking them to write their own three-voices
narratives. Students were able to manipulate genres to varying degrees. While a

few students needed additional instruction, others showed a sophisticated understanding of voice and content. For example, one student bemoaned helping her parents move to another home in an email message to a friend, but wrote a more balanced school essay account which examined the rewards and hardships of moving and concluded with the roles various family members play in joint tasks within the community.

DISCURSIVE ANALYSIS

McComiskey (2000) observes that although the discursive level of evaluation is the most important for understanding the nature and effects of dominant discourse practices, it is the one most undertaught. In our academic English courses, students critiqued institutional, economic, and cultural factors that shape texts to understand the position of the writer and reader in their micro- and macro-environments (see Burke and Hermerschmidt, this volume). Students were encouraged not to see themselves as passive receptacles of information; instead, they interacted with texts, talking back to them as they developed their own stances and opinions. For example, Samoan students read an early (nineteenth century) missionary account of Samoa which suggests that people from this culture are lazy and ignorant. Students used their own experiences and research to counter this racist ideology. Thus, "talking back to the text" encourages student ownership of the text, validates the prior knowledge they bring with them into the classroom, and finally helps them to conceptualize the text writer as subjective rather than the speaker of absolute truths. In this way, students may begin to see how institutions, cultural values, social values, and individual standpoints may constitute the writer, and how students' differing subjectivities may contribute to either passive acceptance of or resistance to the texts they are subjected to (see also Street 2003; Cox and Robinson, this volume). This type of critical, in-depth response also paved the way for learning how to engage in various genres of school writing such as argumentative, comparison and contrast, and position essays.

Technology and Alternative Assessment

The SHALL academic English curriculum includes assessment procedures that reflect our process and discursive orientations. An electronic portfolio project was interwoven throughout the academic literacy courses. This project was designed to help students develop technological skills while documenting their academic progress. The computer lab, which met once a week, was taught by a technology expert (Randy Gomabon) and assisted by an electronic portfolio assessment specialist (Hye-sun Cho, co-author of this chapter). The SHALL instructors worked closely with the technology experts to integrate the curricula of the two courses and utilize assessment procedures to both improve the SHALL courses and allow students to reflect on their progress.

The electronic portfolio differs from its paper counterpart primarily in that portfolio materials are created and stored in a digitized form, such as on a CD-ROM or on a computer network (Hawisher and Selfe 1997). It utilizes electronic technologies that allow the portfolio developer to collect and organize portfolio artifacts in many media types, including audio, video, graphics, and text. However, an electronic portfolio is not a random collection of digitized artifacts; rather, it is a purposeful and reflective tool that demonstrates growth over time (Barrett 2000). In other words, what differentiates an electronic portfolio from a digital scrapbook is the organization of the portfolio around a set of learning goals, in addition to learner reflections and rationale for selecting specific artifacts (Barrett 2000).

Through developing individual electronic portfolios of their work, students learn sophisticated technological applications such as Power Point and I-movie; reflect on their own literacy progress; and engage in critical analyses of school and society. By incorporating both portfolio assessment and electronic technologies, students were able to use electronic media as a way to craft multiple identities and literacies. In other words, electronic portfolio assessment promoted SHALL's overall goals for expanding the notion of literacy (Blair and Takayoshi 1997) and recognizing new ways of capturing the complex ways people read, write, and understand text, including media technology (Flood, Lapp, and Bayles-Martin 2000). For example, teachers use videos in helping students analyze visual representations. The electronic portfolios are also tools for students to accommodate their technological literacy products and expand their knowledge of the rhetoric of electronic environments. In addition, the self-conscious and reflective nature of design in Electronic Portfolio Assessment (EPA) makes a technology-rich context an ideal third space for heritage students who can bring their linguistic and cultural heritage resources to the computer lab, thereby formulating their multiple identities and developing multiple literacies.

The development of multiple literacies in the dominant language, including electronic literacy[14] in today's technology-driven society, is an opportunity for gaining access to Secondary Discourses (Gee 1996), which leads to successful meaning-making across a constellation of expressions, actions, objects, technologies, and other people (Gee 1996, 183). Electronic Portfolio Assessment allows students to juxtapose diverse Discourses so that they can understand them at a metalevel through reflection and dialogue. Equally important is the formative evaluation of EPA that allows teachers to improve curriculum and pedagogical practices on an ongoing basis so as to best meet student needs.

In sum, EPA attempts to better address assessment than standardized tests and other forms of traditional literacy testing, such as multiple-choice tests for reading comprehension and one-off writing tests with prompts. Because of the nature of portfolios as collection devices that contain multiple pieces of student work (including computer lab projects), EPA also offers better validity than other formal assessment procedures. For example, traditional, single-sample approaches to assessing writing do not provide information about the scope of a student's ability to write for different kinds of readers using different kinds of genres. Electronic portfolios, on the other hand, invite students to observe how performance varies from occasion to occasion, how particular strategies and techniques can be adapted for different situations, and how language use varies across genre, audience, and purpose. Consequently, EPA can claim greater validity than essay tests because multiple approaches to multiple literacies development is always more valid than a single measurement.

The motivational impact of utilizing technology in the classroom also has been recognized by a number of researchers (e.g., Becker 2002; Sandholtz, Ringstaff, and Dwyer 1997). Having students construct multimedia presentations enhances their desire to learn and provides them with a sense of responsibility over their projects (Becker 2002). Moreover, students who develop multimedia presentations for outside audiences are rarely satisfied with their

[14]Electronic literacy refers to "a complex set of socially and culturally situated values, practices, and skills involved in operating linguistically within the context of electronic environments, including reading, writing, and communicating" (Selfe 1999, 11). The term further refers to the linking of technology and literacy at fundamental levels of both conception and social practice. In this context, electronic literacy refers to social and cultural contexts for discourse and communication, as well as the social and linguistic products and practices of communication and the ways in which electronic communication environments have become essential parts of our cultural understanding of what it means to be literate (Selfe 1999).

initial designs (see Hawisher and Selfe 1997) and, consequently, they readily engage in a process of reflection and revision that deepens their understanding of curriculum content.

Conclusions

Through engaging in a critical literacy approach to education for linguistic minorities in a public high school in Hawai`i, we discovered that it is possible to promote the classroom as a site of relevance and interest; challenge dehumanizing school actions; and provide opportunities for students to explore identity and exercise power. We offer alternative curricula and pedagogical methods while recognizing the current school structures and demands students and teachers operate under. For example, since standardized tests are administered in schools and expected for application to universities, we coordinated efforts with a federally funded project, GEAR-UP, to provide after-school and weekend training in taking these tests. This training allows students to achieve satisfactory scores to get into university and supports federal expectations for school-wide performance. Yet we also contest assessment procedures based on standardized tests and other narrowly defined forms of evaluation that have failed to capture the complex and multifaceted nature of literacy development. As an alternative to tests that misdiagnose students, we use assessment procedures that enhance student learning and provide information for the ongoing improvement of curriculum and pedagogical strategies.

The SHALL curriculum also refutes damaging approaches to serving linguistic minority students, including those involving decreased expectations for academic success and school work representing low cognitive demands that fail to challenge students or allow them to acquire higher-order thinking skills. Rather than hold minimal expectations and employ rote memorization practices commonly found in low-income schools (Moll 1994), we assume elevated levels of student achievement and provide for use of higher-order cognitive skills through project-centered work (Moll 1994). The community and school research projects allow students to develop a flexible strategy repertoire that enables them to plan, monitor, and evaluate their own learning (Garner 1987).

Teachers and administrators in the high school where the SHALL project is located have recognized the beneficial effects of our alternative approaches to literacy and academic development. We are increasingly hearing from teachers that "students who attend SHALL courses are different" in that they are engaged in their own learning and able to navigate school expectations for academic performance while asking questions about those expectations. In addition, of the 90 students served by the project, 78 percent were on the honor roll and 84 percent achieved perfect attendance. These figures contrast sharply with a comparable student population that achieved only 34 percent honor roll recognition and 43 percent perfect attendance. This acknowledgement of the value of the SHALL program augers well for expanding the use of a critical literacy approach to other classrooms. To facilitate capacity-building, we document curriculum activities and outcomes through films, student products, and reports as well as provide in-service training courses for teachers which present the theories, practices, and products of the curriculum. We intend that this approach to information dissemination will open dialogue with teachers and administrators and, thus, allow for a critical academic language and literacy approach to evolve through our ongoing presence at the school, informal in-service courses, publications, presentations, and workshops. Through teacher workshops and parent nights in which students share their learning experiences, portfolios, and other course products, schools and communities have begun to share the belief that students from disadvantaged backgrounds can excel academically while maintaining a richly diverse cultural heritage.

Although this project takes place at a particular sociocultural site under policies and practices current in the United States, the conditions of inappropriate assessment procedures, low expectations for academic success, and school work that fails to challenge students are common for the linguistically and economically disadvantaged across geographic and cultural environments. Thus, the theoretical principles and classroom practices described here promise to lead to the transformation of policies and practices in the United States and beyond from those that harm or ignore to those that actively aid immigrants and other disenfranchised groups.

References

Barrett, H. 2000. Create your own electronic portfolio. *Learning & Leading with Technology* 27(7): 14–21.

Barton, D., Hamilton, M., and Ivani, R. eds. 2000. *Situated literacies: Reading and writing in context.* London: Routledge.

Becker, M. 2002. *What is all this talk about digital portfolios?* Tahlequah: Center for Teaching & Learning.

Benham, M.K., and Heck, R.H. 1998. *Culture and educational policy in Hawai`i: The silencing of native voices.* Mahwah: Erlbaum.

Bhabha, H.K. 1994. *The location of culture.* New York: Routledge.

Blair, K.L., and Takayoshi, P. 1997. Reflections on reading and evaluating electronic portfolios. In K.B. Yancey, and T. Weiser (eds.), *Situating portfolios: Four perspectives.* Logan: Utah State University Press, pp. 357–369.

Bourdieu, P. 1991. *Language and symbolic power.* Cambridge: Polity Press.

Canagarajah, A.S. 1993. Critical ethnography of a Sri Lankan classroom: Ambiguities in student opposition to reproduction through ESOL. *TESOL Quarterly* 27(4): 601–626.

Churchill, E. 2003. *Construction of language learning opportunities for Japanese high school learners of English in a short term study abroad program.* PhD dissertation, Temple University, Philadelphia.

Coles, G. 2003. Learning to read and the 'W Principle'. *Rethinking Schools* 17(4): 1.

Crawford, J. 2004. *Educating English learners: Language diversity in the classroom.* Los Angeles: Bilingual Educational Services, Inc.

Cummins, J. 1989. *Empowering minority students.* Sacramento: California Association for Bilingual Education.

Cummins, J. 1984. *Bilingualism and special education: Issues in assessment and pedagogy.* Clevedon: Multilingual Matters.

Delpit, L. 1998a. The silenced dialogue: power and pedagogy in educating other people's children. *Harvard Educational Review* 58(3): 280–298.

Delpit, L. 1998b. The politics of teaching literate discourse. In: V. Zamel and R. Spack (eds.), *Negotiating academic literacies: Teaching and learning across languages and cultures.* Mahwah: Lawrence Erlbaum Associates, pp. 207–218.

Egan-Robertson, A. 1998. "We must ask our questions and tell our stories": Writing ethnography and constructing personhood. In: A. Egan-Robertson and D. Bloome (eds.), *Students as researchers of culture and language in their own communities.* Cresskill: Hampton Press Inc., pp. 261–284.

Egan-Robertson, A. and Willett, J. 1998. Students as ethnographers, thinking and doing ethnography a bibliographic essay. In: A. Egan-Robertson and D. Bloome (eds.), Cresskill: Hampton Press Inc., pp. 1–32.

Elbow, P. 1994. *Writing for Learning, Not Just for Demonstrating Learning.* University of Massachusetts Amherst.

Elbow, Peter 2000. *Everyone can write: Essays toward a hopeful theory of writing and teaching writing.* Oxford: Oxford University Press.

Fairclough, N. 1992. The appropriacy of 'appropriateness'. In: N. Fairclough (ed.), *Critical language awareness.* London: Longman, pp. 33–56.

Fine, M., Weis, L., Weseen, S., and Wong, L. 2000. For whom? Qualitative research, representations, and social responsibilities. In: N.K. Denzin and Y.S. Lincoln (eds.), *Handbook of Qualitative Research.* Thousand Oaks: Sage Publishers, Inc., pp. 107–131.

Flood, J., Lapp, D., and Bayles-Martin, D. 2000. Vision possible: The role of visual media in literacy education. In: M.A. Gallego and S. Hollingstorth (eds.), *What counts as literacy.* New York: Teachers College Press, pp. 62–84.

Freire, P. 1970. *Pedagogy of the oppressed.* Translated by Myra Bergman Roamos. New York: Seabury Press.

Garner, R. 1987. *Metacognition and reading comprehension.* Cognition and Literacy Series. Norwood: Ablex.

Gee, J.P. 1996. *Social linguistics and literacies: Ideology in discourses.* Philadelphia: Falmer Press.

Gee, J.P. 2000a. The new literacy studies: From 'socially situated' to the work of the social. In: D. Barton, M. Hamilton, and R. Ivanic (eds.), *Situated literacies: Reading and writing in context.* New York: Routledge, pp. 180–196.

Gee, J.P. 2000b. New people in new worlds: Networks, the new capitalism and schools. In: B. Cope and M. Kalantzis (eds.), *Multiliteracies: Literacy learning and the design of social futures.* New York: Routledge, pp. 43–68.

Gee, J.P. 2000c. Teenagers in new times: A new literacy studies perspective. *Journal of Adolescent and Adult Literacy* 43(5): 412–420.

Hawai'i Council on Language Planning and Policy. May 1997. *Common myths about bilingualism.* Honolulu: Center for Second Language Research, University of Hawaii-Manoa.

Hawai'i Department of Education. Fall 2001. *School Status & Improvement Report.*

Hawisher, G.E., and Selfe, C.L. 1997. Wedding the technologies of writing portfolios and computers. In: K.B. Yancey and T. Weiser (eds.), *Situating portfolios: Four perspectives.* Logan: Utah State University Press, pp. 305–321.

Heath, S.B. 1983. *Ways with words: Language, life, and work in communities and classrooms.* New York: Cambridge University Press.

Hiller, Jennifer and Dayton, Kevin. 64% of schools fail under No Child Left Behind Act: How Hawai'i schools performed. *The Honolulu Advertiser,* September 19, 2003.

Hiller, Jennifer. Our Schools *The Honolulu Advertiser,* December 13, 2001.

Hull, G., and Schultz, K. (Eds.). 2002. *School's out: Bridging out-of-school literacies with classroom practice.* New York: Teachers College Press, pp. 11–31.

Jenkins, J. 2003. *World englishes.* London: Routledge.

Kadooka, J. 2002. ESL: *"A different kind of academics": An ethnographic study of a public high school ESLL program in Hawai'i.* Unpublished manuscript. University of Hawai'i at Manoa.

Luke, A. 1999. Critical discourse analysis. In: J.P. Keeves and G. Lakomski (eds.), *Issues in Educational Research.* Amsterdam: Paragamon, pp. 161–173.

Maybin, J. 2000. The new literacy studies: Context, intertextuality and discourse. In: D. Barton, M. Hamilton, and R. Ivanic (eds.), *Situated literacies: Reading and writing in context.* New York: Routledge, pp. 197–209.

McComiskey, B. 2000. *Teaching composition as a social process.* Utah: Utah State University Press.

Neill, D.M., and Medina, N.J. 1989. Standardized testing: Harmful to educational health. *Phi Delta Kappan* 70: 688–697.

New London Group. A pedagogy of multiliteracies: Designing social futures. *Harvard Educational Review* 66(1): 60–92.

North Central Regional educational Laboratory. 1994. Funds of knowledge: A look at Luis Moll's research into hidden family resources. *CITYSCHOOLS* 1(1): 19–21.

Norton, B. 1997. Language, identity, and the ownership of English. *TESOL Quarterly* 31: 409–430.

Norton, B., and Toohey, K. 2002. Identity and language learning. In: R.B. Kaplan (ed.), *Oxford Handbook of Applied Linguistics.* Oxford: Oxford University Press, pp. 115–123.

Pease-Alvarez, L., and Schecter, S.R. (eds.) In press. *Learning, teaching, and community.* Mahway: Lawrence Erlbaum.

PREL. 1996. *A conversation with parents about language.* Honolulu: Pacific Resources for Education and Learning.

Rethinking Schoools. 2001. Where I'm From. *Rethinking our schools: Teaching for equity and justice*. Milwaukee: Rethinking Schools, Ltd., 12(2): 22–23.

Richardson, P. 1998. Literacy, learning and teaching. *Educational Review* 50(2): 115–134.

Sandholtz, J., Ringstaff, C., and Dwyer, D. 1997. *Teaching with technology: Creating student-centered classrooms*. New York: Teachers College Press.

Sato, C. 1991. Sociolinguistic variation and language attitudes in Hawai`i. In: J. Chesire (ed.), *English around the world: Sociolinguistic perspectives*. Cambridge: Cambridge University Press, pp. 647–663.

Selfe, C.L. 1999. *Technology and literacy in the twenty-first century. The importance of paying attention*. Urbana: NCTE Press.

Street, B. 1993. The new literacy studies, guest editorial. *Journal of Research in Reading* 16(2): 81–97.

Street, B. 1995. *Social literacies: Critical approaches to literacy in development, ethnography and education*. New York: Longman.

Street, B. 1997. The implications of the 'New Language, Literacy and the Curriculum' for literacy education. *English in Education*. 31(3): 45–59.

Street, B. 2003. What's new in NLS? Critical approaches to literacy in theory and practice. *Current Issues in Comparative Education*, Summer 2003.

Swope, K., and Miner, B. 2000. Standardized tests: Common questions. In: K. Swope and B. Miner (eds.), *Failing our kids: Why the testing craze won't fix our schools*. Milwaukee: *Rethinking Schools Ltd.*, pp. 10–12.

Talmy, S. 2001. Historical and political contexts for educational transformation. Washington D.C.: American Anthropological Association Conference Presentation.

Theroux, P. 2001. *Hotel Honolulu*. New York: Houghton Mifflin.

Tonouchi, L. 2002. Dey say if you talk Pidgin you no can . . . *Bamboo Ridge 81*.

Valdés, G., and Figueroa, R.A. 1994. *Bilingualism and testing: A special case of bias*. Norwood: Ablex Publishing.

Wenger, E. 1998. *Learning, meaning and identity*. New York: Cambridge University Press.

Wertsch, J. 1991. *Voices of the mind: A sociocultural approach to mediated action*. Cambridge: Harvard University Press.

Willet, J., Solsken, J., and Wilson-Keenan, J. 1999. The (im)possibilities of constructing multicultural language practices in research and pedagogy. *Linguistics and Education* 10(2): 165–218.

11

Project Freire
Saturday Literacy Academies
Recreating Freire
for High School Students in Brooklyn

Maryann Cucchiara

Literacy makes sense . . . as the consequence of men's beginning to reflect about their own capacity for reflection, about the world, about their position in the world, about their work, about their power to transform the world, about the encounter of consciousness-about literacy itself which thereby ceases to be something external and becomes a part of them, comes as a creation from within them. (Freire/Macedo 1987)

Introduction

No theoretical framework, no pedagogical lens could broaden capacity for reflection about this five year "out-of-school" journey than that of the New Literacy Studies. As I reflect and attempt to make sense, "read the world" of this encounter, this critical engagement with curriculum and pedagogy, I hope to move beyond "the words," the description of the theoretical underpinnings and intersections between Freirean principles and the New Literacy approach. I hope to move to a "rereading" of this world, to an understanding of how this type of literacy intervention broadened educational questions about the teaching and learning of literacy across contexts and the implications of this "out-of-school" journey as it relates to school-based curriculum and assessment.

The "Encounter of Consciousness": The Birth of the Project Freire Saturday Literacy Academies

I had been working as a New York City public school teacher for over fifteen years mostly with immigrant and/or African-American students with varied backgrounds and across multiple languages and dialects. As a teacher and certainly as a coordinator and director of many of the adolescent language and literacy programs in the Brooklyn High School Superintendency, I was painfully aware of the nature of schooling for many students and witnessed the "savage inequalities" which Kozol had described in his 1991 expose on "children in America." Some were blatant and others more subtle, but whatever the evidence, the message remained clear: The public school system was working for some, not all. What I came to recognize along with a core group of educators was a painful but realistic truth about the largest public school system in our nation: The system was working for some, but too many were slipping through the cracks.

In many ways the birth of the Project Freire Saturday Literacy Academies is due to Leonard, a Haitian student of mine who had immigrated to Brooklyn some three years before he was my 10th grade ESL student. I will never forget his words to me as he caught site of a novel by Haitian author Jacques Roumain, *Gouverneurs de la Rosee*. He scanned the book lying on my desk and asked why I was reading it. I told him it was a book required by my college professor and that I was deeply interested in learning about the language and culture of his people/country. "Maybe you can help me with the Haitian?" I asked him. Without hesitation, suddenly and abruptly, he closed the book and returned it to my desk. "Don't read this. We have no culture" was his sobering reply. Enough of a reply for me to reflect , enough of an encounter to begin to make sense of all that I had been experiencing, the explicit and implicit messages that had driven this young man to view his language and his culture as empty and moreover which held no promise.

Fortunately, at the same time of this encounter, I was steeped in my own graduate work in the field of language and literacy and, in particular, immersed in the study of the principles of the New Literacy Studies. My question became more focused on the impact of this deficit mode on Leonard, knowing full well the intersection of language, literacy, identity, and power. If Leonard could not see himself in this Haitian novel, with his people, his language, his culture, then what chance would he have here in New York City to see himself in this strange American curriculum? Without any chance to see the value of himself, his culture, his language, how could Leonard possibly envision himself as part of the "cultural complex of a nation"? As my questions became part of a larger inquiry of a core group of fellow secondary educators, an alternative vision of schooling and in particular of literacy was beginning to emerge along with a strong pull towards Paolo Freire and his literacy work with the oppressed. His tenets seem to become clearer as similar generative words emerged from this one encounter—knowledge, access, power, and freedom.

The Context: An Academically and Politically Charged Arena

The Project Freire Saturday Literacy Academies grew out of funding created as the result of the 1996 New York City's Board of Education Chancellor's Adolescent Task Force. As in 1988, the '96 Task Force found similar results when surveying entering 9th graders and their reading achievement. Significant numbers, in some schools as many as 90 percent of their entering freshman, were entering school reading in the lowest quartile as measured by a variety of standardized reading tests. In addition, the report of the task force surveys identified that the poorest of readers were indeed "concentrated in specific ethnic and socioeconomic groups" (Gee 1991). The New York City public school data certainly mirrored the national school reports. Articles about this "quiet crisis" and as well as the "benign neglect" (Vacca 1995) of adolescent literacy studies begin to appear. In addition to the significant and growing numbers of entering 9th graders falling into this lowest quartile, there was a direct relationship between high percentages of struggling readers and underperforming "schools in need of improvement" with large numbers of uncertified and transient teachers. It was obvious to the emerging Freire group that a "culture of inequality" had emerged and that the "reading crisis" was an outgrowth of this school culture. Surveys did reflect the existence of many literacy programs, but all seemed to be isolated, and in the climate of anti–"whole language," an overwhelming majority of them were skills and phonics based.

Opposing views as to why 'Johnny can't read' were routinely seen in the educational columns of the *New York Times* with educators taking a stance each September as school began in the city accompanied by school report cards detailing the disaster . The two sides were drawn with "analysis on one side and facts on the other" (Gardner and Hirsch 1999) and teachers felt more and more compelled to take sides in an either or manner. Meanwhile, the case of adolescents who can't read, was becoming more significant and harder to ignore.

There was also a charged atmosphere in New York State around speakers of other Englishes. As schools opened in September 1997, the fight over the recognition and/or use of Caribbean Englishes as a potential bilingual model, became heated. As a 1997 New York State initiative called for a recognition of the varieties of Englishes spoken in New York City by the growing Caribbean population (New York State Department of Education 1997), opposition to "First Teach Them English" (Ravitch 1997) was mounting. Since a growing number of our Project Freire students were coming from the "English-speaking" Caribbean, issues around the use of vernacular and its relationship to literacy remained central to our work.

At the same time, New York State was beginning to implement newer high stakes exams that would now require all high schools students to pass five State Regents, including a New York State English Language Arts Regents. Differing from the past, when alternative "minimum competency exams" would suffice, graduation from a New York City high school now would require passing five Regents requiring fairly sophisticated schooled literacy skills. With these new mandates, curricula began to narrow even more and finding room to open new spaces within this system seemed almost impossible.

As the Brooklyn High School Superintendent's representative for this city-wide task force, I was asked to pull together a group of educators to explore those new spaces in the broadest sense. As usual, the abysmal results of this task force report opened the door to funding for alternative literacy programs if they could achieve two goals: raise targeted student's reading achievement and at the same time provide the professional development opportunities for the teachers involved with this endeavor.

How could we redesign the literacy program for these, our neediest of adolescent learners, as well as the professional development opportunities for the teachers who would serve them without sacrificing valuable instruction time for the students who needed it the most? The Saturday Freirean Literacy Academies became our answer, an innovative way that could address the needs of struggling readers in five of the most "at risk" sites in Brooklyn and at the same time help to build capacity of a cohort of secondary literacy teachers. This became our focus and ultimately the vision of the Project Freire Saturday Literacy Academies.

The Saturday Project Freire Literacy Academies: A Studio Model

After a few months of tense talks and at some points heated arguments, a plan was under way in February of 1996. The plan called for a pilot after school literacy academy to be held on Saturday mornings from 9 to 1. There would be a three hour block of time devoted to a Freirean model of literacy instruction, team taught by a lead teacher and two apprentices. The lead teachers had a strong understanding and belief in Freirean pedagogy as well as extensive background and success in adolescent literacy programs. Many of the lead teachers studied Freirean principles and were active participants in both New York City and the North American Freirean popular education movements. The apprentices were newer teachers to the field of teaching or to the field of adolescent literacy who needed additional training, coursework, or support for their regular Monday through Friday school assignments.

Lead teachers and the apprentices would use the Saturday class time as a laboratory of sorts, with the lead teacher serving as a mentor/coach for the apprentices with all three working through the Freirean units. The final hour of this Saturday program would be reserved for the teaching staff and devoted to on-going learning circles for reflection, study, and continued curriculum design.

Without sacrificing valuable school time during the regular week as the more traditional "pull-out" professional development programs did, teachers could continue to provide meaningful instruction for the students who needed it the most and at the same time have a vehicle for meaningful learning circles around the essentials of teaching and learning. The academies would thus serve as "studios" where these newer teachers could observe and serve as apprentices to the lead Freirean teachers who would be directly responsible for the emerging Freirean liberatory curriculum that was soon taking root as the alternative mode of instruction.

Fortunately, there was a small cohort of educators already aligned to the beliefs of Freire, lead literacy teachers in their own rights and a group of newer, less experienced teachers willing to learn and work as apprentices in these Saturday Academies. Fortunately, there were key administrators at the Brooklyn High Schools courageous enough to open a new space and to lend the support for its implementation. Fortunately, there were key outreach organizations willing and ready to work together in this Saturday endeavor. Recruitment for this new Freirean Academy began immediately and Project Freire Saturday Literacy Academies were born. There were to be three major hubs for these high school academies situated in the Bushwick, Flatbush and Bensonhurst areas of Brooklyn.

The Mission

The Project Freire team of educators began to focus on generative questions, questions that would propel our thinking. The first of them was instrumental to the design of this new educational space, the Saturday Academies: *Would an after-school program focused on opening those spaces through a Freirean pedagogy of hope and justice actually be able to facilitate gains in reading scores?*

As Denny Taylor (2002) points out, as the stakes were getting higher, the curriculum was narrowing during these tumultuous transitional New York State assessment years. It became more and more obvious to our team that we needed to find ways to open alternative educational spaces, especially for those high school students who were still "underachieving" vis-à-vis schooled literacy practices. As previously stated, the literacy curricula that did exist were limited and limiting, "subtractive schooling" at its best, paying little or no attention to the background of the students or the community's literacy or language practices and events (Moll 1992). Schooled literacy for these students was most restrictive, and an inordinate number of these students were referred to special education classes.

In order to create a Freirean framework for curriculum development we needed to meet, and meet regularly, on the critical issues before us. An integral part of opening those spaces and an ongoing part of the learning communities created were the routine readings and discussions held after the three-hour instructional block. Freirean staff regularly met both on Saturdays and at our monthly during the weekday meetings. They attended workshops and conferences and worked with other community-based popular education programs. Many of our sessions were co-taught by literacy professors from the New York City area as well as New York State. Generative questions grew in size and in nature and overarching themes became the catalyst of our work. How are we to work with these "unstuperfied" learners? (Lankshear 2002) How are these students making due in very hostile domains? What are the generative themes, the essential questions? These were but a few of the many generative questions that echoed on Saturday afternoons in Brooklyn.

The Freirean team was also ready to challenge the already established and ingrained autonomous model of literacy education offered in the students' Monday through Friday school program. We knew only too well how students in their regular high school language arts program were suffering from "narration sickness"—the banking concept of teaching and learning (Freire 1972). As we became more and more familiar with using an alternative ideological model of literacy education—the New Literacy Studies, the alignment of Freire's vision, which viewed literacy as deeply connected to the lives of the oppressed, and the ideological model which views literacy in terms of power relationships and its interaction with praxis (Street 1999) became more and more apparent. This "synthetic approach," a unique and powerful development in NLS (Welle et al. in this volume) would be our "bifocal lens" as we worked on developing an alternative model of literacy in alternative settings with the goal to move our students to function independently on their roads in academic and workplace settings.

Working in the Educational Borderlands

Work in the arena of new literacy studies reminded our team of the need to have a deep understanding of the two prevailing views at work in the communities of the Freirean Academies (Street 1997) The sociocentric view seemed alive and well, explaining these students' underachievement largely as a factor of home and social background. Less prominent was the school-centric view, which attempts to unpack the impact of curriculum, pedagogy, and school on the academic gap. The borderlands in Brooklyn those years mirrored the borderlands of many of our brother and sister urban areas with struggling readers continually over-represented by African-American males (Gasden 1991), in home schools with material conditions with "savage inequalities" (Kozol 1991), and with results in terms of the National Assessment of Educational Progress indicating that "although the achievement gap appears to be narrowing, African- American and Latino students at all three age levels tested are not learning to read and write as well as their European-American peers" (Mullis and Jenkins 1990).

Once the team's initial recruitment and identification of the first 100 high school students in the Project Freire Saturday Academies began, our first task was to focus attention on getting to know the students as persons as well as learners (Moje et al. 2000).

The majority of these "underachievers" were African American, or Caribbean English or Spanish-speaking immigrants from Puerto Rico, the Dominican Republic, Central America and the English-speaking Caribbean countries and islands. Many of their native languages could best be described as "pariah languages" (Smith 1972), in particular, the English Lexicon Creoles such as Jamaican and Trinidadian English as well as Haitian. We understood that to raise those narratives and use them to inform pedagogy would also call for a radically new vision of pedagogy. How could we integrate students' language and literacy practices and still address school-based literacy skills in "Standard American English"? How could Michael's story and others open spaces for an alternate vision? How could his world count as literacy? How would/could it be measured?

> Politics in Jamaica, it is very vile. When it come to election time, the M.P.'s dem come around, and fren-up the people dey want dem people to vote for dem. If you don't have any work, dey give you road work. Even me, sometimes I get work to sweep up the road. Dey come around and give the women food stamp for dem kids and building stamps to buy clothes or anything. After election and the people dem vote for dem, dey don't remember the people till next election. The people dem start to cuss and say, "is not politics, is politricks . . ." (from Michael's journal, Cucchiara, 1999)

At the same time, all three of these New York City academies were situated in neighborhoods in the midst of major social/political unrest. Police and community relationships were strained and eventually erupted with the Abner Louima case and the Amadou Diallo case, two shocking cases of police brutality against Haitian and African immigrants which drew national and international attention. Both cases impacted heavily on the Freire learning communities, especially the Brooklyn immigrant communities surrounding the hub sites (Goodnough 2000). The atmosphere was a charged one, not unusual for the students and their families and it called for a group of teachers who would be sensitive to the "prevailing winds" (Robinson 1990) and who would know how to integrate the "charge" into the Saturday classes:

> I addvoice I have for police is to get to no people fin out what they like an don't misjude them I no if people scheat police wit ristpuck thay will get back ristpuck . . . Iall the police musch get in the habit of getting to no people don't mater the coluer of they skin so we can have a better life. (from Michael's journal) (Cucchiara 1999)

Theoretical Grounding of the Project: "Reinventing Freire"

The team had worked with Freirean principles before recognizing the power of a liberation pedagogy and was well aware that many "progressive educators" were rediscovering some of Freire's underlying principles. We were determined not to "reduce Freire's leading ideas to a method", not to fall into the same mindset of "transmitting knowledge to otherwise unprepared students" (Aroniwitz 1993). We kept at the forefront of all our learning circles and planning sessions Freire's plea and rejection of the importation and exportation of his methodology: "Donaldo, I don't want to be imported or exported. It is impossible to export pedagogical practices without reinventing them. Please tell your fellow American educators not to import me. Ask them to re-create and rewrite my ideas" (Freire 1994).

Re-creating Freire in Brooklyn

One single sentence strip adorned the Project Freire Learning Centers for our work. It read, "A humanizing education is the path through which men and women can become conscious about their presence in the world" (Freire 1972). As we worked on ways to "read the world" of our students and then "read the word" (Freire and Macedo 1987), we first tried to uncover the world of their "resiliency" and resistance and the role that "cultures have played in creating disabilities" (Ladson-Billings 1994). This reframing, this creation of a newer focus with which to understand our work, work that at best was ambiguous and often scary, gave our team a unique freedom and opportunity to take a new stance and develop our own path here in New York City.

Our inquiry focused on these essential "generative" questions:

- Who are these adolescent learners who struggle with schooled literacy practices/events?
- What are the perspectives as to their underachievement in these literacy practices?
- What do we know about their world and their interests/their resistance to the schooled practices/academic literacies facing them?
- What knowledge do practitioners need to have about their world in order to understand the complexities of the word?
- How could we re-invent Freire and begin to create an atmosphere where learners see themselves as critical readers of the world and the word?

The Tension–The Mission: A Delicate Balance

By refusing to deal with the issue of class privilege, the pseudocritical educator dogmatically pronounces the need to empower students, to give them voices. These educators are even betrayed by their own language. Instead of creating pedagogical structures that would enable oppressed students to empower themselves, they paternalistically proclaim, "We need to empower students." This position often leads to the creation of what we would call literacy and poverty pimps to the extent that, while proclaiming the need to empower students, the are in fact strengthening their won privileged positions (Freire and Macedo 1998).

It was from this tension that our Freirean team adopted two frameworks, two theoretical approaches that would provide somewhat of a balanced checklist when we began the important work of curriculum development. Following Freire, the team recognized his strong belief that being literate meant mastery of the dominant literacy processes where academic and culturally relevant information is coded. Engaging with the New Literacy Studies, we supported the underlying notions of multiple forms of literacies, funds of knowledge, and differences of practices that learners bring to the table as members of distinct communities. It was with this tension that a beginning framework for curriculum development emerged, one which the team would routinely question as to the new insights gained by applying this newer and broader definition of literacy. Because an integral part of the Saturday Freirean programs had a built-in one-hour learning circles, a much needed often overlooked aspect of teaching and learning, this team had a vehicle to examine and question with the hope of ensuring a humanizing and just pathway for literacy acquisition.

Framing Freire: Essential Freirean Core Tenets

The evolving curriculum that emerged as each team designed their Freirean units had as its underpinning seven essential Freirean tenets about teaching and learning about a creative, critical, contextualized, and committed literacy education for the Saturday Academies. Many of these Freirean tenets are completely aligned with the NLS principles outlined in the introduction of this book. (Street, this volume). Those tenets included:

Generative themes: Carefully and collaboratively constructed units would be based on the Freirean notion of "generative themes," which would incorporate student's experiences and interests both in and out of the classroom.

Dialogic: Each unit of study would be rooted in the lives of the participants and directed largely by their input and choice. Student input would be critical and routinely part of instructional practice. The dialogic process would ensure that a view of these experiences were seen through a comprehensive perspective of identity and power, one which would link these experiences with the cultural, historical, and political context of the "world."

Authentic dialogue: Education, as the act of knowing would include acceptance of the inherent need for constant and meaningful dialogue between student and teacher, teacher and teacher, team and students and acknowledgement of learners and educators as equally knowing partners in the process.

Problem posing: Inquiry-based education, where the learners come up with the solutions to problems they pose themselves would be practiced.

Life contextualized: Authentic materials that are relevant to the student's and community's lives and which reflect their needs would be used.

Critical pedagogy: The role of the teacher would be to propose problems about a situation in order to help learners take a critical stance toward what they read, embracing literacy as the key to social transformation.

Telling the Stories: Three Sample Freirean Units in Three Different Brooklyn Communities

In this section, I will describe the practical applications that emerged from the integration, the interplay, and the intersection of these Freirean tenets and the New Literacy Studies approach. All three sites had community-based projects that involved students, teachers, community, and/or local and national organizations. All three sites involved multilingual and multicultural student and teacher populations in communities hardest hit by the social/economic/political instability existing in one of New York City's largest neighborhoods—Brooklyn.

Freirean Academy in Bushwick

The Bushwick section of Brooklyn is a predominantly Latino area with school and community populations from the Spanish-speaking Caribbean islands and Central and Latin America as well as South Americans. Profiles of the students who attended this Saturday site ranged from students born and raised in Brooklyn, labeled LEP (limited English proficient) primarily because of their limited school-based literacy skills, to newly arrived Dominicans, Ecuadorians, and Guatemalan students labeled as SIFE (students with interrupted formal edu-

cation) with limited access to either Spanish or English print. This neighborhood evidences some of the highest child and adolescent asthma and diabetes
rates in the nation (Kravath et al. 1991; Benerji 2002).

Generative questions that emerged from this hub were around the idea of
nutrition, food, illness, and health. *What is good food? Where do we find it? How
do we know? How come we seem to get sick more often? What is it about the air we
breath? What can we do?*

Generative words that emerged led students to know their English alphbet
and to explore the patterns and operations of this language. Word trees, expressions, statements, questions, and answers were displayed around the classrooms,
giving testimony to the literacy skills that were developing:

health	food	air	share
wealth	mood	hair	care
stealth	brood	fair	dare

Dialogue, critical questioning, and student-generated literacy reading and writing centered on some overarching questions: *Is it fair about our air? Who cares?
Which foods keep us the healthiest? How do we know? How healthy is our wealthy
nation? How is our health our greatest wealth? What food do you eat when you are
in a good mood?*

The questions served as a catalyst for life-contextualized literacy events and
practices ranging from bilingual panel discussions, sessions with school administrators, poster campaigns, and a final media project in collaboration with a
nationally recognized New York city–based literacy outreach program—The
Adult Literacy Media Alliance (ALMA). We already had a long and productive
partnership with this organization, specifically through their series of educational videos, TV 411, designed to improve the reading, writing, and math skills
with themes generated from the real-life concerns and issues arising in families
and their communities. Students learned through the media and other hands-
on print material about issues ranging from asthma to fast foods and their impact on families' budget, wealth, and health. Lessons were generated by a team
of ALMA's literacy staff and our Freirean teachers, students, and parents. Outreach at this Saturday center expanded to include not only these high school
students, but their family members as well. Literacy classes spawned new and

innovative ESL classes, which began to integrate the Freirean tenets used in the Freirean academies.

One of the many projects that culminated over the years was a collaborative video project on the Bushwick neighborhood as students, teachers, and ALMA staff created and produced an instructional and entertaining video about the community's health issues and concerns.

Freirean Academy in Bensonhurst:
The Bread and Roses Campaign in Brooklyn's Chinatown

The second hub in Brooklyn is also an immigrant neighborhood, with the predominant immigrant groups arriving from Asia, China, Korea, Pakistan, India, and Bangladesh. Demographics have been quickly changing over the years in what once was a predominantly Italian neighborhood. Some of the students have arrived without parents, much like the old immigrants of a century ago. Once here, they become "New York's youngest and cheapest workers" (Sengupta 1999). Most come from families working in the many garment factories that dot this Brooklyn Chinatown. In this site, our most multilingual hub, ESL Freirean pedagogy became the vehicle for second language and literacy acquisition. Our most populous site, this hub included parent ESL and bilingual programs, extended summer opportunities, and a S.A.V.E. cross-age tutoring component which grew out of a Brooklyn High School initiative—Students Against Violence Everywhere, nationally recognized after the Yusef Hawkins incident in this neighborhood a few years before.

One of the many Freirean units developed in this site was fashioned from an inquiry centered around the generative word *justice*. Inspired by their investigation of the Bread and Roses campaign, students and staff became involved with an investigation of the factories in their neighborhood, their treatment of employers, the inequity in pay, and the conditions that existed in these factories. Students read stories, viewed documentaries, and finally started their own Bread and Roses campaign, demanding a stop to the many injustices they uncovered. Students soon learned the power of boycotting as their investigation discovered that their school was purchasing all of their high school tee shirts from one of the neighborhood's most egregious offenders. Letters to the local newspapers, a poster campaign, meeting with administrators, surveys, and interviews became a routine part of this Freirean classroom as they all became so painfully aware of the harsh realities and injustices in their own community.

Freirean Academy in Flatbush

The final site is situated in the center of Brooklyn, with a predominantly African-American and African-Caribbean population. Student profiles ranged from those learners born and raised here for generations to recently arrived immigrants predominantly from Haiti and the "English-speaking" Caribbean. Ages ranged from 15 years old African-American men to 20-year-old Guyanese men whose most recent job was in the Guyana's gold mines. Mediating the political and racial unrest in this Brooklyn neighborhood became part of the routine work of this Freire Academy. From the turmoil of the police brutality in the case of Abner Louima, a Haitian immigrant from this community, to the student-led protest of the Amadou Diallo verdict (Goodnough 2000), this hub had as its generative work issues of "Power, Race, Hate, and Hope." Working closely with this hub was the New York City–based Theater of the Oppressed, an educational and community-based organization based on the Freirean work of Augusta Boal. The collaboration highlighted how the Freirean concept of reading one's world in light of personal exploration generates a world of language, a world of insight, and hopefully a world of empowerment. As students improved their literacy, they also found ways of "finding voice," of problem solving, of working through the techniques embedded within the Theater of the Oppressed activities to describe, analyze, and transform their reality.

I highlight this site because of its alignment to the Freirean concept of an empowering curriculum, one that goes not only from a descriptive to a personal and then to a critical analysis phase, but also ultimately to a creative action phase (Ada 1989). It was also part of the larger vision of ongoing work with the Freirean teachers in their continued efforts to enhance their own literacy practice. Through a combination of after-school activities, which ranged from the training in the Theater of Oppressed techniques to the weekly reflective writing sessions, to the collective creation of an improvisational ensemble which ultimately culminated in a student/teacher performance highlighting the problem and extending it to a fuller exploration of the democratic process embedded in this experience, the Freirean staff found ways to re-imagine their teaching, not as individuals but alongside their students as a powerful team ready to translate their newly found voices into concrete actions.

Conclusion

Reading the world always precedes reading the word, and reading the word implies continually reading the world (Freire and Macedo 1987).

The Project Freire Saturday Literacy Academies started in 1996 and lasted through 2002. Although the official funding ended for this extended opportunity for both teachers and learners, many of the Freirean team of educators, the ideals, vision, and curriculum remain strong today in high schools throughout New York City. The work in these Brooklyn Academies soon began to attract other boroughs in New York City as well as national attention. The results of this collaborative Freirean journey served as a catalyst for instituting more meaningful and empowering approaches to literacy such as the Freirean innovative literacy curriculum, restructured time to emulate the three-hour block of time in the Saturday programs, and the creation of professional learning communities which integrate the concept of the Freirean apprenticeship model and true collaboration with community and our diverse and multiple outreach partners.

The academic success of this after-school program measured during these five years was fragmented and for the most part anecdotal. Some of the data that emerged was based on informal language and reading inventories and academic review of students' performance in their regular in school programs. Leaps measured in terms of these types of assessment were documented, with an average of two-year growth in reading achievement after a year of Saturday involvement in the Project. "In fact, there is widespread belief, based upon fragmented data and anecdotes, that every 'incarnation' of Project Freire has been successful in boosting student achievement and helping educators to acquire the methodologies and the sensibilities needed to work with adolescent literacy students" (Tewksbury 2001). In fact, many of New York City's leading literacy educators and teacher trainers in the field of adolescent literacy had as their start their work in these Saturday Literacy Academies.

The implications of reading the world and the words emerging from this five-year journey left the team with, as Freire would hope, "a pedagogy of questions rather than answers" (Freire 1972).

As I reflect on this journey, there exists a crucial conflict: the need to find an independent measure of an NLS project such as our Freirean project to evaluate both its strengths and shortcomings and the notion of multiple assessment tools embedded in any NLS project that focuses on building multiple literacy capacities, including out-of-school, home, and community-based literacy practices and events. As we continue to explore Freirean literacy curriculum as we did for these five years, we are still left with questions that arose from this journey:

- How does NLS work within an educational bureaucracy such as this New York City public school work?
- What are the limits of the "local" (Street 1999) and can a Project Freire approach be replicable within the regular school day in a traditionally organized comprehensive high school setting?
- Which elements in these Saturday Academies are directly linked to academic improvement in standardized high stakes exams?
- What counts as literacy?
- What is the hidden curriculum?
- What gets taught?
- How do we measure the growth?
- How do we continue the journey where educators understand their learners as person and as learners? (Moje et al. 2000).
- How do we continue the journey "where students and teachers are committed to creating a place where kids are welcomed, where learning is personal and fun, where all discourse encourages while pushing for print mastery" (Gordon 1999).

As we continue our work and face the many challenges of popular education such as this Freirean work, we continue to see a strong, committed, and growing group of educators willing to develop and sustain this movement. It is our hope to continue to reframe both the methods employed and the approaches to literacy education while continuing to fight against underlying inequalities. We are moved and mobilized by a pedagogy of hope, a hopefulness that refuses to succumb to cynicism. We are left with the hopeful message and warning of Freire as we continue to "unveil opportunities for hope."

> One of the tasks of the progressive educator, through a serious, correct political analysis, is to unveil opportunities for hope, no matter what the obstacles may be. After all, without hope there is little we can do (Freire 1994).

Acknowledgements: The Project Freire Saturday Literacy Academies were supported by the courage and talent of many administrators and educators at the Brooklyn High Schools and our partnerships with university and not-for-profit organizations. A special note of appreciation is extended to Joyce R. Coppin, Superintendent of the Brooklyn High Schools, Winifred Radigan, and Wendy Karp for their vision, belief, and support for this alternative view of literacy education. A sincere thank you to our learning partners: Linda Provenza with the Theater of the Oppressed, Gregory Tewskbury from the Eugene Lang College of New School University, Marian Schwartz and her TV 411 staff from ALMA, Mark Jury from SUNY Albany's Graduate Program in Literacy Studies, and Steven Gordon of the Boston Public Schools. And finally to all the Freirean educators who routinely opened and continue to open those much needed spaces, a sincere debt of gratitude, especially Connie Cuttle, founder of the S.A.V.E. program, Shannon Curran at our Bushwick site, David Temple at our Bensonhurst site, and Peter Kondrat at our Flatbush site.

References

Ada, A. 1989. Literacy for empowerment. In: Cummins, J. *Negotiating Identities: Education for Empowerment in a Diverse Society.* Ontario: California Association for Bilingual Education.

Aronowitz, S. 1993. Paulo Freire's radical democratic humanism. In: P. Freire, P. McLaren, and P. Leonard (eds.), *Paulo Freire: A critical encounter.* New York: Routledge.

Banerji, M.A. 2002. Impaired beta-cell and alpha-cell function in African-American children with type 2 diabetes mellitus—'Flatbush diabetes'. *Journal of Pediatric Endocrinology and Metabolism* Suppl. 1:493–501.

Cucchiara, M. 1999 *Language, discourse, and culture and the teaching and learning of schooled literacy: English lexicon creole immigrant students in an urban high school literacy program.* Excerpt from unfinished dissertation, New York University.

Freire, P. 1972. *Cultural action for freedom.* Baltimore: Penguin Books.

Freire, P. 1972. *Pedagogy of the oppressed.* New York: Seabury.

Freire, P. 1994. *Pedagogy of Hope.* New York: Continuum Publishing Company.

Freire, P., and Macedo, D. 1987. *Literacy: Reading the word and the world.* Hadley: Bergin and Garvey.

Freire, P., and Macedo, D. 1998. *The Paulo Freire reader.* New York: Continuum Publishing Company, p. 106.

Gadsden, V.L., and Wagner, D.A. (eds.) 1995. *Literacy among African-American youth.* New Jersey: Hampton Press.

Gardner, H., and Hirsch, E.D. 1999. Opposing approaches so that Johnny can read. *The New York Times.* September 11, pp. 9–11.

Gee, J. 1991. *Social linguistics and literacies: Ideology in discourses.* Brighton: Falmer Press.

Goodnough, A. 2004. Hundreds of students march against Diallo verdict. *The New York Times.* March 4.

Gordon, S. 1999. Personal letter after a visit to a Brooklyn Freirean Academy by a team of Boston secondary administrators.

Kozol, J. 1991. *Savage inequalities: Children in America's schools.* New York: Harper-Collins.

Ladson-Billings, G. 1994. The dreamkeepers: Successful teachers of African American children. California: Jossey-Bass Publishers.

Lankshear, C., and Michaels, S. 2002. A plenary conversation at the NCTE Research Conference. New York City, February 21, 2002.

Moll, L. et al. 1992. Funds of knowledge for teaching: Using a qualitative approach to connect homes and classrooms. *Theory into Practice* 31(2):132–141.

Mullis, I., and Jenkins, F., 1990. *NAEP 1990 reading report card for the nation and the states.* Princeton: Educational Testing Service.

Moje, E.B., Dillon, D.R., O'Brien, D. 2000. Reexamining roles of the learner, text, and context in secondary literacy. *Journal of Educational Research* 93(3): 165–181.

New York State Department of Education. 1997. *Guidelines for the Education of LEP Caribbean Creole Speaking Students in New York State.* Albany: New York State.

Provenza, L. 1999. *The Project Freire Literacy Academy Theater of the Oppressed Training Guide.* New York City: Theater of the Oppressed. Unpublished.

Rao, M., Kravath, R.E., Abadco, D., Arden, J., Steiner, P. 1991. Childhood asthma mortality: The Brooklyn experience and a brief review. *Journal of the Association of Academic Minority Physicians* 2(3):127–130.

Ravitch, D. 1997. First teach them English. *The New York Times.* September 5, p. A35.

Robinson, Jay L. 1990. *Conversations on the written word: Essays on language and literacy.* Portsmouth: Boynton/Cook.

Smith, D. 1972. *Sociolinguistics in cross-cultural analysis.* Washington, D.C.: Georgetown University Press.

Sengupta, S. 1999. Young immigrants find a hard new land. *The New York Times.* March 14, p. 1.

Street, B. 1997. The implications of the New Literacy Studies for literacy education. *English in Education* 31(3): 26–39.

Street, B. 1999. New literacies in theory and practice: What are the implications for language in education? *Linguistics and Education* 10(1): 1–24.

Taylor, D. 2002. Conceptualizing freedom in contradictory spaces: A Readers' Theater presentation. Presentation, 23rd Annual Urban Ethnography in Education Research Forum, March 2, 2002, University of Pennsylvania.

Tewksbury, G. 2001. Draft proposal for the evaluation of the Brooklyn High School Superintendency's Project Freire.

Vacca, R. 1998. The benign neglect of adolescent literacy. *Journal of Adolescent and Adult Literacy* 1(1) 604–609.

Welle, D., Barnard, G., and Clatts, M. 2004. Not just infatuation: Sexuality and literacy in the age of HIV. This volume.

Section III

Adult Literacies

12

Adults Learning Literacy

Adult Learning Theory and the Provision of Literacy Classes in the Context of Developing Societies

Alan Rogers with Md. Aftab Uddin

Scenario: I am walking across a field late at night in Bangladesh. We are heading for a wattle and thatched building in which are gathered some thirty men, all sitting on the floor around the outside of the room, waiting for their adult literacy class to commence. Three hurricane lights are placed in a row down the center of the room. At one end stands the instructor (facilitator) beside a blackboard. Most of the student learners have a standardized textbook (primer) and a notebook in a neat pile on the floor in front of them. I ask the supervisor with whom I am walking what he is going to look for that evening during his visit. "To see if the teacher is teaching the right page for tonight," he replies.

Traditional Adult Literacy Programs are School Based

This scene can be replicated throughout the so-called 'developing world'. From Nepal to Namibia, there is a standard form of adult literacy class. A group (class) of some thirty learners carefully selected so that they are all deemed to be at more or less the same 'level' of learning; regular (sometimes daily but on occasions less frequent) meetings in a specifically designated location; one 'teacher'; whole-class teaching for most if not the whole time of the meeting; a standardized textbook based on primary school learning processes, even if the contents are asserted to have been adapted to adult concerns; strictly sequential formalized learning from 'easy' to 'difficult'; a pace of learning set by the educators, not the learners; one unvaried mode of learning pursued throughout the class session, usually copying letters chosen by the teacher; the language a nationally approved language in a nationally approved version—these are in most cases the key characteristics of adult literacy centers.

Of course there are some variations and exceptions. The Indian Total Literacy Campaign tended to advocate one instructor to ten learners. Some agencies (mostly NGOs) have developed more intensive (even residential) short-burst learning programs. Various attempts have been made to develop alternative teaching-learning materials—locally generated materials (LGM), the 'language experience approach', 'whole language approach'—but these are mostly employed at the 'post-literacy' stage. A number of national adult literacy programs use what may be called generalized 'real materials' (i.e., typical post office forms, driving license applications, typical bills etc.) inserted into the standardized textbook, and a few encourage their teachers to urge the learners to bring their own reading materials to classes. One or two programs, such as RE-FLECT, have abandoned the textbook approach, using flash cards of words chosen by the learners.

But the fact that these approaches are exceptions serves to demonstrate the strength of the dominant paradigm of adult literacy. It is an assertion by those in power of what is the proper kind of literacy to be learned and what are the proper processes by which it shall be learned. The model they have chosen is primary school, and the epistemology is one of 'learn first and then practice'. Even those programs which have experimented with different models of learning centers adopt a 'single-injection' ideology of literacy learning—one shot and you can become 'literate'.

All of which is a denial of everything we know about the natural learning which all adults engage in.

Adult Learning is Continuous and Chaotic

It is sometimes assumed, even by a number of those who claim to have expertise in adult learning, that adults do no learning outside of some form of 'schooled' experience, that there are some adults who "have done no learning since leaving school." But if there is one thing of which we are now certain, under the impact of the insights of lifelong learning, is that all adults are learning all the time; there is no such person as a 'nonlearner' (Merriam and Cafarella 1999; Aspin et al. 2001; Field and Leicester 2000).

The basic principle of adult learning theory is that each adult learns what he/she wants to learn when and where she/he wants and in the way he/she wants—and that each adult stops learning when she/he wants to stop. Although most adult learning is done within a social context (a community of practice; peer learning; social learning etc.), each adult controls his or her own learning (Brookfield 2000; Lave and Wenger 1991).

We can go further than this. We must of course be careful of over-generalization, for the diversity among adults is enormous, but some general principles can be drawn which should influence adult literacy learning programs.

First, adults are already motivated to learn. They learn what they want to learn at that time, that is to say, at the time and point of what they see as their need. They may not be motivated to learn what we want them to learn (e.g., literacy), but all adults are already motivated to learn something. They have a purpose of their own. To ignore their existing motivation, to try to 'motivate' them to learn literacy when their motivation is elsewhere (on issues of poverty or health, for example, a forthcoming marriage, some family crisis, a festival or holiday, the most recent film, a recent birth or death etc. etc.) is to deny their adulthood, to treat them like children. They have goals of their own.

Adults learn by 'doing'. Children also learn by 'doing', but there is a difference here. For adults, the activities which bring about learning already exist, they lie within their own personal experience. The natural learning process for adults is to learn through real activities in the course of their life. It is not a case of learn first and then practice; rather it is learning through doing for real (learning to cook through cooking real meals; learning to buy and sell in the market by making successes and mistakes when buying and selling in the market; learning to handle a child by handling a child, etc.). Thus adult learning is not preparatory to any activity; it co-exists with the activity. And it is not sequential, starting with easy tasks and moving to more difficult tasks, for life itself is not sequential. Adults learn from the immediate tasks which face them day by day, however difficult these may be.

Adult learning then takes place, not in a dedicated location, but wherever they may be situated. Learning is not confined to any one place. It takes place in the home, in the market, at work, at a religious center, in discussion on the streets, on the buses, in fact, wherever and whenever people are gathered together.

For adults learn by and from their own experience. And this means that learning is highly individualized as well as being collaborative. While each person learns from family, peers, and communities of various kinds (residential, neighborhood, and work communities, for example, or social and religious gatherings etc.), each person makes his or her own meanings. Of course, there are some forms of group learning which adults share. Existing groups will from time to time join together to achieve some joint goal, and the learning will be joint (a music or drama group, a sports club, a developmental self-help group, for example). But such groups will not be all at the same level of illiteracy or literacy; and even here, the group learning will be interpreted individually through the powerful lens of personal experience. Adult learning theory says that every adult learning class needs to take into account what each individual brings to that group and to help each to learn in his or her own way (Coffield 2000; Boud and Miller 1996; Evans 1992).

For adults have by now developed their own learning styles (Rogers 2003a: Kolb 1984). These are not of course fixed in stone; they are still developing. But each adult has built up through experience a preferred way of learning, and these ways of learning vary widely throughout any adult population. One teaching mode is not adequate to cope with these differences.

Adults control their own learning (Candy 1991; Brookfield 1985). Some adults, when they want to learn something, set themselves self-imposed activities—their own reading and writing, asking others, discussing, thinking—working it out for themselves. Others adopt the role (identity) of a 'student'; they choose a more formal style of learning, seeking out a teacher and on occasions others who wish to learn similarly in a group. But even here, they control it, *they* decide when to stop being a 'student'. Others simply perform whatever the task is, less conscious of the learning they are doing (Rogers 2003b).

And this means that all adult learning is partial, never complete. For new concerns, new goals, new motivations come along before the last goal has been fully achieved. Adult learning is never terminal, to be measured by a standardized assessment of achievement. It always leads to further learning, although this may be in a somewhat different field.

All of this is well known. But such characteristics are rarely taken into account when building literacy learning programs for adults. If there is one lesson from all of this, it is that a one-size-fits-all approach to any form of adult learning (including literacy) cannot be effective. Each adult needs to be helped to learn such material at a time and in a way which are appropriate to that adult rather than to a class as a whole. Personalized apprenticeship is more appropriate to adults than standardized academic learning.

This is understood in some areas of development interventions. Much (though not all) agricultural extension is based on individual assistance provided to individual farmers when they feel they need it. Health extension and social work treat all the participants as individuals with their own set of values and beliefs developed over many years through personalized experience. But adult literacy is treated differently; in most cases it regards all 'illiterates' as uniformly ignorant of literacy, seeks to subject them to a common and sequential learning program literally from A to Z, and disregards their individual experience.

Who is to Blame for this Situation?

I have long tried to understand why a primary school–based paradigm of adult literacy learning is so strong through all of Africa and Asia (I have less experience of Latin America but I saw the same thing in parts of the Caribbean). I can suggest a few thoughts but clearly more work needs to be done as to why there is no other viable and tested model on the table.

First, the influence of international educational aid agencies such as UNESCO is enormous. I do not believe that UNESCO really understands the strength of its hegemony in many developing societies. Many times when asking Ministry of Education officials why they are doing this or that, the response comes that UNESCO recommends it. The UNESCO regional office in Bangkok is particularly influential throughout Asia. And the UNESCO main office and regional bodies seem never to have taken adult learning theory seriously—they are strongly school (formal education) based. To my knowledge they have never promoted any serious study of adult learning theory and its implications for adult literacy learning. They have very rarely directly participated in the international adult education field. They have left that to the UNESCO Institute of Education (UIE) in Hamburg, which has pioneered many different approaches to adult education and played a major part in the development of adult education. But UIE and its concerns appear to have been marginalized by UNESCO; it has had to struggle to try to ensure that a specifically adult dimension forms part of any UNESCO program; and the way that the Education for All program has been co-opted to become Schooling for All Children is one example of the strength of the UNESCO education paradigm—that education means schooling and therefore adult education means schooling for adults. Hence the formal literacy classes of thirty learners, one teacher, one textbook, sequential learning, and whole-class teaching.

For the providers who take notice of these international recommendations, such an option, the provision of schooling for adults, is much easier than trying to walk along unfamiliar paths, trying to create new patterns of learning which accord with adult learning theory. This is what they know about, the provision of schooling. So the provision of schooling for adults makes life easier. Managing a uniform learning program with standardized textbooks and agreed learning timetables is a simpler matter than trying to manage a diverse program of learning activities which take each group of learners as the primary source of innovation.

A third reason for the dominant model of adult literacy classes comes from the instructors or facilitators. They have experienced several years of school education, mostly in primary school and some of them in secondary school. They are provided with a few weeks (at the most) of training (we found many who had had no training at all; Rogers et al. 1989). Most of this training was not directed to what is the difference between teaching children and adults but to what is common to both situations. Such a short training will never overcome the years of school experience. Research has shown that when teachers feel unconfident about their role, they fall back onto using the modes of teaching which they themselves experienced. To give one example, in an adult literacy program in India, the facilitators were trained for two weeks using small group learning methods. The manual they used advocated the use of small groups in their adult literacy classes and showed this in picture form. But none of the literacy facilitators visited had ever used small groups; they all used whole class teaching. The reason they gave was that (despite their training) this was the 'right way to teach'. They adopted the identity and roles of a 'teacher', which for them meant a 'school teacher'. Being often less confident, they went back to teaching just as they were themselves taught. Many adult literacy instructors tend to prefer a structured learning program which provides them with scaffolding for their own learning to be a literacy teacher. We must be careful not to blame the teachers. They are simply working within their own dominant experience and very rarely receive support to help them break free from this experience.

A further reason is that many adult learners demand such a form of teaching. They seem to know what 'school' should be, even if they have never been there. A study of adult education with nomadic groups in India revealed that many of the migrants knew what being a teacher meant despite never having been to school themselves, and they insisted that the facilitators who travelled with them should adopt that identity and the roles that went with it (Dyer and Choksi 1998). There are many well-documented instances of adult learners who ask for formal teaching (e.g., Papen forthcoming; Millican 2004). Their argument is that they have never been able to attend school or have never completed their schooling, so they adopt the identity of what they perceive as a student, sit on the floor or at desks which are too small, suspend their adult identities for a time and engage in activities such as copying meaningless letters from the blackboard or textbook into a notebook or even onto a slate. They are very rarely made to feel adult when in an adult literacy classroom. Again we must not blame the learners for this. They too are working within their experience. And this is all they have been offered by the policy-makers and planners who do have a wider range of choices before them.

The model is of course entirely inappropriate for adults and for many developing societies. It is a product of Western Europe. It was (as Faure 1972, and many others have pointed out) created in the late nineteenth century and was designed to prepare the poorer classes in Europe for working in the mills. Its aim was to create obedient, diligent, persistent, and uncritical workers. Many of the buildings erected at the time to house these new experiences were built like mills, with windows high in the walls so that the student-learners should not be distracted from concentrating on what should be their primary activity, work (that is why what is done in schools is called 'work'). Classes of same-level students progressing strictly sequentially formed the core structure (Hamilton 1990; Graff 1979). This model was exported in an early phase of globalization to colonized societies, destroying in full or in part their indigenous learning systems; and on achieving independence, many countries adopted this as the key to the apparent success of the West. The West for a time gave up that model, moving instead to learner-centered and activity-based learning, although today there are signs of some kind of return to more formal processes; but many developing countries have continued to use such approaches continually (Sarangapani 2002). It is therefore no wonder that when literacy facilitators and adult literacy participants (and non-participants) are asked to describe the best way of learning literacy, they describe a formal school.

Which probably helps to explain why there seems to be no viable alternative model which takes seriously adult learning theory. Despite the long experience of some societies of creating alternative learner-centered forms of adult learning programs in many fields, especially in relation to gender (e.g., Walters and Manicom 1996; Jung and King 1999), there is at present no viable and proven alternative model for adult literacy learning in developing societies. The problem is how one can create a learning program which is individualized while at the same time providing scaffolding and developing opportunities for collaborative learning; which uses the immediate purposes (motivations) of each different adult learner; which offers learning programs at their own time; which puts it (including the curriculum and the teaching-learning materials) under their control; which builds on the individual experience of each literacy learner; which takes place at their own pace; and which also takes place in their own spaces rather than in a central location at a given time and in a group.

It is therefore no wonder that policy makers and practitioners alike suggest that the best way to run an adult literacy class is to persuade all the literacy learners to line up on the same starting line and to run the same race. They do not 'start where they are' (a typical adult learning theory slogan) but instead try to motivate 'illiterates' by their need to learn literacy. They exaggerate the benefits of literacy; they exaggerate the problems caused by 'illiteracy' (see Street 1984; Graff 1979; Levine 1985). They deny many of the basic tenets of adult learning theory. They feel that it is easier and cheaper to do it in this mode. This is what they are expert in, running schools for children; so that naturally they feel that running schools for adults is the best way to help adults to learn literacy.

But it is ineffective. The money spent on adult literacy classes in most countries has been largely wasted. Not because, as some have argued (e.g., Abadzi 1994), adults cannot learn literacy after a certain age—there are many cases which prove this wrong. But because we are asking adults to suspend their adulthood and their experience and to become like children and to learn like children in formal schools. And above all, because this is not the way adults learn literacy.

For many adults learn literacy skills without going to school or adult literacy program; and a study of the way such learning is accomplished is very revealing. It will show us that the existing classes do not meet the needs of adult learners, and suggest that there are alternative ways in which adult literacy learning programs can be created which do take serious cognizance of adult learning theory.

Case Studies

A number of case studies made recently in Bangladesh in the course of research into literacy usages in that country help us to see some of the ways in which adults relate their own views of literacy to the literacy learning programs open to them. And they show at the same time how some adults learn literacy skills for their own purposes without ever attending primary school or an adult literacy class. A study of the processes involved may help us to understand some of the key principles involved, which in turn may lead to the development of more appropriate forms of adult literacy learning programs than we use at present.[1]

Abu Sufian[2] saw himself as an illiterate person who was running a grocery shop in a rural market town. He felt that he must learn to maintain accounts if he was to develop his business further. He enrolled in an adult literacy center (class) and was regular, but felt that his new literacy skills from the center were not helping him in performing the daily literacy tasks related to his business. He was struggling to relate classroom education to maintaining his accounts. He felt discouraged and was becoming irregular in attending the class. One day the teacher of the adult literacy center, who also ran a small shop near by, came to Sufian's shop and asked him why he was becoming so irregular. Sufian told him his problem, and the teacher agreed to help him in maintaining his accounts everyday after the end of each class. So they sat together at the end of every class at night at Sufian's shop and the teacher showed him how to write down the daily accounts of the business. Sufian said that within a very short

[1] The case studies have been collected by Md. Aftab Uddin in connection with his PhD studies at the University of Nottingham. They are used here with full discussion with Aftab Uddin and as far as possible have been presented in the language of the case study notes from the field.

[2] All names have been changed for the purposes of this chapter.

time, before the end of that nine months' session, he had learned confidently to maintain his own accounts. In his words, "It was not the class, but the teacher's practical assistance that helped me to learn how to maintain my accounts. I soon became confident." The government's generalized literacy program could not meet the personal literacy ambitions of this shop-keeper.

Such individual assistance occurs time and again; it seems to indicate the need of some adults for such personalized learning under their control. Adults in their own learning choose the form of assistance they feel they need. They will use formal learning when they feel they need it and can cope with it; or they may avoid it as not meeting their individual needs. One of the persons interviewed, Abdul Hoque, learned how to read the Qur'an in Bengali informally in much the same way as Abu Sufian, with the individual help of the teacher outside of the government adult literacy center which he attended. He became confident that he would be able to learn to read the Qur'an in Arabic as well, so he enrolled himself in a maktab (a religious school with many formal characteristics) alongside the young children. He is currently attending the maktab regularly, and says that he can now read the Qur'an properly and that his religious knowledge is improving. He reports that he is interested to learn more.

Others similarly saw the work of adult literacy classes as being irrelevant to their immediate needs and took their own steps to learn literacy without the aid of such programs. Saleh Ahmed went from his village to Chittagong, the major commercial city of the region, where he worked in the construction industry. He quickly developed literacy skills related to his construction work, although he had never attended school. He learned informally how to write the name of the laborers working with him, different items related to construction such as cement, sand, bricks etc., and also transactions. Over the years he learned to maintain the accounts of his work, and he says that he did not have any problem in doing the literacy tasks related to his occupation. However, when he went back to his own village, and changed his occupation, setting up a tea-cum-grocery shop in the village market, he found that his previous literacy skills did not help very much, because in this business the names of the customers, the items to be recorded, and the kind of transactions were all different. So he says that once again he felt illiterate, in much the same way as he felt before learning the literacy skills related to his work as a sub-contractor on a construction site. So initially he had to appoint an assistant to maintain accounts for him. As time went on, however, he again taught himself the literacy skills related to his business, and he dismissed the assistant after a year when he had learned to maintain the accounts himself. However, after a couple of years, he stopped his shop business and became an active worker of a political party; he was elected as a local union (i.e., district council) member. Again, he found difficulties with the new literacy tasks related to his job. Here the literacy practices were different—reading and writing official letters, reading meeting minutes, preparing rural development projects, arranging and coordinating training etc. He again feels as if he is illiterate in these new situations, with new tasks. However, this time he felt that it would be difficult for him to learn the new literacy skills, so he gave up the idea that he would learn again. He is coping with the tasks by asking friends and family members to read and write letters and documents for him, or asking the council staff to maintain accounts for him. He is able to read the written forms of numerals only and he uses these to identify the amounts listed and thus sign the documents. Sometimes, when in an official environment where people ask him to read or write something, he pretends that he could do these literacy jobs, but says that he cannot see anything as he has left his spectacles at home. He says that he feels shy to tell people that he does not know "how to read or write," so he lies. He is not interested in learning the kind of literacy skills taught in a literacy class because he thinks he is now over-aged for such a task and also that it is shameful to go to a literacy class or to ask somebody to help him to learn literacy skills as he did previously. He says that people respect him so much in his new position and he is earning a lot of money, so his nonliteracy is not a big problem in his life. He thinks that the limited but generalized nature of a traditional adult literacy class based on a generic primer is not appropriate for such an adult learner.

The issue here seems to be one of identity more than a simple matter of the transfer of skills from one context to another. As a construction worker and then a shopkeeper, he could admit that he needed help with literacy tasks, for that was common in those fields. And he felt confident to transfer his skills from one field to another. But there are limits to such transfers; as an elected public representative and a political leader, to admit to illiteracy would bring discredit to himself. In his present identity, learning by asking the help of others or attending a literacy class would compound the problem; hence he disguises it. It would seem then that the scaffolding many adults use for their own learning is context dependent—it may take different forms in certain situations or with certain identities.

The central issue here is that many adults perceive that the literacy being offered in the adult classes is irrelevant to their personal and immediate interests. In some of the villages studied, a number of men and women were members of a developmental group organized either by the Government's Rural Development Board (BRDB) or an NGO. They attended group meetings where they were asked to sign papers, read resolutions and minutes, and maintain accounts with the agency in order to take a loan and repay on a regular basis (mostly weekly); thus they needed to read and sign for the amounts of the savings, loans, and repayments as well as for dealing with their pass books. BRDB trained their group members using government literacy primers for six months in a belief that this would help the group members in maintaining their accounts and also that it would encourage them to play a more active role in the group and take better initiatives in using their loans to earn a higher income. But it was observed in these villages that the group members who completed the adult literacy courses were not using the taught literacy skills at all; the group manager or BRDB officials were doing all the literacy tasks on their behalf. Group member Zamila said that they could manage their loan money by themselves without the use of literacy skills, and she added, "We went to the literacy center because we had to and we were given some money for regular attendance." Zamila now possesses accounts with both BRDB and with an NGO working in the village; she claims that she manages her two accounts in a bank in the district headquarters without any problems. When she goes to the bank with her husband, who is also nonliterate, she says that the bank clerks do everything for them; "we just read the figures [which they learned informally] and sign the documents," although it is clear that they also make meaning of the layout of the statements presented to them and interpret the papers more widely than simply reading the written numerals. She knows how much she has in balance in each of her accounts. She can also tell all the transactions in her accounts from the beginning.

As we can see from these examples (and there are many more in the sample), almost invariably adult literacy learning comes after starting some kind of activity. Adults relatively rarely learn in anticipation of some forthcoming event; they normally learn after the experience has commenced.

And they learn just what they feel they need for their tasks and no more. Jahangir Hosen has been running a shop for more than thirty years. When his business was expanding and sales were increasing, he felt that it was becoming more difficult for him to memorize everything, and he thought that it would be very good if he could maintain his own accounts. He only knew the Bengali alphabet but did not know how to read, write, or keep such accounts. He had a barber friend who was a regular customer. Jahangir told him of his intention to learn to maintain accounts. The barber gladly agreed to help him, as he had free time at noon and in the evening. He came to Jahangir's shop whenever he could manage it. He helped him to write the name of the items he had in his shop, the names of his different customers, the quantity of items, and the amount of money due. Initially his friend was writing things for him in his account book and he showed him how to write. Later, Jahangir started writing for himself, and his friend showed him where he was making mistakes. After a few months, Jahangir started maintaining his accounts independently and was asking his friend only whenever he needed to write the name of new customers, new items, or new amounts of money. His friend also showed him how to add or deduct the sums. He says that he came to keep his own accounts as he became more confident. Now he is maintaining his accounts, although he admits that he makes spelling mistakes. His business is now quite big. He buys at wholesale rate and has a large number of retail customers, many of whom buy their goods on credit and pay at the end of the month. He thus has much writing to do. To save time, he developed his own shorthand that only he can read. The researcher looked at his accounts book but found that he could not understand it. Jahangir says that he writes only the initial letter of the item or a symbol, and different symbols for fractions of the amount. He said that his customers trust him whatever he writes, so they do not ask him to show them what he has written. If someone wants to see what he has written, then he reads it to them. He does not know how to read a newspaper or write a letter; he takes help from others for writing or reading letters and for other literacy tasks. However, he can read and write the shopping list of what he needs whenever he buys or sells things; he has at least one hundred items in his shop and he can write the names of all of these items. He can read and write English dates and months, although he does not know what the exact date is; he has some customers who pay him money on the last day or the first day of each month, so whenever they come, he usually asks them if the month has finished or not. The researcher asked why he had not learned these dates, and he replied that he had not had any problem with this so far, so he did not plan to learn these dates.

What and how much one learns then depends on personal choice. And much of adult learning relates to adult identities. Sometimes it is developing and furthering an existing identity, while some of it is connected with changing identities. For identities are multiple and fluid, being made and remade according to different circumstances.

Md. Shamsul Huq is an example of this. Now aged 68, he recounted his life history working in various biri (a locally made cheap quality cigarette) factories, as a day laborer, as a mason, jute mill worker, and so on. The idea that individuals stay in any one occupation for most of their lives is not true of many people in developing societies just as it is not true in other societies, a fact which has important implications for the kinds of literacy which adults need for their daily lives.

Huq recalls an event which changed his life. At the time of his marriage, the marriage registrar (*kazi*) asked him to sign his name. There were many people present. He tried to sign his name with the pen in front of that gathering, but he failed and the people from his in-law's family and their relatives laughed at him. He said that he was so ashamed that he cried; and there and then he promised himself that he would learn how to sign his name. He returned to his work place in Dhaka, the capital of the country, a week after his marriage and asked one of his friends to show him how to sign. His friend asked him to buy paper and pen. He bought them. His friend wrote his name on the piece of paper and he tried it again and again. After a few days, he learned how to hold the pen and also learned how to sign his name. He can still remember that he was so glad on that occasion that he filled the whole book, signing his name again and again. He became confident that he could learn anything if he wanted to, despite the fact that he had never been to school.

He decided to change his profession and to open some kind of business. He went to the post office and asked the postmaster to open a savings account for him where he could save 5 *taka*[3] every week from his weekly earnings. He realized that to run a business, he would have to write and keep accounts of the shop, so that he decided to learn how to read, write, and calculate accounts. At that time, he moved and rented a house with the friend who had helped him to learn how to sign his name. He told his desire to his friend, who agreed to help him in the evenings or whenever they both had free time. Huq bought the

[3]About 5p; there are currently 100 *taka* to the GB £.

books, paper, and pens and started to learn the Bengali alphabet. He asked his friend whenever he needed help. He said he worked hard. He then made words and sentences for himself. He wrote whatever he wanted to write and then asked his friend for correction. He was reading anything available to him. On his way to the jute mill, he collected scrap paper from the road. If there was anything written on it, he tried to read it; if there was nothing on it, he took the paper for his own use to save money buying paper for his own writing. He read posters, signboards, and notices of the factory. He said that his condition at that time was like an addiction. He was also trying to learn how to add and deduct, how to multiply and divide. In two years, he became very confident with his literacy. Then he went to the post office to see how much he had saved so far; he found it was nearly seven hundred taka. He withdrew 500 taka from that account and went back to his village home. He says that he gave two hundred taka to his parents for family costs, and with the rest he started a grocery-cum-stationery shop at his own house, buying goods from the nearby wholesale market. He says that he was making good progress with full confidence. During this time, he learned English numerals and became able to read the English calendar. He did not ask anyone to help him formally to learn these. He said that in his business it was essential to use the English calendar, so he had to learn the dates and months. He observed how other people wrote them; he asked them how they were writing and he followed their example and thus learned. When his children went to school, he did not have enough money to employ someone to teach them at home as others did, so he had to guide them himself; he thus learned the English letters and taught them to his children. He says he can read the letters but he cannot understand the words, although he can make sense of the brand names of the goods in English. He can count in English and write the numerals but not the numbers in words. He says he knows all these things from his daily life experience, not from schooling. He has been running that business for the last forty years. He is now one of the richest men of that area.

It is important for us to realize that Huq is not unusual. Throughout the case studies, we found men and women who taught themselves what they needed when they needed it but only to the limit of what they saw as their need—people who taught themselves how to read the time by asking other people and looking at a clock or watch; people who learned the dates (in Bengali or in English) simply by trying; people who learned to read and write road signs, building names, personal names (their own or other people's) because they felt they needed to in order to fulfil their identities and roles. Masum Ali needed some money for his business of carpentry. He went to the bank, but despite the support of some local elites (as he says), the bank manager refused him a loan as he was unable to sign his name on the bank papers. He felt insulted when the manager told him this in front of other people. He says that he decided to become literate. He bought a Bengali primer and pen and paper; he asked his uncle to teach him, but it did not work as his uncle discouraged and insulted him. Two years later he joined a government adult literacy class which opened in his area but it was soon closed for mismanagement. Seven years later, he joined another course and stayed with it for a year and completed the examination; he says he can still recite parts of the primer off by heart. But this new 'literacy' had no use in his life, and he says that he still "does not know how to read or write." After these different attempts, he feels that he is still illiterate, although he writes his signature in different places. But he can read the various measurements (he uses English tape measures) needed in his carpentry and write them, using his own techniques. He learned how to read the time from other people. He writes the date and month in figures in his notebook. He keeps a daily account of his work and can identify items in the catalogue of carpentry such as locks for doors by looking at the photographs or by asking other people to read them to him.

Such self-teaching does not proceed from the simple to the more complex. It learns to read whatever is needed to be read. There was the garage owner, Miron, who like most of the others in this sample had never been to school. When he started to work in a local garage as a 'helper', he was regularly sent to obtain parts for the vehicles being mended. He first learned their names orally by listening to the mechanics. Then he tried to identify those items individually on the written lists which were provided for him.[4] He said that sometimes he asked the shopkeepers to help him read the names on the lists, and he started to write them down, copying what he read. Over a period of twelve years, he

---

[4]These lists are in Bengali, but the name of each part in the original pack is in English because these are imported. The way the name of each part is pronounced sometimes makes it difficult to relate that item with the name of the part in English. Traders usually give a local name to the parts and write it in that way in Bengali, sometimes using the symbols specially developed for the individual parts of the motorbike. The researcher read one such list and he could not relate it with the parts, although he knows all the names of the parts in English.

became very successful at this. He then started his own garage and employed six persons. Then he thought that he should learn to read newspapers and again he succeeded by teaching himself. He also began to write letters, all of this without going near an adult literacy class. The difficult words were not difficult to him because of his experience and determination.

And they choose their own strategy for learning according to a mixture of opportunity and experience. One man was determined to learn literacy skills in order to get a job in a government office, so he collected an old religious study book, *Islami Shiksha,* of class IV from his village primary school, as he did not have any idea of which book to buy or where to start. He talked to some friends who were students at the local high school; they agreed to help him, so they came to his home whenever he asked them. Usually every evening at least one of them came to help him with his study. He continued for nearly three months and almost finished the book. There was no mathematics in that book, so he did not practice mathematics. On the other hand, there was some Arabic literature in that book, but he did not read that, for as he said, he was not interested in it as it would not help him to earn money or for any other purpose in his personal life. And he did not write anything while he was reading this textbook. He said that he believed that reading was essential for his new identity, but that writing was not so important. In addition to the primer, he began to read other things—the shopping list of the family he worked for who sent him to the market every morning, and the newspapers and magazines at the same house whenever he was free; he read posters, signboards in the street, and notices, letters, and files in the office at his place of work. He was trying to read everything he could find. In the end he secured the government position he sought on the basis of his self-taught skills.

Later one of his friends went to Malaysia for a job, so he decided to learn to write to avoid asking others to write private letters for him. He tried to write for himself what he wanted to tell his friend. He showed it to one of his friends or colleagues to look it over, but there were many spelling mistakes and they often rewrote it for him. But he kept on practicing writing letters, asking people for help whenever he felt he had a problem. Now he says he can write letters by himself although there are still many spelling errors. But he does not have much use for writing in his job, he does not have to write every day. Like many others, he learned English letters, numerals, and dates through the necessities of his work. As he says, he did not learn this from any institution. He observed others; he tried to do it for himself; he asked others for help; they told him and he memorized it; he copied other writings; he practiced and learned from his mistakes. He controlled his own learning at times and places which suited him. He did it to help him to fulfill himself, his own identity and roles.

Of course there are adults who are just as motivated and turn to educational programs for such learning. As we have seen, Abbul Hoque entered a *madrasa* (religious school) to learn Arabic so that he could learn to read the Qur'an accurately and do other religious work; he intended to teach it to other people, again an indication of literacy for a changed identity. Later, when a government literacy center was opened in his village, he enrolled himself in order (as he said) to learn the Qur'an and *hadiths* in Bangla, to learn to read and write letters, since his three sons were abroad, and to maintain accounts, as he was treasurer of the mosque committee. He did not enroll with the center with a view to using his literacy in any income-generating activities or for any other purpose. But on the whole, most of the literacy learning in our case studies was on the job, experiential, unsystematic, certainly not graded and sequential. And it used other helpers.

One man, Abdul Motin, who had decided to go to Malaysia in search of employment, asked his sister to teach him some basic English, some of the English words he might need to survive (he said he had worked out such areas as what to eat, how to travel, how to ask people for help); he learned the English script although he did not know Bengali script at that time. He learned how to sign his name and how to write his address, both of them in English letters (he signed his name on his passport application). When in Malaysia, he learned the Malay language in a matter of months from his work colleagues, not from an adult education class.

Although most of the case studies cited so far have been men, much the same can be seen from the women in the responses. Some attended adult literacy classes but they did not practice what they learned and forgot what they had acquired. Ayesha Begum joined the literacy program for "one long year"; she said she was able to read and write slowly at the completion of the course. But she forgot everything during the five years which followed. Now she does not even know the Bengali letters; but she can sign her name for she does it regularly in the NGO credit group of which she is a member, and she can decipher her loan account, although she checks it from time to time with relatives. Rajia Begum completed her basic adult literacy course for one year; yet she says that she does not know how to read, write, or calculate. Several of the women joined every adult literacy class that came into the village, sometimes four or five of them in succession, but they learned very little effectively, and what they learned was not usable in their daily lives. But like many of the men, they learned what literacy skills they had from family, friends and neighbours, from their work situation, from their changing roles.

Lessons about Adults Learning Literacy

We have I hope demonstrated that adults learn differently from the assumptions made when policy-makers and government officials plan adult literacy classes for adults, whether within the context of so-called 'developing societies' such as Bangladesh or more highly industrialized and postindustrial societies. There are many implications for adult literacy learning programs from these case studies of how adults learn literacy without participating in either formal school or nonformal adult literacy classes. We need to develop literacy learning opportunities which take seriously the important conclusions of studies of adult learning such as these.

The first thing these case studies tell us is that adults can and do learn literacy skills, despite those who suggest that the task is cognitively too difficult for them. The same is of course also true of many children who learn literacy skills well before attending school. And they learn even difficult literacies; they learn whole texts in a specific context, not a set of fragmented and decontextualized words. They "take hold" of literacy and use it for their own purposes with their own strategies. They learn for their own purposes, when impelled by interest or necessity. They learn literacy best when they already know what the text says and means rather than when confronted with unknown and meaningless words chosen by someone else. The ability of adults to learn when they are so minded cannot be impugned.

A good deal of this learning is unconscious learning; the adults concerned are not always aware that they are learning 'literacy'. This is what I have called elsewhere 'task-conscious learning' (Rogers 2003b), that is, learning in the course of fulfilling some task which they have set themselves. They would not call this "literacy," indeed some of them still describe themselves as 'illiterate', that is, they feel that they do not have command of the dominant literacy even though they have a local or personal literacy. For them, 'literacy' is something which is done in the classroom, essentially associated with schooling. And since they do not have schooling, what they do in reading and writing cannot be literacy. This seems to be one reason why so many adults become disengaged from adult literacy learning programs. They drop out or switch off or persist in attending but without any visible achievements. What they are being required to do does not match what they do in 'real life' or what they aspire to do.

And they certainly make no distinction between literacy and numeracy. Most of the examples of self-learning above combine numbers and calculations with words, just as life does. The separation of numeracy in literacy learning programs flies in the face of everything we know about life itself. For to these adults, 'numeracy' per se does not exist. All that exist are accounts, shopping lists with prices, house numbers, etc. But 'literacy' exists for they have been told that many times; literacy is what you learn at school, not what you do in everyday life.

Further, the learning they do naturally does not progress from the simple to the more complex. Reading shopping lists or indeed any scrap of paper which comes their way, writing out items from a construction site, identifying sites and buildings from street names, reading and writing the parts of motor vehicles, etc., all of which these adults do on their own—these indicate that adults often start learning with difficult words which they feel they want to read rather than start with simple words and then move onto more difficult words and sentences.

But there are limits to such learning. The issue of the transferability of literacies from one context to another, from one identity to another, is revealed clearly in some of the case studies and needs much further investigation. But above all there is the question of confidence. Some found in their personal literacy the root of a new confidence to tackle other forms of learning; others felt they did not have enough confidence to undertake what they saw as the difficult schooled literacy.

Again, adults learn freely from their own chosen peers rather than from formal 'teachers'. Many adults choose their own scaffolding; they identify their own mentors; they set themselves into apprenticeship with a self-chosen colleague. Sharing between equals is a key characteristic of much adult learning.

And yet despite this (and perhaps most importantly for our purposes), learning is highly individual. Each adult learns what he/she feels they need at the time and point of need, not at a time when the agencies suggest they should. In all of these examples, the literacy learning sprang from an immediate context and was related to that context (the shop, the workplace, the religious center, the savings and credit group). Much of learning consists of making sense, meaning; and each adult makes personal meaning from their own personal experience. Adults have very varied individual experiences and individual concerns. To suggest that classroom learning situations will suit all adults is a profound mistake.

Using Existing or New Groups for Adults Learning Literacy

There are of course some situations where adults learn in groups. For most adults belong to some kind of group for various reasons—to trade unions, to self-help groups, to religious groups, to local government groups, to informal social groups. Such groups are helping adults to build new identities, to develop new roles for themselves. And such groups engage in co-operative learning. But collaborative learning of this kind is different from the formal classroom where all the 'learners' are treated the same. Indeed, one difference between such groups and the adult literacy class is that these groups consist of persons with mixed literacy competences. Some members will have developed considerable formal and informal literacy skills; others will have no such skills at all (Rogers 2000). This is one possible avenue for the creation of adult literacy learning programs. In some cases, we can use the group as a whole, with its peer learning, so that those with greater experience and confidence help others with less experience and confidence. Distributed learning such as this is after all (as we have seen) how much adult learning is done in real life (Rogoff 1998; Chavajay and Rogoff 2002). In other cases, it may be appropriate to separate those with greater need for developing their literacy skills from the others and provide for them special learning programs. But the immediate relevance of such learning programs to the activities of the group will need to be clear to all involved; the texts used for learning need to be clearly related to the tasks of the group rather than being of 'the cat sat on the mat' variety, divorced from the life of the group.

Another approach would be to identify some common activities (new identities and new roles) which some men and women come to face at a special time. For example, all parents of children entering school for the first time will share a temporary common bond in relation to the school and/or to their children's school work. Running a literacy program related to these immediate concerns, these new identities and roles, may work; at least it is worth trying. Literacy in such contexts will be set within a framework of other learning, not separated from other activities as it is in most traditional adult literacy classes. Learning to be a new parent of a schoolchild; learning to relate to the school and teacher; learning to read school reports and notices; learning to help children with their schoolwork can all be related to specific literacy practices. Some parents will have considerable literacy skills, experience and confidence; others will have less. The members of such a group can help each other.

Literacy learning thus needs to be set in a context, since it is from their own particular context that adults learn literacy naturally, as we have seen from our studies. No adult ever learned literacy without a purpose, and that purpose cannot be divorced from the learning process itself. We need to use the existing goals of adults to help them to learn the literacy they feel they need.

Building Individualized Literacy Learning Programs

But the key problem is how to help individuals rather than groups to learn literacy at a time when they need it for their own purposes. Some of the respondents in our study wanted to learn at a time when there was no class running in their area. Two strategies may be proposed to help individual adults learn literacy skills.

The first is the so-called drop-in center or 'flexible learning center'. This approach to adult literacy learning has been described elsewhere (Aderinoye and Rogers 2004), with an example from Nigeria. A drop-in center is a building staffed and open to all comers (including those who will never go to adult literacy classes) to provide learning assistance with literacy and other basic education skills to those individuals who come to it (see Hamilton and Bergin 1994). It provides assistance at the time and point that the clients/customers themselves feel they need it. It can be staffed by volunteers with adequate training and support; they will offer help with the personal and immediate literacy tasks of those who come in. It will be demand-led, not supply-led, highly individualized and immediate, practical and personal. There will be no pre-set outcomes.

In order to fulfill such a role, a drop-in center needs to be situated where people are. In the Nigerian example, the center was located in a shop in one of markets of Ibadan. It needs to be in a building where people who may be reluctant to go into a school will feel comfortable in visiting. For its chief aim is to help adults to learn the literacy which they feel they need when and how they need it.

Such a purpose would indicate the mode of operation. The aim of such a center is not just to assist those who come with a specific task and text, but at the same time to help them to learn, if only in a small way, their own literacy skills on the spot. For a drop-in center is not intended simply to do the literacy tasks for the persons who come to it; that would be to deny both adult learning theory and indeed its essential purpose, which is to help those who come to develop their own skills through doing their individual literacy tasks and in the process to reflect on their literacy activities. This is a very difficult task for the facilitators, not to do too much and at the same time not to expect the clients to do too much.

The drop-in center has proved to be very effective in certain circumstances (Mark and Donaghy 2003; McGivney 2000).[5] It is of course most appropriate to urban contexts with a high population density. It is less appropriate for rural areas except when combined with a major element of new technologies, which are as yet rarely available in rural areas of most developing countries. For such areas, an extension service, such as is used for agriculture and health, may be more appropriate. Such an approach, while intensive in terms of staffing, is highly flexible, has a long tradition behind it, and is built on adult learning theory. Group activities and individual learning activities can both be comprised within it. Like agricultural extension, which provides on-going direct and specific assistance to individual and groups of farmers with their immediate tasks and needs, like health extension, which helps individuals and families with urgent issues on an on-going basis, a literacy extension service could provide regular learning support for adults with their wide diversity of purposes and learning styles. It will be more expensive than the current provision of adult classes but since these have proved to be so ineffective, it is not clear why we should continue to provide them any longer except as token activities to demonstrate politically that the state is doing something about adult literacy.

[5]I owe these references to Juliet Merrifield.

Conclusion

I do not wish to argue that this analysis applies only to so-called Third World countries; nor that it applies only to adults. I am trying to indicate that there is a natural learning process for both children and adults which is individualized and highly context dependent; that this is life related and very unlike the formalized learning that goes on in classes; and that we need to try to develop learning programs for adults which build on the natural learning processes which they engage in rather than ignoring such learning (Rogers 2003b). (The same may be true for children.)

Both of the approaches suggested above—the drop-in center and a literacy extension service—have the advantage that, unlike the adult literacy class, they can provide on-going learning support. They are not single-injection modes of learning literacy. The idea that you only need to learn literacy once in your life and will remain 'literate' for ever thereafter is one of the larger myths of literacy which keeps the traditional classroom approach to adult literacy learning alive. But it is essential to develop programs which get away from the standardized one-size-fits-all approach, which help individual adults as they develop new identities and roles and the skills appropriate to those new roles. These will use the 'real' literacy tasks and texts of the literacy learners for their learning (Rogers 1999). They "break out of the educational silo" (LitAfr 2000:13) of the schooling model—away from classes consisting of only 'illiterates'; from formal whole-class teaching rather than collaborative learning; from standardized learning texts felt to be appropriate for all adults. Above all, they will get away from a pre-set sequential learning program based on a false idea that adults need to learn simple things first and harder things later. As we have seen, reading shopping lists, writing out items from a construction site, identifying sites and buildings from street names, reading and writing the parts of motor vehicles, and so on, which many adults do on their own, indicate that adults often start learning with difficult words which they feel they urgently want to read rather than start with simple words and then move onto more difficult words and sentences. To talk about 'levels' of literacy for adults may be meaningless: what is the level of literacy for someone who can read and write car mechanic items but not read a newspaper? Why is reading a newspaper to be regarded as 'higher' than writing construction industry wage lists or keeping a record of shop accounts or clients' measurements?

Adults can and do learn literacy naturally in the course of their daily living. Our task is not to ignore this and put them into a school-room type of situation separate from life but to help them to build on it, to develop more systematic literacy skills able to deal with a wider range of literacy activities than if they are left on their own.

References

Abadzi, H. 1994. Adult literacy: is there hope? Washington D.C.: World Bank.

Aderinoye, R., and Rogers, A. 2004. Urban literacies: the intervention of the literacy shop in Bodija Market, Ibadan, Nigeria. In A. Rogers (ed.), *Urban Literacy: communication, identity and learning in development contexts*. Hamburg: UNESCO Institute of Education.

Aspin, D., Chapman, J., Hatton, M., and Sawano Y. (eds.). 2001. *International handbook of lifelong learning*. London: Kluwer.

Boud, D., and Miller, N. (eds.). 1996. *Working with experience: Animating learning*. New York: Routledge.

Brookfield, S. (ed.). 1985. *Self-directed learning: From theory to practice*. San Francisco: Jossey Bass.

Brookfield, S. 2000. Adult cognition as a dimension of adult learning. In J. Field and M. Leicester. *Lifelong learning*. London: Routledge Falmer.

Candy, P.C. 1991. *Self-direction for lifelong learning: A comprehensive guide to theory and practice*. San Francisco: Jossey Bass.

Chavajay, P., and Rogoff, B. 2002. Schooling and traditional collaborative social organization of problem solving by Mayan mothers and children. *Developmental Psychology* 38: 55–66.

Coffield, F. 2000. *The necessity of informal learning*. Bristol: Policy Press.

Dyer, C., and Choksi, A. 1998. Education is like wearing glasses: nomads' views of literacy and empowerment, *International Journal of Educational Development* 18(5): 405–413.

Evans, N. 1992. *Experiential learning: Assessment and accreditation*. London: Routledge.

Faure, E. Et al. 1972. *Learning to be*. Paris: UNESCO.

Field, J., and Leicester, M. 2000. *Lifelong learning*. London: Routledge Falmer.

Graff, H.J. 1979. *The literacy myth*. New York: Academic Press.

Hamilton, M., and Bergin, S. 1994. Who's at the Centre? The experience of open learning in adult basic education. In: M. Thorpe and D. Grugeon (eds.). *Open learning in the mainstream*. London: Longman.

Hamilton, D. 1990. *Learning about education*. Milton Keynes: Open University Press.

Kolb, D. 1984. *Experiential learning: Experience as the source of learning and development*. New Jersey: Prentice Hall.

Jung, I., and King, L. 1999. *Gender, innovation and education in Latin America*. Hamburg: UNESCO Institute of Education.

Lave, J., and Wenger, E. 1991. *Situated learning: Legitimate peripheral participation*. Cambridge: Cambridge University Press.

Levine, K. 1985. *The social context of literacy*. London: Routledge and Kegan Paul.

Literacy in Africa 2000. Paper prepared for Ministers of Education, Africa. Paris: UNESCO.

Mark, R., and Donaghy, M. 2003. *Using ICT as a hook.* Belfast: Queen's University.

McGivney, V. 2000. *Recovering outreach: Concepts, issues and practices.* Leicester: NIACE.

Merriam, S.B., and Cafarella, R.S. 1999. *Learning in adulthood: A comprehensive guide.* San Francisco: Jossey Bass.

Millican, J. 2004. "I will stay here until I die:" a critical analysis of the Muthande Literacy Programme, In: A. Robinson-Pant (ed.), *Women, literacy and development: Alternative perspective.* London: Routledge, pp. 195–205.

Rogers, A. 1999. Improving the quality of adult literacy: The 'real literacies' approach. *International Journal of Educational Development* 19: 219–234.

Rogers, A. 2000. Literacy comes second: Working with groups in developing societies. *Development in Practice* 10(2): 236–240.

Rogers, A. 2003a. *Teaching adults.* 3rd edition. Buckingham: Open University Press.

Rogers, A. 2003b. *What is the difference? A new critique of adult learning and teaching.* Leicester: NIACE.

Rogers, A. (ed.). 2004. *Urban literacy: Communication, identity and learning in developing countries.* Hamburg: UNESCO Institute of Education.

Rogers, A., Elias, M., Ranjanidas, R.P. 1989. *Partners in literacy.* Reading: Education for Development.

Rogoff, B. 1998. Cognition as a collaborative process. In: D. Kuhn and R.S. Siegler (eds.), *Cognition, perception and language.* New York: Wiley, pp. 679–744.

Sarangapani, P. 2002. *Constructing school knowledge.* Delhi: Sage.

Street, B.V. 1984. *Literacy in theory and practice.* Cambridge: Cambridge University Press.

Walters, S., and Manicom, L. 1996. *Gender in popular education: Methods for empowerment.* London: Zed Books.

13

"Not Just Infatuation"

Sexuality and Literacy in the Age of HIV

Dorinda Welle, Michael Clatts, and Glen Barnard

The main site that I go to inside this website is the health section, the one about how to protect yourself from serious diseases, and how to know some tricks and all that, you know, health tips. So I love that. But when I'm getting tired of knowing all about gay people, then I go to chat with them. So I usually go to the chat all the time, chat for hours and hours and hours, as long as this person is interesting. (Interview, Sammy)

At its best, anthropology is largely about utilizing the powerful experience of being "the outsider" to gain unique insights into everyday contexts and practices not immediately transparent to even the most privileged "insiders." We join in this discussion of New Literacy Studies as relative "newcomers" variously conducting ethnographic human immunodeficiency virus (HIV) behavioral research and providing prevention services among lesbian, gay, bisexual, transgender, and questioning (LGBTQ) youth, but not directly involved in literacy programming. However, in the course of launching an ethnographic study of LGBTQ youth in New York City, it quickly became apparent that we would need to address a range of literacy issues facing our mixed in-school and out-of-school sample. The field of HIV prevention has largely bypassed questions of how literacy practices might intersect with sexual or drug-related risk. By exploring intersections of sexuality and literacy practices evident in a set of narrative ethnographic data, we hope to illustrate how the perspectives afforded by a New Literacies approach can enrich our understanding of risk and protective contexts and practices in the lives of LGBTQ youth.

Explicating Shared Autonomous Models

Just as literacy has traditionally been defined and taught as a set of technical practices that students must master (Heath 1983; Street 1993), so sexuality has been commonly understood and approached as a set of technical practices accompanied by a fair amount of anxiety about mastery. Research conducted in the context of the AIDS pandemic has only further entrenched an understanding of sexuality as a constellation of disembodied acts alienated not only from the actor but also from the relational context of sexual encounters (Clatts 1998). Not unlike autonomous definitions of literacy which privilege "standard" practices such as reading and writing, what could be considered autonomous definitions of sexuality typically remain focused on a relatively limited set of "standard" sexual practices anchored within discrete "sexual events." By treating situated, relational practices as "acts," and by treating "identities" as predictive of individual behavior, autonomous models of sexuality (whether referencing heterosexual or LBTQ orientations) reify or invest agency in "things" rather than persons.

In addition, autonomous understandings of literacy and sexuality variously focus on "transmissibility," particularly in the transmission of knowledge through literacy practices, and the transmissibility of HIV through sexual (and drug injection) practices. These two autonomous models most clearly intersect in public health approaches to HIV prevention "messages," which are viewed to have the power to alter sexual behavior (if individuals are adequately "exposed" to these potent phrases). Two decades of HIV prevention education experiences have demonstrated the limits of an autonomous literacy model which assumes that the accumulation of knowledge and skills (through the transmission of prevention messages) will suffice to empower young adults to protect themselves from exposure to health risks. Similarly, the limits of both public health and literacy approaches that overemphasize "testing"—HIV testing, standardized educational testing—have become quite clear (for critiques of HIV testing, see Rowe et al. 2004; Bayer and Fairchild-Carrino 1993; for critiques of standardized educational testing, see Sacks 2001; Orfield and Kornhaber 2001).

The potential for overlap of autonomous, technical models for both literacy and sexuality immediately throws a certain shadow upon any project aiming to practically and conceptually link sexuality and literacy practices. Thus, we wish to provide some clarification about our conceptual orientation. We are not proposing a notion of "sexual literacy" in the sense of achieving sexual competence, sexual knowledge, or sexual skills. Nor is this project about defining or assuming some notion of "cultured" sexuality, "literate" sexuality, or "academic" sexuality (although it is hoped the linkages we explore are novel and make for a good read). In fact, the majority of social research on lesbian, gay, bisexual, transgender, and questioning youth has been derived from samples of college students immersed in academic literacy environments; here, we are interested in finding ways to make relationships between sexuality and literacy contexts and practices explicit rather than implicit, as well as identifying out-of-school contexts for the intersection of sexuality and literacy in social practice.

As a final disclaimer, we are not interested in defining some "essential" relationship between literacy and sexuality, but rather aim to explore literacy and sexuality "in use" and "in context," "in play" and "at work." Far from bringing us to some singular definition of a relationship, such a project involves examining the multiple contexts, multiple configurations, multiple functions, and multiple meanings of intersecting literacy and sexuality practices. With this emphasis on "the multiple," we ought to attend as well to the possibility of numeracy practices (Baker, Street, and Tomlin 2004) at work in these configurations of literacy and sexuality. Certainly HIV research has had its numeracy moments, tallying numbers of sexual partners and calculating the density of risk as it accumulates within sexual networks.

We need to ask not only how autonomous definitions of literacy legitimize hierarchical roles and statuses within education systems; we also need to conduct a kind of archaeology of the autonomous model, exhuming its artifacts in the stratifications of students' adult lives, particularly in their identities and relationships. As an early model of social inequity both based upon and competing for primacy with caretaker-child relationships, the teacher-student relationship serves as a site of socialization for other (uneven yet meaningful) adult relationships. How do the meanings and statuses invested in literacy inform and organize the distribution of power within relationships?

More specifically, how might the "positive" meanings and statuses invested in literacy inform partner selection and the assumption of risk-bearing roles within sexual encounters? These are difficult questions to ask, not only because the autonomous model masks the ways that schooling produces gendered and sexual subjects; but also because the autonomous model would prohibit an examination of how students, as adults, may appropriate the autonomous model for themselves, in their intimate relationships, in their efforts at economic survival, and in ways that may engender unanticipated consequences for their health. We need to understand ethnographically how students and out-of-school youth apply the criteria implicit in the autonomous model of literacy, particularly in how they use autonomous assumptions about literacy and education in their assessments and selections of sexual partners. By equating partners' literacy and education levels with "health," and by equating their own literacy proficiencies as unduly protective, LGBTQ youth and heterosexual youth face potentially serious unintended health consequences. At the same time, by examining intersections of sexuality and literacy in context, we aim to disrupt autonomous, homophobic discourse that represents gay educators as predators and students as victims, instead bringing questions of agency and desire into focus.

An autonomous literacy model generates the impression that sexuality is only relevant to the sexual "other"—e.g., gay, lesbian, bisexual, transgender, or questioning students. However, the intersection of sexuality and literacy has significance across sexual and gender orientations. For example, Stein and Mamabolo (this volume) detail how the African AIDS pandemic—driven largely by heterosexual transmission of the HIV virus—intervenes in the lives of rural South African students and their families, and raises questions about the sustainability and contemporary relevance of autonomous forms of schooling.

In the following ethnographic case study, we aim to demonstrate a number of juxtapositions of literacy to sexuality in the everyday life of Sammy, a homeless, immigrant gay youth in New York City. However, we should note that, unlike autonomous approaches that problematize "illiteracy," our particular interest in learning from Sammy's narratives is informed by our initial observations of the value and centrality of literacy in Sammy's narration of himself as a sexual subject. His narratives are rich in description of the various modes of textual and sexual communication he employs. In addition to writing text and reading text, Sammy engages mixed modes of communication (Kress 2001), augmenting written (email, instant messages) with visual mode (photographs), written (poetry) with spoken mode, and the multiple modes and multiple actors that comprise interactive video (Kress and Van Leeuwen 2003).

However, this is not necessarily about celebrating some sort of postmodern multiplicity and fluency of modes. Extending research on modes of communication, we ask how various modes of literacy-and-sexuality practices might not only construct *identities* and convey *meanings* but also construct and convey forms of *risk* and *protection, agency* and *vulnerability?* Using this bifocal lens of literacy-and-sexuality practices (Cuchiara similarly uses a bifocal lens of NLS and Freirean approaches; this volume), can we identify discrete contexts and modes that seem variously protective or facilitative for HIV transmission? Stated more broadly, how might the lens of literacy-and-sexuality practices illuminate the possibilities for—and constraints on—agency and subjectivity for LGBTQ youth?

The 2Grown Project

The 2Grown Project is a four-year longitudinal ethnographic study of developmental complexity (Noam 1996) among street-involved LGBTQ youth. Examining how the AIDS epidemic complicates adolescent development and sexual identity development for LGBTQ youth, the study employs life history interviewing, participant-observation, and ethnographic follow-up interviewing focused on sexual and drug use–related risk and protective behaviors and individual participants' life history themes. We first became interested in the significance of literacy in relation to developmental complexity in our pilot phase, when it became clear that LGBTQ youth not only reported extensive harassment in school (see Savin-Williams and Cohen 1996), but also described how their experiences of harassment affected their grades and participation in school. We also became aware of how LGBTQ youth in our preliminary research considered "getting an education" as a potent counter to negative stereotypes of LGBTQ youth. These themes of literacy and education now constitute an important focus of the ongoing research.

The Case Study: Meeting Sammy at The Internet Warehouse

Parallel to the description in Sammy's opening quote, the 2Grown research team started the first weeks of the project in the "health section," reading the HIV literature "about how to protect yourself from serious diseases" and reading the available literature on LGBTQ youth and sexuality. But, like Sammy, once we were saturated with reading "all about gay people," we felt ready to start the pilot phase and "go to chat with them." However, at this point, we encountered a problem that faces nearly all LGBTQ youth: how to go out in public and identify (other) LGBTQ youth and "chat with them" without directly asking about their identity or implicitly identifying them as "gay"? For LGBTQ youth, this is a concern as much about personal safety as it is about identity disclosure. For our research group, it was a concern about protection of the youths' confidentiality, as well as an ethnographic confrontation with the nonverbal signs we were "reading" to signify lesbian, gay, bisexual, or transgender identities and inform our recruitment.

One of our early strategies then, in utilizing a venue-based or street-based recruitment approach (Clatts, Welle, and Goldsamt 2001), involved conducting participant-observation at a large commercial Internet venue in one of the tourist districts of Manhattan. We reasoned that, if LGBTQ youth at Internet venues were comfortable "disclosing" their identity via the websites appearing on their publicly-visible computer screens, that they would be amenable to confidential recruitment in such a setting. Through the barriers we encountered to public recruitment of LGBTQ youth, we became familiar with the social and environmental contingencies that make the Internet such a popular venue for LGBTQ youth to connect with each other.

"Sammy" was the first individual recruited into the pilot phase of the 2Grown study. Stationed at one of the 800 computers housed in the two-story Internet Warehouse, Sammy sat in the middle seat of a bank of six computers, keyboards set close together along a mass-produced plastic surface, monitors attached to a bare plank of plywood. The cavernous warehouse, filled with Internet users, was eerily silent except for the sound of typing. Glen and Dorinda sat down at a computer across from Sammy, whose monitor displayed a Gay.com screen. Once Sammy logged off, we asked if we could interrupt him and tell him about a study we were doing. He agreed, and expressed interest in the study's themes. Sammy explained that he is 19 years old, currently homeless, and "always on line." Born and raised in Sri Lanka, he later immigrated with his family to London, where he came out to his parents. Within a year of disclosing his sexual orientation to them, everyday life became intolerable, and Sammy immigrated alone to New York, which he believed would be "more free than London."

In New York, his stay with relatives of his mother was short-lived; as the relatives began to "suspect" that Sammy was gay, they accused him of trying to "poison" them, and he left their household for a homeless shelter. He explained that by staying "for free" at homeless shelters, he can utilize the money his mother gave him for tuition to finish a two-year college degree. He pulled a necklace out of his shirt, showing us a silver military dog tag with vivid rainbow colors imprinted on the metal. "This is the rainbow of the gay people, and I always wear it. At school, I wear it backwards so they don't see the colors. But some people I show them the rainbow side."

Dressing Up for Autonomous Literacy: Gendered Schooling, Genetic Sexuality

Mixing descriptions of sexual difference and gender difference, Sammy introduced his life history with descriptions of growing up "a gay person" and dressing like, feeling like, and acting "like a girl" during his early childhood in rural Sri Lanka.

> I was born September 22nd, 1983, in Sri Lanka. And I grew up as, really, like, a gay person, because I remember at age 6 going around fanning myself with a piece of skirt and walking down the street like a girl. And everybody thought I was a girl. Everybody. And I was really open about myself, even during that tender age. My mother was not against it, my father died two years before I even became myself, like, dressing up like a girl. I was about 2 years old, something like that (when he died). I was still crawling. So, at about 6 years old, I started going around with skirts and all that. Some people had a problem; my mom didn't have a problem. I felt like a girl when I was dressed like a girl, acted like a girl. I go outside, buy stuff, groceries, all that.

Sammy describes his six years "dressed like a girl" as a kind of developmental phase that predated puberty and his entry into private school. Suggesting a vertical move into a masculine presentation that afforded him access to a quality educational setting, Sammy recalled when he started "dressing up" like a boy.

> After that, I grew up, actually, when I was about 12. That's when I got some flesh and bones, when I started dressing up like a boy. . . . I couldn't wear all those (girls' clothes) at a private school. I had to wear pants, you know? You

can't wear all that in a private school. . . . But that feeling (was) still there, and the gene (was) still inside me that says that I am a gay person. So I (went) to school normally, I graduated from (high) school in 1998.

Since Sammy associated being "a gay person" with dressing, feeling, and acting "like a girl," his shift into a "normal" gender presentation at school generated a movement of the site of sexuality signifiers. Previously located on the body's surface where it could be "read" in social context, upon Sammy's entry into private school, the "text" of sexual orientation relocated to the body's deepest interior, where it could be "read" (only by Sammy) as genetic code. This interiority was further illustrated when Sammy explained,

> I suppressed the feeling. I mean, you can't express (same-sex attractions), you'll be chucked out of the school, you know.

Thus, school effectively represented a moment when certain (autonomous) texts could remain external and comprise the focus of autonomous literacy practices, while the text of sexuality became "suppressed" (see Foucault 1978). In this way, homosexuality and gender difference are institutionally constructed to appear as "ideological," invested with desires that schooling enables LGBTQ youth to identify but requires LGBTQ youth to deny. One effect, then, of the autonomous model, is the projection of ideological (sexual) content and interests onto "the student/other" (as well as the "teacher/other"). Since heterosexual desires are typically assumed to be neutral and "natural," those students experiencing homosexual and gender-different desires are most "at risk" of exposing the autonomous literacy model as in fact thouroughly invested with ideological (e.g., heterosexual) content, functions, and structures.

In this institutional/educational context that dares not expose its own reproduction of conventional power relations, "ideological" sexual practices are set against "autonomous" literacy practices. An enormous burden subsequently falls on LGBTQ students, who weigh the delights of flirting against the costs of flunking. Sammy perceived that if he were to let these feelings "come out," he would run the risk of being "chucked out" of school. In this context, we can begin to see the significance of generating a reciprocal dialogue across the fields of literacy and sexuality. Just as Stein and Mamabolo (this volume) claim that "pedagogy is not enough," here we claim that a critical dialogue with autonomous and new literacy approaches is not enough. In concert with putting forward "home" literacy practices, for example, there is a need to identify the normative (autonomous) content of "home" and inquire into its ideological underpinnings, including normative (autonomous) models of sexuality. It is through this analogy with sexuality that the ideological content of even new literacy approaches can become transparent. A creative and dialogic "self-critique" of new literacy approaches appears throughout this volume, as various authors juxtapose "other" fields with New Literacy Studies. Stein and Mamabolo bring in practices from the field of social work to critique and transform normative literacy models in South Africa. Similarly, Hopson brings in theories of identity and power to illuminate and transform autonomous models of literacy with Appalachian youth, making possible as well the identification of problematic assumptions in liberatory approaches to literacy and pedagogy.

Coming Out in the Context of School: "Literally Shocking"

The timing of LGBTQ youths' decisions to "come out" needs to be considered in relation to their school careers (Mauk, Welle, and Clatts 2004; Fuller, Welle, and Clatts 2004). In Sammy's life history narrative, we see a deferral of coming out until after graduation from the private high school in India. Having achieved a successful graduation, he feels free to come out. However, this implicit plan becomes complicated by various unanticipated circumstances. Immediately after his graduation, Sammy's mother and step-father move the family to London, where Sammy faces an additional two years of schooling to meet English educational standards.

> After (graduation), I moved to England. And I went there for two years (of) high school, just two years, because, you know, I finished already but they just wanted to test me because this is at English standards, (which) are much more, so . . . It was during this time that I came out myself as a gay person. Openly came out to the world as a gay person. And my family was shocked. They were shocked, literally.

As anthropologist Brackette Williams (1994) demonstrated in her ethnographic research in Guyana, the social source of "getting a shock" often can be traced to moments when autonomous models of social life are exposed as ideological and/or claimed as such. In other words, when the hierarchical organization of assumedly neutral relationships is made explicit, or the distances structured into hierarchical relations are momentarily bridged or re-organized, members of the immediate or larger social group "get a shock."

In Sammy's life history narrative, his disclosure of his sexual orientation to his mother and step-father occurred in the context of his disclosure of his desire to "run away" with a male instructor at his London high school. Introducing—or rather, acknowledging—sexual and romantic desire into the teacher-student relationship, and demonstrating this "autonomous," formal structure as "self-interested" and potentially intimate, Sammy exposed one of the fundamental social features of the autonomous literacy model: namely, that the pedagogical relationship partakes in power relations that are variously gendered and sexualized. As David Halpern (2003) has noted, "hierarchy is hot," but discussing the structuring of sexual desire is not. Demanding a silencing of sexual desire while actively silencing the everyday sexualization of the pedagogical relationship, the intersection of autonomous models of literacy and sexuality places students of all sexual orientations in a fragile situation in which the potential for sexual desire (through the uneven structuring of teacher-student relations) is great, but the costs of articulating and trying to understand this reality seem greater.

Sexy Literacy and Literate Sexuality

Sexuality and literacy intersect most directly in life history context and in developmental context as students explore their own sexual attractions while attending school. In Sammy's life history narrative, sexual desire overlaps with his respect for educators and education. Willing to "dress up" to attend private school, discipline his gender, and accumulate the social-educational capital that this promises, Sammy first experienced same-sex attractions in the context of attending school.

> The first time was when I was in the private school. I was staying in a boarding (school) in Sri Lanka. There was this instructor, I was madly in love with him. Not just infatuation.

Similarly, his "coming out story" is interwoven with a story of running away with a male instructor at his high school. Sammy described how gay youth at his high school in Sri Lanka experienced "severe economic hardship" after coming out; they were effectively banned from the local workforce. By identifying with male educators, Sammy counters the "negative" status assigned to homosexuality or gender difference with the "positive" status and respect invested in teachers and others in the profession of education.

As a young adult in New York, Sammy applies the autonomous model of pedagogy and utilizes its criteria in his selection of sexual partners. He describes consistently selecting sexual partners who are variously "associated with" schools and who exhibit the markers of educational success. Here Sammy describes his most recent partner that he met on the Internet.

> He's got a very cute voice. He's a singer. He's also a school administrator. Well-dressed. And, um, you know, a lot of things about him which I really admire. So, we took his car and we drove. We had dinner in a very exclusive restaurant. It's called Tea for Two.

In these encounters, Sammy largely remains the "student" who "admires" the slightly older, more educationally established partner. It is the partner who can provide the "class" in this encounter, and who has achieved the autonomous subjectivity (if that is not an oxymoron) worthy of "admiration": the "voice," the looks, the car, the salary—all of the things that a good education promises to "buy." By going out on this date and partnering with a "literate" individual while struggling for survival as a homeless youth, Sammy gets to temporarily or at least imaginatively occupy the same (social if not economic) "class" as his partner. The educational metaphor is certainly not lost in all of this class positioning.

Class positioning at dinner was followed by sexual positioning in what Sammy recalled was "the greatest moment" of his life.

> We're in the car, and he stopped in a very quiet parking lot with a lot of scenic beauty outside, with the moon hanging out, and we start kissing, and we had sex. In the car! It was the greatest moment of my life.

Having sex with someone who has presented himself as a school administrator represents for Sammy a grand and memorable moment when literacy and sexuality merge in a scene so idyllic it could have originated from a romance novel (what with the quite literary—and perhaps also literal—moon hanging out).

Literacy did not just constitute a "status symbol" embodied in the partner's livelihood; literacy practices also directly informed sexuality practices in this romantic encounter. When asked about whether Sammy asked his partner to use a condom during anal sex, he responded:

> Yeah, we used condoms. We used condoms. Actually, he was very honest about his being, him being HIV-negative. He showed me all the papers.

Thus, the partner showed Sammy written documents to "verify" his health status. "Showing one's HIV papers" is a common autonomous literacy practice that calls upon the officiality, the authority, and, as Sammy implies, the naïve "honesty" of documents, while playing upon implicit assumptions about the truth-value and the permanency of written information. As any HIV educator will explain (usually without intending a pun), "HIV test results are only as good as your last sexual encounter." However, in sexual encounters, "HIV papers" are often reified, decontextualized, and treated as tantamount to travel authorizations, granting one "safe" and "sanctioned" access into "unknown" or "foreign" territory or affording "sexual citizenship."

Here we might reflect on how the autonomous model of literacy, as it requires the suppression and interiorization of sexuality into the unreadable depths of the body, might also contribute to the "success" of the literacy practice of presenting one's HIV papers. For many LGBTQ youth, as Sammy's narrative illustrates, their schooling experience socializes them into the dual experience of interiority of sexuality and exteriority of autonomous written documents. Certainly the interiority of the HIV virus, combined with the exteriorization of "official," written HIV status, duplicates the bi-directional experience of the intersection of autonomous (formally documented) literacy and autonomous (interiorized, unreadable) sexuality. One can imagine this as effecting a "tearing apart" of the subject by pulling in opposite directions. Just as the autonomous literacy model insists that students not be "torn" over their sexual orientation, so its relationship to autonomous, interiorized sexual health helps insure that LGBTQ students not be unduly "torn" over the possible HIV status of their sexual partners, as long as superficial, visually "readable" signs of health are available.

Reciprocally, Sammy's "viewing his partner's HIV papers" constitutes an autonomous literacy practice, in its uncritical acceptance of written medical "facts" authorized by recognized institutions. Not only did Sammy not interrogate his partner's "HIV papers," he declined to produce his own: a reciprocity that would befit an encounter between two "versatile" partners. Weeks after the romantic encounter with the school administrator, Sammy called Glen from the emergency room to reschedule an upcoming ethnographic interview. Days later, he explained that shelter staff brought him into the emergency department, where he was kept overnight for a round of intravenous antibiotics for an unspecified infection.

Although currently a health major in college and aspiring to become a pharmacist, Sammy did not learn the name of the condition which the hospital staff was treating. "Some kind of throat infection. It's in my medical records, I'm sure." Two weeks prior to this hospitalization, Sammy went for an HIV test, but hadn't returned for the test results. And he didn't seem to be "torn" about what to do, having managed to "write off" written information about his health status as the purview of doctors and anonymous medical staff. Autonomous literacy does not inquire either into the meanings of those documents one does read, nor the meanings of refusals to read what has been documented. By refusing to read his own medical records, Sammy is able to retain the role of student, still needing to "learn" about his health status while remaining available to "learn" about his partners if not himself. What remains at stake in the failure of autonomous literacy models to address sexual risk for HIV is the increased likelihood of having to "learn"—of course, always too late—from so-called "experience."

Intersections of Sexuality and Literacy in the New Work Order

> I wake up at about 7, and eat breakfast. And then I get dressed up, and then head to school. I reach my school at about 9, 9:15. 9:30 I start my (first) class, Customer Service . . . beautiful course . . . This should help me in, you know, finding a job.

Gee et al. (1996) eloquently detailed the characteristics of The New Work Order, which makes new demands on the content, application, and social organization of literacy practices. As Street (2001) has noted, the autonomous model of literacy is profoundly inadequate to the team-oriented marketing practices informing The New Work Order. Sammy's life history narrative further underscores this inadequacy, as the aims of his schooling direct him into the traditionally low-paying, traditionally female, and now emergent, low-paying gay male economic role of Customer Service. As a homeless youth, as an immigrant, and as a gay male youth of color, Sammy implicitly recognizes that Customer Service may be his best chance—"a beautiful course"—but he also recognizes the exploitation built into this particular level of the economy.

> I've heard that (The Gap) uses prison employment, which is very bad. . . . I'm totally against, you know, like, prison employment. So that's why I don't want to work at the Gap. I find that cruel, you know, for any company to treat people . . . like prisoners, having prisoners to, you know, work for them, to make the clothes and all that.

While Sammy recognizes the direct exploitation involved in prison-based manufacturing, his language indirectly refers to the economic confinement that such Customer Service roles might eventually impose on him. Illustrating the local realities of this economic confinement, our prior research with young men who have sex with men identified two main economic niches for YMSM in New York City: (1) legal customer service roles at global clothing franchises which typically utilize LGBTQ imagery in their marketing and (2) illegal street-based sex work (Welle et al. 2002). Currently, Sammy is located in "the gap" between these two available economic niches: preparing for a career in Customer Service and familiarizing himself with the Internet as a potential sex work venue. At a juncture between finishing school and entering the workforce, Sammy also straddles two autonomous models of sexuality: one, anchored in school contexts, that references heterosexual scripts, and another, anchored in cyberspace, that references sexual scripts between men who have sex with men. As we will see below, what these two models of autonomous sexuality share is a mainstream economic discourse that authorizes and naturalizes "service" relationships between sexual partners.

Searching: MyRichUncle.Com

Returning to the homeless shelter after being informed that, as an international student, he did not qualify for any scholarships at his two-year college, Sammy stopped at The Internet Warehouse thinking about money. Initially, he went onto the Internet as a way of making a kind of magical wish, searching for the possibility of limitless wealth.

> And then, I went to the Internet, I went to this website called MyRichUncle .com. (The name) just clicked in my head, I don't know how. I said, "Okay, let me try to go to the Internet." And when I clicked—oh! (laughs) I re-member. I wrote, you know, in that search, in that search gap, Yahoo search gap. I just wrote, "RICH UNCLE." I just was wishing for it. And I click, and there it was: MyRichUncle.com. It was such a funny incident.

However, in the land of Uncle Sam, "My Rich Uncle" turned out to be a bank willing to send students into debt.

> I've got some papers in (my backpack). It's basically about the loan that you could get. You don't pay till you graduate and get your job and all that. . . . It's more like a loan, a loan site. There's some bank affiliated with it.

Granted a small scholarship by his homeless shelter, but pressed to come up with money for daily living and school expenses, Sammy turned his interests to hooking up with financially stable "professionals," "international bankers," and other "educated types" through Internet chat rooms.

Stripped-Down Text: Modes of Communication

Analyzing video- and audio-taped classroom sessions, Kress (2001) has provided nuanced descriptions of the various modes through which classroom literacy practices are conveyed and realized. By identifying the material modes of writ-ten communication that Sammy uses and encounters on the Internet, we can gain insight into the structuring of HIV risk. However, as Kress notes, captur-ing reciprocal modes of communication is particularly complex. Here, we take a unique approach and rely upon Sammy's ethnographic narrative account (see

Hymes 1996) of these Internet-based literacy practices: an approach with both strengths and limitations. On the one hand capturing Sammy's experience of discrete modes, and on the other hand missing altogether modes that Sammy might fail to describe, this narrative approach provides a starting point for future elaborations of ethnographic method and analysis of Internet-based literacy-and-sexuality practices.

Not long after posting a written profile on a gay website, Sammy learned that written text alone was not considered "sexy." Text had to be accompanied by a visual image of the body.

> I was at my friend's house, he took a picture. And he said, you know, if you want to attract somebody . . . you have to put some sort of picture that really attracts people. And it did . . . a picture with just my underwear on. I was like, on the computer. It's not really, but some people find it sexy. Whenever I'm there, I'll get, like 20 windows popping at a time.

Inviting a "stripped-down" conversation at the computer, Sammy struggled to view his own photo as "sexy," noting that he wore "cheap underwear" that he hoped the computer would partially hide. Rather, "sexy" is defined through the number of "windows" that "pop up" when his photo appears. These windows can be fairly easily managed, affording Sammy substantial control in deciding whether to exchange text messages with one or more men. On winter afternoons until his shelter's curfew, Sammy would sit in the upstairs level of the Internet Warehouse trying to stay warm and engage in hours of text exchange on line.

He got involved in webcam chats through the friend who initially took his photo. Sammy's descriptions indicate webcam communication as both multimodal and multidirectional.

> We were chatting. We were chatting with the webcam on. So basically, he was telling me, "Okay, take off your shirt." I said, "If it really excites you. I mean, I really don't care." So I basically did for him. But I didn't realize that after I started doing, stripping off, and stopped, I got, like, 20 messages saying, "Do it again. Do it again." I realized that a lot of people were watching me.

The use of a webcam also introduces what could be considered a Customer Service model of communication, in which one individual is expected to visually "service" another, who acts as the "customer." In the quote above, Sammy is not thoroughly invested in this model; he "really (doesn't) care" what his viewer wants, and describes providing the performance in a casual manner.

In contrast to Instant Messaging, where Sammy can craft his own responses to others' emails or messages and go into more "private" chat rooms with selected individuals, the webcam is operated by his friend, who chooses how "Sammy" will respond to viewers' demands for repeat performances, and who opts to multiply rather than limit the viewing audience.

> My friend was operating that, you know, the whole (webcam) thing, and he clicked on "Yes," and "Yes," and "Yes," and "Yes," and "Yes." I mean, it comes, like, do you want somebody to, this guy to watch this, and you say, like, "Yes" or "No." If you say "Yes," it comes on the screen.

Critically describing his friend's role as "director" of the webcam production, Sammy describes a hierarchical organization of webcam communication: his friend "behind" the camera, protected from exposure, and Sammy "in front of" the camera and the audience, "stripping down."

> And he keeps clicking "Yes." Without knowing (whether) I was going to do that. So basically, when he chats, then, you know, he always clicks "Yes" to everything. He doesn't care. He doesn't strip down. But for me, I did.

Having stopped the script in its tracks by refusing to continue, Sammy generated a flood of responses that "froze" the computer.

> They started sending messages, thousands of messages, until the computer froze because there was too many messages coming over (saying), "Why did you stop?" "Oh, go on, please." . . . "Hi cutie," this, that. "I really want to meet you, where are you?" I just happened to respond to one boy. I said, "I'm in the United States. Of America." He got angry (laughs).

Responding by presenting himself as remote and inaccessible, Sammy took pleasure in breaking a cardinal rule of Customer Service by making a customer "angry."

When the computer re-booted, Sammy was effectively confronted with an image of himself: a young man, nearly the same age, also going through hardships in his life.

Boot(ed) back up. I saw this guy from Brooklyn. He was so cute. I'm meeting him tomorrow. Oh my God. I was in Gay.com chat, and I was not doing any computer, you know, webcam. And he said, "I like you." I said, "How could you like me? You didn't even see me." He said, "I like your picture. . . ." I didn't even go a sentence further, he started saying, "Okay, let me tell you the truth. . . ." He said, "Okay, I worked all my way up here, I'm 25 years old, and you know, I really have struggled in my life. I do this, I do that. . . ." You know, lot of things. And then I said, "Okay, let me see your face. . . ." So we got our, you know, webcam, started chatting. I thought he just wanted some sort of striptease or something like that. I started, you know, taking off my clothes. And he said, "This is not at all—I just wanted to meet you. I don't want you to do that for me." And I was, like, shocked. He looked at me, the whole chat was just looking at me. I mean, I could just see his face. His face was angelic. He was just so cute. I couldn't say anything. I was dumbfounded.

As a moment of crisis in the coherence of an autonomous literacy model, this encounter introduced the possibility of "telling the truth" in the context of socially-scripted exchanges, of moderating one's own level of "exposure" to an unknown audience, and of breaking out of the expectation of "servicing" someone. Instead, Sammy "encountered" someone and, in the process, encountered himself. Through Sammy's critical exposure and rejection of the Customer Service approach to Internet encounters, he experiences a momentary transformation of the usual hierarchical organization of power, and revels in innocence, seeing a potential partner as "true," "angelic," "cute," someone to "like" rather than "service." In this instance the Internet audience witnesses a different kind of naked moment, one when an autonomous model of literacy can no longer naturalize an autonomous model of sexuality and a kind of "shock" occurs. In this dis(course)juncture, both writing and speech fail Sammy and he is momentarily "dumbfounded:" unable to speak, yet "found," not just seen but recognizing himself in a dialogue about biography and desire.

Discussion/Chat

Given the severe tensions in the development of subjectivity in "the era of the death of the subject" (Passerini 2002; Noam 1996b), ethnographic investigations into the intersection of literacy-and-sexuality can support inquiry into the social construction of desire among students and out-of-school youth: What literacy practices do individual students value, and why? What kinds of partnering practices do individual students value, and why? Since autonomous models of literacy and sexuality rarely facilitate youths' identification of their own unique desires and sources of pleasure, ethnographic interviewing can become a potent process of exploration and documentation of the ongoing social construction of desire and pleasure.

Academic treatments of desire and pleasure typically overemphasize "the sexual," overlooking other domains and forms of pleasure, enjoyment, and engagement. The importance of discovering what is "fun"—an everyday construct which seems to bring together learning and pleasure—resonates in several chapters in this volume (e.g., Larson; Hopson; Davies). As described in Larson's chapter, fieldtrips outside the classroom anchor "sleep-overs" in educational contexts and settings, linking educational empowerment with students' experiences of intimacy, friendship, play, and physical comforts with adults and age peers.

As we have seen in this chapter, autonomous models of literacy re-locate sexuality in the forbidding depths of biology and the body, robbing students of "accessible" discourses about sexuality and making "the coming out process" a profoundly wrenching one. Through a process of externalizing or "releasing" the very narratives that autonomous models suppress, ethnographic and life history interviewing can provide a platform for individual learners to transform disciplinary "biopower"—i.e., the power invested in an individual's genetics, identities, biology (Foucault, 1977)—into a meaningful biography that can "realize" the self and "impact" others (Welle and Falkin, in press). In particular, ethnographic research can provide a nonjudgemental context for students and out-of-school youth grappling with the extended process of "coming out" and desiring confidentiality protections. In our current research, many LGBTQ youth report speaking with school counselors focused on enhancing students' "time management skills" and little interested in life history themes that may include sexuality or the impact of coming out stressors on educational achievement. School counselors' use of confidential life history interviewing may also encourage LGBTQ youth to exercise their "biographical" power while contemplating "coming out" at school: In constructing a "coming out story," literacy and sexuality practices are mutually operant.

The approach to literacy-and-sexuality we have detailed here has potential to inform HIV education and prevention curricula, pedagogy, and practices, as well as the development of sex education curricula (Barnard, Welle, and Clatts 2004). Future ethnographic research on HIV prevention can elaborate health-related literacy practices, such as those related to partner selection, scripting of high-risk behaviors, safer sex education, and HIV testing and treatment. We need to better understand how the autonomous model of literacy and its diffusion into school settings variably impacts the education experiences and literacy practices and outcomes for lesbian, gay, bisexual, transgender, questioning, and heterosexual youth. By applying ethnographic interviewing as well as observational and archival methods in nontraditional, out-of-school settings, we can gain a more thoroughly grounded understanding of youth in contexts of HIV risk and contexts of educational engagement. Two decades into the AIDS pandemic, and two decades into the standardization crisis in public education, it is imperative that educators and researchers begin to explore intersections of literacy and sexuality in local and global contexts.

Acknowledgements: Research reported in this chapter was funded through a grant awarded to Dorinda Welle by the National Institute for Child Health and Human Development (Grant R01 HD 41723–01) and support from National Development & Research Institutes, Inc. Views expressed in this chapter do not necessarily represent those of NDRI or the U.S. Government. We acknowledge the essential contributions of the 2Grown Project team: Amy Braksmajer, Sebastian Fuller, Daniel Mauk, Damaris Wortes, and Kristine Ziek, and are especially grateful to Sammy and his peers for their ongoing participation in this project.

References

Baker, D., Street, B.V., and Tomlin, A. 2004. Maths as social: Understanding the relationship between home and school numeracy practices. *For the learning of mathematics* 23(3): 11–15.

Barnard, G.H., Welle, D.L., and Clatts, M.C. 2004. Layering the sex ed cake: LGBTQ youth at risk. Presentation, 25th Annual Ethnography in Education Research Forum, February 26–28, Philadelphia, Pennsylvania.

Bayer, R., and Fairchild-Carrino, A. 1993. AIDS and the limits of control: Public health orders, quarantines, and recalcitrant behavior. *American Journal of Public Health* 83(10): 1471–1476.

Clatts, M.C. 1998. Ethnographic observations of men who have sex with men in public: Notes and queries toward an ecology of sexual action. In: W. Leap (ed.), *Gay Sex, Public Space*. New York: Columbia University Press.

Clatts, M.C., Welle, D.L., and Goldsamt, L.G. 2001. Reconceptualizing the interaction of drug and sexual risk among MSM speed users: Notes toward an ethnoepidemiology. *AIDS and Behavior* 5(2): 115–130.

Foucault, M. 1977. *Discipline and punish: The birth of the prison*. New York: Pantheon.

Foucault, M. 1978. *The history of sexuality*. Volume 1. New York: Random House.

Fuller, S.S., Welle, D.L., and Clatts, M.C. 2004. "A little sugar in her tank": The challenges of gender transitioning and school. Presentation, 25th Annual Ethnography in Education Research Forum, February 26–28, Philadephia, Pennsylvania.

Gee, J., Jull, G., and Lankshear, C. 1996. *The new work order: Behind the language of the new capitalism*. Sydney: Allen & Unwin.

Halpern, D. 2002. *How to do the history of homosexuality*. Chicago: University of Chicago Press.

Heath, S.B. 1982. What no bedtime story means: Narrative skills at home and school. *Language and Society* 11: 49–76.

Hymes, D. 1996. *Ethnography, linguistics, narrative inequality: Towards an understanding of voice*. Philadelphia: Taylor & Francis.

Kress, G. 2001. *Multimodal discourse: The modes and media of contemporary communication*. London: Edward Arnold.

Kress, G., and Van Leeuwen, T. 2003. *Literacy in the new media age*. London: Routledge.

Mauk, D., Welle, D.L., and Clatts, M.C. 2004. "The rainbow cloud": The public and private lives of a "popular" gay student. Presentation, 25th Annual Ethnography in Education Research Forum, February 26–28, Philadephia, Pennsylvania.

Noam, G.G. 1996a. High-risk children and youth: Transforming our understanding of human development. *Human Development* (39): 1–17.

Noam, G.G. 1996b. Reconceptualizing maturity: The search for deeper meaning. In: G.G. Noam and K.W. Fischer (eds.), *Development and Vulnerability in Close Relationships*. Mahwah: Lawrence Erlbaum, pp. 135–172.

Orfield, G., and Kornhaber, M. 2001. *Raising standards or raising barriers?: Inequality and high stakes testing in public education*. New York: Century Foundation Press.

Passerini, L. 2000. Becoming a subject in the time of the death of the subject. Presentation, 4th European Feminist Research Conference: Body, gender, subjectivity: Crossing borders of disciplines and institutions. September 28–October 1, Bologna. Full text available at www.women.it/cyberarchive/files/passerini.htm.

Rowe, R.E., Garcia, J., and Davidson, L.L. 2004. Social and ethnic inequalities in the offer and uptake of prenatal screening and diagnosis in the UK: A systematic review. *Public Health* 118(3): 177–189.

Sacks, P. 2001. *Standardized minds: The high price of America's testing culture and what we can do to change it*. Boulder: Perseus Publishing.

Savin-Williams, R.C., and Cohen, K.M. 1996. *The lives of lesbians, gays, and bisexuals: Children to adults*. Belmont: Wadsworth.

Street, B.V. (ed.). 1993. *Cross-cultural approaches to literacy*. Cambridge: Cambridge University Press.

Street, B.V. 1995. *Social literacies: Critical approaches to literacy in development, ethnography and education*. London: Longman.

Street, B.V. (ed.). 2001. *Literacy and development: Ethnographic perspectives.* London: Routledge.

Welle, D.L., Clatts, M.C., Lankenau, S., Goldsamt, L.G., and Yi, H. 2002. Globalization and market-level sources of risk among young men who have sex with men (YMSM) involved in sex work. Poster, 2002 International Conference on AIDS. Barcelona, Spain.

Welle, D.L., and Falkin, G.P. In press. "Bio"power and bodies of righting: Women inmates in drug treatment. *Pre/Text: A Journal of Rhetorical Theory.* Volume 18 ("Prison/Literacy/Culture").

Williams, B.F. 1991. *Stains on my name, war in my veins: Guyana and the politics of cultural struggle.* Durham: Duke University Press.

14

What Does "Finding Out" Literacy Practices Mean?

An Exploration of Some of the "Hard Issues" in a College English Class Tutoring Project with Appalachian Children

Julie Eastlack Hopson

We worry about using [Appalachian school tutees] as lab rats basically and this is something we need to bring up . . . In my darkest moments when I think we just have to stop this, I don't know what else, how else I would teach. I know this is really, really good for our students but I doubt it does much real good out in the community and that drives us crazy. Those are the really hard issues of service learning. Is there such a thing? Can we serve a community? What are we trying to accomplish? Even if you go and do the ethnography and find out the literacy practices of the people you're dealing with, etc., etc., what do they want out of this? And then we just get into political agendas and ideologies and does the university like this, that caters to the elite liberal arts class—does it really want to be out there working for social justice? What is social justice? What is economic justice? All those sorts of things? We're back to structural issues. What is the schooling you want to do? How much a part of the community does it really want to be?
—Lithman College, Professor Nevis[1]

[1]All names have been changed.

Introduction

In this chapter, I discuss ethnographic research designed to "find out" some of the New Literacy Studies (NLS) literacy practices (Street 1993a; Gee, 1991) Professor Nevis refers to and I offer possible answers to his question "what do [those being "served" and researched] want out of this?" In doing so, I describe how I enhanced the NLS theoretical framework with situated learning (Lave and Wenger 1991; Lave 1996; Wenger 1998), identity (Holland and Lave 2001), and power (Foucault 1976; 1977) frameworks to better understand how such after-school literacy intervention projects might be improved.

To illustrate my findings, I use an exemplar—a 9-year-old school tutee, Oliver, his college student tutor, Roberta, and her English professor, Nevis—drawn from a larger ethnographic study (Hopson 2002) of five English composition classes at Lithman College. In Lithman's program, a form of academic literacies (Street 1996) based on critical pedagogy was enacted in conjunction with a service-learning (mandatory community service) tutoring project with Appalachian migrant elementary school children from the East End neighborhood of a nearby city. This curricular practice—combining critical pedagogy (Freire 1970; 1985; Giroux 1983; 1995) and service-learning (Bok 1982; Coleman 1976; Coles 1993; Kolb 1984; Schon 1987) theoretical strands—is not unusual in composition studies in the Academy.

Activist writing teachers have long been inspired by Freire's (1974) method of teaching literacy based on his theory that if teachers were to ask students to question their own (or others', such as school tutees') positioning in the world, such "problem-posing" might very well motivate those students to resolve the conflicts such positioning are said to cause by learning to read and write better and thereby improve their own and perhaps others' lives. In addition, since the early 1990s, writing teachers at Lithman and other institutions of higher education have become attracted to the growing service-learning movement because they believe it offers a convenient venue for employing Freirean pedagogy through community action—the "service,"—and at the same time offers college students possible opportunities to connect that action to knowledge—the "learning" (Stanton et al. 1999). The approach in the five courses I studied at Lithman College was derived from a strand of the tradition of cultural literacy in the Academy that Peck, Flower, and Higgins (1995) classify as "the literacy of social and cultural critique," which "openly addresses issues of power, defining social relationships in terms of economic and ideological struggle" (204).

Problem Investigated: "Some Real Road Block"

I had begun the year-long study (1997–98) of Nevis and two other professors, fifteen college student tutors, and eight 3rd-or-4th grade "at-risk" school tutees, hoping to better understand why various participant groups reported differing perceptions of outcomes. During the pilot study, I had learned that a number of Lithman College administrators and uninvolved faculty criticized this particular English composition service-learning program for straying too far from writing instruction and too close to politics; that the professors teaching those writing courses believed combining critical pedagogy with community service to be the best way to promote their Freirean-based social justice agenda even though it did not appear to benefit school tutees scholastically; that the elementary school staff viewed the tutoring program as primarily a "social rehabilitation" project, since 4th-grade test scores did not improve as a result of the tutoring; that a majority of college student tutors were disappointed with their efforts to help the school tutees do better in school; and that the school tutees thought the tutoring experience was "fun" and gave it very high marks. The major thrust of my inquiry, then, became to understand this disparity of opinions by investigating literacy practices within the tutoring community itself.

On the one hand, I chose to look at what the professors taught in the writing classes, how the college student tutors learned and what they did with the theories about literacy that were taught to them, and why this learning turned out to be disappointing in practice. Nevis told me that the program goal was to encourage the college student tutors "to spark intrinsic motivation [in school tutees] and get their heads back in the game." This had never happened, however. Nevis explained the problem this way:

> It's just like they [the college student tutors] can see the world described in a different way but then when they hit some real limit situation, some real road block, they seem to snap back into how they were raised to see the world, and can't get past that.

At the same time, I also investigated the tutoring program from the perspective of the recipients' literacy practices, asking what "at-risk" children like Oliver appeared to gain from the tutoring interactions. I learned from the elementary school principal that although Nevis had explicitly requested that the college student tutors work with "at-risk" school tutees who were predicted to fail state-mandated 4th-grade exit exams, the elementary school teachers "did *not* select only the lowest-functioning child." Instead, the principal told me that the waiting list of children "at-risk" who needed tutors was so long that teachers selected low-achieving children "also for social reasons, looking at who would benefit, who had no positive experiences at home because the [college student tutors] filled the need for a positive relationship, to see how someone else behaves." It appeared, then, that most of the school tutees were chosen to participate as part of another experiment, tapped because they were "at-risk" not just for school failure, but for being different. In this sense then, as well, Nevis's fears that the school tutees were being used as "lab rats" appear to be doubly justified.

It is worth noting that I found no evidence more generally that short-term tutoring projects like the Lithman College English program end up working in ways school personnel expect. And I could locate no sustained empirical research to support this form of imported Freirean literacy intervention in terms of school achievement. This is not surprising, since studies of even more traditional one-on-one literacy remediation initiatives (e.g., Ritter 2001; Wasik 1998; Wasik and Slavin 1993; Shanahan 1998) show that benefits of any form of tutoring to low-achieving readers have been problematic. Reports like these substantiate what many NLS theorists have contended, that there may be some issues around schooling and literacy that remedial reading instruction models may not recognize or solve, such as differences in early socialization contexts (Heath 1983) related to family literacies (Taylor 1997) which may not mesh with conceptions of literacy associated with particular school-based notions of teaching and learning (Street and Street 1991; Hull and Schultz 2001; 2002).

Research and Theoretical Frameworks

I chose the NLS framework because NLS researchers (e.g., Heath 1982; Camitta 1995; Probst 1993; Rockhill 1995; Weinstein-Shr 1993) suggest NLS's emphasis on the concept of literacy practices as a broad cultural conception (Street 1993a) offers a promising way to promote better understandings of problematic theoretical issues in literacy-program designs. I selected the ethnographic research methodology because literacy theorists (Barton 1994; Collins 1995; Gee 1990; Heath, Mangiola, Schecter, and Hull 1991; Street 1993a; 1993b; 1995b; 1997; 2000; Taylor 1997), in response to concerns about rising rates of "illiteracy" and the failures of a variety of interventions to improve achievement based on schooled-literacy standards, have called for more sustained ethnographic inquiries in order to "test out" theories of how attending to local literacy practices might help transform literacy intervention programs instead.

The concept of "literacy practices" is central to the NLS framework. Certainly, there are those who see "literacy practices" as simply "what people do with literacy," as Barton, Hamilton, and Ivanic (2000, 7), have noted (but do not advocate), an interpretation that might allow for a photographer to represent a practice. In this study, however, I considered "literacy practices" as a broader concept intended "to incorporate not only 'literacy events' as empirical occasions to which literacy is integral, but also 'folk models' of those events and the ideological preconceptions that underpin them" (Street 1993a, 12–13). This "ideological" model (Street 1984) of literacy practices then, "attempts to handle the events and the patterns of activity around literacy but to link them to something broader of a social or cultural kind" (Street 2000, 21).

I also adopted the NLS frame because it builds on the notion that inquiries into the nature of "cultural models," such as learning theories (Gee 1999) of different social groups, may help to explain what literacy learning means in different situations. This means that understanding some of those meanings for participants in the tutoring project might help explain how they could find spaces for productive resistance and accommodation, as Foucault (1976) postulated when he said power was to be considered as a process, moving about everywhere (rather than as a fixed property of oppression residing exclusively in one class to be employed against another). In Foucault's conception of power, the arrangements affected by culture may work to the advantage of one class over another under certain conditions. Foucault's model meshes well with the NLS notion of how culture works; Street has suggested that "culture is a verb . . . a process that is contested, not a given inventory of characteristics" (2000, 19). I hypothesized that these notions of literacy and power might be fruitfully employed for tracking resistances within power relations in local literacy learning contexts, and then allow educators to make use of those discoveries productively to recommend ways to facilitate changes on behalf of marginalized groups.

New Literacy Studies does not incorporate a theory of learning, however. For that piece of the model, I incorporated communities-of-practice theories (Lave 1996; Lave and Wenger 1991; Wenger 1998). Aware that "recent studies of language and literacy learning show it is a social endeavor often most effective when it is the result of activities in actual situations" (Roberts, Byram, Barro, Jordan, and Street 2001, 9), I interpreted the tutoring group's literacy practices as processes within particular kinds of learning communities. This approach locates learning "squarely in the processes of coparticipation" (Hanks 1991, 13), which is, of course, what tutoring depends on. Essential to understanding my findings is the theoretical assumption that "acquisition of knowledge is not a simple matter of taking in knowledge; rather, things assumed to be natural categories, such as 'bodies of knowledge,' 'learners,' and 'cultural transmission,' require reconceptualization as cultural, social products" (Lave 1996, 8). This approach "takes as its focus the relationship between learning and the social situations in which it occurs" (Lave and Wenger 1991, 14). What this means for literacy inquiries is that, as Lave and Wenger (1991) say, "Rather than asking what kinds of cognitive processes and conceptual structures are involved," literacy researchers who choose this approach "ask what kinds of social engagements provide the proper context for learning to take place" (14), to understand learning, particularly successful learning, wherever it occurs. Another important aspect to the community-of-practice framework, one that played an important role in my interpretations of the school tutees' literacy practices, is that it takes into consideration the "subjectively selective character of time-space relations" (Lave 1996, 4).

In addition, I incorporated notions of identity theorized by Wenger (1998) and Lave, who, with Holland (2001), have been influenced by Bakhtin (1986; 1990). They have postulated that identities are inexorably connected to and implicated in processes of socially situated activities and relate such identification practices to broader structural forces. I decided to weave these theories of learning and identity into my analytical approach because they offer a way of understanding how school tutees who may feel they are at a disadvantage can participate in "communities-of-practice" (Lave and Wenger 1991; Wenger

1998) by managing the "address-and-answer processes" (Bakhtin 1981; 1986) in order to make themselves known. This notion, Bahktin suggests, assumes that persons actively use the words and verbal genres of others in ways that are not simply faithful reproductive acts, but rather problematize boundaries and offer spaces for possibilities for new identity formation processes. Wenger (1998), whose framework for looking at "communities of practice" formed a key resource in the interpretation portion of this study, says identity is "a way of talking about how learning changes who we are and creates personal histories of becoming in the context of our communities" (5). In his social theory of learning model, identity (learning as becoming) is one of four components. The remaining three are practice (learning by doing), community (learning as belonging), and meaning (learning as experience). Wenger predicates his component inventory on the notion that people are always organizing their lives to get things done and that the most important ways of learning arise from these organizational activities. He says this process happens in schools in a variety of ways:

> Students go to school and, as they come together to deal in their own fashion with the agenda of the imposing institution and the unsettling mysteries of youth, communities of practice sprout everywhere—in the classroom as well as on the playground, officially or in the cracks. And in spite of curriculum, discipline, and exhortation, the learning that is the most personally transformative turns out to be the learning that involves membership in these communities of practice. (6)

This communities-of-practice approach resonated with what I learned about Appalachian identity and played an important part in my interpretations of the school tutees' literacy practices. The importance of the identity link for literacy educators is eloquently expressed by Low (this volume) when she says: "Who one imagines oneself to be is vital to what and how one will learn." I discovered that Appalachians, mostly poor whites living in or transplanted to larger towns and cities from rural areas, have historically felt marginalized by schools, which often have attempted to categorize them in terms of deficit models. Purcell-Gates (1995), in her study of an Appalachian mother and son with low literacy skills in Cincinnati, calls Appalachians "a white underclass" and says "[t]he discrimination and stereotyping they face from mainstream communities is not as visible as for minority people of color, but the effects are just as insidious and as costly to society" (2). Yet, despite how the outside world might like to label them, Appalachians tend to be independent and overwhelmingly reject the labeling process for the stigma it represents. Banton (1988) postulates that this happens because of people's consciousness of how differences can vary according to circumstances, suggesting that it may follow that Appalachians believe ethnic identities can be defined in new situations as well. Thus, he says that when Appalachians move to larger towns and cities, they try to shed that "naming" aspect of their identities.

Findings

I determined that the college student tutors did not experience the "connected learning" expected from the service-learning tutoring experience because they could not reconcile different conceptions of how knowledge and power were supposed to work. They struggled to balance what they already believed about how and what people should be motivated to learn, what their professors and the critical pedagogy theorists (Freire 1970; Giroux 1983; 1995; MacLeod 1995) expected empowerment-based teaching to accomplish, and then what they experienced as they began to "know" what and how their school tutees preferred to learn in the after-school tutoring setting. One frustrated college student tutor in Nevis's course described the dilemma this way: "It didn't seem right for me to come in with all these ideas about how to help this kid when I hadn't taken the time to find out what help he needs." By the end of each term the pattern was the same; the college student tutors, rather than accomplishing their professors' social justice agenda—"empowering" the school tutees to resolve conflicts with school by reentering the school game on their own terms—accommodated the school tutees' literacy practices and came to feel increasingly disempowered. And despite their hopeful rhetoric in the classroom, by the end of each term, all three professors privately expressed a certain sense of futility.

At the same time, my study of literacy practices suggested that the school tutees liked being involved with the tutoring program because it gave them chances to bridge sense-making systems—their working-class Appalachian "lifeworlds" (Habermas 1987) and those school-based institutions which both the elementary school and the college student tutors appeared to represent. The school tutees became part of a "community-of-practice" (Lave and Wenger 1991; Wenger 1998), participating in social practices (or performances) of resistance, assertion, and collaboration in order to create opportunities to promote identities as independent, competent, and valued learners. These findings suggest that the Appalachian school tutees echoed the same "identity shedding" actions when moving from school to tutoring as Philliber and McCoy (1981) and Banton (1988) suggest Appalachians appear to do when they move from the country to the cities. My interpretation is that the school tutees began the tutoring program feeling disempowered by the labelings that got them there, then generated their own productive capacities for control, in effect "empowering" themselves to enact a set of local literacy-learning practices designed to mediate among differing conceptualizations of learning models.

Case Study of Oliver and Roberta

The experiences of one school tutee, Oliver, and his college student tutor, Roberta, may offer insights into how this NLS-enhanced research, analysis, and interpretative approach suggested these findings.

Roberta, an English major, came from a white, upper middle-class Catholic family. She and her younger three siblings had spent all of their K–12 schooling in parochial schools. At the beginning of the 1997 Fall term, soon after walking Oliver home after tutoring, Roberta wrote a "reflection paper" in which she described how her "isolated" schooling and family experiences in the past limited her understanding of people from different cultural and racial backgrounds and she described the dilemma she expected to experience with Oliver:

> My efforts to overcome my limited experience become a difficult cycle; I cannot come to an understanding of the area until I am able to communicate with the people, but I cannot gain the trust needed to communicate with anyone until I have some understanding of their interests and backgrounds.

The third of four children, Oliver lived with his mother. His grandparents lived next door. His mother read at home with him and his sister helped with math homework, using flash cards for his "times tables." He was in the elementary school free lunch program. In an attempt to both separate himself from some of his peers in his neighborhood and describe his own sense of disempowerment, he told Roberta that "other kids" at his elementary school "get in trouble a lot because they come from a bad place, East End."

Oliver was overweight, moved slowly, and did not own athletic shoes, so he was not among those asked by the other children to play basketball outside at the end of tutoring. At the same time, because he was admired for being adept with technology, he often interrupted a computer session with his own college student tutor to respond to calls to assist another school tutee at a nearby terminal. (He did not have a computer at home, but had learned on the school classroom and library computers.)

Oliver worked on math with Roberta for their initial tutoring session. She said at the time, "He is so intelligent and well behaved that I am curious to see why he was chosen for tutoring." Roberta talked with Oliver's classroom teacher, Mrs. Kitts, who said Oliver was nominated for tutoring because, while he was good at math and science, he needed help in spelling, reading, and writing. Aware that Oliver wanted to be a chef someday, Roberta devised a cookbook "chemistry" project that involved creating different recipes in the school microwave and keyboarding them into the computer.

After the cookbook project was finished, they began reading stories together. When, during one session, Oliver shared with Roberta that he would like to be able to change the endings of stories he read in school, she believed she had "found" his intrinsic motivation and suggested he write an imaginary tale, one that combined his love of food with his desire to create his own conclusion. Together, they wrote a ghost story that included a recipe for "ghost cookies." Oliver baked the cookies and distributed them to delighted tutees in the tutoring program, but he did not share his literacy-project cookbook with the other children, evidence that he worked to straddle different ways of presenting himself in and out of school.

A vignette from a different literacy event one in which Oliver talked about ways he was both attracted to and resisted a certain form of literacy, shows how he enjoyed making sense of a character's identities and values in a chapter book. Like many Appalachians who are known for the cultural practice of storytelling (Heath 1982; 1983; Philliber and McCoy 1981; Wolfram 1984), Oliver enjoyed and looked forward to reading aloud with his tutor.

In this particular interaction, Oliver introduced the themes of "good" and "bad" that would be repeated throughout the term in his conversations with her. Roberta and Oliver shared reading an *Encyclopedia Brown* (Sobel, 1992) mystery-format storybook; she read the story to him, then asked him to read the solution to her. When, at the end, she asked Oliver what he thought about a 10-year-old who knew so much, he at first said, "It would be good," but then added, "It would also be hard because people would make fun of you." This statement by Oliver made an impression on Roberta, who wrote in an essay:

> I think Oliver feels that he must suppress his energy and curiosity because they will only cause trouble for him in the classroom. If Oliver expressed in school all his thoughts and opinions, his interest in learning how to run a business like the restaurant we pass on the way home, or his desire to re-write the stories in which he and his classmates are required to write the correct word on the line, he would be like Encyclopedia Brown—knowing too much.

Roberta's interpretation was insightful; Oliver needed to be careful how he related to books or displayed what he knew or he would assume an identity not valued in his East End home community, and one culturally at odds with mainstream behaviors valued at school. He would face ridicule if he appropriated Encyclopedia Brown's "Discourse" (Gee 1999) style. In school and at home he needed to assert different identities than he did within the private conversations with his college student tutor in an after-school program.

Despite some success in overcoming her initial "limitations" by understanding the background and interests of her school tutee, by the end of the term, Roberta said, "I am concerned that my work with Oliver will be inconsequential to him after I leave. I know he enjoys the cooking, but it is not exactly a 'conflict-resolving' project." In contrast to her initial positive assessment, Roberta had came to see Oliver as deficient because his literacy learning preferences differed from the Freirean template proffered by Nevis. She had come to view her own expectations for helping him through the lens of critical pedagogy and service-learning had come up wanting. Yet, I would argue that those theories offered no way for her to see that Oliver *had* dealt with a variety of conflicts—social and psychological ones—throughout their times together, successfully struggling to manage their interactions in ways that allowed him to learn more while navigating culturally treacherous waters.

Social Practices and Purposes

In conjunction with documenting literacy events, of the kind summarized above, I compiled a list of social practices and purposes for the school tutee group as a whole. As time went on, I noted patterns and was able to "winnow" (Wolcott 1994) the school tutees' social practices down to three main categories: *resisting, asserting,* and *collaborating.* For example, in the literacy event involving Encyclopedia Brown, I described Oliver's social practices as "directing," for he was on top of all of the processes involving interaction around this text. "Directing" fell under the summary category "asserting."

In tandem with the process of determining patterns, I tentatively identified underlying uniformities that might produce categories of "purposes" that I could associate with "identities" in this setting. I eventually winnowed the school tutees' purposes down to three categories, ones reflecting their desire or need to be seen as *independent, capable,* and *valued* learners.

To illustrate, my analysis and interpretation of Oliver in the Encyclopedia Brown literacy event suggests independence in his need to control how he related to texts and how he learned from them. And, conscious of his own frustration level and how he could be perceived by others, he needed to manage how he displayed what he knew and was capable of doing. In this sense, he wanted to be valued, but on terms he could live with within his community. This is the *Encyclopedia Brown* literacy event depicted on Oliver's chart:

Literacy Events			Social Practices and Purposes				Identity
Activities	Text	Literacy Behaviors	Social Practices	Summary (Categories)	Purposes		Summary (Categories)
Library	Book	Read Listen Talk	Directing Attending Narrating	Collaborating Asserting Resisting	Interest & Control Cross boundaries Explain Choices		Independent Valued Capable

Sequence of Changes

The master chart of literacy events for the school tutee group as a whole revealed that two of the three social practices categories (resistance and assertion) predominated for the group as a whole, indicating that the school tutees appeared to be in charge of transforming the learning dynamic. Over both terms, I was able to document and track a similar process, one in which the elementary school tutees and their college student tutors changed roles. Only when the college student tutors acquiesced, gave up their own plans, and accommodated the school tutees' agendas, did the school tutees cooperate and agree to work together. Teacher and learner identities transferred; the would-be apprentices became the masters, and vice versa. I later learned that Hull and Schultz (2002) have also noted these kinds of reverse behaviors; they state that practices of learning in after-school settings, such as youth centers, "can reorganize learning such that typical student-teacher relationships and participant structures are turned on their heads" (47). I found that the sequence of changes in interactions among all of the college student tutors and school tutees in the study fell into five successive stages: passivity, agreement, compromise, a change in activity, and closure.

In Oliver's case, some of the sequences can be seen in Roberta's report of a literacy event involving the cookbook project: Roberta had insisted at first that Oliver write and, to add credibility to her ability to help him with this, she told him her goal in life was to be an author. Here is her journal account of writing a recipe on the computer:

> I had Oliver type some, but he is slow and much prefers to read and have me type. (This provides ample opportunity for him to use the mouse when I make mistakes, which apparently is quite a thrill.) Oliver was wound-up enough to insist that "writing is my worst nightmare" but I did convince him to "help" me write the recipe since it was short. Oliver typed the first sentence but there was another learner playing a game on the computer next to his, and he kept being distracted. Finally, I let him read the end of the recipe to me while I typed.

Until Oliver told Roberta that "writing is my worst nightmare," Roberta may not have realized that she had placed herself in his category of frightening creatures. He had, however, offered a cultural model that placed himself in opposition to her passion, and eventually, she gave way to his preferences. Thus, Oliver's resistant social practices also included verbal and physical cues designed to "slow down" the writing assignment such that his college student tutor's agenda for that literacy-related task would change. Notice that Oliver took on the role of "helping" Roberta, rather than the reverse, which the usual tutoring model assumes. Attend also to how Roberta first "read" Oliver's social practices in terms of her own school-based expectations—a need to keep him focused on her literacy-teaching agenda—then acquiesced in order to get the project finished (in large part because she needed it for her own grade in Nevis's composition course). Thus, in the small spaces allowed them, aspects of Oliver and Roberta's identities were exchanged as they attempted to behave productively for their own ends. Oliver became the leader, feeling happier about the tutoring situation, and Roberta became the follower, feeling less successful with her service assignment.

Differing Conceptions of Time and Space

It appeared then, that the school tutees constructed their "literacy" tutoring sessions so the college student tutors would help them mediate between different sense-making systems that included emphases on constructing different meaning-making contexts. The question to ponder next then was how could these differences be understood and accommodated to enhance learning? My interpretation was that the school tutees conceptualized the dimensions of time and space differently.

Analyzing discourse around literacy events revealed patterns, particularly within complaints. For example, Roberta said Oliver "spent too much time" negotiating roles and became frustrated before completing tasks when he sensed that she thought he was "taking too much time to write." Oliver continually asked Roberta for "more time to work on the computer," "more time away from the tutoring room," "more time to hang out," and "more time to be with other kids." These kinds of "whining" commentaries and appeals suggest that Oliver evaluated the segments of a clock and spaces within learning settings differently.

Such findings suggest that realigning time and spaces to support school tutees' mediating literacy practices could help them to become more capable learners. Perhaps time allotted to tasks could be less structured and more flexible, allowing independent students (like Oliver) to have a voice in what they did and when and where they did it. Oliver's abilities in science and math proved that he could read in a content area in which he was interested. Perhaps he could be offered broader choices among reading materials, including science fiction books, that included those topics. Like his fellow school tutees, Oliver liked working with others. Collaborative learning arrangements which would allow him to move about, both within and among groups, might promote higher interest in school. As for writing, Oliver quickly learned the word-processing system on the school computer; the incorporation of innovative technology options could offer him opportunities for endless forays into "virtual space."

Conclusions

At the beginning and end of each term, I conducted a survey in which I asked the college student tutors to define "literacy." Roberta changed her perspective. She had defined literacy at the beginning according to the "autonomous" model (Street 1984), as "being able to communicate through both written and oral methods." At the end, she wrote, "the same, but also being able to 'read' yourself and your community," a shift towards a broader understanding. As Mamabolo (in this volume) found, "Pedagogy is not enough." In her final essay, Roberta wrote:

> The [tutees' elementary school] curriculum is focused around skills that could be important—writing, spelling, and grammar—but these skills are taught in ways completely irrelevant to their use in daily life. . . . It is a system far too caught up in looking good for parents and political leaders to truly be of service to its children.

Roberta's observation offers a glimpse of what "finding" literacy practices might mean in the case of school tutees like Oliver. Although she had not been exposed to the theoretical tools to discern or name Oliver's mediating literacy practices, Roberta had learned enough from working with him to know the significance of the "disconnects" between his learning in school and ways of learning of "use in daily life" outside school. And she also knew some of the hard issues these "disconnects" presented; given what she knew Oliver faced in school each day, she believed she had failed him even as she had accommodated him. She wrote in her final paper:

As for Oliver, I don't know where I leave him. He has learned the basics of a word processing system, he has become more confident in describing our project to outsiders, and he has completed a story and several recipes, but I don't know if any of that is of lasting significance. If this academic game is poker, I have perhaps given Oliver the chance to get rid of one of his cards by teaching him that *learning can be good as well as bad.* Whether or not Oliver will chose to make the trade I don't know, and he is still left with four not-so-great cards in his hand. So much for my desire to redeal.

Roberta began the term feeling hopeful about helping a nice kid from the East End and ended the term feeling disappointed with herself. Such negotiations of roles and reexamination of goals formed part of a larger conversation, I would argue, that both the college student tutors and the school tutees should have had a part in changing. My findings suggest that the school tutees' mediating literacy practices—created in order to negotiate a shared understanding that might link their own different ways of knowing to school-based learning—can be related to larger social goals and practices associated with redefining deficit labels. Even "tutee," a term often associated with the term "at-risk," is derived from educational practices based on "culturally arbitrary and cross-culturally foolish tasks" (McDermott 1996, 284) like filling certain "right" words in the blanks so the stories' endings match those the teacher expects.

Implications

Such findings of research into literacy practices suggest that college service-learning and other literacy intervention projects could benefit by building on theoretical frameworks such as NLS and situated-learning linked to notions of power like Foucault's (1976; 1977). Unfortunately, as a general rule, English composition professors tend to underestimate the importance of understanding social theories of literacy, learning, and identity and incorporating them into service-learning tutoring projects, relying instead on certain interpretations of service-learning and critical pedagogy approaches that may actually serve to undermine those projects. Low's chapter (this volume) shows how the "cultural studies" model has been constructively linked to literacy work. The academic literacies concept speaks directly to this contrary turn of events: Critical and service-learning educators in composition studies (as do many mainstream educators, such as the principal and teachers in this study) often share a theoretical vision of the kinds of educational communities which they want their students to "learn" to take part in co-constructing, predicated on expectations of those students' acquisition of certain predetermined or highly preferred ways of thinking and behaving. This means knowledge and power are conceptualized as objects than can be transferred in predictable ways. When these expectations do not materialize, the tendency is to blame various participants and institutions "on the ground," as Nevis and Roberta did, rather than on various theorists "in the books."

I would argue that participants in such projects would be better served if concepts such as "literacy," "knowledge," "learning," and "power" were redefined as parts of processes of literacy practices considered within contexts of culture, community, and identity. These theoretical approaches could also help explain how expectations may be thwarted and rationales might be misdirected. Roberta might better understand how she had wrongly assumed responsibility for losing a game Oliver never thought he was playing. Nevis might better understand why college student tutors traveling through his service-learning courses become adept at avoiding "road blocks" by seeking more productive, alternative routes that keep them closer to home.

References

Bakhtin, M.M. 1986. *Speech genres and other late essays*. Translated by V.M.McGee. Austin: University of Texas Press.
Bakhtin, M.M. (Ed.). 1990. *Art and answerability: Early philosophical essays*. Austin: University of Texas Press.
Banton, M. 1988. *Racial consciousness*. London: Longman.
Barton, D. 1994. Literacy: An introduction to the ecology of written language. Oxford: Blackwell.
Barton, D. 2000. Researching literacy practices: Learning from activities with teachers and students. In: D. Barton, M. Hamilton, and R. Ivanic (eds.): *Situated literacies: Reading and writing in context*. London: Routledge, pp. 167–179.
Barton, D., Hamilton, M., and Ivanic, R. (eds.). 2000. *Situated literacies: Reading and writing in context*. London: Routledge.
Bok, D. 1982. Beyond the ivory tower: Social responsibilities of the modern university. Cambridge: Harvard University Press.
Camitta, M. 1995. Vernacular writing: Varieties of literacy among Philadelphia high school students. In: B.V. Street (ed.), *Cross-cultural approaches to literacy*. Cambridge: Cambridge University Press, pp. 228–246.

Coleman, J. 1976. Differences between classroom and experiential learning. In: M.T. Keeton (ed.), *Experiential learning: Rationale, characteristics, and assessment.* San Francisco: Jossey-Bass, pp. 49–61.

Coles, R. 1993. *The call of service: A witness to idealism.* Boston: Houghton Mifflin.

Collins, J. 1995. Literacy and literacies. *Annual Review of Anthropology* 24: 75–93.

Foucault, M. 1976. Power as knowledge. In: C. Lemert (ed.), *Social theory: The multicultural and classic readings.* Boulder: Westview Press, pp. 518–524.

Foucault, M. 1977. Truth and Power. In: P. Rabinow (ed.), *The Foucault reader.* New York: Pantheon Books, pp. 51–75.

Freire, P. 1970a. *Cultural action for freedom.* Vol. viii. Cambridge: Harvard Education Review.

Freire, P. 1970b. *Pedagogy of the oppressed.* New York: Seabury Press.

Freire, P. 1974. *Education for critical consciousness.* New York: Continuum.

Freire, P. 1985. *The politics of education: Culture, power, and liberation.* London: Macmillan.

Gee, J.P. 1990. *Social linguistics and literacies: Ideology in discourses.* 2nd ed. London: Taylor & Francis.

Gee, J.P. 1999. *An introduction to discourse analysis: Theory and method.* New York: Routledge.

Giroux, H.A. 1983. *Theory and resistance in education: A pedagogy for the opposition.* South Hadley: Bergin and Garvey.

Giroux, H.A. 1995. Who writes in a cultural studies class? Or, where is the pedagogy? In: K. Fitts and A.W. France (eds.), *Left margins: Cultural studies and composition pedagogy.* Albany: State University of New York Press, pp. 3–16.

Habermas, J. 1987. *The philosophical discourse of modernity: Twelve lectures.* Translated by G. Lawrence. Cambridge: MIT Press.

Hamilton, M. 2000. Expanding the New Literacy Studies: Using photographs to explore literacy as a social practice. In: D. Barton, M. Hamilton, and R. Ivanic (eds.), *Situated literacies: Reading and writing in context.* London: Routledge, pp. 16–34.

Hanks, W.F. 1991. Foreword. In: L. Lave and E. Wegner (eds.), *Situated peripheral learning: Legitimate peripheral participation.* Cambridge: Cambridge University Press.

Heath, S.B. 1982. Protean shapes in literacy events. In: D. Tannen (ed.), *Spoken and written language: Exploring orality and literacy.* Norwood, NJ: Ablex, pp. 348–370.

Heath, S.B. 1983. *Ways with words.* Cambridge: Cambridge University Press.

Heath, S.B., Mangiola, L., Schecter, S., and Hull, G. (Eds.). 1991. *Children of promise: Literate activity in linguistically and culturally diverse classrooms.* Washington, D.C.: National Education Association.

Herzberg, B. 1994. Community service and critical teaching. *College Composition and Communication* 45(3): 307–319.

Holland, D., and Lave, J. 2001. *History in person: Enduring struggles, contentious practice, intimate identities.* Santa Fe, NM: School of American Research Press.

Hopson, J.E. 2002. "Seeing practices of hope": Rereading critical pedagogy and service-learning in a liberal arts college English program. Unpublished doctoral dissertation. Philadelphia: University of Pennsylvania.

Hull, G., and Schultz, K. 2001. Literacy and learning out of school: A review of theory and research. *Review of educational research* 71(4): 575–611.

Hull, G., and Schultz, K. (eds.). 2002. *School's out: Bridging out-of-school literacies with classroom practice.* New York: Teachers College Press.

Kolb, D.A. 1984. *Experiential learning: Experience as the source of learning and development.* Englewood Cliffs: Prentice Hall.

Lave, L., and Wenger, E. 1991. Situated learning: Legitimate peripheral participation. Cambridge: Cambridge University Press.

Lave, J. 1996. The practice of learning. In: S. Chaiklen and J. Lave (eds.), *Understanding practice: Perspectives on activity and context.* Cambridge: Cambridge University Press, pp. 1–32.

MacLeod, J. 1995. *Ain't no makin' it.* Boulder: Westview.

Maloney, M.E. 1997. *The social areas of Cincinnati: An analysis of social needs.* 3rd ed. Cincinnati: University of Cincinnati, School of Planning.

McDermott, R.P. 1996. The acquisition of a child by a learning disability. In: S. Chaiklin and J. Lave (eds.), *Understanding practice: Perspectives on activity and context.* Cambridge: Cambridge University Press, pp. 269–305.

Peck, W.C., Flower, L., and Higgins, L. 1995. Community literacy. *College Composition and Communication* 46(2): 199–222.

Philliber, W.W., and McCoy, C.B. (eds.). 1981. *The invisible minority: Urban Appalachians.* Lexington: University Press of Kentucky.

Probst, P. 1993. The letter and the spirit: Literacy and religious authority in the history of the Aladura movement in western Nigeria. In: B.V. Street (ed.), *Cross-cultural approaches to literacy.* Cambridge: Cambridge University Press, pp. 247–271.

Purcell-Gates, V. 1994. *Other people's words: The cycle of low literacy.* Cambridge: Harvard University Press.

Ritter, G.W. 2001. The academic impact of volunteer tutoring in urban public elementary schools: Results of an experimental design evaluation. Unpublished doctoral dissertation. Philadelphia: University of Pennsylvania.

Roberts, C., Byram, M., Barro, A., Jordan, S., and Street, B. 2001. *Language learners as ethnographers.* Clevedon: Multilingual Matters Ltd.

Rockhill, K. 1995. Gender, language and the politics of literacy. In: B.V. Street (ed.), *Cross-cultural approaches to literacy.* Cambridge: Cambridge University Press, pp. 156–175.

Schon, D.A. 1987. *Educating the reflective practitioner.* San Francisco: Jossey-Bass.

Shanahan, T. (1998). On the effectiveness and limitations of tutoring in reading. In: A. Iran-Nejad and D. Pearson (eds.), *Review of research in education.* Vol. 23. Washington, D.C.: American Educational Research Association, pp. 217–234.

Sobol, D.J. 1992. *Encyclopedia Brown solves them all.* New York: Yearling Books.

Stanton, T.K., Giles, D.E., and Cruz, N. 1999. *Service-learning: A movement's pioneers reflect on its origins, practice, and future.* San Francisco: Jossey-Bass.

Street, B.V. 1984. *Literacy in theory and practice.* Cambridge: Cambridge Univerity Press.

Street, B.V. 1987. Lieracy and orality as ideological constructions: Some problems in cross-cultural studies. *Culture and history.* Vol. 2. Copenhagen: Museum Tusculanum Press.

Street, B.V. 1993a. Introduction: The New Literacy Studies. In: B.V. Street (ed.), *Cross-cultural approaches to literacy.* Cambridge: Cambridge University Press, pp. 1–21.

Street, B.V. (ed.). 1993b. Literacy in cross-cultural perspectives. Cambridge: Cambridge University Press.

Street, B.V. 1995a. Literacy and power. Paper presented at the Literacy in Development Conference, Harare, Zimbabwe, August 6–9.

Street, B.V. 1995b. Social literacies: Critical approaches to literacy in development, ethnography and education. London: Longman.

Street, B.V. 1996. Academic literacies. In: D. Baker, J. Clay, and C. Fox (eds.), *Alternative Ways of Knowing: Literacies, Numeracies, Sciences.* London: Falmer Press, pp. 101–134.

Street, B.V. 1997. The implications of the New Literacy Studies for literacy education. *English in education* 31(3): 26–39.

Street, B.V. 2000. Literacy "events" and literacy "practices": Theory and practice in the "new literacy studies." In: K. Jones and M. Martin-Jones (eds.), *Multilingual literacies: Comparative perspectives on research and practice.* Amsterdam: John Benjamins, pp. 17–29.

Street, B.V., and Street, J. 1991. The schooling of literacy. In: D. Barton and R. Ivanic (eds.), *Writing in the community.* London: Sage, pp. 143–166.

Taylor, D. 1997. Many families, many literacies: An international declaration of principles. Portsmouth: Heinemann.

Wasik, B.A. 1998. Volunteer tutoring programs in reading: A review. *Reading Research Quarterly* 3(4): 266–293.

Wasik, B.A., and Slavin, R.A. 1993. Preventing early reading failure with one-to-one tutoring: A review of five great programs. *Reading Research Quarterly* 28(2): 179–200.

Weinstein-Shr, G. 1993. Literacy and social process: A community in transition. In: B.V. Street (ed.), *Cross-cultural approaches to literacy.* Cambridge: Cambridge University Press, pp. 272–293.

Wenger, E. 1998. *Communities of practice: Learning, meaning, and identity.* Cambridge: Cambridge University Press.

Wolcott, H.F. 1994. *Transforming qualitative data: Description, analysis, and interpretation.* Thousand Oaks: Sage.

Wolfram, W. 1984. Is there an Appalachian English. *Appalachian Journal* 11: 215–225.

15

Nontraditional Students in Higher Education

English as an Additional Language and Literacies

Constant Leung and Kimberly Safford

Introduction

This chapter focuses on the conceptualization of academic literacy development issues with reference to ethnic and linguistic minority school students who are interested in going to university. These London students are settled residents, not overseas students. The discussion will draw on findings of a research project that worked with a group of 17- and 18-year-old London students who attended a voluntary Academic Language Development (ALD) course run by a local university as part of its Widening Participation program. These students were at various stages of developing their English as an additional language (EAL) and were preparing for university matriculation examinations. Their interview accounts and reflections highlight the complex and long-term processes of becoming a confident user of academic literacies in English. Their experiences also raise questions about the assumptions underpinning higher education widening access policies and programs in the United Kingdom—and more generally—which sidestep the need to examine the specific educational experiences, and the language and literacy needs of these students.

Terminologically we generally prefer terms such as 'academic literacies' and 'literacy practices' to signal that we, like researchers working within the New Literacy Studies tradition (Street 2003, among others), understand that people use language and other semiotic means to do things in multiple ways in different contexts. Established terms such as 'academic literacy' will be used whenever they are appropriate in the context of the unfolding meaning.

Widening Participation in Higher Education

Widening participation in higher education has been a catchcry in British educational and social policy in recent years. According to the Department for Education and Skills (DfES 2003, 7), the gap in university admissions between 'higher and lower social classes' has grown wider in Britain since the 1960s. There is also official concern about drop-out rates. Some 30,000 students who start first-time degrees do not complete them (National Audit Office 2002).

The British government's stated goal—for 50 percent of the population under the age of 30 to be in higher education by the year 2010—has been accompanied by policy directives requiring universities to "attract, retain and promote the progress of students from under-represented groups" (Department for Education and Skills 2003, 19). Officially "differential rates of application rather than any bias in admissions procedures" are the main cause of under-representation (11). Therefore, universities must do more to "raise aspirations of students from backgrounds where studying at university is not part of the family or community tradition" and "understand why students may be put off from applying to their institution" (13).

It is now becoming a standard practice that British universities, as part of a commitment to recruiting a broad spectrum of students, offer 'widening access' or 'widening participation' programs through which 'nontraditional' secondary school and other post-16 students may experience a fore-taste of university life. The term 'nontraditional students' is often used to refer to those who have been under-represented in higher education; the under-represented groups include people with low(er) socioeconomic backgrounds and/or from ethnolinguistic minority communities. Outreach activities are often organized by universities to create pre-university contact points with nontraditional students. These activities range widely, from 'liaison' visits by university staff to schools and university open days, to one-day workshops focusing on particular skills such as writing or using Information Communication Technology (ICT) and master classes in particular disciplines and summer schools.

Once these nontraditional students enter university, there is further support, such as mentoring programs, advice clinics, study support, work experience programs, and retention strategies for undergraduates. For instance;

> The University of Greenwich seeks to widen access to Higher Education for people from communities and socio-economic groups who traditionally would not go to university. . . . To achieve participation with success is the primary goal of our Widening Participation Strategy. This linkage constitutes an explicit recognition that widening access to University programs only has value if those students who are recruited into the University continue and succeed in their studies. (Greenwich University, 2002)

> London Metropolitan University aims to be at the forefront of widening participation in support of the Government target of 50% participation in HE by 18–30 year olds by 2010 . . . the rates of retention and progression of students are lower than can be accepted as a norm for the medium and longer term. It must be recognized that many of the students who have been attracted to higher education by the University are less than averagely prepared and supported for the experience. (London Metropolitan University, 2003)

These types of policy statements express considerable anxiety and concern about retention of nontraditional students. While there are many factors contributing to high rates of noncompletion (Medway et al. 2003; National Audit Office 2002), cultural distance, and understanding and the ability to use academic language are widely regarded as among the most challenging aspects of university study.

As Medway and colleagues (2003, 1.4) point out, universities, particularly the ones that conform to more traditional values and practices, can be formidable institutions and they can make some students feel out of place socially and culturally. It is often thought that nontraditional school students do not have the necessary social and cultural knowledge and background experience to feel comfortable in an academic environment. The purpose of widening participation programs often appears to be the induction of low(er) social class and ethnic minority students into the 'ways' of university life, what Lea and

Street refer to as the 'academic socialisation' model (1998): the assumption here is that nontraditional students will succeed if a set of behaviors for study, interaction, and writing can be learned.

Academic literacy is often conceptualized as a 'strange new language' that everyone in higher education will have in common. For example, Crème and Lea (1997, 5) urge students to "think, and write down as much as you can, about your own personal linguistic history . . . ways in which you have written, read and spoken in your life." The authors go on to describe university as ". . . a foreign country, far away from you and your familiar setting. . . . You feel awkward at first . . . but it gets easier. The more you take part the more you are bridging the gap between what you came with and a different way of thinking and speaking" (15). Generally speaking, language-oriented improvement programs, e.g., 'academic writing' and 'thesis writing', are designed to cater for students who seem to lack appropriate levels of language knowledge, study skills, and/or cultural knowledge about writing conventions in British universities. Where English for Academic Purposes (EAP) programs are offered, the focus on grammar and specific language skills suggests that they are an extension of EFL/TOEFL style teaching for students who come from abroad to study at British universities. For example, it is by no means exceptional to see this gloss for an EAP course: "[This course is] mainly for students intending to study at British universities. The course aims to improve your all-round English language proficiency while developing study skills and an understanding of British university culture" (Nottingham University).

Students from Ethnolinguistic Minority Communities: Subsets of Nontraditional Students

It would seem that notions of cultural distance and academic literacy in university settings have tended to be conceptualized as associated with specific groups of students, for instance, EAP for overseas/foreign students and academic literacy for 'home' students. In large conurbations such as London there is a good deal of movement (and settlement) of people of diverse backgrounds. In London schools it is not unusual to find 30 percent or 40 percent (or more) of the students from ethnolinguistic minority homes (Baker and Eversley 2000).

These students often have different language and social experiences than the so-called mainstream or 'home' students. They are 'home' students with a difference. (For a further discussion see Leung, Harris, and Rampton 1997.)

Widening participation programs often explicitly include members of eth-nolinguistic minority communities who are settled residents in Britain in their list of target groups. The conceptualizations (and the problems) of cultural distance and academic literacy, as suggested above, appear to be assumed to be valid for these students. In other words, ethnolinguistic minority individuals have generally been subsumed into the larger and nondifferentiated 'nontraditional students' category in educational discourse and policy response. Case studies of access programs sometimes refer to the provision of some teaching resources and university prospectus information in languages such as Bengali and Turkish (Woodrow and Yorke 2002, 143). Minority languages and diverse community experiences seem to be submerged in the cultural distance/ academic literacy model where 'everyone' is learning a 'new language' and a 'new culture' at university. A question here is: Are the prevailing formulations of cultural distance and academic literacy appropriate for local (not overseas) school students from diverse ethnolinguistic backgrounds?

Our professional experience suggests that experiential and pedagogic issues specifically related to ethnolinguistic difference, such as learning English as an additional language, transcultural encounters with pedagogic practices in local educational institutions, and multiculturalism/multilingualism at the individual and local social network levels, have not generally been discussed in detail in policy and curriculum statements. It is with these issues in mind that we now turn to some of the findings of a research study involving fifteen school students.

Developing Student Accounts

The students participants in this study[1] formed roughly half of a cohort that attended a non–fee-paying voluntary course in Academic Language Development (ALD) in 2002/3 run by a university in London. The fifteen students were a core group that attended the course regularly. The course was one of several

[1]The research team comprised Carys Jones, Anne Morgan, Amanda Bellsham-Revell, Roxy Harris, PascAline Scalone, Brian Street, Annabel Tremlett, and the two present authors.

strands within the university's Widening Participation program. Unlike other one- or-two-day access activities or workshops, the ALD class met twenty-five times on Saturday mornings during the academic year.

The students were recruited from London secondary schools on the recommendation of school teachers. They were 17 and 18 years old, and all but two had arrived in London within the previous two to five years with little or no English. With one exception, they had been placed in local schools where they normally had several weeks of induction that included a peer 'buddying' arrangement to help them adjust to school routines. This was usually followed by in-class EAL support for a short period of time, or separate EAL classes where coursework would be explained. The students' countries of origin were Algeria, Ethiopia, Somalia, Brazil, Taiwan, Vietnam, Gambia, Serbia, Cameroon, Iran, Zimbabwe, and Pakistan. One student was born in England and had attended Farsi supplementary school since the age of 5.

Most of the students were studying maths and sciences and were preparing for university matriculation examinations. The aim of the ALD course was to offer additional opportunities for students such as these to develop their knowledge of English language and academic literacies. The classes covered topics such as uses of academic registers and genres in different teaching and discussion contexts, the concept of 'argument' in academic writing, note-taking as part of meaning-taking and meaning-making, understanding examination questions, making sense of teacher feedback, developing oral communication in group work and for presentations, and writing personal statements for university application.

We were interested in exploring how these students viewed themselves as language learners/users, and their understandings and uses of academic literacies. We were interested in not only gaining further understanding of the students' perceptions and needs, but also using the findings to assist the development of effective and sensitive pedagogic practices when working with this type of student.

In this discussion we will mainly draw on the data produced by the semi-structured interviews with the students. The students were interviewed individually at or near the end of the year. All interviews were audio-recorded. The interviews covered a range of topics, which included questions about their educational and life experiences prior to coming to the United Kingdom, their arrival in the United Kingdom and initial experiences in London schools, how they had learned and were continuing to learn English, what they were currently studying and how they felt they were progressing, how and when they used their first and additional languages, and their ambitions for future study and work. The interviews lasted up to an hour and they were conducted in a conversational style in an effort to get 'insider' perspectives.

The young people on this ALD course were by no means an unusual group in London, yet there has been very little relevant background research information. Initial literature and information surveys conducted by the research team, covering sources such as the British Museum oral history archives, the United Kingdom Millennium Voices Project, the Museum of the City of London, and university archives in the United Kingdom and the United States, found ethnic minority experiences documented as early childhood memories, as struggles (and successes) of adaptation, or as experiences in building settled communities with distinct cultural identities. We were not able to find publicly available recorded individual or group accounts and experiences of language and literacy learning by members of ethnolinguistic communities in large population centers such as London and California.

Student Experiences

We will now try to draw out some of the themes that have emerged from the interviews. All students cited have been given pseudonyms. The student quotes are shown here to reflect the key issues emerging from the accounts of their experiences.

English is a Multilevel and Multidimensional Struggle

One of the clear themes in the interviews was the immense complexity of learning and using English in real everyday contexts. Students with little or no English described their initial experiences of entering secondary schools as "scary" and "depressing" because "you don't know what anyone is saying" (Rosa) and as a result many retreated into silence: "I didn't speak for the first year" (Walid).

> *Serouse:* It was terrible. I was sitting in the class, not understanding a word the teacher is talking about at all. I couldn't even understand 'hello' when I came here.

Students experienced prolonged difficulties in using English in an array of contexts. They were learning English as a language. At the same time they were learning to use English as a means for studying, dealing with educational and other social institutions, and socializing with others, which involves a range of literacies. As language learners they were grasping the nuances of pronunciation, grammar, and vocabulary, and trying to use appropriate registers in speech and in writing; and many had to learn new scripts as well.

> *Li Sin:* In my language there is no past tense, past perfect, things like that and . . . we don't have difference between 'the' and 'a'. . . . So prepositions for and the tenses and also the words that could link the sentence together. . . . The simple things: 'I was', 'I am', things like that. English have a lot of way to express a sentence . . . I found it very difficult . . . I only know how to use the simple one.

> *Minh:* I think I have a big problem with writing. It's lack of words. Some people can use one word to describe everything they want to say, but I don't know that word. . . . The way people write in my country and the way people write in English is different.

As young people they were trying to 'fit in' socially to a new environment and often felt isolated.

> *Walid:* I couldn't even say 'my name is that'. So I was just not saying any word. So some people—basically boys—hated me for that . . . You know, it's rude when you talk to some one and he is not responding. . . . Teachers do understand [how difficult it is, not speaking any English] sometimes. But students take it the wrong way. . . . At first, I had a couple of fights, because of that.

> *Rosa:* I think I was very lucky, I had a really good friend who would help me and stand by me. I think that's what got me through all those years . . . she was English. Even though we couldn't really talk . . . we just . . . stuck together. It's nice to see if people bother, care for you, if they see you can't speak the language, so I think I was quite lucky about that.

Some students experienced conflicting emotions and loyalties in learning and using English. They felt the attrition of their first languages and a sense of alienation from their language communities in London.

> *Walid:* They think: 'English wannabee', because I forgot the words, or I can't put them together. I can see it in their eyes they think I'm rude.

Yussuf: Now it's just English. Even at home, my sisters, we're not allowed to speak Arabic, only English. It's kind of a rule: English, only English . . . my dad says . . . 'they are in England now, let them learn English.'

No English, Can't Do Much

Students who arrived with little English, but with formal school experience in their first languages, reported being given infant picture books to learn how to read. It would seem that in the specific instances experienced by the students the schools associated students' lack of English with low cognitive need and a lack of any background learning. Some students had to argue vigorously to gain recognition of their academic qualifications and experiences.

Yussuf: Do you know those characters, 'Biff & Chip'? [the Oxford Reading Tree series] That's how I learned to read, from those books.

Serouse: At the beginning, I was going to this library that had these books with tapes, for babies. I would open them, trying to learn them.

Minh: I asked to study AS[2] Economics and [the teacher] he shocked me. He said, 'OK, economics is a really hard subject, especially for you, a student who comes from another country'. He tried to scare me. . . . Because I did a foundation course, they think I'm not a good student. The thing is, I come from another country, so it's a transition step. In science I do very well. They think, 'amazing'! I know what they think about me.

Natasha: When I came here it was a bit of a shock because I had to speak English, although I was very advanced in writing and listening, but I couldn't express myself. . . . When I came here they asked me to do GCSEs[3] because I didn't have GCSEs, and I complained because in my country I was the top student. I said no. They tested me, a general test. Then the teacher said yes I could start from ASs.

Developing English as an Additional Language in a Tough Curriculum Environment

The students who attended separate English as a Foreign Language (EFL) classes said the content of these classes was often not related to their academic subject classes.

[2]Advanced Subsidiary level examinations which can be taken at the end of the first year of the two-year matriculation (subject-based) examination courses.

[3]General Certificate of Secondary Education—school leaving examinations for secondary students at the age of 16 in England.

Li Sin: They have quite a lot of foreign students in my college and they have all departments specially for foreigner to learn English.

(Q: And were those classes linked to what you were studying in GCSEs?)

Li Sin: No we study bibles, we study English with religion studies. . . . They provide the class just for foreign students and they teach you writing, speaking and reading but they use the book of religion study.

Some students who joined subject classes soon after they first arrived reported that during this initial period they often had to wait until the end of the school day to have their classwork explained in 'homework club'. For the most part, new arrivals sat mutely in class and tried not to call attention to themselves.

Serouse: When I first came there was this teacher, and she wouldn't talk much. She would just sit there and the rest would sit in silence. She would ask them to do something, and they would just get on with it . . . everyone was scared of her for some reason. I was quite scared of her, of asking questions of her. So I would do nothing for the whole two hours of the lessons, sitting there, copying people next to me . . .

You're on Your Own

Some of our student informants appeared to use a good many coping strategies. They reported that self-study played a crucial role in making up for their lack of comprehension in subject classes; they appeared to have spent long hours in background reading and research, and they were unwilling to engage in questioning in class to clarify understanding.[4] The students would disguise their lack of understanding until they could find time to research and work out questions for themselves, in private or at home with family help. Rost (1994, 113) observed that university students with EAL regularly experience confusion in lectures and commented that this ". . . may seem to project a rather pessimistic picture of L2 learners groping in confusion . . . however L2 learners— from their perspective—are developing realistic strategies for instruction." Likewise we see these efforts by our students as determined attempts to cope with the challenges they faced and not signs of ineptitude.

[4]Interestingly, Manson (1994) has documented this same strategy among PhD and MBA students with EAL.

Some expressed strong reluctance to ask questions in class, because they might be assessed as 'stupid' and wasting teachers and other students' time.

> *Minh:* You have to understand what the teacher is saying, and what people are saying, and I *do* understand. . . . A girl in the class made me feel uncomfortable. She said, 'I've lived here longer than you, your English is so bad'. Sometimes they make you feel like you are stupid.

> *Li Sin:* When I came to study here in England I'm afraid to ask questions, I felt shy to ask [a] person. Now I will ask but *after* the class and not during the class. [Because] other people, they might already know. Then it's a waste of time for them. . . . I will ask it after the class . . .

> *Amadou:* If I take for instance chemistry, back home we don't do many experimental practicals, so when I came here some of the apparatus that we use I've not ever seen them in my life before. [W]hen you want to ask the teachers in front of the students they think maybe [you] are dumb or something. . . . One of my chemistry teachers, he was Irish, so the accent oh my god I cannot get it, but later on I found I became used to it and almost whatever he says I understand. I look at your emotions and your body language. I get what you say . . .

> *(Q: Have you ever talked to your teachers about that?)*

> *Amadou:* Nah, I've never spoke to them about it. I just try my best, but if I tell them they'll think I'm telling them that the way they speak is not good or their English is not good That's why I try to open my ears and listen very well.

One student described waiting for the teacher to write something on the board throughout her first science class; he never did, and she could only guess at the content of the lesson.

> *Minh:* On my first day in school, it was a science lesson, and the teacher he talked for the whole lesson, and I kept waiting for him to write something on the board, but he never did! I kept waiting and waiting for him to write a few words so I would know what it was about.

In one or two instances where students reported that when they did ask teachers for help their requests were often brushed aside.

> *Li Sin:* Every time I ask a teacher what extra information can I read of the subject, they will say 'don't worry about it, in the end you will under-

stand' . . . and they don't really tell you what extra thing you can read that [would] help me understand about the area of the subject. Maybe they can't understand how difficult [it is] for me.

Walid: Because I came at the end of Year 10, I didn't have to do GCSEs, so they said 'don't worry about it, just go to classes, learn what you can'. But in Year 11 I had to do my GCSEs. I had to learn and do coursework and all that. So I suffered, because it took me ages just to do English coursework. People do five pages and I do just one page and I look at it and say 'Oh God!' . . . English, geographic, all those, I just got in and listened, I got no clue what they said.

Because they often did not understand their teachers and were reluctant to ask for help, some of the students regularly did a great deal of extra work outside of school, relying on their families and the Internet. Some students had their own textbooks at home which they found more familiar and useful than school textbooks.

Natasha: After the first lesson, I went to the library and got a dictionary and tried to translate every single word to see what it meant. I did that every time [class] for the first two weeks. . . . [Now] I read a lot related to my subjects . . . I do reading before the lesson to get the idea, so when I get to the class I will understand it quicker.

Farrukh: Whenever the teachers give us, he or she speaks in the class, sometimes teachers go so fast all you can do is note down the bullet points. I take my notes in bullet points. When I reach home, I will do as an essay. And I have some textbooks, from GCSEs as well as from Pakistan, and I think many old books can help you with your A-levels.[5] So . . . I take some bits from these books, take some bits from that book . . .

Walid: [All the other students] they do their homework in the class. It was so easy for them, they could do it in the class. For me, I got to research for it, go home, check it. Even at home, no one speaks English, we're all trying it. My whole family is doing my homework.

Minh: If you want good grades, you don't just read from the textbook from the school. You have to read and have extra exercises . . . I check the books myself . . . I don't depend on the teacher so much . . . In a sentence,

[5]Advanced Level examinations, subject examinations taken at the end of matriculation courses.

maybe there is one important word . . . if you miss it, you miss everything. It's a problem for overseas students, that's why we have to spend a lot of time for extra work.

Natasha: Sometimes I just leave my paper blank and I say okay, that's my homework (laughs) because it's hard . . . sometime I do it at home because the books you have in the lab, I don't find it as useful as such, I have another book at home which I find very useful I like it better than the one we use in the lab . . .

For some of the students, a strategy for academic success was to re-take subjects they had already studied before they came to England, even though the academic content may have been undemanding.

Paul: The stuff we were doing, I had already done it back home, so it was a bit of a breeze, yeah, it was easy. . . . Back there [Zimbabwe] for A-level we do Cambridge examination papers. So I thought it would be more of the same.

Li Sin: Well I find it very relaxed really apart from the English problems. I pick up the resources very quickly. The hardest part is to use English, express my answer or reading the question and answer the right question.

(Q: So you think that because you knew already more or less the content of the course that kind of helped you?)

Li Sin: It helped me improve my English . . . because I know what does it mean in my language.

A Hidden Multilingual World

From their descriptions many of our students seemed to live in multilingual communities and social networks. Many of them could read, write, and speak more than one language and were often learning other languages in addition to English through school or family and social networks. One student had attended Farsi school since the age of 5 and was taking A-level examinations in Farsi. The students described complex family multilingualism, with some parents speaking, reading, and writing in a range of languages such as Somali, Farsi, and Russian, others watching satellite television in Urdu, Panjabi, and Hindi, and yet others using the Internet in Somali, Arabic, and Mandarin Chinese. Students reported family and friends, especially other students with EAL, being significantly more important than school teachers in learning English. The affective dimension seems prominent in their accounts.

> *Walid:* Most of it is friends. If you have some one who doesn't speak [your] language to you, you'll try to speak English to him, because you can't speak his language . . . more people come in, new, then you just go to them. I know how you feel, come here, we'll start! Anyone comes, you just join the group, so I started like that and most of us now find it easier. . . . Some one comes new, you just know how they are suffering, so you might as well help.

> *Serouse:* [I've got] friends from other places—China, Brazil, Portugal, everywhere. . . . I have to admit, the first words I learned were swear words. . . . They throw in a new word and you say 'what did you mean by that?' and they will tell you . . . I don't understand from the teacher. I understand from my classmates. . . . You just ask, and there is no embarrassment because sometimes the teacher will say 'ah you are so stupid!'. Even if your friends say that, I can answer them back. The teacher I can't answer back.

> *Li Sin:* Being a foreign student it's much easier to [be] close with another foreign student . . . I can speak two languages, it means I have wide range of friends. And I can know a lot of things, knowledge and the culture in other countries . . . I have lot of opportunity to speak English in school and when I'm going with my friends but at home I mainly speak Chinese with my sister. I also speak a little bit Japanese . . . my sister's boyfriend is Japanese and he live with us and I have some Japanese friends . . . I learn from them . . . and now I'm trying to learn Cantonese . . .

Although they valued their multilingualism, students' first and other languages were not mentioned as living languages in school processes but rather as reified cultural objects. Minority languages had no place in curriculum activities but only in extracurricular cultural celebrations, where teachers responsible for EAL pupils would organize events such Eid celebrations (a Muslim event).

> *Farrukh:* Day before yesterday, my head of EAL was asking when is Ramadan finishing, because she has to make a party. I told her it is finishing 27 November. She said, oh we'll make a party first week of December, so I know she will give me one responsibility to prepare the invitation cards and go to the photographic room to laminate this or photocopy that, making the food list, decorating.

One of the students, Kamal, who was fluent in Farsi and was taking an A-level examination in Farsi reported using this language "only with the lads here [at the ALD course] and sometimes with lads at school, only outside [the class-room], never inside." No student reported accessing academic materials in a language other than English in school, and in some cases this was perceived by them as a factor in the attrition of their first languages.

> *Serouse:* I can't get hold of [Farsi] books [for academic subjects]—otherwise I would. . . . Actually my Persian has got quite terrible now. I can't spell in it. I can speak, got difficulty reading, just a bit, writing is just terrible.

Developing Academic Language and Literacies

In the interviews some of the students offered their opinions on the usefulness and relevance of the activities in the ALD program. These statements, covering a range of knowledge and skills, and contexts of use, can be seen as indirect re-flections of the students' perceived needs. From the standpoint of the present research they are seen as discursive indices of what the students construed as the constituents of a developed capacity to tackle the tasks and challenges they faced. We will first show some of the students' views on the value of their work in the ALD program. We would like to emphasize that these student remarks are not taken as direct evaluation of the usefulness or validity of the ALD program.

Readiness to Engage

> *Yussuf:* It [the student's university admission interview] was good. I had to sit down with all the rest of the students and we were called up one by one by the interviewers and basically I was called by this new guy, he was a doctor from Germany, and he asked me why I liked mathematics. I said because it's like a game to me, I never get bored of it. He asked me what aspect of mathematics I liked. He was being tricky, because when I told him what I liked, he asked me a question straight away. I did his question. I told him that I come to King's [the ALD course] anyway. I was going to go for the tour, he goes: you don't need to go for the tour, stay with me

even longer! So I spent even longer with him and he liked me. He goes: you're a keen mathematician, I'd love to see you back next year!

Natasha: It has helped me a lot in the way I should communicate . . . Now I'm confident in something like presentation. I feel confident if you ask me to stand in front of people to speak or present something.

Literacies for Real

Yussuf: Basically these lessons have very improved my vocal skills. You have to speak out loud and explain so people understand. What I talk about, they don't do the same subjects as me, and I have to put it in a simple context. . . . Presentation, even in school now, when the students have to do something, I think I have a better advantage because I came here [to the ALD course] not knowing anyone. I had to interact, to get to know them, and speak in front of them.

Serouse: Taking notes, I found quite helpful, because I never take notes in my [school] classes. This year for the first time in a computing lesson I had to take notes because the teacher would explain on the board and I had to take notes. The rest [of my classes] are all textbooks and exercises.

Getting the Right Register and Genre

Amadou: It has helped me a lot in my writing. . . . We had new terms and vocabulary that you use in higher education, and if I'd not come to this place [the ALD course] maybe when I get to university . . . I'll be consulting my dictionary but here there are people who are in the university telling me what it means. If I don't understand it I ask them and they clarify, so I would say that's really helped me. In my writing I've learnt new terms in the higher education sense.

Serouse: Coming to this class has helped [my writing]—how to plan it. . . . The worst thing about writing is thinking what you want to write and then what order you want to put it. . . . When I was writing, I noticed that between the lines I used certain words three or four times. . . . After these classes, when I sat my English GCSE [examination] the second time around, the writing was quite easier. Planning and actually writing it. It was easier, after this class. . . . When I look back on my first coursework, it was very basic. When I looked at the new one, it was more structured. . . . It helped me understand how lectures work at university, because this is how it would be. . . . And also sharing with your classmate sitting next to you. That's how it works.

Walid: Before, when they said 'Oxford' I used to say 'oh that's just a dream', forget it, there's no point even thinking about going to university! But now I want to go to university and I think I can do it . . . You gave us some papers about what does it mean, 'to evaluate' [and also explain, report, contrast, analyse, argue] and we had to do evaluation in class at school, so I said let me see, let me check those papers again. It does help. I saw the word 'evaluation' but I never knew what it means. The teacher said, all right what happened? What went well, what went wrong? Now I can see, I know how to do that, I'm more confident. I used to hate to do reports. Now they say 'report' I say, ok, I can do a report. Like 'describe' and 'explain', I had a hard time with that [the difference], and I didn't really find the difference until when I came here.

The above student statements clearly do not represent the full spectrum of language and sociocultural knowledge and skills needed to develop a capacity to perform effectively in academic tasks. In a sense the kinds of knowledge and skills mentioned are unremarkable in that activities such as learning new vocabulary and doing class presentations are commonplace in different areas of school curriculum; our students must have been involved in, for instance, vocabulary learning activities regularly in school. The fact that these activities and experiences were identified by the students with reference to the ALD program signals the importance of the opportunities for engaged interaction, the opportunity to do a variety of academic language and literacy activities with a heightened sense of awareness, and through the use and interaction to reflect on their own learning. Without wishing to suggest that all learning phenomena are individual psychoaffective and cognitive issues in a reductionist way, our data here point to, *inter alia,* the need to address the question of student identity. This will be one of the issues discussed in the next section.

Academic Literacies and Nontraditional Students

The glimpses of our students' experiences, as seen in the interview data, strongly suggest that there are at least two conceptual and pedagogic points that need to be addressed. First, our group (and other similar groups) of nontraditional students should not be regarded as *tabula rasa* in relation to the development of academic literacies. We saw earlier that academic literacy was sometimes likened to be 'a new language' in a 'foreign country'. This metaphor invokes the imagery of a first-time visitor to an unknown land. Our students were, however, already dwellers of the land, to push the metaphor further. They were already active participants in their local communities and social networks; more importantly, they had already experienced academic education in general (it would seem that this point was not always recognized by those they met in British education) and the learning of English (and other language/s) in particular and had first-hand knowledge of what it felt like to be a novice language user. Their perceptions and their responses to their on-going experience would inevitably be carried over into their learning and use of English and academic literacies. Therefore, as Leki (2001, 26) argues, it is important to listen to students' voices to give us "a better idea of 'the nature of people and systems' . . . and perhaps of how to stimulate 'further reflection' . . . among ourselves." As Street notes in the Introduction to this volume, in contrasting the academic socialization model that dominates thinking about student writing in higher education with an academic literacies approach:

> The academic literacies approach builds on NLS to direct educationalists' attention away from the narrow and formal features of literacy in education, such as, for example, initial acquisition and learning of the alphabet in primary school; mastery of English spelling and grammar for English as a second language learners in secondary schools; and development of study skills in higher education. The academic literacies approach, rather, directs our attention to the broader and more socially based uses and meanings of literacy. In the educational context this means making explicit both the particular genres, styles, and discourses associated with the literacies required for educational purposes and the underlying institutional power relations in which such literacy practices are grounded.

On this view, what the ALD program has taught us is that we need to take account of not just what students need to learn but also how they have experienced and perceived their past and present learning experiences. These experiences are rooted in relations of power and of identity, as many of the quotations form students above indicate. All students would readily agree that, for instance, learning to do written assignments according to teacher requirements is a good thing. But not everyone becomes good at knowing how to do this in the course of everyday schooling; many find school language and literacy practices a daunting challenge, as our student accounts readily testify. Our group of students appeared to have experienced classroom and school practices in a variety of specific ways; they also encountered "particular genres, styles, and discourses associated with the literacies required for educational purposes," some of which were problematic for them. Paying attention to the lived experiences of these students is a first step in the development of responsive pedagogy. The kind of student experiences we have seen here, for example, can help us appreciate, from these students' standpoint, the learning complexity that may underlie apparently straightforward tasks such as "say something/write about yourself" in an academic context.

Second, educational policy discourse tends to emphasize the responsibility of the individual. For instance, in a speech given by the Home Secretary to a group of ethnic minority young people the following point was made:

> Having confidence in yourself and holding on to a dream of what you can achieve is so important. Nothing should hold you back in reaching your full potential. I want a society that gives you these chances, a society where each of you, regardless of colour or race or religion has an equal opportunity to succeed. (Teacher Training Agency, 2000, 7)

The individual is presented as in some sense ultimately 'in charge' of what they succeed to do, or in this discussion, to learn. The student accounts we have seen here have shown instances where pedagogic practices in the classroom and curriculum provision have precluded any meaningful engagement with English and with subject content through English. In the field of Second Language Acquisition a number of studies have investigated the impact of social and cultural factors on language learning. For instance, in a study of adult migrant women in Canada, Norton (2000) shows that the women's opportunities to use and develop their English at work and in the family were intertwined with their job status, social standing, gender, and other social factors in the eyes of their peers. In an ethnographic study of four Chinese immigrant students at high school in California, Harklau (1994) provides an account of the different learning opportunities and demands in different areas of the school curriculum. One of her observations was that the classroom-teacher talk in the subject (not

EAL) lessons was difficult for the English language learners because the teachers assumed that they were working with mainstream students, i.e., fluent in English. The findings of these studies, while not directly concerned with issues of academic literacies, support a general point raised by our student accounts—that pedagogic and curriculum practices, in Lea and Street's terms, the 'academic literacies'—of school can have an important impact on the quality of learning as experienced by ethnolinguistic minority students. In this connection Cummins' (2000, 44) notion of 'coercive relations of power' is salient—"... in the transmission of knowledge, culturally diverse students were required to acquiesce in the subordination of their identities and to celebrate as "truth" the perspectives of the dominant group. . . ." In the context of the classroom we can clearly see that when teachers and educators adopt classroom and curriculum practices which do not accommodate nontraditional students' language and literacy needs, some sort of coercive power, in all likelihood unwittingly, is being exercised. It is beyond the scope of this discussion to engage with moral and ethical questions concerning coercion in education. It is, however, germane to the consideration of language and literacy development if pedagogy and curriculum work to exclude the possibility of learning.

Widening Participation, Widening Conceptualization

In this discussion we have seen some of the challenges and difficulties faced by a group of ethnolinguistic minority students when trying to participate in school learning. In addition to the already tricky and knotty issues of learning academic registers and genres (which all university students have to address), these students had to deal with other equally urgent and complex 'problems' which are specifically associated with their ethnolinguistic backgrounds. These include learning English as an additional language, making sense of different pedagogic and curriculum practices, learning to live with the marginalizing effects of not being seen as a fully paid-up member of the local society, and coping with the loss of cultural and linguistic capital encoded in their other languages (and its consequences in terms of academic performance). The student accounts have provided some helpful insights for further work on the conceptualization of academic literacies from the point of view of these young people. A lot more fine-grained work needs to be done. Woodrow and Yorke (2002,

169) argue that "[t]here is a need for greater understanding of pedagogic practices that are effective in facilitating the development of those students for whom Higher Education is a particularly formidable challenge . . . there is a need for more formal research but it can be looked at during 'activities' as well." We would endorse this view in relation to academic literacies for the types of young people we have been talking about.

References

Baker, P., and Eversley, J. (eds.). 2000. *Multilingual capital: The languages of London's schoolchildren and their relevance to economic, social and educational policies.* London: Battlebridge Publications.

Creme, P., and Lea, M.R. 1997. *Writing at university: A guide for students.* Buckingham: Open University Press.

Cummins, J. 2000. *Language, power and pedagogy: Bilingual children in the crossfire.* Clevedon: Multilingual Matters.

Department for Education and Skills. 2003. *Widening participation in higher education.* Retrieved 28-04-2004, from http://www.dfes.gov.uk/hegateway/uploads/EWParticipation.pdf.

Greenwich University. 2002. *Teaching and learning strategy 2002-2005.* Retrieved 28-04-2004, from http://www.gre.ac.uk/quAlity/learn/learning.htm.

Harklau, L. 1994. ESL versus mainstream classes: Contrasting L2 learning environments. *TESOL Quarterly* 28(2): 241–272.

Lea, M., and Street, B. 1998. Student writing in higher education: An academic literacies approach. *Studies in Higher Education* 23(2): 157–172.

Leki, I. Hearing voices: L2 students' experiences in L2 writing courses. In: T. Silva (ed.), *On second language writing.* Mahwah: Lawrence Erlbaum Associates, pp. 17–28.

Leung, C., Harris, R., and Rampton, B. 1997. The idealised native speaker, reified ethnicities, and classroom realities. *TESOL Quarterly* 31(3): 543–560.

London Metropolitan University. 2003. *Strategic Plan 2003-2008.* Retrieved 28-04-2004, from http://www.londonmet.ac.uk/services/quAlity-&-standards/aspc/publications.cfm.

Manson, A. 1994. By dint of. In: J. Flowerdew (ed.), *Academic listening: research perspectives.* Cambridge: Cambridge University Press, pp. 199–218.

Medway, P., Rhodes, V., Macrae, S., Maguire, M., and Gerwitz, S. 2003. *Widening participation by supporting undergraduates: What is being done and what can be done to support student progression at King's.* London: Dept. Of Education and Professional Studies, King's College London.

National Audit Office. 2002. *Improving student achievement in English higher education executive summary.* London: HMSO.

Norton, B. 2000. *Identity and language learning: Gender, ethnicity and educational change.* Harlow and New York: Longman.

Nottingham University. Undated. *English as a foreign language/English for academic purposes.* Retrieved 28-04-2004, from http://www.nlc.ntu.ac.uk/EFL/eap.html.

Rost, M. 1994. One-line summaries as representations of lecture understanding. In: J. Flowerdew (ed.), *Academic listening: Research perspectives.* Cambridge: Cambridge University Press, pp. 93–127.

Street, B. 2003. What's "new" in New Literacy Studies? Critical approaches to literacy in theory and practice. *Current Issues in Comparative Education* 5(2): 1–14.

Teacher Training Agency. 2000. *Raising the attainment of minority ethnic pupils: guidance and resource materials for providers of initial teacher training.* London: Teacher Training Agency.

Woodrow, M., and Yorke, M. 2002. *Social class and participation; good practice in widening access to higher education; the follow-up report to 'From elitism to inclusion' (1998).* London: Universities UK.

16

There is No Place Like Home

A Teacher Education Perspective on Literacies Across Educational Contexts

Jennifer Rowsell and Dorothy Rajaratnam

Second distancing: I return home—this return can be purely mental or physical as well—but this 'home' is less close to me than it was before: I can now cast at it the look of a foreigner, comparable to that which I turned on the foreign society. Does this mean that I have become split into two, half a Persian in Paris and half a Parisian in Persia? No, unless I succumb to schizophrenia: my two halves communicate with each other, they look for common ground, translate for each other until they understand each other. *(Todorov 1984, 4)*

I see rows and rows of girls seated in a classroom wearing gleaming white uniforms and neatly combed hair. A teacher enters the class and everyone stands up in unison to greet her with respect. Whenever a teacher addresses a student he or she stands to answer. We started each day gathering at chapel to say morning prayers. The first lesson of the day is mathematics. We completed lessons in workbooks with drill and practice exercises. Language comprises grammar, essay writing, and reading from a classic novel like Dicken's *Great Expectations.* What stands out in my mind is the school environment. I was educated in a tropical country where seasons never change. We had huge, shady trees and ponds all around the school. Ponds are filled with fish, tadpoles, frogs and lily pads. I felt tied to nature and to such biological facts as seed dispersal, animal life cycles, and habitats. *(Interview, Dorothy Rajaratnam)*

Introduction

This is the story of Dorothy Rajaratnam, who was born in Jaffna in the northern part of Sri Lanka but raised in its capital, Colombo. Dorothy comes from a middle-class family and was educated in a girl's-only private school. Her early years of schooling took place at a Christian mission school where most of the children came from affluent families. In the excerpt from an interview, you see a description of the context in which Dorothy was educated.

As her instructor and supervisor over the course of her Bachelor of Education program in Canada, Dorothy stands out in my mind as a thoughtful, intuitive, keen learner. From the outset, Dorothy exhibited 'exemplary practice' as it is viewed within our program: Her planning and teaching were inclusive and integrative; she appealed to different learning styles; she had strategies in place to deal with the linguistic divide felt by ESL students; she combined informal with formal assessment; and more than anything else, she was engaging, and creative. She received exceptional evaluations of her teaching in her practica and she secured a job upon graduating. Dorothy's gift for teaching became apparent to me after my first observation of her teaching. After getting to know Dorothy and familiarizing myself with her story, I concluded that much of her gift derives from a dual identity, or as Todorov describes it, two halves communicating with each other until they understand each other.

In this chapter, we (the pronoun we will use in the rest of this chapter to indicate our co-authorship) break apart her dual identity to place it at the center of her vocation and her art. We illustrate Dorothy's dual identity by presenting teaching artefacts—a lesson plan and her classroom design—to illustrate the slipping and sliding of Discourses (Gee 1996) and practices. What is clear from other studies in this volume (e.g., Stein and Mamabolo; Larson) is certainly true of our chapter: *Literacy is not a neutral set of skills that we teach and that children learn.* Rather, literacy by its very nature demands that we bring parts of ourselves into the process. In short, *subjectivity is formed in the space of practice.*

Our notions of self and our histories derive from strings of language moments during school and nonschool language teaching. What is more, who we are and where we come from impinge on the way we learn and, as Gunther Kress argues in *Before Writing,* the way we *make* language (Kress 1997, xvi). The concept of language-making is particularly helpful because it draws our attention to the subjective nature of speech specifically and meaning-making more generally. To learn and to teach literacy, we build on what we know and what we have experienced. In this way, we not only make language in the way we speak in different contexts, but equally and more importantly, we make ourselves.

The methodology we used for our research together was a series of observations and two informal interviews. In their work Brandt and Clinton maintain that social context organizes literacy as opposed to literacy organizing social context (Brandt and Clinton 2002). In an *autonomous model of literacy* (Street 1984) texts dictate terms for the reader, whereas in an *ideological model of literacy* (Street 1984), the reader and the context dictate the terms of how a text is read and understood. Such a shift in thinking gives more power to the reader and the context as carriers of their own meanings, discourses, and ideologies. If we locate the way we embed our culture and our history into our literacy teaching and learning, and equally, the way students embed their culture and history into their literacy learning, we are that much closer to understanding where our literacy skills and assumptions end and where global influences begin.

The chapter looks at Dorothy's two halves (Sri Lanka and Canada) and reflects on their benefits as she moves across contexts. Chronicling her story demands that we account for and understand what anthropologist Dorothy Holland calls 'history-in-person' (Holland et al. 1998). Holland defines the notion of history-in-person as:

> . . . the sediment from past experiences upon which one improvises, using the cultural resources available, in response to the subject positions afforded one in the present. The constraints are overpowering, yet not hermetically sealed. Improvisation can become the basis for a reformed subjectivity. (Holland et al. 1998, 18)

Analyzing moments in our lives when two cultures collide and catalyze teaching or learning is essential to coming to grips with the role of culture in our teaching. It is a process that Duranti and Ochs observed in their work and which they call *syncretic literacies*. Syncretic refers to the blending of different practices from different sources and cultures (Duranti and Ochs 1996). An added layer in Dorothy's story is dissecting how she speaks and uses signs and the visual to present herself and how these modalities are components of her identity. In this chapter, we present the mixing and melding together of Dorothy's unofficial social world and official school world.

In former work, Rowsell describes the mixing and melding together of multiple Discourses (Gee 1996) we carry with us—as teacher, as mother, as carrier of belief systems—into modes (visual, gestural, linguistic, etc.) of texts of all kinds—lesson plans, classroom space, etc.—as "materializing Discourses in multimodality" (Rowsell 2000). Writing this chapter with Dorothy and engaging with other work in this volume is an act of materializing an eclectic mix of Discourses into the modalities of a particular book written at a specific moment in time speaking to a certain audience.

There are questions that emerge from such a study: Is this discursive and multimodal scaffolding an unconscious or conscious act? Does it serve as a strength in our teaching and learning or merely an enrichment? Is our slipping and sliding from one discourse community to the next or from one cultural practice to the next a way of positioning and repositioning ourselves? And importantly, does bringing in cultural practices and 'history-in-person' into the classroom improve our teaching? These questions lie beneath the surface of our work together and we attend to their implications at the end of the chapter. To answer such questions, we adopt a lens that promotes an understanding of how people are culturally socialized into routines, and how cultural practices play themselves out in contexts at particular times.

Theoretical Framework: Instructional and Interactional Positioning in an Elementary Classroom

We begin from the perspective that speech and cognition are mediated by social interaction and cultural practice. What this means in practice is that language, literacy, and discourse derive from social and cultural practice (Scribner and Cole 1981). Literacy and learning practices are embedded in various Discourses, or ways of knowing, doing, talking, reading, and writing, which are constructed and reproduced in social and cultural practice and interaction (Gee 1996; Heath 1983). That teacher and student language practices shape classroom instructional and interactional discourse practices is clear from a survey of current research (Cazden 1988; Gee 1999; Gumperz 1977; Lemke 1990; Moje 2001).

In particular, the work of James Paul Gee and Gunther Kress has significantly influenced our theorizing of Dorothy's literacies across educational contexts. For the purposes of the chapter, we also use Kress's concept of 'motivated signs' (Kress, 1997, 6–7). Given that we are spotlighting Dorothy's teacher preparation year, we will look at artefacts of her practice as opposed to moments of her teaching. That is, although Dorothy taught significantly before the Bachelor of Education program, we are charting how she has evolved as a teacher and how her artefacts reveal this evolution. For instance, Dorothy's description of how she would design her classroom exemplifies how she sediments her migrations from one culture to another into her teaching. We combine Kress's belief that "signs arise out of our interest at a given moment" (Kress 1997, xii) and these signs manifest the interest of the makers with Gee's belief that "out in the world exist materials out of which we continually make and remake our social worlds" (Gee 1999, 191).

The different ways of speaking and being in situated speech (Gee 1996), and practices (Barton and Hamilton 1998; Street 1993) that are required in the classroom, can draw from the social and everyday Multiple Discourses that we bring to the classroom. For example, Dorothy focuses on language, particularly the acquisition of literacy skills, in her elementary teaching. As such, she not only embeds her own repository of knowledge and experience within language teaching from her childhood and disparate teaching experience, but also knowledge she acquired over the course of her teacher preparation year.

Like other studies in this volume (Burke and Hermerschmidt; Low; Larson; Stein; and Welle), our study promotes a greater understanding of the funds of knowledge (Moll 1992) we bring to classrooms and, what is more, our students bring to classrooms. One simply has to look to the rich vein of inquiry within studies on 'outside' literacy practices and home literacies (Barton and Hamilton 1998; Cairney 2002; Heath 1983; Hull and Shultz 2002; Hymes 1972; Luke and Carrington 2001; Marsh and Mallard 2000; Pahl 2002; Scribner and Cole 1981; Street 1996) to appreciate the invaluable nature of a deeper understanding of the implications of culture on learning in general and language development in particular. Culture in this sense is not simply a colorful set of alternatives but a highly charged and contested space—it is 'ideological.'

To view 'school learning' as a form of cultural socialization, we should account for three dimensions of the process: family and community practices; the nature of academic disciplines; and classroom practices. Accounting for culture within the classroom space concerns not only linguistic dimensions and discursive practices but also ideological practices. That is, how cultures come from different epistemologies of teaching and how learning is not universal and cut and dried, but instead fluid, moving with the practitioner according to his or her beliefs, bias, and backgrounds (not to mention those of the students in the classroom). Aspects of a teacher's past and present can be seen in such elements of practice as classroom talk and classroom design. But, what happens when students' understanding of subjects like history or mathematics based on their 'unofficial' knowledge meets 'official' knowledge of these subjects in school?

Invoking Luis Moll's notion of *funds of knowledge* is helpful here in that the funds of knowledge that teachers and students bring to classrooms represent resources that facilitate stronger ties with and understanding of 'school learning' or 'schooling knowledge.' Moll (1992) and Gutierrez (2001) build on Bhabha's notion of a *third space* (see also Davis et al., this volume) to describe a bridge between community/home ways of speaking and reading/writing and school-based literacy practices. This third space is a space where students can be supported to move their literacy practices into a school domain of knowledge.

The Outsider Looking In

As teachers, we carry with us assumptions about learners based on observations and different bits of information we acquire over the course of our teaching. With respect to Dorothy, I, as teacher educator, assumed that she was a shy, thoughtful learner who was diligent but less eager to contribute and participate in class compared to her peers and that these same traits would transfer into her teaching. Wittingly or unwittingly, I presumed that her teaching would display the same thoughtful, measured quietness.

It was with surprise that I first heard of Dorothy's dynamic, inspired teaching from a colleague who observed her teach in her first practicum.[1] Indeed, Dorothy stood out in her program and other than a strong work ethic and creative and inclusive planning, I was curious to determine what ingredients made

---

[1] Students in our program have two month-long teaching blocks during the autumn and winter terms of their teacher preparation year.

her such a powerful teacher. Dorothy was always and everywhere aware of the teaching-learning continuum. From early on in her schooling Dorothy harnessed her learning to her method of instruction. This instinct for understanding the nuances of teaching imbued flexibility into her teaching methodology. In our interview and discussions, Dorothy consistently referred to moving between and among different models of teaching from traditional to progressive to skill-based to holistic in order to speak to each learner.

On a sociocultural level, Dorothy is adept at foregrounding her background into her teaching to befit her class, or a learner, or a group of learners. Her interweaving of cultural practices and experience relates back to the important concept of third space that Elizabeth Moje builds on in her work on the discourse of science teaching; Moje uses this concept to illustrate the merging of disparate Discourses (Gee 1996) in a science teacher's method of instruction:

> These alternate positionings as teacher/scientist/expert or fellow community member seemed critical to Maestro Tomas's abilities to construct instructional congruence, or a third space that wove different Discourses together without sacrificing or dismissing the importance of either set of experiences and ways of knowing the world. When he connected personally with students' experiences, he was better able to merge these Discourses (referring to students and himself as "us"). Moje 2001, 479.

Moje describes 'third space', based on the work of Moll and Gutierrez, as "the mediational context and tools necessary for future social and cognitive development" (Moje 2001, 474). In Dorothy's teaching, she consciously or unconsciously inhabits a third space, bringing her life and her learning to bear on her teaching. We are arguing that Dorothy actively creates a *third space* within her practice.

James Gee (1996) argues that Discourses are located in cultural models that are shaped by the practices of different people. Discourses grow from practices and from knowledge that is produced within specific contexts such as workplaces, homes, schools, and so on. Gee refers to Moll's notion of "funds of knowledge," from which individuals draw in their speech. For example, a language arts teacher draws from knowledge about cognitive development; knowledge about reading theory; knowledge about teaching methodology; knowledge of assessment; research in literacy education, and so on.

In the course that Dorothy took, students were acquainted with studies on language development. They were encouraged to acknowledge the importance of understanding language teaching methodology (e.g., paired reading vs. guided reading) *and* the importance of understanding the ideological nature of speech (e.g., the concept of Discourse communities and embedding parts of ourselves and our culture into the way we speak). Gee's concept of Multiple Discourses and Moll's notion of funds of knowledge provide a vehicle for understanding language on a deeper, perhaps more profound level. The present case examines how Dorothy draws on these notions and moves in and out of her speech communities to empower her teaching.

In the diagram below, we represent how Discourses are instantiated into practice and texts. The diagram illustrates how Multiple Discourses (as in both language and cultural models that are associated with Discourses) become modes or 'stuff' we use to make texts. Our 'history in person' guides the practices we use in making texts of all kinds. What results from the merging of multiple discourses–history in person–into text mode is a third space.

Multiple Discourses	→	Multiple Modes

Multiple Discourses → **Multiple Modes**
History in person (Holland 1998) ↔ Practices
Discourses → *Identity with funds of knowledge* (Moll 1992) → Texts
THIRD SPACE (Moll 1992; Moje 2001)

In the diagram, we visually depict the process of embedding our ways of being into texts we produce. We use texts in the broadest sense as artefacts of our identity. Texts range from how we design our classrooms or offices to how we write lesson plans and memos. Bits of our hybrid experiences and history in person (Holland 1998) can be found in the multitude of texts we make, read, and touch. By examining two of Dorothy's texts (a lesson plan and classroom design), we break apart how she deftly interweaves her multiple voices.

According to Gee, individuals acquire their Primary Discourse within the immediate context of their community and their home. In other words, language development occurs in the Primary Discourse. For example, Dorothy's basis for understanding teaching derives from the Discourse of teaching and learning in Sri Lanka (which is a hybrid of the English system and local schooling practice) and this Primary Discourse informs her burgeoning teacher Secondary Discourse at OISE/University of Toronto, which sits within a teaching discourse.

The Discourse of an elementary language teacher brings with it theories of cognition; theories of language and literacy development; the Discourse of language textbooks; different models of language development such as phonics and whole language; and curricular models and expectations for language development like the National Literacy Hour. Although several intersecting Discourses and practices can be at work in one classroom, for the purposes of the chapter, we are focusing on how Dorothy tacitly applies an understanding of how her own culture and background enhance her language teaching. For example, her belief in structure and skill-based teaching of grammar and language conventions is tied to her more traditional Sri Lankan education (her funds of knowledge), but at the same time, is coupled with her belief in understanding the semantic/meaning level of narratives which she acquired in a language arts course during her Bachelor of Education program. The efficacy of her teaching lies in this third space—a merging of cultural practices to inform her teaching of students from similar backgrounds and similar stories of migration.

Dorothy's Story

When I began to peel back the layers of her history in the second term of her teacher preparation program I came to appreciate the origins of Dorothy's inspired teaching. To begin with, Dorothy had some teaching experience in Sri Lanka and Montreal before entering the Bachelor of Education program at the University of Toronto. However, the story behind Dorothy's exemplary teaching goes further back than her years as an 'untrained' teacher.

Her reflex to foreground and background culture in teaching derives from an eclectic education. As a child, Dorothy went to a private school and due to her more privileged access to private education, she was refused entry into university. The Sri Lankan system limits its entrance to university on a district basis. This means a student from an 'underprivileged' village, with the same results, would be admitted before someone from a more privileged background. University is free in Sri Lanka, which provided an opportunity for less fortunate individuals to advance in life through higher education.

Dorothy therefore faced a crossroads: Her parents could not afford to send her overseas like some of her classmates and she was refused entrance to university given her privileged status. At the time, there was an opening for a grade one teaching position and she was granted the position. She found the experience a challenge having to piece together, on her own, what it means to be a teacher;

in her words, "although I enjoyed the company of children, I didn't know much about teaching at all. I learned by observing the teacher teach in a very structured and disciplined environment." It was around this time that Dorothy developed an ability to be a voyeur of teaching practice. What grew from this was an awareness of a teaching-learning continuum. What is more, it began a series of events in which she honed the art of being an outsider looking in.

Dorothy has therefore been a teacher for some time, having taught in primary school in Sri Lanka and later on in a preschool in Montreal. These two seminal experiences set the stage for her professional training in teaching. From the beginning, Dorothy appreciated that good teaching demands that a child "needs to be engaged to stay on-task." Dorothy tacitly integrates multiple subjects (language-science-music) into lessons so that there is not a language lesson and then a science lesson, but instead a language lesson with scientific dimensions with arts infusion (music, dance, drama, or visual arts). Dorothy identifies students' needs while at the same time providing support necessary to help students struggling in literacy or in numeracy.

Dorothy's family immigrated to Canada in 1992. They left Sri Lanka because her family was affected when riots broke out in 1983. Their house was badly damaged and looted. They ended up in a refugee camp and were displaced to the north of Sri Lanka. The traumatic experience resulted in their move to Canada.

In November of 1992 she landed in Montreal. Dorothy worked in a day-care center for a year, and then worked part-time in a preschool, which was followed by getting a Bachelor of Arts in Child Studies at Concordia University in Montreal. In 1996, Dorothy returned to Sri Lanka and married and lived there for four years, during which time she had two daughters, Patricia, now 5, and Sarah, now 3. Shortly after giving birth to her second child, Dorothy worked as a grade 3 teacher in a prestigious international school. This teaching experience set the foundation for teaching students at the elementary level. After experiencing more political strife they moved to Canada in July 2000, ostensibly for good. Dorothy maintains that she hopes some day to return to Sri Lanka and that it remains her home.

The Researcher Looking In

In relation to the structure of the volume, Dorothy's story clearly illustrates Street's belief that,

. . . in order to build upon the richness and complexity of learners' prior knowledge, we need to treat 'home background' not as a deficit but as affecting deep levels of identity and epistemology, and thereby the stance that learners take with respect to the 'new' literacy of the educational settings. (Street 1997)

Certainly it became clear to me over the course of teaching and supervising Dorothy during her teacher preparation year that the strength of her teaching resides in her dual identity, the result of having grown up in Sri Lanka and in her twenties moving to Canada. Dorothy speaks of being aware of a continual dialogue between her native culture and her adopted culture and she plays on the strength of both in her teaching.

Although Dorothy was diligent, she tended to be less of a 'presence' within the group of teachers-in-training. After several discussions, Dorothy and I decided to chronicle her story and share it as evidence of the strength of cultural modeling in teaching. Dorothy presents herself as having multiple, often converging identities, and she encourages students to view themselves in this light. For example, Dorothy brought in the sari she wore to her own wedding and asked students (in a multicultural, inner-city school) about traditions and clothes worn within their cultures and how they compare to those of their host culture (Canada). Students thereby made connections between their tacit/cultural understanding *and* reasoning strategies relating them back to strategies they are expected to acquire.

During her second practicum, as a culminating task for a unit on multiculturalism, Dorothy asked each student to present their culture to the class. In our interview, Dorothy described the assignment with animation: "I told children to research on which country they came from, bringing in some interesting facts and incorporating a drama activity with it." Dorothy followed up her description by saying, "it was a real mix of different worlds together in one setting. There was a girl who presented Hawai`i and dressed up in a grass skirt and performed a traditional Hawaiian dance."

Given her gift for adapting her teaching to suit the particular needs of a student, it is fitting that Dorothy is now working as an ESL and special education teacher at an elementary school in Toronto. The special education model she implements in her teaching is "an integrated approach where I work with students in their classrooms and only withdraw them when necessary." In this way she makes students feel that "they are part of their home class rather than being withdrawn and feeling isolated." Dorothy imbues a philosophy in her teaching that people learn to make sense of experiences in the world through a process of cultural socialization. Dorothy has kindly allowed me to present her story as a case study of cultural modeling.

Dorothy's Pedagogy

Dorothy's mantra in teaching is making "it as clear and as interesting as possible for the learner." Dorothy's teaching is a hybrid of quite structured teaching harnessed to a cooperative model of teaching she learned in her teacher preparation year at OISE/University of Toronto.

Dorothy, however, believes in direct instruction. Much of her own education took place within structured teaching environments, or as she articulates it, "in Sri Lanka it is so structured that the teacher is seen as the person who has all of the knowledge." During her schooling, Dorothy's predominant form of assessment was "ongoing monthly tests" whereby you were only judged by your final marks. Assessment was mostly by skill-based tests that would demonstrate performance and understanding of subject matter. Although she eschews such a traditional approach to assessment and evaluation, in our interview she confesses that her rather traditional schooling gave her "prior knowledge" (Street 2004) and very much informs her teaching. Dorothy made it clear that she believes in focusing on skills like spelling, grammar, and arithmetic to make learning as clear as possible.

However, there is a merging of pedagogic models derived from a more rigorous schooling with her comparatively more progressive teacher training. As she expressed it, "I think people in Canada are much more open-ended in discussions where you think critically and have control over learning. Whereas, in Sri Lanka, it is so structured that the teacher is seen as the person who has the knowledge." In the first artefact, a lesson plan (see Figure 1), we see vestiges of different parts of her 'history-in-person' (Holland et al. 1998) and these traditional funds of knowledge—her love of nature, her structured schooling, her preference for cooperative-based activities, and her preference for integrated teaching. The lesson continues a unit she taught on dinosaurs. In her learning expectations, she proposes that students:

(text continues on page 339)

Figure 1.   **Planning The Lesson**

Curriculum Area: Science and Technology
Unit of Study: Dinosaurs
Title of Lesson: Triceratops

Background Information: This lesson takes place in the middle of the unit on dinosaurs. Students are now learning different types of dinosaurs. They have finished learning about things that existed in prehistoric times, extinction, fossils and paleontologists.

Objectives
Science and Technology:
- demonstrate curiosity and a willingness to explore and experiment
- demonstrate understanding of and care for the natural world
- say that fossils are evidence that dinosaurs, and other plant and animal life, existed on earth many years ago, even though we cannot see them today
- classify dinosaurs as either plant eaters or meat eaters

Language:
- listen and respond to others in a variety of contexts (e.g., pay attention to the speaker; take turns speaking in a group)
- follow simple directions and respond appropriately to familiar questions
- ask questions, express feelings, and share ideas
- use language to connect new experiences with what they already know
- listen and respond orally to language patterns in stories and poems

Assessments: Students will answer questions correctly. They will use their critical thinking skills to answer them. They will ask questions to clear doubts. Work sheets will indicate understanding.

Materials:
Visual aids
Books about dinosaurs (Structure of teeth and feet)
Dinosaur learning wheel (meat eaters, plant eaters)
Head dress (3 horns)
song

Figure 1. continued

Implementing The Lesson (20 minutes)

Activating Prior Knowledge:
Look at what Dino is wearing on his head.
Dino: "Which dinosaur's head looks like my head?"
It has 3 horns, so it must be Triceratops.

Stating the Purpose/Objectives of the Lesson:
Today we are going to learn about Triceratops. We will learn about how he kept his enemies away, what he ate, and how his body looked.

Body of the Lesson: (Teaching strategies include input, check for understanding, and practice)
Why do you think this dinosaur was called TRICERATOPS?? (Because it had 3 horns)

I will show a picture of a tricycle and ask them what it is. Some may say it is a bicycle. Then I'll tell them that bi means two. But the picture has three wheels. Therefore it has to be Tricycle. Tri means three. That is why the three horned dinosaur is called Triceratops.

How do you think it kept its enemies away? By poking them with its horns. The horns were a defensive structure. Just like the way a country trains its soldiers to defend in a war, the Triceratops defends itself by butting the enemy with its horns.

Let's look at its teeth and feet. Does it have sharp spiky looking teeth? No. So is it a plant eater or a meat eater? Plant eater.

The Triceratops had a beak like a bird's beak. It was a timid dinosaur.

If you go to the zoo today. You will see an animal that looks similar to the Triceratops. Who can tell me what that animal is? It begins with the letter "R" (Rhinoceros)

Concluding the Lesson:
Song: (Sung to the tune of Do You Know The Muffin Man)
Children will suggest the actions for each verse of the song)

> Do you know the Triceratops?
> It had 3 horns on its head.
>
> And every time a T-rex came
> It went poke, poke, poke, poke!
>
> It always ate green, green plants
> It was a plant eater.

Review questions after the song:
How many horns did a Triceratops have?
How did it protect itself from his/her enemies?
What type of food did it eat?

(text continued from page 336)

- Demonstrate curiosity and a willingness to explore and experiment *(B.Ed. Discourse and practice)*
- Demonstrate understanding of and care for the natural world *(Personal philosophy and pedagogy)*
- Say that fossils are evidence that dinosaurs, and other plant and animal life, existed on earth many years ago, even though we cannot see them today *(Standard teaching pedagogy)*
- Classify dinosaurs as either plant eaters or meat eaters *(curriculum expectation and structured school pedagogy)*

The use of worksheets in the lesson provides an evaluation component, adding the requisite rigor Dorothy demands from her teaching and her pedagogy. The words in italics signpost Dorothy's history-in-person. Within the lesson we see vestiges of her postgraduate schooling; her cultural epistemology and personal philosophy; and her adherence and reverence for pedagogy and curriculum.

Dorothy's Classroom as a Semiotic Mediation of Cultural Models

The eclectic influences and Discourses in Dorothy's life materialize in the "semiotic domain" (Gee 2003) of her classroom space. Jennifer's interpretations of multimodality (the mixture of different types of modes, from interview-speak to math centers) are the realization of Discourses—the Discourse of teacher preparation, Discourse of Tamil education, the Discourse of primary math. According to Gee, Discourses are always and everywhere "embedded in a medley of social institutions" (Gee 1999, 18). Equally, Kress contends that modes "indicate that we make signs from lots of different 'stuff', from quite different materials" (Kress 1997, 7). In the diagram presented earlier in the chapter, we illustrated the process of Discourses becoming modes in texts, and our depiction of Dorothy's classroom underpins our analysis of the artefact.

Essentially, Dorothy's classroom as a semiotic space objectifies, sediments (Pahl 2001), and naturalizes her Multiple Discourses in the form of modes. A mode could be a nature mode—by featuring tropical plants in her classroom she objectifies her memories of growing up in Sri Lanka with its lush, green

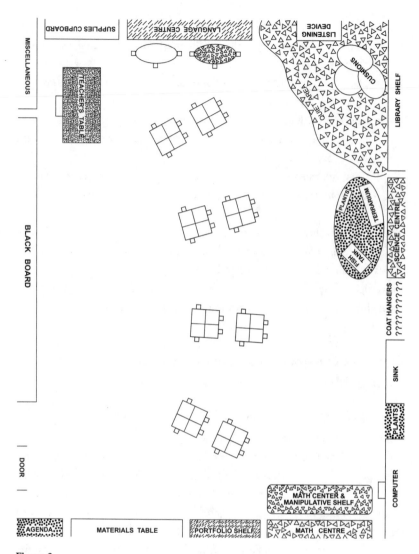

Figure 2.

vegetation. During our interview, Dorothy spoke at length about how she would design (see Figure 2) her classroom as a reflection of her philosophy of teaching. What we see in Figure 2 is a depiction of Dorothy's ideal classroom design.

The shapes within components like the math center differentiate parts of Dorothy's history-in-person (her Discourses, her practices, her beliefs, her education). The triangles represent what she learned over the course of her teacher preparation: math needs to be interactive and engage the student (i.e., learn by doing); independent and paired reading should take place in a comfortable environment; the tables situated in the language center are for guided-reading sessions. Differentiated by dots, the plants, fish tank, and terrarium represent Dorothy's love of the environment tied to her childhood in tropical Sri Lanka. The agenda is also differentiated by dots—larger ones—signifying her belief in having children always aware of what they are studying and when they are studying it. Finally, the diagonal lines represent her own bias—the teacher's desk is not front and center but instead at the side—physically and psychologically—as a constant support but "without spoon feeding." Dorothy strongly believes in displaying student's work as well to celebrate their successes.

Dorothy's classroom combines the rigor of her schooling in Sri Lanka with centers focused on skills development—a math center, a language center, and a science center. Around the "library shelves" are soft-covered cushions, forming what Gemma Moss describes as a partitioned area exuding "the possibilities of domestic leisure" (Moss 1999, 12). Dorothy emphasizes the importance of a listening center for ESL students who may need the extra support. The language center is a separate area devoted to developing literacy and language skills. There are several visuals displayed as a support for students struggling with language skills and tables to conduct reading sessions. In our interview, Dorothy spoke about looking at color in saris for visual arts and examining patterns in the saris to teach math concepts like tessellations. Culture and cultural practices thereby serve as vehicles to skills development.

A key component of the science center is the "green area" with plants, a terrarium, and a fish tank. This area is a cynosural force in the classroom and is tied to her Sri Lankan roots. As Dorothy articulates it, she is inextricably tied to the environment and to the greenness of her upbringing in Sri Lanka:

> First of all, I would like to take care of the environment, which is very degraded; and I'm a person who was brought up with a lot of nature; back in Sri Lanka, it is a very tropical country; so I would make sure there are a few plants in the class to give that effect because that puts something extra to motivate and a lot of visual aids to support students.

Beside the science center, there are coat hooks, a sink, and more plants as a reminder of the ecological, green theme that is central to her program and to her classroom. To forge a strong connection among technology, math, and science, Dorothy places a computer station in between the math and science centers. Dorothy derives a strong part of her math and science pedagogy from her years of instruction in Sri Lanka. Nonetheless, she has adopted a more holistic, less skill-based approach to teaching math in the light of the integrative, interactive math instruction she received during her Bachelor of Education teaching. Dorothy believes in acquiring math skills using math manipulatives and math activities that invite an understanding of meaning as opposed to a rote understanding of math that she learned as a child.

Implications for Practice

Literacy is socially situated: language that is spoken, read, acquired, learned within particular classrooms by particular teachers. As we move across sites, we carry with us practices intrinsic to these sites. Dorothy's story serves as a telling case study of how to mediate culture within teaching practice. Vestiges of past and present literacy practices and assumptions about literacy can be seen in such aspects of our teaching practice as our classroom design; our lesson and unit planning; the nature of our assignments; the types of texts we use; and the visuals we use to explain written texts.

If we regard literacy *as a global and social practice,* then we must analyze how we communicate across cultures in our teaching and learning to access embodied understandings in language for ourselves and for our students. In the words of Brandt and Clinton, "objects are animated with human histories, vision, ingenuity, and will, yet they also have durable status and are resilient to our will. Our objects are us but more than us, bigger than we are" (Brandt and Clinton 2002, 340).

Forms of literacy that go beyond our immediate context and classroom are literacy for establishing and maintaining relationships (e.g., e-mail and texting); literacy for skills development (e.g., using multiple modes—animation, gesture, movement, words, visuals—in written assignments); literacy for pleasure and self-expression (e.g., creating websites); literacy for displaying information (e.g., PowerPoint). Victoria Purcell-Gates et al. (2002) speak of using objects from everyday experiences to encourage students to draw on their lived experience in their language learning. Like Dorothy, students should incorporate their cultural practices and views of the world into classroom events to enrich their literacy learning.

What Dorothy's story tells us about literacy teaching and learning is to be aware, to be explicit, and to celebrate the dynamism of our histories-in-person (Holland et al. 1998, 18) and to use our funds of knowledge (Moll 1992). We should take from contexts that which is a strength and move beyond constraints and deficits. The key point here is to address the assumption that Dorothy's education in Sri Lanka was somehow backward, 'traditional', or perhaps even out-of-date undermines the strength of it in her teaching.

If she remained in a deficit model, she would be doing her students a disservice; instead, she has developed a capacity to use her background to move students forward. What is more, having the psychology of an outsider, she gives her students more space (linguistic, symbolic, emotional) to find a place in her classroom.

What Dorothy and Jennifer appreciated in writing this chapter is the importance of directing our attention to broader and more socially based uses and meanings of literacy, which are often rendered vague or absent in literacy curricula. As Street notes in his introduction, in educational contexts this ability to build on our prior knowledge helps us make explicit what was formerly vague.

Practitioners adopting a New Literacy Studies framework would argue that effective literacy learning in current educational climates could occur only *outside* of school settings. As practitioners, we should bring these theories into the classroom and use them as a framework for language teaching; to think about race and language; to incorporate multimodality into literacy teaching and learning; to diversify and blur gender lines; and to account for our students' funds of knowledge and actively create a third space in our planning and our teaching.

References

Barton, D., and Hamilton, M. 1998. *Local Literacies*. London: Routledge.
Barton, D., Hamilton, M., and Ivanic, R. (eds.). 1999. *Situated literacies: Reading and writing in context*. London: Routledge.

Brandt, D., and Clinton K. 2002. The limits of the local: Expanding perspectives of literacy as a social practice. *Journal of Literacy Research* 34(3): 337–356.

Cairney, T.H. 2002. Bridging home and school literacy: In search of transformative approaches to curriculum. *Early Child Development and Care* 172(2): 153–172.

Cazden, C.B. 1988. *Classroom discourse: Language of teaching and learning.* Portsmouth: Heinemann.

Duranti, A., and Ochs, E. 1996. *Syncretic literacy: Multiculturalism in Samoan American families.* Research Report No. 16. University of California, Santa Cruz. National Centre for Research in Cultural Diversity and Second Language Learning.

Gee, J.P. 1996. *Social linguistics and literacies.* London: Routledge Publishing.

Gee, J.P. 1999. *An introduction to discourse analysis—theory and method.* London: Routledge.

Gumperz, J.J. 1977. Conversational inference and classroom learning. In: J. Green and C. Wallat (eds.), *Ethnography and language in shcool settings.* Norwood: Ablex, pp. 3–23.

Gutierrez, K.D. 2001. Smoke and mirrors: Language policy and educational reform. In: Larson, J. ed. *Literacy as snake oil: Beyond the quick fix.* New York: Peter Lang Publishers, pp. 111–112.

Heath, S.B. 1983. *Ways with words—Language, life, and work in communities and classrooms.* Cambridge: Cambridge University Press.

Holland, D., Skinner, D., Lachicotte, W., Cain, C. 1998. *Identity and agency in cultural worlds.* Cambridge: Harvard University Press.

Hull, G., and Shultz, K. 2002. Locating literacy theory in out-of-school contexts. *School's Out! Bridging out-of-school literacies.* New York: Teachers College Press.

Hymes, D. 1972. *Language in culture and society.* New York: Harper Collins.

Kress, G. 1997. *Before writing: Rethinking paths to literacy.* London: Routledge.

Kress, G. 2003. *Literacy in the new media age.* London: Routledge.

Lee, C., Beale Spencer, M., and Harpalani, V. 2003. "Every Shut Eye Ain't Sleep": Studying how people live culturally. *Educational Researcher* 32(5): 6–13.

Lemke, J.L. 1990. *Talking science: Language, learning, and values.* Norwood: Ablex.

Marsh, J., and Millard, E. 2000. *Literacy and popular culture: Using children's culture in the classroom.* London: Paul Chapman.

Moje, E., Collazo, T., Carillo, R., and Marx, R. 2001. "Maestro, What is 'Quality'?": Language, literacy, and discourse in project-based science. *Journal of Research in Science Teaching* 38(4): 469–498.

Moll, L. 1992. Literacy research in community and classrooms: A sociocultural approach. In: R. Beach, J.L. Green, M.L. Kamil, and T. Shanahan (eds.), *Multidisciplinary perspectives in literacy research.* Urbana: National Conference on Research in English & National Council of Teachers of English, pp. 211–244.

Moss, G. 1999. Texts in context: Mapping out the gender differentiation of the reading curriculum. *Pedigodgy, Culture and Society* 7(3): 507–522.

Pahl, K. 2002. Ephemera, mass and miscellaneous piles: text and practices in families. *Journal of Early Childhood Literacy* 2(2): 145–165.

Pahl, K. 2001. Texts as artefacts crossing sites. *Reading* 35(3): 00–00.

Purcell-Gates, V., Degener, S.C., Jacobson, E., and Soler, M. 2002. Impact of authentic adult literacy instruction on adult literacy practices. *Reading Research Quarterly* 37(1): 70–92.

Rowsell, J. 2000. Publishing practices in printed education: British and Canadian perspectives on educational publishing. Unpublished Ph.D. thesis, King's College, University of London.

Scribner, S., and Cole, M. 1981. *The psychology of literacy.* Cambridge: Harvard University Press.

Street, B.V. 1996. *Literacy in theory and practice.* Cambridge: Cambridge University Press.

Street, B.V. 1997. The implications of the 'New Literacy Studies' for literacy education. *English in Education* 31(3): 45–59.

Street, B. And Street, J. 1991. The Schooling of Literacy. In: D. Barton and R. Ivanic (eds.), *Literacy in the community.* London: Sage, pp. 143–166.

Todorov, T. 1984. Knowledge in social anthropology. *Anthropology Today* 4(2): 2–5.

17

Deconstructing Academic Practices Through Self-reflexive Pedagogies

Penny Jane Burke and Monika Hermerschmidt

Introduction

In light of current developments in educational policy, which could deepen divisions between theory and practice, we will draw attention to the connections between practice and theory in academic writing that are often ignored. We argue that the power relations in the teaching of academic writing need to be reflexively examined and transformed through pedagogies that reposition students as active participants in the writing process. Two theoretical frameworks shape our understanding and practice of teaching academic writing. First, we conceptualize academic writing as a social practice, drawing on New Literacy Studies (Street 1984; Lea and Street 1997; Ivanic 1998; Lea and Street 2000; Lillis 2001; Street 2001). This approach "allows a broader, more institutional and socially-sensitive understanding of the processes in which writing in higher education is embedded" (Jones, Turner, and Street 1999, xix). Second, our self-reflexive pedagogical approach is located in poststructural feminist positions (Lather 1991; Luke and Gore 1992; Gore 1993; Ellsworth 1994; Ellsworth 1997). This approach allows students and tutors to explore "the relations to one's self that emerge from particular practices or discourses" (Gore 1993, 154). Both theoretical frameworks conceptualize research, teaching, learning, and academic writing practices as socially and culturally embedded. Our paper draws on our collaborative work in the context of academic writing courses in a British postgraduate institution of higher education.

The authors in this volume share a perspective of literacies as social practices, which involves us, as writers and teachers, in considering the social and cultural contexts within which the students we work with approach their writing and learning. Self-reflexivity necessitates that context is a central concern in exploring and understanding the ways in which writing is shaped by, and shapes, material structures and discursive practices. Working in higher education is a privileged position, not just for us, but also for the students. This position needs to be recognized and examined in order to make connections between academic writing practices, processes of knowledge construction, and wider social contexts and relations. This kind of examination allows us to see that there is a stark contrast between the contexts in which we, and our students, work and the contexts within which Pippa Stein and Tshidi Mamabolo (this volume) work. Neither Stein, as a teacher-educator, nor Mamabolo and her pupils, can ignore the significant material constraints they face in South Africa where "not enough children are learning to read and write because there is no food on the table." While the types of material and discursive constraints that we face in a postgraduate higher education institution are different, they must be examined and made part of the discussions about how and what we write, because writing is not just embedded in those contexts but may, if not critically examined, perpetuate local and global inequalities and injustices.

Writing this paper, we are aware of the deeply embedded institutional structures and divisions that situate 'academic writing provision' in the margins of the academy. There appears to be a wide gap between those who teach academic writing and those who do research. Researchers, who are interested in pedagogies in higher education, might not necessarily focus their attention on the teaching of academic writing. On the other hand, teachers, who teach academic writing, might not necessarily have the resources or the institutional status to conduct research and write academic papers. With this paper we want to engage with teachers of academic writing and researchers who want to contribute to bridging this gap.

The teaching and learning of academic writing is institutionally separated from disciplinary teaching and constructed as 'remedial' and skills-based. Students participating in academic literacy provision are often constructed as 'non-standard' or 'non-traditional' through classifications such as international, access, mature, ethnic minority, and working class (Webb 1997; Ivanic 1998, see also Hopson's discussion of 'deficit labels' in this volume; Lillis 2001). These classifications are often taken for granted and understood as 'measurable' in neutral and objective ways. However, these categories are constructions that label students "as 'outsiders' who do not have the 'requisite values, knowledge, and skills to belong,' who 'lack these necessary qualifications'" (Zamel 1998a, 193, citing Cooper and Holtzmann). Tutors who provide academic literacy support are also located at the margins of the academy in social positionings that construct them as language experts rather than academics and are granted only 'second-class intellectual status' (Rose 1998, 17). They are often excluded from theoretical debates in higher education and not given access to the institutional resources that would allow them to enter those debates. Through this paper we enter those debates to reveal and deconstruct currently privileged discourses that reinforce such exclusions (Ellsworth 1994; Rose 1998; Zamel 1998a; 1998b; Lillis 2001). Students and lecturers experience discursive struggles through the ways in which they are positioned and/or position themselves in the academy. Conceptualizing academic writing as a social practice and reflexive pedagogies challenge these hierarchical divisions and reveal connections between theory and practice. We understand teaching and learning to be interventionist rather than value-free. Teachers do not come as neutral subjects to 'deliver' their sessions. Pedagogical processes are always tied to epistemologies, that is, what can be known and what counts as knowledge, whether conscious or not, and involve the making of meaning rather than the transmission of knowledge. The design and interpretation of sets of course materials are implicated in power relations and embedded in selective and contested practices.

In our own teaching, we aim to engage the students in processes and practices of self-reflexivity in their learning and writing. We draw on reflexive methodologies in order to deconstruct or unpack our subjectivities, rejecting the notion that teachers or learners can be objective agents and that 'skills support' is all that is needed. There is a large body of work on the concept of reflexivity, particularly in the context of ethnographic and qualitative research (Lather 1991; Adkins 2002; Skeggs 2002; Mauthner and Doucet 2003). Self-reflexive processes enable writers and researchers to think critically about the link between their autobiographies and the decisions they make in their research. As Mauthner and Doucet explain:

The 'choices' we make in our research with regard to ontological and episte-mological positioning, methodological and theoretical perspective, and the adoption of particular research methods are bound not only with our per-sonal or academic biographies, nor are they motivated exclusively by intellec-tual concerns. The interpersonal, political and institutional contexts in which researchers are embedded also play a key role in shaping these 'decisions' (Mauthner and Doucet 2003, 421).

We have drawn on those understandings and, in this paper, we will explain how we have used the concept of 'self-conscious reflexivity' (Bourgois 2002) in our teaching and writing practice. We have used reflexivity as a tool to exam-ine our own subjectivities, values, and approaches, while recognizing that this is always a partial process (Lather 1991; Gore 1993; Ellsworth 1997). If lec-turers and students become aware of the power relations that underpin aca-demic conventions and practices, they can challenge the ways that these re/pro-duce the privileging of culture-specific knowledges. The connections between our theoretical understandings and our practices of teaching, learning, and writing in higher education came to light through our reflexive discussions of our course design. Through such discussions teachers, researchers, writers, and learners can benefit from reflexively examining the social relations and processes they are implicated in.

Deconstructing Academic Practices: 'Being Explicit', 'Being Critical', and 'Referencing'

The focus in this section is on some of the academic practices that are taken for granted in academic communities. Assuming only one shared meaning makes it difficult for many students to recognize the contested nature of academic conventions. Our aim is to deconstruct those practices, in order to reveal the social processes and practices they are implicated in. We use the poststructural tool of deconstruction to expose sets of assumptions and to unpack some of those taken-for-granted practices in writing in higher education in order to re-veal the 'enactment of the institutional practice of mystery' (Lillis 2001). De-construction draws on poststructural frameworks to foster a powerful critique of existing knowldges and the hierarchical power relations they defend. For example, postmodernism questions the taken-for-granted nature of categories such as race, gender, and heterosexuality and suggests that these seeming "biological truths" constitute social constructions. By focusing on marginalised, excluded and silenced dimensions of social life, postmodernism destabilises what has been deemed natural, normal, normative and true (Collins 2000, 41).

Recently, academic practices such as 'being explicit', 'being critical', and 'referencing' have been deconstructed (Lillis and Ramsay 1997; Lillis 2001; Nichols 2003). For example, Lillis exposes the multiplicity of expectations hidden in the instruction/assessment criterion 'be explicit' (Lillis 2001, 57). Tutors seem to use 'be explicit' as a shorthand for a range of meanings that remain hidden to the student and yet that the tutor assumes the student will understand. Lillis draws up a list (Lillis 2001, 57, Figure 3.1) that includes all the meanings that she has uncovered while she was exploring 'be explicit' with one of her student-writers. Her list "challenges any presumed straightforward notion of 'explicitness', pointing instead to a number of specific meanings within the context of student academic writing" and shows that these meanings include:

a. Make clear the link between claim and supporting evidence.
b. Avoid such vague wordings, as 'etc.', 'lots of . . .'.
c. Check that it is clear what 'this', 'these' refer back/forward to.
d. Make clear why a particular section was included.
e. Say why particular examples are used.
f. Make links between sections.
g. Say why particular punctuation is used.
h. Show that you understand key terms.
i. Show how you are using contested terms.
j. Link content with essay questions.

When tutors take the term 'be explicit' for granted, students are left to believe that they have misunderstood what has been explained. We argue that the responsibility to work out those meanings lies both with the individual student and with the tutor but, more importantly, is located at institutional, cultural, and social levels. This involves that tutors and students examine the interconnections between their individual responsibility and the wider social contexts and relations within which they write. Taking that responsibility engages teachers and students in deconstructing academic conventions, such as 'being critical', and in examining the ways in which these practices are institutionally embedded in hierarchies of knowledge construction.

'Being critical' as an academic practice is itself highly problematic and might operate as an exclusionary device. As Nichols (2003, 140) points out,

> 'Critical thinking' occupies an interesting position in current discussions about diversity. It is discussed both as an outcome of a university education and as an essential pre-requisite for success. References to critical thinking in various guises (e.g., 'analytic skills', 'independent thinking', 'reasoning ability' etc.) appear in every version of the graduate outcome statements. . . . If certain groups of entrants are seen as starting with a deficiency in critical thinking, then it is not surprising that these groups will become a focus for anxiety and remedial action (Nichols 2003).

Her discussion sheds light on the ways in which hegemonic definitions of 'critical thinking' act as gatekeeping mechanisms through re/privileging gendered, classed, and racialized assumptions of what it means to be critical. She examines the implications of being included or excluded from access to those re/privileged practices. In those hegemonic definitions, according to Nicols, citing Plumwood (1993), the key words are:

> 'reasonable', 'focused' and 'deciding'. Critical thought is rational; it is purposive; and it results in decisions about belief. . . . The terms in which critical thinking is defined support the notion of an ideal critical thinking subject. At the same time, they imply a problematic non-critical other. If we take the reverse of the terms in this definition, we can construct a definition of this other; one that is irrational, unreflective, unfocused and indecisive. If we recall that the inability to think critically is seen as a marker of cultural difference, such definitions position the cultural Other as such an irrational subject, consistent with colonialist strategies of representation (Plumwood 1993). (Nichols 2003).

We argue that academic writing should be reconceptualized as competing and contested sets of writing methodologies and social practices rather than as homogenous sets of skills. This would involve tutors and students reflexively considering 'critical thinking' practices not only as writers, but also as readers. The approach to reading that we take in the sessions takes into account that students will not all share the same perspectives and experiences of 'being critical'. We deliberately challenge narrowly defined reading styles such as skimming and scanning and take students to deeper and critical questions to be asked of texts. We break down with the students what is involved in 'being critical' in academic writing and reading.

The students on our writing courses come from a wide range of disciplinary and professional backgrounds and courses. This is a challenge, but also an opportunity to engage them in deconstructing the assumptions and taken-for-granted truths embedded in the reading and writing they encounter in the contexts in which they work and study. On their subject-specific courses students are often presented, not only with the kinds of mystifying instructions we have discussed above, but also with lengthy reading lists that are constructed as if they were the key to 'unlock' and 'get into' the knowledge of the field. Moreover, reading lists are presented as neutral and value-free and as if the students' only task was to gain entry to the knowledge inside. Students often are left feeling that, before they can write, they need to 'have' that knowledge. As one of the students on the course put it:

> The temptation is high to read a book as a whole, forgetting my own question. . . . When reading I feel like being in a discussion with a prestigious author and the more he speaks the less I have to say.

This student vividly captures the power relations involved in her experience of academic reading by painting an image of the author as prestigious and male. She describes reading as a "discussion," and yet still feels that "the more he speaks the less [she] has to say." A self-reflexive pedagogy of reading and of writing can help students to understand that their individual experiences as readers and writers are interconnected with wider power relations and social practices. Reflexivity enabled this student to make her observation and the pedagogy created the space for her to share such an insight with the class.

The student's observation also has implications for the ways in which referencing is understood and taught. Referencing tends to be conceptualized as a mechanical procedure such as "use the Harvard system." This fails to recognize that referencing involves much deeper concerns about making connections between concepts/theories in the field. It also ignores that students struggle to give authority to their writing, as the following student comment shows:

> I try to stick as much to references as possible. I have to have the relevant data. . . . In the actual essay I don't interject myself. . . . I just go with everything that somebody can actually go back and check . . . because I'm not an authority. . . . The problem is when you are writing there is always a tendency to forget the academic side of it and you go and put in anecdotes and whatever and you think 'good' and you think everything is flowing. So sometimes you think you'll have a go but you know that is wrong and you have to cut it out (Creme and Lea 1997, 99).

Taking a mechanistic approach to referencing, which explains citing in relation to referencing systems, does not allow student writers to explore the connections between giving authority to their writing and bringing other voices in the field into their texts. We argue that 'referencing' is one of the academic conventions that are often taken for granted and understood as mechanical procedures. In our courses, we have drawn on the concept of "orchestration of voices" (Lillis and Ramsey 1997) to move students to an understanding of referencing as a social practice. In the discussions we had with students about this concept, students were able to recognize the complex nature of the academic convention of referencing. They noted, for example, that citing authors with status in the academy gives authority to their writing, that subjective processes are involved in selecting and excluding authors from their writing, that they are writing within and outside of academic communities, and that the concept "orchestration of voices" helps them to see themselves as the writer/'conductor'. This concept helps move students away from positioning themselves as just a 'singer in the choir', as one student put it, to taking on the responsibility as the 'conductor' who brings out and supports some voices while subduing other voices. Lillis and Ramsey's metaphor helps students to understand the relationship between subjectivity, power, authorial voices in the literature, and the ways in which they position themselves in their writing. The 'orchestration of voices' brings to light the ways in which referencing is a social practice and contributes to the construction of knowledges.

Putting a Self-reflexive Pedagogy into Practice

We will now provide a detailed account of how we put a self-reflexive pedagogy into practice. The account centers on one of our sessions, which aimed to provide the tools for the students to make responsible and confident decisions in their reading and writing. In this session, we considered what critical reading might involve. With the students, we discussed how readings shape our writing both theoretically and methodologically and how we come to select, discard, or reject certain texts. This highlights that writers and readers actively make decisions that are always informed, consciously or unconsciously, by their different positionings and perspectives. We used the following extract from an MA course handbook, which gives the students valuable advice about how to 'unpack' their reading but is often overlooked by students:

> An important aspect of your writing will involve understanding and critically discussing other people's writing in the area you are working on. As part of this process, try and engage with the literature. This involves asking yourself who the authors are, which viewpoints they write from and why they take this view [*sic*]. Try to work out who they are in conversation/dialogue/dispute with and what kind of methodologies they draw on and they [*sic*] evidence they use and why they use this. Then reflect on how you respond to their work and what the reasons for your responses are. Your thinking on these themes needs to be crafted into the arguments and analysis you make in writing good course work and reports/dissertations. Thinking about reviewing and evaluating the literature in the field is an essential component of the degree. (Excerpt from Institute of Education, 2002–03, MA course handbook)

From this excerpt, we extracted the questions below and used them, with the students, as tools to understand and put into practice the processes involved in critical reading.

- Who are the authors? Which viewpoints do they write from and why do they take these views?
- Who are they in conversation/dialogue/dispute with?
- What kind of methodologies do they draw on?
- What evidence do they use and why?

We added a second set of questions from a different source (Richardson 2000).

- What is the central argument and how is it presented?
- Who is the presumed audience?
- How does the author claim authority over the material?
- Where is the author?

Richardson's questions foster self-reflexive perspectives on reading and writing. We used them to work with the students towards a deeper understanding of the contested meanings that different texts and disciplinary fields carry in relation to 'argument', 'audience', 'claim to authority', and author position. As there is no single right or wrong 'author position' or 'reader position', students as readers and writers engage in processes of 'world-making' (Usher, 1997).

An aim of the session was to move the students away from 'passive' approaches to reading towards positioning themselves as readers who have something to say in response to a text. Currently academic writing provision is framed by institutional expectations of both teachers and students, which construct the students as passive recipients of the teachers' instruction and guidance. However, constructions of passivity are problematic, as they reinforce binary oppositions and conceal that there is no 'passivity'. Taking up a passive position is always an active process of privileging certain discourses over others and legitimizing particular academic practices and conventions that are considered neutral, objective, value-free, and asocial. Our courses aim to uncover these active processes that enable the students to make connections between their social positionings, their identities, their values, their readings and to make these links explicit in their writing. The following two questions engaged the students in making these connections:

- Where are you in the text?
- How do you respond to the text and why?

For our teaching we select published academic articles for the students to work with that are not just different in the way they are written but also in the way they are framed theoretically and methodologically and how that is 'made explicit', or not, by the authors. Working across academic fields puts us in the difficult but also advantageous position of being able to interweave texts from different disciplinary locations and to examine the epistemologies and methodologies that go with them. The questions above generate rich discussions that engage students in critically considering their response to a text but also enable them to interrogate their responses.

However, there were always constraints and limitations, which could not be fully resolved. For example, the students experience time pressures because the academic writing courses are not run as part of their main program. Academic writing courses are conceptualized as add-on 'support' sessions that provide quick answers, and the time frame, determined institutionally, reinforces this. This causes frustration, which students have expressed in the courses and in end-of-term evaluation forms. Students need time to engage with the kinds of questions above if they are to understand what is involved in 'critical reading'. When designing and teaching the course, we too recognized the time limitations imposed by institutional structures, which impede reflexive pedagogical processes.

Other constraints relate to the different kinds of academic writing that students come into contact with as writers and as readers. Because students are encouraged to read published professional academic literature, which is given authority through their reading lists, they have less time to look for and read Masters dissertations or pieces of course work that were written for assessment. This poses particular difficulties for students in understanding the expectations for *student* academic writing. Student writing for assessment is expected to 'be explicit' about and justify the decisions made by the student writer/researcher to the reader/examiner. This itself is not made explicit and adds to the institutional mystification of student academic writing. Rather than explaining that expectations may be different for students than for professional writers, students are often given professionally written academic texts to use as 'models' for their writing, putting students into a contradictory position. Any approach to (the teaching of) academic writing, that does not conceptualize it from a social practice perspective, will be in danger of taking for granted and reinforcing tacit power relations, which have a profound effect on the students' experiences of academic writing (Ivanic and Simpson 1992; Ivanic 1998). While students are mainly exposed to texts that are written with an authorial voice of power, expertise, and prestige, they cannot write from that authorial position themselves (Geisler 1994).

This has implications for the way in which students approach and write their dissertations or research reports. The guidelines that are provided to students about how to write a research paper are often presented in the form of outlines of chapter headings (introduction, literature review, methods, data findings, and conclusion) and in the form of stages of the research process. This language limits the ways in which students might understand "doing research" and suggests the "stages" are separate, unique moments. Yet, what happens in research is interconnected, interdependent, complex, and overlapping (Griffiths 1998). In the session, we used the following quote from Griffiths to point out that the decisions we make about our research, often even before we begin the project, are underpinned by epistemology, whether we are conscious of that or not:

> The order of the questions in the logical framework should not be confused with when things happen in practice. Logically, the abstractions of epistemology come first, followed by methodology and finally methods and techniques. But this, chronologically and psychologically speaking, is hardly ever descriptive of research as it happens, where the order may be reversed, at least in the early stages, after which there are cycles of adjustment in understanding of methods, methodology and epistemology. During these cycles, the research is developed and refined (Griffiths 1998, 108).

However, professionally written research, as well as the advice that is given in student handbooks, often does not account for the connections between epistemology and research practices. This may leave students to believe that research is a linear, smooth, simple set of steps and stages. More importantly, this may leave students unaware of the implications of the decisions they make with regard to methodology and methods. Methods are often understood as 'packages' that can be picked 'off the shelf'. The same goes with theoretical frameworks, which can sometimes be misunderstood by students to be ready-made packages that they simply select and then apply to sets of data. This limits students to certain theoretical frameworks and restricts the kinds of questions they can ask. This also leads to anxiety, when students think that they have not found the 'right' theory that matches their questions. These misconceptions, left unexplored, contribute to a lack of awareness of the processes involved in drawing on specific theoretical and epistemological frameworks and how those evolve in the course of research and writing (see also Davis, Cho, and Toohey, this volume, for a discussion of writing and revision as nonlinear, "continual, iterative, and interactive" processes).

Self-reflexive Discussions
of Our Own Writing to Inform Our Pedagogy

Self-reflexive pedagogies necessitate the interrogation of *our own* writing practices to become critically aware ourselves of the processes involved in the construction of a piece of writing. This, in turn, informs the teaching of writing in ways that provide access to writing processes that otherwise might remain hidden and unexplored. This kind of interrogation also forces us as writers to critically explore and question the ontological and epistemological positions that shape the texts we produce.

In this section, we use extracts from a previous paper we have written collaboratively (see Extracts 1 and 2 below) to illuminate how this self-reflexive approach helped us to critically discuss *how we write* and the implications of this for *what we say*. While rewriting the earlier draft (Extract 1), we noticed that by using "on the one hand" and "on the other hand" we created an opposition that oversimplified the argument we were trying to make. Rewriting and discussing it helped us to recognize that there was a contradiction between our theoretical perspectives and the highly logical, rational, positivist terms implied in the language we were using. Using "however" and "moreover" in the redrafted version does not resolve this contradiction, but it avoids setting up a simplistic binary opposition. Other words, such as "examine" and "explore," which seem to be embedded in positivist discourses and in gendered notions of the scientific experiment and of the explorer, also kept entering our text. We were often locked into the available language and had to struggle against the connected hegemonic discourses. Writers cannot always get away from classed, gendered, and racialized vocabularies, even if they are aware that by using these words they are reinforcing the implicit power relations. These are some of the issues that reflexivity cannot simply resolve, but nonetheless need to be deconstructed to understand the ways in which writing is socially, culturally, and historically embedded. We argue that self-reflexive discussions will go further to engage students with the complex social and cultural issues involved in writing and help them to recognize that sign posts or linking words, such as "however", do not simply link ideas but also operate to privilege one perspective over another. A self-reflexive approach highlights that language is socially embedded in, and constructs, teaching, learning, and writing practices.

Extract 1 (early draft):

We are concerned about the power, status and recognition attached to academic practices and conventions. This raises certain kinds of tensions and contradictions that we need to address. **On the one hand,** students need to have access to those practices and conventions which are sets of cultural capital. **On the other hand,** students also need to understand the power relations behind those academic conventions and practices. It is important to recognise the value of diverse and different knowledges and the practices connected to those. Power relations are not only discursive but are interconnected with material inequalities. We feel we cannot 'write out' those inequalities in the discussions and the design of academic writing courses.

Extract 1 (redrafted):

Issues of access and knowledge construction are interconnected with power, status and recognition. This raises certain kinds of tensions and contradictions that we need to address. We recognise the importance that students have access to the practices and conventions that are privileged within academic communities because they are sets of cultural capital. **However,** it is also important to recognise the value of diverse and different knowledges and the practices connected to those. [Therefore] Students, and teachers/tutors/ lecturers, need to understand the power relations behind academic conventions and practices and the ways that these reproduce the privileging of culture-specific knowledges. **Moreover,** power relations are not only discursive but are interconnected with material inequalities. We feel we cannot 'write out' those inequalities in the discussions and the design of academic writing courses.

Using Extract 2 below, we explain how self-reflexive discussions have helped us to refine and clarify, in our writing, our positioning in the theoretical debates about power and discourse. For example, in the earlier version of Extract 2, we used "dominant," although our discussions made us aware that we shared concerns about how processes of power and privilege are being conceptualized. "Dominant" seemed to be connected to notions of power as fixed, expressing relations of power in simplistic oppositions such as dominant/oppressed, rather than understanding them as fluid and as continually being struggled over. Through our discussions, we decided to use "hegemonic," drawing on poststructuralist frameworks, to capture the complex relations of power, and to use "privileged" to define what we meant by "hegemonic."

Extract 2 (early draft):	Extract 2 (redrafted):
We are taking a reflexive approach because we are committed to issues of access. By this we mean access to engaging with and contributing to meaning making in a way that takes serious forms of knowledge that don't fit into the narrow frame created by some of the academic conventions and wider hegemonic discourses. We both feel that there is a lack of institutional spaces that could allow students and lecturers alike to explore some of the assumptions that they bring to their learning and teaching. Currently available spaces in lectures and seminars, and the 'dominant' concepts of knowledge construction, seem to work within a frame of transmission of knowledge rather than transformation of knowledge.	We are taking a reflexive approach because we are committed to issues of access and processes of knowledge construction. We understand 'access' to mean engaging with and contributing to meaning making in a way that takes serious forms of knowledge that do not fit into the narrow frame created by some of the academic conventions and wider **hegemonic** discourses. Currently, the concepts of knowledge constructions that are being **privileged** work within a frame of transmission of knowledge rather than transformation of knowledge. We both feel that there is a lack of spaces in institutions of education that could allow students and lecturers alike to explore some of the assumptions that they bring to their learning and teaching.

Deconstructing our own writing in these self-reflexive ways helped us to recognize the value of involving students in similar discussions of their writing in order to question the ways they employ language to highlight, foreground, legitimize and privilege certain epistemological and conceptual positions or subdue, reject, and undermine them.

We argue that the teaching of academic writing should involve self-reflexive discussions of (student) writing and explorations of how ontological and epistemological positions shape how and what we write. Even seemingly neutral language, for example, signposts or linking words, connect with much more complex issues related to power, representation, identity, and knowledge debates. Teaching students how to signpost and link ideas will help them, to some extent, to learn how to structure their writing. It does not point to the ways, though, in which writers make meaning through structure. It also limits the students' understanding of writing processes and keeps them in a dependent and vulnerable position where they look to the teacher for answers. This reinforces assumptions that leave students dependent on others to instruct them 'how to' write, rather than enabling them to decide how to write based on a critical understanding of the implications, individual and social, of academic writing.

Conclusion

Current and mainstream academic writing provision constructs students as passive recipients of language instruction, which is problematic as we discussed above. It also locates students of academic writing and their teachers in subordinate and low-status positions, setting up a contrast with those in 'real' academic positions, thus creating a 'hierarchical model' (Zamel 1998a). At the moment, the status and prestige attached to the teaching of academic writing is seen to be of a lesser kind in the academy than teaching within the disciplines. Teachers of academic writing are usually constructed, and construct themselves, as language experts which we argue is a barrier to the development of pedagogies that are able to address the issues we are raising in this paper. Zamel identifies the dangers connected to this creation of hierarchies within the academy:

> One danger is that teaching toward what is viewed as the 'real stuff' of academia forces conformity and submission and limits and undermines both our own expertise and that of our students. . . . Yet another danger that stems from a hierarchical model is that it sets up the unrealistic and unwarranted expectations that ESL and writing courses will complete the process of 'initiation' and that in the case of students who are found 'underprepared' or 'deficient', these courses will serve a gatekeeping function in the institution. (Zamel 1998a, 192–193).

These two key dangers that Zamel identifies here are deeply embedded within the structures that have been set up in higher education institutions not just in the United States but also in the British context. Academic writing provision is understood as merely supporting the 'real' academic work done in the university and reinforces perceptions that academic writing teachers provide a service and are not, themselves, academics. Yet, academic writing teachers must be granted the same resources as other academics to carry out scholarship and research, in order to be able to draw on and contribute to the rich body of research in the field of academic literacies and other interconnected fields. As we argued earlier, there is an inextricable link among theory, teaching, and practice, which also applies to the work of those academics teaching academic writing. We address this paper to a range of different audiences: those who teach academic writing and those who, within the disciplines, are interested in writing and research methodologies. We emphasize that writing and research methodologies are not separate. Consequently, the teaching of research must consider writing processes and the teaching of writing must consider research practices. This argument is also relevant for those decision and policy makers in and outside the academy who are also interested in the teaching and learning of academic writing.

Self-reflexive pedagogies position students and tutors as active participants in writing and research practices and view academic conventions as socially, culturally, and historically embedded. In current academic writing provision, students are constructed as passive recipients of the tutor's advice, and the tutor is constructed as the expert who instructs the students about 'how to' write. These constructions are problematic and contribute to the way students are perceived as 'those who can' and 'those who cannot' produce the particular kinds of writing expected in academic contexts. This constructs a 'problem' that appears to be located with individual students or tutors rather than in complex social, cultural, and educational contexts and power relations. A key theme running throughout this book is a concern to shift this current focus from a 'deficit' perspective to a critical understanding of academic literacies as social practices.

A self-reflexive and collaborative approach helps to uncover the operation of subtle power relations within different formal and informal educational contexts. Exploring our subjectivities as readers and writers is central to deconstructing the assumptions and values that we carry with us, which are interconnected with how we write and what we say. For students to be in a position to contribute to an academic field they need to think about not just the individual and institutional but also the wider social implications of the decisions they make in their writing. Self-reflexivity provides spaces that enable tutors and students to challenge some of the currently privilaged writing practices in higher education. Reflexivity involves examining processes of constructing an authorial voice and the representation of contested perspectives and meanings.

Although the value of self-reflexive pedagogies and methodologies has been recognized, higher education institutions make only very limited space and time available for both students and staff to practise self-reflexivity in their work (Mauthner and Doucet 2003). Teachers of academic writing are located within those constraints but must recognize their responsibility to contribute to the development of understandings of academic writing. This responsibility involves a shift in the identity positioning of teachers of academic writing so that they are positioned, and position themselves, as 'real' academics. Teachers of academic writing, who inadvertently position themselves as outside of academic work, risk excluding themselves and their students from wider social debates about the production of knowledge through writing and research in higher education. Self-reflexive pedagogies contribute not only to deconstructing writing practices in the classroom and in our own writing but also to reconstructing the institutional discourses that construct meanings of academic writing and knowledge production. Regardless of constraints of space and time, it is imperative that, through self-reflexive approaches to academic writing and research, we challenge the current perpetuation of local and global inequalities and injustices. This would involve reconceptualizing, academic writing provision, as the teaching and learning of competing and contested sets of writing methodologies and social practices.

References

Adkins, L. 2002. Reflexivity and the politics of qualitative research. In: T. May (ed.), *Qualitative Research in Action*. London, Thousand Oaks and New Delhi: SAGE Publications, pp. 332–348.

Bourgois, P. 2002. Respect at work: 'Going legit.' In: S. Taylor (ed.), *Ethnographic Research: A reader*. London and Thousand Oaks and New Delhi: SAGE Publications in association with The Open University, pp. 15–35.

Collins, P.H. 2000. What's going on? Black feminist thought and the politics of postmodernism. In: E.A. St. Pierre and W.S. Pillow (eds.), *Working the ruins: Feminist poststructural theory and methods in education*. New York and London: Routledge, pp. 41–73.

Creme, P., and Lea, M. 1997. *Writing at university: A guide for students*. Buckingham and Philadelphia: Open University Press.

Ellsworth, E. 1994. Why doesn't this feel empowering? Working through the repressive myths of critical pedagogy (1989). In: L. Stone and with the assistance of G.M. Boldt (eds.), *The education feminism reader*. New York and London: Routledge, pp. 300–327.

Ellsworth, E. 1997. *Teaching positions: Difference, pedagogy and the power of address*. New York and London: Teachers College Press.

Geisler, C. 1994. *Academic literacy and the nature of expertise: Reading, writing, and knowing in academic philosophy.* Hillsdale and Hove: Lawrence Erlbaum Associates.

Gore, J.M. 1993. *The struggle for pedagogies: Critical and feminist discourses as regimes of truth.* New York and London: Routledge.

Griffiths, M. 1998. *Educational research for social justice: Getting off the fence.* Buckingham and Philadelphia: Open University Press.

Institute of Education. 2002–03. *Gender and international development,* MA course handbook. London, University of London.

Ivanic, R. 1998. *Writing and identity: The discoursal construction of identity in academic writing.* Amsterdam and Philadelphia: John Benjamins Publishing Company.

Ivanic, R., and Simpson, J. 1992. Who's who in academic writing. In: N. Fairclough (ed.), *Critical language awareness.* London and New York: Longman, pp. 141–173.

Jones, C., Turner, J., and Street, B. 1999. Introduction. In: C. Jones, J. Turner, and B. Street (eds.), *Students writing in the university: Cultural and epistemological issues.* Amsterdam and Philadelphia: John Benjamins Publishing Company, pp. xv–xxiv.

Lather, P. 1991. *Getting smart: Feminist research and pedagogy with/in the postmodern.* New York and London: Routledge.

Lea, M.R., and Street, B. 1997 *Student writing and staff feedback in higher education: An academic literacies approach.* Swindon: Economic and Social Research Council.

Lea, M.R., and Street, B. 2000. Student writing and staff feedback in higher education: An academic literacies approach. In: M.R. Lea and B. Stierer (eds.), *Student writing in higher education: New contexts.* Buckingham: The Society for Research into Higher Education and Open University Press, pp. 32–46.

Lillis, T.M. 2001. *Student writing: Access, regulation, desire.* London and New York: Routledge.

Lillis, T.M., and Ramsey, M. 1997. Student status and the question of choice in academic writing. *Research and Practice in Adult Learning Bulletin,* Spring, pp. 15–22.

Luke, C., and Gore, J.M. eds. 1992. *Feminisms and critical pedagogy.* London and New York: Routledge.

Mauthner, N., and Doucet, A. 2003. Reflexive accounts and accounts of reflexivity in qualitative data analysis. *Sociology* 37: 413–432.

Nichols, S. 2003. "They just won't critique anything": The 'problem' of international students in the Western academy. In: J. Satterthwaite, E. Atkinson, and K. Gale (eds.), *Discourse, power, resistance: Challenging the rhetoric of contemporary education.* Stoke on Trent and Sterling: Trentham Books, pp. 135–148.

Richardson, L. 2000. Writing: A method of inquiry. In: N.K. Denzin and Y.S. Lincoln (eds.), *Handbook of qualitative research.* 2nd ed. London: SAGE Publications, pp. 923–948.

Rose, M. 1998. The language of exclusion: Writing instruction at the university. In: V. Zamel and R. Spack (eds.), *Negotiating academic literacies: Teaching and learning across languages and cultures.* Mahwah and London: Lawrence Erlbaum Associates, pp. 9–30.

Skeggs, B. 2002. Techniques for telling the reflexive self. In: T. May (ed.), *Qualitative research in action.* London, Thousand Oaks and New Delhi: SAGE Publications, pp. 349–374.

Street, B. 1984. *Literacy in theory and practice.* Cambridge, New York and Melbourne: Cambridge University Press.

Street, B. 2001. The new literacy studies. In: E. Cushman, E.R. Kintgen, B.M. Kroll, and M. Rose (eds.), *Literacy: A critical sourcebook.* Boston and New York: Bedford/St. Martin's, pp. 430–442.

Usher, R. 1997. Telling a story about research and research as story-telling: Postmodern approaches to social research. In: G. McKenzie, J. Powell, and R. Usher (eds.), *Understanding social research: Perspectives on methodology and practice.* London: Falmer Press, pp. 27–41.

Webb, S. 1997. Alternative students? Conceptualizations of difference. In: J. Williams (ed.), *Negotiating access to higher education: The discourse of selectivity and equity.* Buckingham: SRHE and Open University Press, pp. 65–86.

Zamel, V. 1998a. Questioning academic discourse. In: V. Zamel and R. Spack (eds.). *Negotiating academic literacies: Teaching and learning across languages and cultures.* Mahwah and London: Lawrence Erlbaum Associates, pp. 187–198.

Zamel, V. 1998b. Strangers in academia: The experiences of faculty and ESL students across the curriculum. In: V. Zamel and R. Spack (eds.), *Negotiating academic literacies: Teaching and learning across languages and cultures.* Mahwah and London: Lawrence Erlbaum Associates, pp. 249–264.

Index